*On the Side of My People*

# On the Side of My People

A Religious Life of Malcolm X

Louis A. DeCaro, Jr.

New York University Press

NEW YORK AND LONDON

NEW YORK UNIVERSITY PRESS
New York and London

Library of Congress Cataloging-in-Publication Data
DeCaro, Louis A., 1957–
    On the side of my people a religious life of Malcolm X / Louis
A. DeCaro, Jr.
        p.   cm.
    Includes bibliographical references (p.     ) and index.
    Contents: Black nationalist religion before the Nation—The
Nation before Malcolm X—A Garveyite son—Early life and
religious training—Wayward youth—Crime, imprisonment, and
redemption—Early ministry—Evangelism and Nation-building—
From Harlem to the dark world—The making of an emissary—
Religious apologist—Foreshadowing Mecca: between cult and
orthodoxy—Fame and fury—Banished from the Nation—The
pilgrim convert—The realities and ideals of witness—The final
year—Religious revolutionist—Fighting in the way of God—
Closing the book—Epilogue: now he's gone.
    ISBN 0-8147-1864-7 (alk. paper)
    1. X, Malcolm, 1925–1965.   2.  Black Muslims—
Biography.   3.  Afro-Americans—Biography.
I.  Title.
BP223.Z8L573334   1996
297'.87'092—dc20          95-4404
[B]                              CIP

New York University Press books are printed on acid-free paper,
and their binding materials are chosen for strength and durability.

Manufactured in the United States of America

10 9 8 7 6 5 4 3 2 1

To Dad, Mom, and Frank
and
to the Brokenborough Children,
Tiffany, Aaron, Rachel and Jessica,
with love.


*"And by my God have I leaped over a wall."*
—Psalms 18:29b

# Contents

# Illustrations

All illustrations appear as an insert following page 174.

1. Malcolm X speaking at the 1958 Marcus Garvey Day celebration in Harlem.
2. Malcolm X with Elijah Muhammad in 1958 at Harlem's Park Palace.
3. Malcolm and other Nation dignitaries listen to Muhammad speaking at the Park Palace, 1958.
4. Malcolm X attending the opening of Abdul Basit Naeem's "Shalimar International Travel Service" in New York, ca. 1962.
5. Demonstration by the Nation of Islam at Manhattan's Criminal Court building, January 11, 1963.
6. Malcolm X confers with Muslim associates at the demonstration scene.
7. Flier prepared by Malcolm X for the January 1963 demonstration.
8. Flier/poster advertising an "African Bazaar" sponsored by Mosque No. 7 in Harlem, featuring Malcolm X as keynote speaker.

# Preface

In the early stages of my research, I called a writer who has done significant work on Malcolm X's life story. When I was greeted over the phone by his wife, I explained my reason for calling. Without hesitating she lamented, "Not another one! Poor Malcolm!" I would like to think that I am not "another one" determined to publish a few fast-and-easy pages at Malcolm's expense. However, this book is hardly just "another one." Indeed, *On the Side of My People* is thus far the only book exclusively devoted to the study of Malcolm X's *religious* life.

Those who know little about Malcolm X may wince and say—as one staid Christian man said to me—"There won't be much to write about, will there?" However, the fact is that Malcolm's story is highly religious, *not* just in connection with his famous pilgrimage to Mecca in 1964, but literally from the beginning to the end of his life. This should not surprise anyone, for religious life is really a birth-to-death experience, as is religious learning.

Only Allah may write the ultimate biography. The rest of us must admit that we are limited by certain boundaries, some of which are imposed upon us, while others are of our own making. Like the Malcolm X books that have preceded this one, *On the Side of My People* lacks an author's interview with Malcolm's widow, Betty Shabazz. Throughout the period of my active research, I endeavored to speak with Dr. Shabazz. Perhaps she was besieged by too many callers and interviewers, particularly during the production of the Spike Lee movie on Malcolm X. I had, or assumed I had, a connection to Dr. Shabazz through an academic official at New York University. To my disappointment, nothing materialized in this regard. After many unsuccessful follow-up telephone calls to her office, my research time had expired and I abandoned all hope of interviewing her; soon afterward I left New York City to begin writing. I was also denied an interview with Malcolm's elder half-sister, Ella Collins, whose son thought it best not to share with me what might be revealed in his own intended memoir. Consequently, where either Dr. Shabazz or Mrs. Collins speak in this book, they do so in other people's interviews.

Fortunately, I was warmly received into the home of Wilfred and Ruth Little Shabazz, Malcolm's eldest sibling and his wife. Wilfred kindly answered many questions and encouraged me to rely on my own personal spirituality, reminding me that all of us have a part to play in the telling of Malcolm's story. Both patient and capable of great recollection, Wilfred proved to be a most precious resource—especially in helping me to appreciate the unique religious values of the Little family and how those values shaped him, Malcolm, and their other siblings. I soon realized, however, that Wilfred is to be cherished in his own right. He is invariably sought out and identified as Malcolm's brother, but he certainly has his own poignant story to tell and his own special wisdom to share with those privileged to meet him.

Along with extensive material from those memorable meetings and telephone conversations with Wilfred, I was especially pleased to meet with Clarence Atkins, an old friend of Malcolm during his now famous "Detroit Red" days in Harlem. Atkins, who is a music critic and freelance journalist, provided a rare, unique, and honest insight into the much-distorted and exploited character, Malcolm the hustler. Thus, while I cannot boast hundreds of interviews with Malcolm's playmates, classmates, and colleagues, my interview experiences have been more than compensated by their depth and quality.

I believe that religious education—as in Malcolm's case—has the potential to provide a bridge over the race and culture chasm. Consequently, I hope that *On the Side of My People* will prove to be worthy of its subject. As the leading voice of the Nation of Islam in the 1950s and early 1960s, Malcolm X was undoubtedly committed to black folks, speaking as he did from a cultic Muslim platform. As the most promising voice of Islam among African Americans in 1964–65, Malcolm did not surrender his revolutionary struggle on behalf of black people—but set it within the broader framework of theistic humanism. Consequently, race and racism are issues inseparable from his entire life story. Yet because Malcolm X was always very religious and made no secret about his commitment to religious life, perhaps a religious study will help us understand him better—and at the same time limit neither the subject nor the reader to the racial arena. If *On the Side of My People* accomplishes that much, then perhaps its other limitations may be forgiven.

*Maran Atha*

# Acknowledgments

I am grateful to my advisers and instructors at New York University who assisted me in the studies, research, and writing that culminated in the first manifestation of this book in the form of a doctoral dissertation: Gabriel Moran, Richard Hull, LaMar Miller, and Marc Crawford. Mr. Crawford also provided me with one of my most dynamic interviews, energizing me with his own vivid recollections of Malcolm X. Also at New York University, Dean Earl Davis was kind enough to share with me some of the Malcolm X tape recordings in the archives of the Institute of Afro-American Affairs. Thanks go also to Malik Mubashshir of Philadelphia, an accomplished scholar of both Islam and the Nation of Islam, who has read my manuscript and offered vital criticisms and suggestions. I am likewise grateful to Paul Lee and Henry Lewis, director and business manager, respectively, of Best Efforts, Inc., Highland Park, Michigan. Their interest and support greatly augmented my work, also providing criticism, counsel, and encouragement along with archival resources.

I was unable to draw directly from all of my interviews in preparing this book. However, whether or not I have done so, every opportunity to ask questions and converse with those who knew Malcolm X has been extremely helpful to my work. Accordingly, warm thanks go to Robert Haggins, Malcolm's personal photographer from 1960 to 1965, who first opened his door to me as a graduate student doing research. Mr. Haggins generously shared his time, showed me his photos, and offered me rich remembrances of Malcolm X. I would also like to thank Wilfred Little Shabazz (see the Preface), Robert Little, Charles Kenyatta, Percy Sutton, Yuri Kochiyama, Peter Goldman, Claude Lewis, Wyatt Tee Walker, Justice Jawn Sandifer, Richard Jones, Claude Frazier Sharieff, Jeremiah Shabazz, and Benjamin Karim (with whom I spoke over the telephone) for taking time to speak with me. Thanks also go to Charles Keil and Joan Durham, who in their college days encountered Minister Malcolm X of the Nation of Islam, and have shared their writings about those encounters with me.

My research was particularly enriched by the extensive support of Marlayna Gates and her assistants in the Interlibrary Loan Department of New York University. Marlayna and her staff patiently worked with me in tracking down numerous newspaper articles and other materials. Thanks also go to Dr. Janet Wilson Knight, Jaymie Derderian, and James Palmer of the Department of Correction, State of Massachusetts, who made Malcolm's prison and parole files available. I also received kind assistance from Kenneth Cramer, archivist of the Dartmouth College Library, and Elizabeth Sage, assistant archivist at the University of Chicago Library. At the Schomburg Center for Research in Black Culture, New York City, I was amiably assisted by Victor Smythe and Diana Lachatanere.

Thanks go to Niko Pfund, editor in chief, and Despina Papazoglou Gimbel, managing editor, at New York University Press, who have been immensely helpful and encouraging in bringing this book to publication. Others provided various kinds of assistance and timely support, for which I am also appreciative: Bettie Brewer, Gil Noble, Michelle Robinson, Michael Horan, Omar Farooq, Rosalyn Akalonu, and Tina Rice; also Deacon J. Walker Sturdivant of the Gospel Spreading Church of God, Washington, D.C.; Bishop Wilbert McKinley of the Elim International Fellowship, Brooklyn, New York; and Joyce M. Ford. A special note of thanks goes to Randall Schuler and Susan Jackson of New York University, who provided me with much needed employment throughout the sojourn of manuscript preparation.

Finally, thanks go to my parents, the Reverend Louis A. DeCaro and Clara J. DeCaro; to my elder brother Frank; and to the DeCaro and DeCapita families for their loving support. My parents in particular have played an important role in encouraging me, and after more than a decade of independence, allowed me expediently to return home while I read, pondered, and wrote about Malcolm X. I am especially grateful to them.

*On the Side of My People*

# Introduction

*My Life Has Always Been One of Changes*

Malcolm X's role in the Nation of Islam (henceforth "the Nation") and his later independent role as a so-called militant black leader have to date been portrayed primarily from a political perspective. While Malcolm X was alive, most of what people knew about him was based on news from the mainstream press, and their attention was invariably focused on the Nation's rejection of integration and the white man—at best a partial analysis that served to sell newspapers. It would have been considerably less shocking if the Nation had been described along the lines of other separatist religious communities. In addition to this social and political misrepresentation, the Nation was virtually never presented as a religious movement. Few journalists concerned themselves with the religious teachings and experiences that buttressed Muslim-oriented blacks in the United States, especially Malcolm X.

In their own way, Malcolm's white revolutionary supporters have also tended to limit his persona to politics. Malcolm X was a political man, and after he achieved a painful independence from the Nation in 1964 he was finally free to become politically active. However, throughout his life, Malcolm pursued religious ideas and came to reflect deeply on the relationship between God, the oppressed, and the oppressor. His story is itself a religious story, a double-barreled conversion narrative that inevitably reveals that he was a man with personal religious interests—that he was a man who was as concerned with redemption as with revolution.

This religious aspect has long been ignored, and even suppressed, by white revolutionists who embraced Malcolm during his lifetime and in the decades since his tragic assassination in 1965. These white allies must be acknowledged for keeping Malcolm's speeches on the bookstore shelves, making his words accessible to those of us who never heard him speak in life; but these works have been edited and packaged with a tendency to secularize him, since—in the Western world—revolution is an agnostic endeavor.

Furthermore, when the religious Malcolm X has been discussed, it has usually been done in very parochial terms and before relatively small audiences. Some traditional Muslims have written reflective pieces on Malcolm X, but this work tends to be abstract, reading sophisticated Islamic ideas into his story for the sake of devotional or didactic purposes. The current leading manifestation of the Nation led by Louis Farrakhan (several others are entirely overlooked by the media) also addresses the religious Malcolm X, though it always interprets him according to an organizational agenda. Farrakhan seems to have remained an admirer of Malcolm as the leading spokesman for the Nation's "Honorable Elijah Muhammad" who died in 1975. This version of Malcolm dominates the memory of the Nation, it seems, because the Nation's rendition of his story enhances their organizational claims. In Farrakhan's rhetoric, Malcolm X is "the fruit" of Elijah Muhammad, who was "the tree that produced him." However, this is hardly the whole truth.

In fact, Malcolm had been deeply impressed with religious and political ideas since childhood, and he, along with his siblings, brought those ideas with them into the Nation in the late 1940s. While Elijah Muhammad gave a great deal to Malcolm X, his role was perhaps more of the catalyst—inadvertently assisting Malcolm in the development of his mature ideas. Thus, when "the fruit" finally fell, it fell far from the tree. In contrast, Louis Farrakhan and others are genuinely the offspring of Elijah Muhammad and therefore rest much closer to the roots of his movement.

As significant as these various representations may be, the most important voice to speak about Malcolm X is the man himself. In this regard one must first consult *The Autobiography of Malcolm X*—his story as he told it through the pen of author Alex Haley. Haley admitted in the epilogue that Malcolm X wished for him to act as a "writer" and not an "interpreter." However, it appears that Haley ultimately acted as more than amanuensis in structuring the final version and in his interpretive epilogue—inevitable, perhaps, given Malcolm's sudden, tragic death before the publication of the book.

In the same epilogue, Haley recalled that after Malcolm X returned from Mecca, his inclination was to "re-edit the entire book into a polemic against Elijah Muhammad." Fortunately, Malcolm reconsidered and, according to Haley, "never again asked for any change in what he had originally said." Despite the fact that massive reediting was avoided, it is still clear that *The Autobiography of Malcolm* X bears interpolations that seem entirely consistent with Malcolm's thinking after being ejected from the Nation in early 1964. In fact, these interpolations—explanations, clarifications, and corrections—document Malcolm's conversion from the religion of Mr. Muhammad to the traditional Islam of the East. They represent a second layer of narrative, a redactive voice that seems to be authentically Malcolm's own, or is at least consistent with his voice.

For instance, in "Minister Malcolm X," one of the original chapters of the autobiography, Malcolm recounted his courtship and marriage to Betty Shabazz and concluded the chapter by discussing the 1957 beating of a New York Muslim by the police—an incident that proved to be a red-letter event in Malcolm's career in Harlem (and one that was ready-made for the cinematic version of his story thirty-five years later). However, the discussion of Betty seems to have been enlarged after Malcolm's second trip abroad in 1964.

"I guess by now I will say I love Betty," Malcolm added later with Haley's assistance. It seems that Malcolm affirmed his feelings for his wife this way because he had spent an extended time abroad and was all the more appreciative of her sacrifices during his long absence—he had "been away as much as five months" on his second, more extensive trip to Asia and Africa, from July to November 1964. Malcolm not only mentioned cabling Betty from Cairo, Accra, and Mecca during this time, but used her as the model of a "good Muslim woman and wife" while extolling the superiority of a Muslim marriage to that of the "Western 'love' concept." As a faithful servant of the Nation, Malcolm undoubtedly made similar claims on behalf of Mr. Muhammad's "Islam," but this interpolation seems to reflect an orthodox Malcolm—the one who returned in late 1964 as a bona fide Muslim evangelist after being ordained at Cairo's Al-Azhar University, which he called the "seat of Islam."

Alex Haley had spent much of 1964 writing the book according to his extended interviews with Malcolm X during 1963. After the first draft was completed, Haley edited his work with the assistance of Murray Fisher, an associate editor for *Playboy*. The manuscript was revised twice before it actually went to press.[1] In his epilogue, Haley recalled that Malcolm would "frown and wince" as he read the edited work, but agreed not to change his original narration. Malcolm was similarly disturbed by an abridged version of his autobiography that appeared in *The Saturday Evening Post* in September 1964, while he was still in Cairo. After the publication of the magazine version, Malcolm X was firm with Haley about clarifying the changes in his racial perspective due to his conversion to Sunni Islam.

Even though Haley had completed *The Autobiography* about two weeks before Malcolm's assassination, the manuscript remained vulnerable to further editing. If Haley took advantage of the situation, this can be explored further by students of Malcolm and his autobiography.

What *is* clear is that two chapters were deleted from the final, published version, chapters that Malcolm X had initially designed to bring his story to a stylized religious climax. The omission of the chapters entitled "The End of Christianity" and "Twenty Million Muslims," was in fact completely consistent with the changes that had taken place in Malcolm's religious life by 1964. His conversion to traditional Islam mandated the disavowal of his former religious vision as a "Black Muslim," as, apparently, related in the two fanciful chapters.[2] If these sections, which were written in the voice of a devoted cultist—the representative of a religious movement that was both antithetical to Christianity and irreconcilable with traditional Islam—are ever published, they will likely confuse and distort popular interpretations of Malcolm X unless they are read in the context of his entire religious life story.

*The Autobiography of Malcolm X* has been read uncritically even when Haley's influence as interpreter and editor is considered. This is particularly so in the exclusion of critical religious and theological observations. Autobiography, regardless of the author, is self-interpretation in its purest form—an attempt to explain one's life in some ultimate sense. An author will stylize, exaggerate, emphasize some things and deemphasize others. Malcolm's autobiography bears all of these traits, though it does not mean that Malcolm X was somehow hiding some secret childhood fears, masking a troubled life with a manly hero's tale, as one discredited biography has suggested.

*On the Side of My People* fundamentally accepts Malcolm's autobiography as a brilliant religious story, originally conceived as a way to enhance and glorify Elijah Muhammad. Malcolm X wrote it as if from an ultimate perspective, an attempt to explain and reconcile his former beliefs with the new path he chose to take in the Nation. Still, *The Autobiography of Malcolm X* carries an organizational burden. Malcolm modeled his life and conversion with intent to strengthen the Nation, and his own standing in the movement at a time when he privately realized the need was great. In 1962–63, Malcolm X was fighting the increasing hostilities of the government, the police, and the media while also facing the antagonism of his enemies at the highest echelons of the Nation. Unquestionably loyal to Elijah Muhammad, Malcolm's self-told story on behalf of the Nation was thus his fullest and final tribute to the man who had pulled him out of prison and into the salvation of "Islam."

At the time that he was writing his autobiography, Malcolm X was also dealing with his own religious growth—a maturing of ideas that had been in process for years. A kind of religious pregnancy, Malcolm's inclination to follow traditional Islam began to show in the early 1960s. Though he argued otherwise, virtually until he was excommunicated in early 1964, Malcolm X had in fact begun to outgrow the religious world of the Nation. For many years a faithful son, he stayed in Mr. Muhammad's cultic backyard, conversing with traditional Muslims outside and eyeing the intriguing Islamic world just beyond the Nation's black picket fence. For this reason, *The Autobiography of Malcolm X* is actually two conversion stories. Just as it bears Malcolm's Nation self-portrayal, it suddenly breaks into the story of Malcolm's conversion to traditional Islam.

*On the Side of My People* provides an alternative reading: it tells the story of a religiously driven revolutionist, reading *The Autobiography of Malcolm X* back into Malcolm's life from a religious standpoint. It is a biography, but it does not follow a strict biographical format. *On the Side of My People* is built around Malcolm's two conversions—to the Nation and to traditional Islam. Political issues are not entirely ignored—they serve as a background for the ample religious themes of the story. The conversions are presented as "moments"—though not literal ones, of course, but rather as moments that emphasize what was religiously pivotal in Malcolm's life.

To gain these insights, I have drawn on a diverse collection of sources, including several extensive interviews, a variety of interviews with Malcolm (some of which have never been referenced in any publication), FBI and police surveillance documents, Malcolm's personal and published correspondence, prison and parole files, recorded speeches, and other primary resources. For secondary sources, I have prepared an extensive bibliography, featuring popular and scholarly writing on Malcolm X in books, newspapers, journals, and magazines, including the largely nonindexed black press. In addition to his extensive work in the development of the Nation's *Muhammad Speaks* publication, Malcolm X was an accomplished newspaper columnist; even as a reader he penned fervent letters to newspapers, many of which have been recovered for this book.

*On the Side of My People* is also a religious study and therefore requires religious terminology. The terminology that seems most appropriate to me is that of orthodoxy versus cult, the experience of traditional religion as opposed to that of new religion. (Muslims may rightly object to references to "orthodox Islam," since orthodoxy is fundamentally a Western theological conception that has no absolute counterpart in Islam. However, Islam has a *kind* of orthodoxy in the idea of the faithful community and its developing tradition, just as it has its own kinds of heresy.) Furthermore, the Nation was, for all of its identification with Islam, a Western phenomenon that drew many of its religious conceptualizations from Christianity and biblically oriented cults. In his last days, Malcolm X himself employed the term "orthodox Islam" in speaking of his newfound faith; he likewise cast the Nation in specific cult references. I have therefore taken the liberty to use "orthodox Islam" interchangeably with "traditional Islam" and "Sunni Islam" within the context of this religious study.

When Malcolm began to face the grim reality of his widening breach with the Nation in 1963, he was undoubtedly aware that his autobiography was going to be affected. Alex Haley had made a practice of salvaging Malcolm's "scribblings," those little jotted writings that Haley came to realize held great value for gaining insight into their interview sessions. It seems possible that Malcolm intended as much, or at least came to surmise that Haley appreciated his off-the-record messages scribbled on newspapers, index cards, and paper napkins. In the final months of 1963, one of the scribblings Haley retrieved after an interview read: "My life has always been one of changes." Malcolm was perhaps hinting to his writer that changes were afoot, and that such changes would have a significant impact on their autobiographical project.

Finally, when it became clear that the Nation had rejected Malcolm, he adjusted his publishing royalties and the dedication in his book to favor Betty and their children instead of his former beneficiary, Elijah Muhammad. In a note to Haley written around the time he announced his independent movement in March 1964, Malcolm X added a postscript: "How is it possible to write one's autobiography in a world so fast-changing as this?" This represented perhaps a deeper recognition than did his first assurance to Haley that he would not rewrite his story, but leave it "the way it was" when he was still in the Nation. It was impossible for *The Autobiography* to remain "the way it was," for shortly afterward, in April 1964, Malcolm X made his famous pilgrimage to Mecca, forever altering the nature of his story.

Had Malcolm been spared the brutality, vindictiveness, and malevolent intrigue that culminated in his assassination, he would—at this writing— have reached the age of seventy. One can only speculate with a certain awe what would have become of this man, now advanced in age and wisdom, upon whom had flowed in youth such an unusual anointing of history and providence. My guess is that Malcolm X would still be difficult to categorize, politically and religiously. This is precisely why he is constantly invoked in poetry and prose, re-formed in the human clay of theater and cinema, and profiled by artists, scholars, and other admirers. All somehow want to bring Malcolm X back, to vindicate his words and shame his enemies, to salvage the troubled youth of our nation's cities, and to help us ride the waves of change.

"In life," Malcolm wrote to Alex Haley in his later days, "nothing is permanent; not even life itself." Malcolm's words were warm and thoughtful, but he was actually urging Haley to rush the autobiography's production. Not only was Malcolm aware that his days were numbered, but in terms of his autobiography, he knew that the events in his life were occurring so swiftly that much of their writing project could easily become "outdated." Malcolm's life did change rapidly, so much so that the literary boundaries of *The Autobiography* really could not contain the fullest account of his development. Yet, in committing his life story ultimately to the forces of change, Malcolm's autobiography transcended its prior parochial identity and became a classic in the chronicles of religious experience.[3]

In the final paragraph of his epilogue to *The Autobiography*, Alex Haley passed the baton of interpretation to a still rising generation of Malcolm X biographers and scholars. Our last glimpse through Alex Haley's eyes is of a living Malcolm stepping into the pages of history. *On the Side of My People*, therefore, is one attempt to grasp the baton and pursue Malcolm X into those same pages of history—hopefully to return with some evidence of a genuine and meaningful encounter.

This religious study will surely some day be complemented by other religious analyses, especially Muslim analysis. Even more certain is the fact that Malcolm's story will be told and retold often, and that he will continue to have presence in a society he intimately understood and ultimately wished to salvage. Disagree with him, fear him, malign him, or exclude him,

Malcolm X the religious revolutionist remains, his long legs striding through the pages of history, his legendary smile still comforting friends and disturbing enemies, his words still penetrating to the very marrow of our society. Whatever scholarly or historical contributions *On the Side of My People* provides, it is also a reminder that Malcolm X has strangely challenged the forces of mortality, as even Alex Haley concluded in 1965. It is still difficult to imagine him gone.

# PART ONE

# Prophets and Messiahs of a Black God

*The Lord your God will raise up for you a prophet like me
from among you, from your countrymen, you shall listen
to him.* —Deuteronomy 18:15

*Then if anyone says to you, "Behold, here is the Christ," or
"There he is," do not believe him. For False Christs and
false prophets will arise and will show great signs and won-
ders, so as to mislead, if possible, even the elect.*
—Matthew 24:23–24

# 1

## Black Nationalist Religion before the Nation

*A God in our own image.*

The organization which Malcolm X brought to national attention in the early 1960s was a far cry from the movement as it existed in its earliest stages. Indeed, the Nation had significantly changed even by the time Malcolm joined it as a newly paroled enthusiast in the summer of 1952. The Nation began, in fact, not in the civil rights era, but in a far less hopeful time in the thinking of African Americans.

The Nation's philosophy, which was characteristically oppositional, was born in an era when—and a place where—black people were realizing anew the longevity, adaptability, and extensiveness of white people's racism. That era was the Great Depression, and the place was the urban ghetto of Detroit, Michigan—one of many industrial centers where African American laborers from the southern United States had migrated in search of a better life for themselves and their children.

While contemporary European immigrants were able to surmount the native xenophobia of the United States, African Americans invariably found themselves both practically and theoretically overlooked in the white man's program of "Americanization." Nevertheless, African Americans were always fundamentally involved in the culture of the United States—a fact observable, for instance, in the era just before the Great Depression, more popularly known as "the Jazz Age"—an era that celebrated the classical-music contribution to U.S. society by African Americans. Yet it was not "cultural lag" that hindered the advancement of black migrants in the North, but racism.

African Americans, in fact, had already been migrating northward during the years preceding World War I. Very quickly the black migrant vanguard saw that racial lines were being increasingly tightened. In the World War I era, when migration of African Americans from the South to the North became particularly heavy due to wartime employment opportunities, so also did the burden of racial animosity from whites. Black migrants were invariably treated as invaders, being physically assaulted and killed and blocked from purchasing property by white realtors and so-called neighborhood improvement associations.

The inevitable outcome of this racist system was the development of the black northern ghetto, which became increasingly crowded as African American migrants arrived, finding nowhere to go besides the "safety" of the urban slums in which their brethren were dwelling. By 1930, the year in which the Nation was born in a Detroit ghetto, 2.25 million black migrants had left southern farms and plantations for the urban North. Between 1910 and 1920 the black population in Detroit increased by 611 percent, and the overall black population in the North increased from 75,000 to 3 million.

When World War I ended and white northerners began to return from the service, the pangs of racism struck the African American community even deeper: black people suddenly found themselves losing their jobs en masse to white veterans who had returned home. Black urban dwellers, who had fled the South to escape the perils of racial violence and economic despair, now found all hope of a better life vanish before their eyes.

The stream of black migrants did not cease to flow after World War I. The ghetto existence of the African American migrants and their families was only intensified with the arrival of more and more unskilled and often illiterate southern blacks—refugees of the bitter sharecropping system of the South. "Soon," one scholar concluded, "there was hunger and crime and delinquency—and trouble with the police. The bright promise of the North had failed. Hope turned to desperation." It was in this troubled era that Marcus Garvey appeared on the scene, as James Weldon Johnson has noted, stirring the imagination of the black masses as no African American leader had done before.[1]

Garvey's organization, the Universal Negro Improvement Association

(UNIA), was both controversial and influential among early-twentieth-century African Americans. Garvey characterized his organization as a militant opponent to white supremacy as well as an advocate of the unification of African peoples globally. Controversy surrounded Garvey and the UNIA, not only among whites (from whom Garvey wanted to separate completely) but also among integrationists such as the National Association for the Advancement of Colored People (NAACP). The latter accused Garvey and the UNIA of being nothing but a black version of the Ku Klux Klan and an "impractical, visionary and ridiculous" venture that had misled "poor, ignorant negroes . . . promising them a competence for life from their investments in his enterprises."

Marcus Garvey was a Caribbean black, born in Jamaica in 1887 of humble background. In his youth he visited various places in the Americas and witnessed the dire economic and social condition of the African peoples of the West. He enjoyed an extended stay in England, and visited a variety of European countries as well. Garvey's travel experiences and his reading of various black writers reinforced his own blossoming sense of leadership in the struggle for black liberation. In 1914 he founded the UNIA, which grew rapidly among African Americans once Garvey arrived in the United States in 1916.

In time, Garvey founded branches of the UNIA not only in the United States but among scattered Africans in the Western Hemisphere as well. By the middle of the 1920s the UNIA had eleven hundred branches in over forty countries, most of them in the United States. The fact that the UNIA appealed to black peoples in many parts of the world shows a common experience of racial oppression among Africans worldwide. Garvey and his followers observed in history that wherever Europeans and their descendants confronted black peoples, a consistent pattern of racism evolved.

However, it was Garvey's organizational philosophy and operations that stirred so much controversy and undoubtedly threatened the status of other liberation movements vying for the attention of the black masses. The UNIA was different from the integrationist-styled movements of that era, which Garvey chided as being the "tools of white people," in that it departed from the established civil rights strategy that was based essentially on egalitarian presuppositions. Instead, Garvey and the UNIA preached, as both racial presupposition and priority, the total liberation of black people.[2]

The black nationalist spirit of the UNIA was a revitalization of the theme of separation and repatriation to Africa that had been argued—with varying characteristics—by nineteenth-century African American leaders such as

Martin Delaney and Bishop Henry Turner. Particularly in Turner's case there was a rebirth in the UNIA's idea that a successful African state would win the respect of whites. But unlike any of his predecessors or nationalist contemporaries, Marcus Garvey was able to establish a mass movement.

The program which Garvey himself delineated, and which became popularly termed a "back to Africa" philosophy, did not call for the repatriation of black peoples worldwide to the African continent. Rather, it subordinated the national identities of colonized black peoples worldwide to an Africentric worldview. That worldview, whose motto Garvey proclaimed as "One God! One aim! One destiny!" was particularly committed "to establish a universal confraternity among the members of the Black race." In Garvey's thinking, this would be accomplished by strengthening continental African peoples, building independent black nations, and promoting the wholistic development of African peoples worldwide. Africa was the central concern of Garvey and the UNIA, and the liberation of Africa from European colonialism was the "prerequisite for the dignity of Black men all over the world."

"Let no man pull you down, let no man destroy your ambition," Garvey preached. The white man "is not your lord; he is not your sovereign master." Garvey's ideology was thus both nationalist and racial: "He advocated racial purity, racial integrity, and racial hegemony." This does not, however, suggest that Garvey sought to realize a reversal of the status quo. It was not his dream for African peoples to dominate Europeans, but only to be separate from them and build a separate power of their own: "If you cannot live alongside the white man in peace . . . then find a country of your own and rise to the highest position within that country."[3] Garvey believed that by finding their homeland and working within it, black people worldwide could build their own place in the sun.

The UNIA did not limit itself to theory and rhetoric, but sought to implement programs of economic cooperation in and through black solidarity. To this effect, the organization published its own international newspaper, the *Negro World*, a weekly that carried stories designed to advance the movement's philosophy and develop black pride. While the *Negro World* was essentially Garvey's voice, it enjoyed the contributions of some of the finest African American editors and achieved a global readership. In time it was perceived as a threat in many colonial headquarters.

Under the umbrella of the Negro Factories Corporation, the UNIA sought to develop factories and businesses in all the large industrial centers of the Western world. Grocery stores and other service industries were developed, as was a publishing house. Perhaps the best-known business venture was the

Black Star Line, a steamship company that was supposed to link black peoples worldwide.

Garvey's UNIA expressed its racial solidarity in a variety of other ways, including a black political organization, the Negro Political Union, that was designed to consolidate and apply black political power in domestic politics. Various components of the UNIA, which functioned as auxiliaries, touched every aspect of the black community, and did so with a touch of pomp and circumstance. Auxiliaries like the Universal African Legion, the Universal Black Cross Nurses, the Universal African Motor Corps, and the Black Flying Eagles were all uniformed groups.

The program and public image of Marcus Garvey was thus a threat to black organizations that preferred to approach the problems of African-Americans in the United States from the standpoint of citizenship and the black wish to be a part of society. Garvey's universal African approach undoubtedly exacerbated the bad feelings of both white and black critics by the universal manner in which he applied his nationalism. This was perhaps no more clear than in his treatment of the Christian religion.

In a rally of the UNIA, Marcus Garvey proclaimed: "God tells us to worship a God in our own image. . . . We are black, and to be in our image God must be black . . . we have been worshipping a false god. . . . We must create a god of our own and give this new religion to the negroes of the world." Garvey had boldly inverted the orthodox theological premise of the Hebrew and Christian scriptures, that is, that humans are to worship a God in whose image they are made.

Quite to the contrary, Garvey asserted, black people must "create" their own god and religion. To be sure, Garvey was not advocating the invention of an entirely new religion, nor was he proposing—as the Nation would later—that the God of the Christian religion be disclaimed altogether. What Garvey appears to have advocated was the creation of a "black theology" that would be manifested both in the exterior and inward aspects of the religious lives of Africans worldwide—thus acting as a corrective to the white man's religion.

Though the UNIA had no religious affiliation, Garvey and his followers were closely aligned with the African Orthodox Church, over which presided an ordained Orthodox bishop, George Alexander McGuire. McGuire, who carried Garvey's religious ideals to their logical conclusion, publicly urged black Christians to destroy pictures of white Madonnas and white Christs in bonfires. Such symbols of white religious devotion were to be replaced with images more appropriate to the spiritual needs of the black family: "Let us start our negro painters getting busy . . . and supply a black Madonna and a black Christ for the training of our children." In another public statement, during a rally of the UNIA, McGuire declared: "If the white man is going to impress on the children of my race that everything good is white and that everything that is of the devil is black, then let us here at this convention begin to rewrite theology."

Besides being a social and political organization, the UNIA had undeniably established itself as "a spiritual movement."[4] Garvey and his followers were clearly dedicated to uprooting European theology in the thinking of black people, and to replace it with an Africentric Christian theology:

Our cause is based upon righteousness. And anything that is not righteous we have no respect for, because God Almighty is our leader and Jesus Christ our standard bearer. We rely on them on that kind leadership that will make us free, for it is the same God who inspired the Psalmist to write "Princes shall come out of Egypt and Ethiopia shall stretch out her hands unto God."[5]

However essential his impact was upon black Christian thinking, it appears that Garvey and his followers may have inadvertently cleared the way for Islam among black nationalists in the United States. In a purely theological sense, Garvey's personal religion was ecumenical. Not only was he influenced by Edward Wilmot Blyden's earlier, positive assessment of Islam,[6] but he seems to have personally minimized the differences between Christianity and Islam. Thus, despite the close ties between the UNIA and the African Orthodox Church, Garvey provided Muslim missionaries in the United States with a friendly platform. Indeed, some members of the UNIA were themselves converts to Islam; there is, in fact, testimony that Elijah Muhammad—who would later lead the Nation—was originally a member of the UNIA.

The glory days of Marcus Garvey in the United States peaked in the early 1920s, during which time he had been able to capture massive black support from southern laborers residing in northern cities, struggling small business owners and students, and soldiers who had recently returned from World War I battlefields. Garvey's powerful oratory and progressive agenda had captured their imaginations and provided them hope at a time when, overall, the experience of blacks in the United States was one of disenchantment with the nation and its recalcitrant racism.

The movement was not without its problems, however, the major one being its inability to manage its businesses. Most notably, the Negro Factory Corporation and the Black Star Line failed due to incompetence, mismanagement, and other problems. The Black Star Line suffered in particular, not only from criminal exploitation by employees, but from the sabotage of white engineers. Throughout his career in the United States, Garvey had faced legal skirmishes, mostly pertaining to libel suits filed against him; but these were small concerns compared to the more serious legal problems he would face over matters pertaining to the Black Star Line. As in the case of the Nation years later, Garvey and the UNIA were under surveillance by the government, which entailed many forms of harassment—including legal suits. Thus, the legal problems over the Black Star Line represented the climax of the assault on Marcus Garvey by the United States government.[7]

Ultimately, Garvey was convicted of knowingly, and with criminal intent, using the mails to promote the sale of Black Star Line stocks with full knowledge that the Line had failed. He was convicted on the basis of what one writer calls "extremely thin" evidence: a single, empty envelope with the Black Star Line stamp was used as proof of Garvey's alleged crime. After Garvey lost an appeal of his case, he was imprisoned in Atlanta in 1925, and was deported in 1927 after President Coolidge commuted his sentence.

Marcus Garvey's movement did not end with his deportation. As in the case of Malcolm's parents, Garvey's followers in the United States persisted in the UNIA's mission of African redemption. However, Garvey was never able to re-create elsewhere the success known by the UNIA in the United States. By 1940, when he died in London, his political force was only a shadow of what it had been. Yet he had irrevocably planted his black nationalist philosophy in the soil of the black liberation movement of the United States. And perhaps the boldest stroke of that contribution was the creation of a black religion and a black God.

While the Marcus Garvey movement left a budding black theology among nationalist-oriented African American Christians, not all black nationalists were content to remain members of such a revolutionary black Christianity. Dissenters felt no theological affinity to either the African American Christian church or the orthodox tenets of Christianity, and did not hesitate to deny the divine nature of Jesus—even that of a black Jesus. This theological departure from black Christianity was most pronounced in the development of black nationalist Muslim and Jewish organizations among urban African Americans in the era of Garvey's movement in the United States.

According to one scholar, even before Marcus Garvey had arrived in the United States there was already a spreading flame of "psychological emigrationism" moving through the South, particularly through the Carolinas. This wave emphasized the theme of African Americans being "the lost sheep of Israel." Assuming this to be correct, then perhaps there was a black *zeitgeist*, providing an alternative stream of nationalism that eventually fed into the Garvey movement. Inevitably, such a stream would have become diversified in a number of black nationalist religious currents—including that of the non-Christian movements that blossomed after the UNIA had declined.[8]

Among these non-Christian movements, most notable was the Moorish Science Temple, led by Noble Drew Ali, who was born Timothy Drew in North Carolina in 1886. Drew Ali migrated northward and secured employment on the railroad, settling in Newark, New Jersey. Drew Ali was apparently not well schooled, but he was sufficiently self-educated to have developed a taste for religious literature, including religious materials of an apocryphal and exotic nature.

Drew Ali's belief was that blacks could find salvation only when they discovered their "national origin"—their real identities as an "Asiatic" people, the Moorish American descendants of the ancient Moabites of northwest and southwest Africa. Indeed, he fervently rejected references such as "Negro," "colored," "African," or "Ethiopian." Drew Ali's movement spread from Newark, where it had been founded in 1913, and Moorish temples were established in cities with significant black populations such as Pittsburgh and Detroit. The Moorish movement eventually found its way to Chicago and was registered with the state of Illinois in 1926 as an organization dedicated to uplifting "fallen humanity" and instructing "those things necessary to make men and women become better citizens."[9]

Having been established in Chicago, Drew Ali now faced both his greatest hour as a leader and his bitterest time of disappointment, opposition, and division. While the movement enjoyed success, it was invariably exposed to hustlers, opportunists, and others seeking to exert their personal interests in the guise of the black liberation movement. Likewise, Chicago's Moorish followers were much more aggressive in expressing their racial dissatisfaction and began to accost whites on the streets, creating minor disturbances and drawing negative attention from the police. In his own publication, *Moorish Literature*, Drew Ali felt obligated to issue a "Divine Warning" to his followers, urging them to desist from "radical agitating" at work or on the streets. "We are for peace and not destruction," Drew Ali concluded.

Unfortunately, peace did not prevail in the Moorish movement. While Drew Ali apparently had a number of rivals, he faced significant opposition from one who called himself "Sheikh" and launched what became a bitter contest for supremacy in Chicago. However, in March 1929, while Drew Ali was out of the city, his rival was murdered; when he returned to Chicago, Drew Ali was arrested and jailed. During his incarceration, he issued what was apparently his last message. In a "warning and appeal," Drew Ali declared to his followers that he had been imprisoned for them and their cause, and that he had redeemed those who still believed "in me and my father, God."

The legacy of Noble Drew Ali, like that of Marcus Garvey, is vital to understanding the development of the Nation. While Garvey contributed the idea of a black religion with a black divinity, Drew Ali left an alternative black religious legacy that harkened back to an "Asiatic" identity in a Moorish homeland. Thus, while Garvey benignly opened the door to Islam, Drew Ali endeavored to step through that door, leading his followers toward a nominal Islamic religion.

Drew Ali's step toward Islam was hardly orthodox—another contribution to the black nationalist legacy that would eventually blossom in the Nation. Despite the fact that he lauded Islam and called it the "least appreciated" and "most misunderstood of the world's great religions," Drew Ali only added misunderstanding by introducing his own cultic errors in the name of Islam. This is epitomized in the fact that his organization's *Holy Koran* was not the Qur'an of the Islamic world, but rather a heavily plagiarized version of two documents, *The Aquarian Gospel of Jesus the Christ*, and a Tibetan writing entitled "Infinite Wisdom." *The Aquarian Gospel* was an apocryphal document first published in the early twentieth century; apparently Drew Ali merely made superficial modifications in his version, especially by changing "God" to "Allah."

Though Drew Ali apparently rejected the divinity of Jesus, he was hardly consistent with Islam by claiming he was the third reincarnation of the Prophet Muhammad—who was himself supposedly the reincarnation of Jesus Christ. Indeed, even Drew Ali's conception of God seems to have been more akin to the divinity of classical deism than that of the true Muslim.

Drew Ali showed respect to the United States and its Constitution from a purely nationalistic standpoint, and apparently he tended to minimize open condemnation of whites. A nationalist and separatist, he criticized the integrationist blacks for their "sinful ways of action," believing that the best way to coexist with whites was to maintain a strong, separate national identity, and practice the Moorish religion. However, his writings did contain mild criticism of the "Europeans," and one of his catechisms allude to the descendants of Adam and Eve being "Satan, Devil, Dragon and Beast." These words may hint at Drew Ali's private analysis of whites within the confines of the Moorish movement, though they would ultimately be expanded to more dramatic proportions in the Nation's teachings. Overall, Noble Drew Ali's movement clearly foreshadowed the Nation, which later appropriated his notion of a black Islamic-styled religion, a philosophy of racial separatism, and identification with an Asiatic nationalism. [10]

# 2

## The Nation before Malcolm X

*I am the one you were expecting.*

          The history of the Nation prior to Malcolm is actually two stories: the foundational organization of a mysterious peddler-turned-prophet, and the revision of that organization by a Southern migrant with aspirations to religious preeminence. In the thinking of the Nation, of course, there was an unbroken continuity between the original founder, W. D. Fard, and his black successor, Elijah Muhammad—just as today's leading manifestation of the Nation, under Louis Farrakhan, undoubtedly sees itself in unbroken continuity with Elijah Muhammad. However, the continuity that each version of the Nation has enjoyed is not so much organizational, but ideological. In the case of every dominant version there was a point of disintegration—at the disappearance or death of the leader—after which the Nation was reinvented, each organization claiming succession to the previous manifestation.[1]

The Nation that Malcolm entered was in fact the movement's predominant second manifestation under the leadership of Elijah Muhammad. By the late 1940s and early 1950s, Muhammad had proven himself a capable administrator and teacher. Despite the diminutive size of his movement, Muhammad had led his Nation into an institutional phase, with several temples in various cities and a small but loyal following of ministers and laypeople. The fact that Malcolm was eventually able to expand the Nation's borders is not only testimony to his organizational skills, but also to the able leadership of Muhammad, who was a capable organizer in his own right.

When the first manifestation of the Nation occurred in Detroit Elijah Muhammad was still Elijah Poole, a Georgia-born migrant. Having witnessed from childhood the brutality that the South demonstrated toward blacks, Muhammad had developed a keen analysis of whites. Though intimately acquainted with the Baptist church, Muhammad had early displayed the tendency to reject orthodox Christianity—a tendency that perhaps his father, an unordained "jackleg" preacher, also shared. Muhammad's life in the South, as later in Detroit, was characterized by hard work and a tireless, often agonizing, search of the Bible for an answer to his people's dilemma. Muhammad's answer apparently came, or so he believed, when he attended one of the Nation's meetings in 1931.[2]

The man whom Muhammad had come to hear was known among his black followers as W. D. Fard, though this name seems to have been a distortion of Farrad. He was also known as Wallace Farrad Muhammad—though Fard seems to have been the preferred reference among the Nation's membership. Fard's origins are somewhat mysterious, though it seems likely he was previously involved in both Garvey's UNIA and Drew Ali's Moorish Science Temple movement. Ironically, by appearance, W. D. Fard could even have passed for a white man of the Mediterranean type. Fard himself claimed to be of the lineage of the Prophet Muhammad, and that his origins were in Mecca. A variety of theories exist as to his descent, and though Fard may have been of Eastern descent it is almost certainly the case that his claim to Meccan lineage was bogus.

Fard appeared in Detroit in 1930, though neither as an activist nor a messiah. Rather, like the many Arab and Syrian salesmen of Detroit in that era, Fard used the peddler's guise to make his first contacts in the migrant black community. Selling raincoats and silks, Fard apparently won the affection of his clients by his genuine interest in their welfare and his desire to provide advice and information. He stimulated the interest of his customers by making repeated references to *their* homeland, and *their* people's ways and customs in that homeland. Fard advised them especially on matters of diet, and his concern for them apparently led to unorganized house group meetings.

During these home meetings, Fard began to expose the people to deeper teachings, particularly his caustic view of white people, Christianity, and the

Bible. Despite the fact that they were all too familiar with white racism, Fard's audiences were shocked at his drastic rejection of the cultural and religious norms of society. However, Fard was soon able to win them over, using in his defense the harsh realities of the racial status quo. Having established the loyalty of his listeners, Fard formed the Nation, which was also called "the Lost Found Nation of Islam," signifying his teaching that blacks were actually a lost Asiatic tribe, wandering in the "wilderness of North America."

The Nation was quickly organized in a place of worship and instruction that Fard called a "temple." This nomenclature was a tell-tale sign of the Nation's dubious "Islamic" heritage. Indeed, the Nation kept its "temples" for thirty years—until Malcolm X and Elijah Muhammad went to the Middle East in 1959–60, an experience that apparently shamed them into calling their sanctuaries "mosques."

Fard's operations undoubtedly reflected prior planning and experience. In a short time he had developed auxiliaries for men and women, as well as written and oral catechisms for the entire membership. He appointed assistant ministers and even began a "University of Islam," a parochial school for the Nation's children. Fard also organized the Fruit of Islam, a kind of elite Muslim guard that provided security for the temple and its ministers.[3]

A sample of Fard's oral catechism, the *Secret Ritual of the Nation of Islam*, provides some insight into his original religious teachings: "Me and my people who have been lost from home for 379 years have tried this so-called mystery God for bread, clothing and a home. And we receive nothing but hard times, hunger, naked and out of doors. Also was beat and killed by the ones that advocated that kind of God."[4] In short, Fard recommended the abandonment of Christianity by virtue of its supposed failure, and the failure of the "so-called mystery God" to grant provision and liberation to black people. At a purely religious level, it appears Fard saw no reason to salvage Christianity as Garvey had done; his negative allusion to the "mystery God," which Elijah Muhammad continued to echo for decades afterward, was clearly a reference to the essential mystery of the divine nature in Christian theology and not just a rejection of the cultural form of white Western Christendom.

Fard understandably clashed with the local black church and its ministers. As the Nation continued to prosper, he had undoubtedly deprived the churches of members, and his scathing religious criticisms could hardly have escaped notice within a predominately Christian community. Fard's role in the community was not limited to religious teachings, yet it was not merely racial leadership, either. Fard's social and racial teachings were inseparably bound up with his alternative theology, and everything he taught his black followers was premised on the notion that their God, Allah, was a black divinity.

Fard was able to hold the respect of his followers, even when he was opposed by the community's Christian clergy in a public confrontation. Even though Fard was apparently stifled by their "baffling questions," he had at least convinced the Nation of his supernatural powers and knowledge; they believed Fard's claim that he even knew the inner thoughts of the preachers. He also claimed to know the real names of his followers—their "Asiatic" identities, which he revealed to them after they had paid a registration fee and signed onto the movement. The names Fard gave his followers were no more authentic African names than were the European slave names they had inherited in the South. However, they happily received their "original" names, Asiatic names such as Sharrieff, Pasha, Karriem, and Mohammed.[5]

Fard reined in his followers in more practical ways beyond catechism and organizational structure. The Nation had a rigorous ethical and dietary code that restricted members to a strict life-style. Alcoholic beverages and tobacco products were forbidden, and consumption of pork, among other dietary regulations, was forbidden. Sexual ethics were likewise strict, with both premarital and extramarital relations prohibited.

By late 1932, however, Fard's problems had begun to accumulate. He began to make fewer public appearances, probably because of harassment from the police as well as competition from other "Moslem" and race-oriented leaders. Apparently two of his assistant ministers had proven to be especially troublesome, and one of them in particular tried to lead the Nation into the Moorish movement. It was during this time of crisis that Fard increasingly turned to his young assistant, Elijah Muhammad, to maintain stability in the Nation's temple.

Unlike the other ministers, it seems that Elijah Muhammad had an amazingly credulous faith in W. D. Fard. This was undoubtedly based on Muhammad's own previous social and religious experiences, and his apparent hunger for a racially messianic solution to the black man's situation in the United States. After he had heard Fard speak only for the second time, Elijah—still using the last name Poole—approached him, meekly declaring: "You are that one we read in the Bible that he would come in the last day under the name of Jesus. . . . You are that one?" Fard, who was probably taken aback by this naive expectation, responded: "Yes, I am the one that you have been looking for the last two thousand years; I am the one."

Thereafter, a special chemistry seems to have developed between the two. After that conversation, it seems that Fard began to reveal his messianic identity to the movement, assuring his black followers that "I am the one you were expecting." Muhammad was apparently overjoyed. He began to bear witness to Fard's messianic advent, announcing that his long-awaited salvation had come. He would even go home and get into his closet, where he would pray to W. D. Fard, "who brought us the truth that I was longing to hear."

In the temple, Elijah was at first given the name Karriem, but it was eventually changed to Muhammad. His claims to omniscience notwithstanding, Fard had mistakenly given Elijah and his two brothers three different last names. However, it is probable that Fard gave Elijah the name Muhammad later, especially after he proved to be his most faithful and devoted minister. Muhammad had accompanied Fard to Chicago for preaching expeditions, and had even begun to deify his leader in his speeches. Not surprisingly, Muhammad frequented the Detroit temple to monitor the other assistant ministers in the Nation, reporting back to Fard, who by late 1932 had withdrawn from the movement.

In May 1933 Fard was exiled from Detroit after harassment by police that resulted in several arrests. He apparently tried to rebuild his movement in Chicago, but was driven out of that city by the police as well. He was last seen at the Chicago airport in February 1934, where he bid farewell to his followers. "Don't worry," he promised, "I am with you; I will be back to you in the near future to lead you out of this hell." However, Fard never returned, and his movement was left to fragment—just as Noble Drew Ali's movement eventually succumbed to divisive strife from within.[6]

After Fard's banishment, most of his Detroit following either went back to the Christian church or allied themselves with various "Moslem" factions. Probably because of his loyalty to Fard, Elijah Muhammad found himself opposed, and even threatened, by other claimants to the prophet's mantle. Muhammad persevered but eventually felt constrained to leave Detroit with his family, who comprised the nucleus of his temple. Moving to Chicago, Muhammad established the Allah Temple of Islam—Allah, in this case, referring to W. D. Fard.

In Chicago "the Temple People," as Muhammad called his movement, did not find great success, either. They soon discovered they could not maintain a stable location for their temple and were constantly being forced out of leases by landlords—who were themselves probably under pressure from law enforcement agencies. This antagonism was likely heightened by the bold resistance to government and police that characterized Muhammad's followers, especially in Chicago. Drew Ali's Moorish followers in Chicago had distinguished themselves by their aggressive response to whites; it also seems likely that Muhammad had acquired some of Drew Ali's followers in his Chicago congregation. Not surprisingly, Muhammad's Temple People clashed with police on at least two occasions, with one fracas taking place inside a courtroom. Yet Muhammad's tribulations were only beginning.

Having apparently established two small congregations, Muhammad was still facing rivals whose threats were all too real. No longer safe even in Chicago, Elijah Muhammad took to the road, living as a kind of leader in exile, fleeing from city to city and using pseudonyms to protect his identity. Leaving Detroit's Temple No. 1 and Chicago's Temple No. 2 in the hands of assistants, Muhammad left in 1935. Moving through Wisconsin and finally settling in Washington, D.C., Muhammad was known as "Mohammed Rasool" and "Gulam Bogans." During this time, matters worsened when Muhammad's assistant ministers in Detroit and Chicago seceded, taking followers with them.

In May 1942, shortly after the United States had responded to Japan's attack by declaring war, Muhammad was arrested in Washington, D.C., for inciting his followers to resist the draft. Back in Chicago, police completely closed down Temple No. 2 on the pretext that the Temple People were affiliated with the Japanese (a charge that may have held some truth with respect to Fard). Muhammad, as Gulam Bogans, told a grand jury in Washington that he had been advised by Allah to have nothing to do with war or fighting.

Though Muhammad's family and followers eventually posted bail for their leader, he was moved back to Chicago for trial and was ultimately sentenced to five years in a federal correction facility for encouraging draft resistance. In fact, during World War II, more than one hundred of Muhammad's followers served jail sentences for refusing to register for the draft according to their leader's instruction. The immediate effect on Muhammad's movement was devastating; with many of its men imprisoned and the Chicago temple shut down, the movement was once again temporarily reduced to a house meeting format. Having lost members through secession, imprisonment, and intimidation by law enforcement agencies, the Temple People persevered. While Muhammad was serving his prison sentence, his followers first rented then purchased their first property in Chicago.[7]

Ironically, Muhammad and his organization seem to have benefited from prison life. During his incarceration, Muhammad apparently began to plan economic strategies with his followers, which they implemented upon release. He emerged from prison with a "new vision"—the conviction that his movement had to transform itself into an organization that was no longer an underground movement. Without renouncing his former commitment to W. D. Fard's deity, Elijah Muhammad nevertheless sought a more progressive agenda. He encouraged his followers to expand their thinking and even welcomed the advent of the television into his home. After he established new businesses in the community, the movement began to cultivate a friendly presence there.

In the teachings of the movement Muhammad was equally astute. After getting out of prison, he aggressively collected the remaining materials that had been produced by Fard. "He took those things out of circulation and then he began himself to interpret, to preach, and put the emphasis where he wanted the emphasis to be." While Muhammad's actions undoubtedly reflected a genuine concern for his religious heritage, it seems he was also exerting a control that he knew would be necessary if the movement were to survive and grow. In this regard, Muhammad was undoubtedly successful.

One knowledgeable witness wrote in 1951: "Elijah Mohammed now follows the steps of Fard in all the details of his thought and actions." Muhammad's leadership had been developed and established, the observer wrote, "by the support that he has acquired from Fard first and by his exact imitation of Fard himself later on." Though an imitator, Muhammad was clever enough to centralize himself as "the maintainer of the ideology and morale of the group." By controlling and manipulating all the instrumentalities of the movement, Elijah Muhammad became the undisputed "stimulator of a kind of coordinated and collective action." No longer a fleeing, persecuted teacher, Muhammad was now a religious magnate with the last word on all matters of the movement.[8]

Muhammad's teachings remained nationalistic, though in the sense that his followers perceived themselves as an exclusive black nation with roots in the Asiatic city of Mecca. Though Fard had never actively claimed divinity, Elijah Muhammad now expanded the notion of the Mahdi to Christian proportions—applying a divine nature to Fard as the Messiah. Upon joining his movement, Muhammad's followers did not receive "Moslem" names from him as Fard had done. Instead, new members were required to drop their last names, replacing them with "X." Since their former names were considered the legacy of slavery, the "X" was itself a personal rejection of the white man's world and a demonstration of their conviction that someday Fard would return to grant them their true names.

Separation from whites remained central to the teachings of Elijah Muhammad's organization, and the doors of the movement were opened only to blacks, even though there was a non-black Muslim presence in Chicago. Unlike Garvey, Muhammad did not tie his nationalism to Africa; however, neither did he look forward to repatriating black people to Asia. When land was demanded, it was usually couched in the language of reparations, not repatriation. Ultimately, Muhammad's call was vague, urging blacks to "return to their own," which may have hinted at a separate racial settlement in the United States, yet as an idea remained fluid enough to fill any black nationalist's cup.

The moralism and dietary restrictions prescribed by Fard were carried over into Muhammad's organization. The life-style of the followers of Muhammad's "Islam" evidenced a fervent devotion to the morality and self-help philosophy of the movement. Indeed, Muhammad instructed his followers to eat only one meal per day. Men were to dress in suits and women were attired in Muslim outfits, complete with head coverings. Children were strictly reared and disciplined, and—if possible—were enrolled in Muhammad's version of the University of Islam.

Muhammad's temple worship and rituals were not in accordance with the prescribed traditions of true Islam. In essence, Muhammad's meetings were lectures, with little prayer and none of the hymn singing that his people would have known from the Christian church. Readings were taken both from the Bible and the Qur'an, but the greater emphasis in these presentations seems to have been placed on the Bible. Prayers were conducted in the followers' homes, but not in correspondence to the five daily prayers of the Muslim world. Later, Malcolm X probably led the movement toward more authenticity in their worship; the Nation's 1957 publication, *Muslim Daily Prayers*, a devotional guide, evidenced a greater inclination toward orthodox Islam.

Still, there was a fundamental unorthodoxy about Muhammad's teachings, insofar as Islam is concerned. All the aspects of the movement were bound up with the claim that Fard had been a divine manifestation, and that Muhammad himself was Fard's sole representative, the "Messenger of Allah." This became the assumption under which both the Bible and the Qur'an were studied and interpreted. Similarly, just as Fard's divine nature was intrinsic to Muhammad's program, so also were the teachings built upon the prerequisite belief that Satan was not a supernatural being but rather the inherently evil and inferior white race. The theology of Elijah Muhammad turned completely on this doctrine and upon the notion that Allah (Fard) was going to unleash a final, devastating catastrophe upon the white man's world from which only his black followers would escape.

Interestingly, it was only after his new, progressive agenda had been implemented that Elijah Muhammad claimed complete succession to Fard. Probably in the late 1940s, Muhammad changed the name of his organization to "the Nation of Islam," finally appropriating the full identity of Fard's movement. Having survived many crises and competitive attacks, his success was apparently complete. Elijah Muhammad now led his followers into an institutional stage that no other "Moslem" leader had ever achieved in the realm of black urban religion. The new Nation had gained the stability that could allow further growth without threat to its established leadership.[9] The stage was now set for Malcolm X.

# PART TWO

# The First Moment

*Woe to me, my mother, that you have borne me as a man
of strife and a man of contention to all the land!*
　　　　　　　　　　　　　　　　*—Jeremiah 15:10a*

While Malcolm's conversion to the Nation had its dramatic and even revelatory aspects, it was really not a sudden conversion. He thought that the biblical account of St. Paul's conversion was similar to his own, though he wrote in his autobiography that he did not mean to compare himself with the saint. "But," Malcolm added, "I do understand his experience."[1] Actually, Malcolm X identified with Paul the Apostle much more than he was willing to share with his readers. While he clearly associated elements of his conversion story with Paul's dramatic rebirth, Malcolm was also quite fond of Paul's role as an ecclesiastical leader.

In a letter written in 1960, Malcolm X told Elijah Muhammad that, from the onset of his ministry in the Nation, "I have studied those in the [B]ible who did most to help spread the 'Gospel of Jesus' and tried my best to copy them or to walk in their footsteps without anyone knowing it." Of course, Malcolm meant that he was imitating "their tactics and efforts," not the Christian theology they espoused, and he went on to cite a number of biblical models he sought to emulate, such as Aaron, the priest and brother of Moses the prophet. He also noted that he sought to avoid being a "doubting Thomas," a "denying Peter," or a "betraying Judas." But Malcolm made it clear that he had a particular attraction to the ministry of Paul the Apostle: "I've secretly tried to be a Fisherman, a Gospel spreading Paul, a letter-writing (Journalist) Paul, a traveling Paul, a diplomat to all classes of people . . . and ALLAH has blessed me. I would never tell this to anyone but you because no one else would understand me."[2]

With such feelings about emulating Paul, it is not surprising that Malcolm minimized his identification with the apostle in the autobiography. These feelings were so personal that he shared them only with Elijah Muhammad, and then only after six years of ministry in the Nation's New York Temple. Apart from revealing Malcolm's deep commitment to Elijah Muhammad, these words reflect a number of important aspects of Malcolm's life and work in the Nation. First, they make it clear that his zealotry in promoting Elijah Muhammad and the Nation was not only premeditated, but very carefully planned and executed. Second, Malcolm's words reflect not only how he found in the Nation a reason and motivation for study, but how he appropriated the Bible for the betterment of Mr. Muhammad's cause.

Finally, these words also reveal how Malcolm perceived his role in the Nation. Whether an Aaron or a Paul, Malcolm X cherished his function as right-hand man. However, he did not aspire to usurp Elijah Muhammad's place, nor to assume a divinely appointed headship as his successor. Rather, Malcolm X believed his role in the Nation was unique, even as Paul's role was unique to the foundation of the Christian church.

Neither a messiah nor one of Christ's original disciples, Paul was the late-born witness, the thirteenth apostle whose mission emanated from a revelatory vision rather than a three-year apprenticeship with Jesus of Nazareth. Unlike the original twelve disciples, Paul's mission was inherently different. None of the twelve were prone to advance their faith outside the racial-religious sphere of first century Judaism; they were apparently content to keep primitive Christianity a Jewish sect. In contrast, Paul wanted to extend the boundaries of Christianity to include the gentile world, as well as the distinct worlds of women and slaves.

Malcolm X seems to have been quite conscious of these Pauline aspects, and he clearly applied them to his own ministry. He was not an eyewitness to the cultic ministry of W. D. Fard, nor was he present at the foundation of Elijah Muhammad's Nation. When he entered the ranks of the Nation's clergy, Malcolm was younger than the small number of established ministers in the movement. His enthusiasm, energy, and vision were refreshing to the Nation, which by the early 1950s was settling into an institutional phase in the black community. Malcolm X was dissatisfied with the Nation as he found it, not only because it was too small for his evangelistic appetites, but because the organization had apparently become satisfied with its marginal but secure presence in the urban black setting. Like Paul, Malcolm X was determined to push his religious community to the regions beyond—driven by his zeal for Muhammad's message, his love for black people, and the enduring force of his own conversion.

In this regard, Malcolm undoubtedly relished the story of the transformation of Saul the persecutor to Paul the apostle. He was particularly drawn to the crisis moment when—as Malcolm described it—Paul "was so smitten that he was knocked off his horse, in a daze." Nevertheless, Malcolm was not so much focusing on the instantaneous nature of the conversion as he was on the crisis theme of a sinner facing divine light. "Only guilt admitted accepts the truth," Malcolm declared in the same context. It seems, then, that this is how he may have understood and identified with St. Paul: in their former lives both had committed sin and rebelled against the very divinity who—in the moment of religious crisis—was revealed to them.

Suddenly blinded by the light of truth on the road to self-destruction, Malcolm identified his conversion with Paul's spiritual arrest on the road to Damascus. Malcolm felt that he, like Paul, had been rescued by a power far greater than he could have imagined, or believed, in his former life. The truth that came to him, Malcolm said, "was like a blinding light," and the first thing that it seemed to reveal to him was his own guilt. "The very enormity of my previous life's guilt," Malcolm confessed, "prepared me to accept the truth."[3]

Accepting the truth, as Malcolm would come to know it in the Nation, was an acceptance that required a process of transformation before it would be complete. This process, however, seems to have been sealed by a sudden and dramatic moment of crisis and revelation—a moment that would serve to fuse the youthful Malcolm Little to the Nation for the next sixteen years of his life. As such, that moment proved to link him with the movement's past, present, and future. Unlike St. Paul's moment of religious crisis, however, Malcolm Little's moment came neither in broad daylight nor on an open road.

The moment came for Malcolm, rather, during the night, as he lay on a bed in his prison cell. As he recorded in his own autobiography, "I suddenly, with a start, became aware of a man sitting beside me in my chair." Malcolm's description of the apparition is as vivid as it is eerie: "He had on a dark suit. I remember . . . he wasn't black, and he wasn't white. He was light-

brown-skinned, an Asiatic cast of countenance, and he had oily black hair
. . . I couldn't place him racially—other than that I knew he was a non-European. I had no idea whatsoever who he was."[4] Malcolm says he continued staring through the shadows into the face of this figure, who was apparently sitting close to his bed. "I didn't get frightened," Malcolm maintained. "I knew I wasn't dreaming." For those few moments Malcolm and his mysterious guest were transfixed, as if frozen. Malcolm made no exclamation, and the man in the chair said nothing. Then, as suddenly as he had come, the silent figure in the chair was gone.

Malcolm seems to have drawn no immediate conclusions from the incident. The man he had seen was entirely unknown to him. Yet, as we will see, the vision occurred at a pivotal time in his relationship to the Nation, an almost mystical purview that he would later believe had given him a glimpse of someone yet unknown to him. Only after Malcolm had solidified his role as a devoted follower of Elijah Muhammad did he claim to know the true identity of the mysterious "light-brown-skinned" apparition. He concluded it was a "pre-vision"—a vision "of someone whom you never have seen before . . . exactly as he looks." He came to believe, in time, that this "pre-vision" was none other than the mysterious "Asiatic" founder of the Nation, W. D. Fard, who had been missing for nearly two decades.

Of the many exceptional scenes in *The Autobiography of Malcolm X*, this scene of the mysterious apparition is certainly one of the strangest and, not surprisingly, one of the most overlooked aspects of Malcolm's story. When the ghostly figure *has* been discussed, however, it has been minimized—presented as a self-induced illusion or as some supposed evidence of psychological family weakness.[5] In this religious study, however, neither psychological assumption is acceptable to me. I do not share the antisupernaturalist presuppositions of psychoanalysis and maintain that Malcolm indeed experienced some sort of metaphysical phenomenon, and that his narrative should be respected as testimony of an authentic religious experience.

The mysterious apparition of the seated guest, as a religious event, occurred at a critical hour in Malcolm's relationship to the Nation. As such, it heavily impacted upon his worldview, family relationships, and theological perceptions. At first it seemed to provide him with a personal mystery that he sensed was somehow sacred, and later it served as proof that his conversion had been both authentic and special. Undoubtedly, it also provided Elijah Muhammad with the means of pulling Malcolm into the heart of the movement, convincing the young disciple of the divinely inspired mission of the Nation.

This "pre-vision" becomes the key to understanding the first moment of Malcolm's religious sojourn—his conversion to the Nation. Certainly, as a climactic point in his life, it becomes the watershed in the flow of his experiences before exposure to the Nation. Likewise, as a devout convert, follower, and servant of Elijah Muhammad, the pre-vision became Malcolm's beatific vision. It authenticated Mr. Muhammad's claims and fueled Malcolm's own increasing involvement in "Nation-building."

This first moment, then, becomes the basis for reviewing Malcolm's youth and conversion and for discussing his quintessential role in transforming the Nation from a small, marginalized institution to an ambitious, expansive, and sometimes notorious movement.

# 3

## A Garveyite Son

*Whenever a black man was outspoken, he was*
*considered crazy or dangerous.*

Since childhood, Malcolm Little's life had been characterized by all of the essential themes that would later underscore his message to a generation of black people engulfed in crisis. In the particular sense of racism, Malcolm would come to know from his youth the reality of white racial animosity and insouciance toward the black struggle. That reality would increasingly press in on his human experience as he grew from childhood into manhood.

Ironically, however, just as Malcolm's story can easily be said to typify the black experience in the United States—especially the Northern urban experience—his beginnings were not at all typical in some significant ways. In fact, these uncommon, even unique aspects of his foundational years gave his work and message distinctive features that became key to his success as a black leader in an era when many organizations and leaders were competing for the devotion of blacks.

Malcolm Little was born on May 19, 1925, in Omaha, Nebraska—an unlikely nativity for the man who would become the icon of the urban black struggle in the later twentieth century. At the time of Malcolm's birth, Elijah

Poole, not yet christened Elijah Muhammad, was working in a factory in Detroit, still searching for some kind of revelation to appease his messianic appetites. At the same time, Noble Drew Ali's movement was at its peak in Chicago, and Marcus Garvey was imprisoned in Atlanta, where he would remain until his deportation in 1927.

It is perhaps no coincidence that Malcolm was born in this era of crisis, when the failure of the United States to resolve its racial injustices in the nineteenth century had been passed into the twentieth. Bitter legacy as it was, "the Negro problem"—which was really the national curse of white racial dysfunction—was inherited by yet another generation of whites who would not own up to the truth, and another generation of blacks who could not escape the consequences of white people's self-deception. Some black men thus passed on to their sons and daughters the hope of integration, and the dream of acceptance. Other black men, such as Earl Little, a follower of Marcus Garvey, passed on a different legacy to their children. And thus it was the birthright of Earl's son, Malcolm, to embrace a black God, a black aim, and a black destiny.

Malcolm's father was J. Early (Earl) Little, a native of Reynolds, Georgia, and his mother was Louise (Louisa) Norton Little, who had emigrated from the Caribbean to the United States. Both were enthusiastic supporters of Marcus Garvey, and both were actively involved as organizers in Garvey's UNIA. Earl Little traveled around preaching Garvey's ideas, often from behind the pulpits of African American churches—the memory of which left the mistaken impression in the mind of a young Malcolm that his father was an itinerant, unordained Christian preacher. However, Earl Little, who was lauded with the honorary titles of the "Reverend" and "Elder," made no claim to being a minister. His frequent appearances in black churches was surely a matter of political expediency and security. "He mostly used the church as a means of getting to the people to talk about Marcus Garvey's philosophy," recalled Wilfred Little.[1]

Young Malcolm Little was inevitably immersed in the atmosphere of his parents' political activism since infancy. In his autobiography, Malcolm writes that even as a boy he preferred the cool, intelligent behavior of the Garveyites to the excitement and emotion of the Christian church, which he said "confused and amazed" him. In his childhood memories Malcolm clearly recalled the Garveyite meetings, along with the UNIA's slogans and trappings. More important, Malcolm also remembered—undoubtedly with filial pride—the grinning expression of one elderly black woman as she lauded his father's Garveyite speech: "You're scaring these white folks to death!" Scaring white folks to death would also become Malcolm's unique birthright.

It is probably no exaggeration to say that the influence of his parents, both by virtue of their philosophy as well as their temperaments, was the major factor that molded Malcolm's future. Certainly others would influence him in his later years and undeniably he was strongly influenced by Elijah Muhammad in particular. Yet the heart of Malcolm's activism and struggle was formed in the character and commitment of Earl and Louise Little and his later reflection upon their lives.

This is explicit, for instance, in Malcolm's words in a speech delivered in April 1964 about the deaths of blacks killed as a result of racism. He included his father along with slain African leader Patrice Lamumba and Medgar Evers, the civil rights activist assassinated in 1963. Implicitly, the force of his mother's valiant struggle to keep her family together without her husband, and under great stress, remained with Malcolm all of his life. In the epilogue to Malcolm's autobiography, Alex Haley recalled his own initial difficulties in assisting Malcolm in the writing of his story, and noted how deeply moved Malcolm became in recalling his mother's struggles.[2]

The Little household laid the foundation for the critical aspects of Malcolm's later ideas, just as it gave to him his personal characteristics and traits. For Malcolm, intelligence was an especially admirable trait, and he respected learned people. No doubt this was a reflection of his early exposure to the Garveyite meetings, which Malcolm remembered as intelligent, purposeful, and organized—"it made me feel the same way." In his earliest memories of home, Malcolm recalled parents whose first love was to disperse information and provide social education to blacks in the name of liberation.

This remains key to understanding the development of Malcolm as a social and political leader in his own right. As we will see, even after Malcolm broke with the racialist presuppositions of Elijah Muhammad, he was still fundamentally grounded in a Garveyite worldview. Garveyite research of the UNIA's *Negro World* has provided insight about the involvement of the Littles in the movement.

Earl Little was not only a Garveyite organizer, but he was president of the Omaha branch of the UNIA, which was apparently a large enough group to create concern among organized white racists. The success of Mr. Little's leadership in Omaha was typified by his branch's ability to obtain its own "Liberty Hall," which was the central meeting place designated for Garveyites, much as the Nation would later centralize meetings in their own temples or mosques.

Malcolm was perhaps too young to note the extent of his mother's involvement in her husband's Garveyite labors. Maybe because of the novelty of the experience, Malcolm was able to recall attending UNIA branch meetings with his father. But his elder brother Wilfred also remembers that because there was no UNIA Liberty Hall in their hometown of Lansing, Earl Little would drive down to Detroit, sometimes leading other cars. In his autobiography Malcolm neglects to mention, probably because he didn't know, that his Caribbean-born mother contributed articles to the "News of Divisions" section of *Negro World.* Mrs. Little's articles, in fact, verify Malcolm's statement that his parents went to work in Milwaukee after leaving Omaha, and they provide brief glimpses into Mr. Little's UNIA activities as well.[3]

Malcolm was the fourth of Earl and Louise's seven children, though Earl already had three children from a previous marriage. Earl and Louise were married in Montreal on May 10, 1919, and lived for a while in Philadelphia, where Wilfred, their first child, was born. The other children—Hilda, Philbert, Malcolm, Reginald, Wesley, and Yvonne—were born in Omaha or elsewhere in the Midwest, since the Littles moved from Omaha, then to Milwaukee, and finally into the Lansing, Michigan, area.

Malcolm described his father as "a big, six-foot-four, very black man," and his mother as a slender woman with very light skin and long dark hair. Yet the cultural contrast between his father and mother was equally striking. Earl Little was from Georgia, the environment of which must have been intensely racist and therefore extremely limiting to his development—almost certainly substantiated by his limited schooling, having completed, according to Malcolm, only the third or fourth grade. Undoubtedly a man of strong will and character, Mr. Little was largely self-educated and self-motivated in his organizational, professional, and business achievements.[4]

Louise Little was born on "the isle of spice," Grenada, ninety miles northeast of the larger island nation of Trinidad. Grenada was colonized first by the French, who had slaughtered most of the indigenous Carib people of the island in the mid-seventeenth century. The island was ceded by the French to the British in the Treaty of Versailles in 1783, and the British managed to maintain control of the sugar-producing colony despite later French attempts to win it back. By the mid-nineteenth century Grenada had been transformed into a cocoa- and spice-producing colony, and the majority black population, which had been emancipated in 1838, was augmented by

imported black freedmen and other laborers from Portugal and the Mediterranean island of Malta.

Malcolm explained in his autobiography that his maternal grandfather
was a white European, a fact that both he and his mother lamented. Louise,
unlike her husband, was not only well schooled, but she was also educated
in the more exacting Anglican tradition, which also seems to have included
French language lessons. Her work as a reporter for the UNIA's publication
showed that while sharing her husband's zeal for the black struggle, she more
than shared in the burden of his work.[5]

To say that Malcolm and his siblings were reared in a Garveyite home is
no exaggeration. The Little children were undoubtedly accustomed to hearing their father's powerful baritone voice leading the Garveyites in prayers
and hymns; likewise, they regularly enjoyed sitting around the stove while
Louise told them stories about their proud ancestry as black people. "She
told us we came from great people that were onetime rulers," Malcolm's
brother Philbert recalled. Indeed, the influence of Garvey's philosophy permeated their entire family life, particularly in two respects.

First, the self-help emphasis of Marcus Garvey was not taken merely as a
model for the masses, but as a principle of the household. "We always lived
outside of the city, where we had some land to be independent," Wilfred
Little remembers, adding that "my father wanted that independence." Independence, especially to a Garveyite organizer, was both an economic and
political expedient, especially since Mr. Little, who was apparently a freelance craftsman, was frequently blackballed because of his political activities.
Living in the rural area of Lansing, the Littles raised their own food, and
Louise canned the produce, both for the family's consumption and for the
market. The Littles had their own cow for dairy products, and raised chickens
and rabbits for sale to the largely white community in which they lived.
What the children could not sell to people driving by the Little's property
they would sell wholesale to produce dealers at the city market.

The self-help philosophy was integrated into chores and small projects for
the Little children as well. Strictly disciplined, the children supported their
parents' independent philosophy by working in the garden and doing other
chores. Malcolm remembered asking his mother if he could plant his own
personal garden, and he tended and cared for it with great pride—particularly at the thought of adding its fruits to the family table. But Malcolm was
no exception: apparently all of Earl and Louise's children were allocated
ground for personal gardens. The children would send for seeds through a
mail-order catalog, often preferring to experiment with exotic or unusual

produce such as banana musk melon. In short, the whole family was expected to participate in the economics of self-help that characterized Marcus
Garvey's gospel of black nationalism.

A second feature of Garvey's influence that filled the Little home, and
was undoubtedly rooted in Malcolm's thinking, was Africentrism. Malcolm
stated in his autobiography that his childhood conception of Africa was much
like that of other children in the United States, picturing it as the stereotypical dark continent—a place of steaming jungles filled with natives and wild
animals. Yet in pointing this out, Malcolm was underscoring that such
misconceptions were incongruous to the essentially African emphasis of his
home life.

Though young Malcolm may not have had a proper understanding of the
African continent for a time, he was quickly sensitized to black internationalism. This he knew simply because his mother was a black woman who was
in some ways different from the other black people he knew in Lansing. In
mentioning that Louise Little had an accent that "didn't sound like a Negro's," Malcolm was showing his childhood exposure to black cultural diversity. He likewise remembered his mother pointing out that besides herself,
only a few other Caribbean blacks lived in their area of Michigan, including
their good friends, the Lyons family.[6]

The Littles received not only *Negro World*, but they also regularly read
other black publications, including newspapers from the Caribbean. At the
dinner table, the Little children would hear their parents discuss the philosophy and concerns of Garvey's "scattered Africa," undoubtedly making Malcolm sensitive to Africentrism. "So we were more or less international type
of thinkers," Wilfred recalls of those early days. "We grew up thinking in an
international sense because we were exposed to that. We were keeping up
with what was going on in the Caribbean area and parts of Africa; and we
were keeping up with what was happening around the country as far as the
[Garvey] movement was concerned."[7] Drawing from these roots years later,
Malcolm would declare to an audience of black people, "That's what we
are—Africans who are in America. You're nothing but Africans." This was
the international black perspective nurtured in the family of Earl and Louise
Little that would, in full flower, make Malcolm a global African.

Malcolm's autobiography begins with the disclosure that just before he
was born, the family home in Omaha was attacked by the Ku Klux Klan
(KKK). According to Malcolm's account, his father was away at the time,
and the Klan took advantage of the situation in an attempt to intimidate
Louise Little by breaking all the windows and demanding that the family

leave town. The veracity of this incident has been challenged, even though Wilfred recalled the attack quite vividly, saying he and Hilda, his younger sister, clung fearfully to their mother's skirts while the sound of breaking window glass and the shouting of threats filled the night air.[8]

It is a historical fact that the KKK was active in the North and West at the time of Malcolm's birth, though it was not quite the same as the original nineteenth-century southern racist organization. Still, the twentieth-century version was equally belligerent toward blacks, but now their hatred was directed at Roman Catholic foreigners and Jews as well. Malcolm's account of the attack on his home verifies that "the Klan's willingness to use coercive means to gain its ends was its distinguishing characteristic."

There is historical irony in the fact that the KKK voiced a distorted support of Garvey, but only in the sense that Garvey's UNIA advocated racial separatism. The KKK criticized integrationist black leaders such as A. Philip Randolph for opposing the UNIA, and at one point they even tried to coerce him to support black separatism. And though Garvey and his UNIA opposed the KKK, Garvey gave them a back-handed tribute by acknowledging they were "perfectly honest and frank" about their racism. Garvey assured the UNIA that any effort to fight the KKK would bring about no change because it represented the "invisible government" of the white nation.

Although there was no organizational cooperation between the UNIA and the KKK, Garvey's integrationist enemies rallied against him, calling him an ally of organized white racism. Still, Garvey and his followers recognized and acknowledged what the black integrationists did not—that "there was no clear, categorical distinction between Klan power and legal authority."[9] The Little family became aware of this time and time again.

By 1929, the Littles had relocated to the Lansing area and purchased a three-lot property with a small, one-and-a-half story house. The deed to the property contained a racial exclusion clause, of which the Littles seem to have been unaware. According to the Michigan state police, their white neighbors "resented the presence of the colored family" enough to initiate legal proceedings that resulted in a court ruling requiring their eviction.

Before the eviction could occur, Earl and Louise were awakened in the early morning hours of November 8, 1929, by an explosion. They quickly discovered that their home was set ablaze. Salvaging a few personal items, they escaped with the children, though their infant daughter was nearly left behind amid the confusion. Malcolm recalled the incident as "the nightmare night" and noted that his father had shot his pistol at the two fleeing white men who had apparently set the fire. Young Malcolm was amazed that, while the family stood outside, undressed and helpless before the flames, "white police and firemen came and stood around watching as the house burned to the ground."

It has been suggested that the firemen from Lansing did not show up because the fire occurred outside the city limits, though the official report of the Michigan State Police Department states merely that the fire department "refused to come." In such a case, one would have to assume that there was *no* fire department service to any of the households outside of Lansing—a notion that is untenable. It seems safe to assume that the fire department would not have refused assistance to a white family in the same situation.[10]

Even allowing for a degree of literary license, Malcolm's account of the destruction of his home is essentially correct. Like the rest of his childhood recollections, this scene must be read in the context of the racist society in which he lived. The Littles were a black family living in a white neighborhood where most whites made no secret of their prejudice. Even more, the Littles were black activists who refused to conform to the assumed standards of either the white or black communities.

Given the thin line that separated many whites from the organized white racists of that era, it is entirely probable that white officials would refuse to assist the Littles, and they may even have come, unofficially, to watch the house burn to the ground. This possibility is given credence by the fact that the Michigan state police investigation was undertaken on the premise that Earl Little was an arsonist—that he had set the fire himself.

To cast doubt on Malcolm's account of the incident, an elaborate explanation has been concocted by one biographer, allegedly based on the same police report. It suggests that Earl Little had run through his sleeping neighborhood knocking on doors, and then returned home to set his house ablaze in an attempt to give the impression that others had set the fire. Furthermore, the investigators are said to have suspected this deception, and thus didn't believe Earl's claim that two white men had set the blaze. In truth, however, the police report contains no such speculation on the part of the police. But it is significant that the police did not even record Earl Little's statement about two white men—though Wilfred Little specifically recalled his father telling the police about them.

This wildly contradictory and speculative account obviously goes to great lengths to try to prove that Earl Little was an arsonist. The very same police report reveals that the Little family was at the time legally fighting the unjust eviction, and that their lawyer was determined to bring the case to the state supreme court. What weighs all the more heavily against the concocted account is that, at the time of the fire, Earl Little had no insurance on his home. He had let the policy lapse, either out of forgetfulness or—more probably—because of financial stress. The morning after the fire, Little apparently went to the insurance office to make a payment on the policy, making no mention of the fire until later that day. His behavior suggests that the fire caught him completely off-guard, and he had hoped to be able to salvage something after the disaster by reactivating his insurance policy.

The state police report about the incident shows that the authorities had far more interest in the gun that Earl Little had used to shoot at the arsonists than in the fire itself. They asked him virtually no questions about the details of the fire, yet, according to Malcolm, they asked him repeatedly about the gun and searched for it—which is verified by the state police transcript. Earl had temporarily given the weapon to a neighbor whom he must have trusted, and later he transferred it to a hiding place. It is clear that the police trumped up the charge of "suspected arson" by Earl to cover up their search for the black man's gun. "It was a typical actualization of the Klan mentality, a mentality not limited to those who were members of the KKK," since by searching for the handgun the police "evidently hoped to disarm the defender and thereby to defend his attackers." [11]

Indeed, the attacks on the Little family in Omaha and Lansing were not isolated incidents, but "they must be understood as skirmishes in an ongoing war between Garveyites and members of the Klan." Other Garveyite organizers endured similar attacks and, along with their families, were forced to live under great stress because of organized racism as well as individual white prejudice. In fact, the Klan-like "Black Legion" referred to by Malcolm in the autobiography was active in Michigan a year before the Little home was burned down. Bombings and murders were part of its program of racial warfare in Ohio and Michigan, and their infiltration into police and fire departments, as well as other agencies, is a matter of record.

Not surprisingly, it is at this point in the story that Malcolm recalled increased "friction" in the family's home life, especially between his parents. Though the Littles were able to rebuild their lives in another part of the Lansing area, it is likely that whatever domestic problems the couple may have had, they were dealing with pressures Malcolm did not yet understand. Wilfred Little would later recall that his Garveyite parents lived under the stigma of being "oddballs"—often the targets of ill feelings of both whites and blacks because of their political activism. Readers of Malcolm's autobiography probably do not know enough of "the tremendous outside pressures impinging upon the domestic tranquillity of the families of activists of that time."

Things proceeded from bad to worse for the Little family. In 1931, Earl Little was killed, purportedly in a streetcar accident. The black community in Lansing, however, was whispering that Little had actually been brutally attacked and was left on the tracks to be run over by a streetcar. A coroner's inquest established that Little's death was an accident. According to the state police report, Little was found lying on the streetcar tracks, bleeding profusely but still conscious; police noted "blood under the rear truck of Car No. 624."[12]

Malcolm would later freely speak of his father's death as a racially motivated murder. Malcolm's assistant minister recalls that Malcolm said his father had been found with a gag in his mouth. However, when he spoke at Michigan State University in 1963, Malcolm preferred to refer to the incident as an accident, perhaps because it had occurred in that vicinity. However, it seems that Malcolm wasn't certain about the circumstances of his father's death and suspected that his death had been made to look like an accident. In 1963, at the height of his career in the Nation, he informed Elijah Muhammad that he had retained both a lawyer and a private detective to investigate the incident.[13]

Like the rest of his family, Malcolm viewed his father's tragic death through the lens of a racist system. He pointed out to Kenneth Clark: "Whenever a black man was outspoken, he was considered crazy or dangerous. And the police department and various branches of the law usually were interwoven with that Klan element, so the Klan had the backing of the police, and usually the police had the backing of the Klan, same as today."[14] Interviewing Malcolm in 1964, an *Ebony* writer drew a similar conclusion about Malcolm's thoughts regarding his father's death: "The killing, Malcolm says, was officially listed as a traffic accident. 'I was only six years at the time, but I had already learned that being a Negro in this country was a liability.' "

Malcolm recalled that the black community, which—politically speaking—had no great love for his father, still whispered their suspicions about the tragic death. The accident report itself is suspect in its lack of Earl Little's testimony regarding the event even though he was conscious at the time he was found by the police.[15] Were Earl Little's words about the supposed accident disregarded in the police report, as was his previous insistence that two white men had set his house on fire?

# 4

## Early Life and
## Religious Training

*A brainwashed black Christian.*

For Malcolm to state "I was born in trouble"[1] was no exaggeration. His childhood was directly and indirectly affected by white racism and
the troubles of his Garveyite family. Nevertheless, Malcolm was still a child
seeking the things that children seek, getting in trouble and learning the
lessons of life through adventures and misadventures. And though it might
not be so obvious in *The Autobiography of Malcolm X*, it appears that some
of his boyhood adventures involved his first religious experiences.

One of Malcolm's more thoughtful adventures was his discovery of contemplation, which he seemed to find at once comforting and affirming.
Many years later, he recalled with a great deal of reflection what he had
considered a significant contemplative aspect of his youth: "Out behind our
house, out in the country from Lansing, Michigan, there was an old, grassy
'Hector's Hill,' we called it. . . . I used to lie on the top of Hector's Hill, and
look up at the sky, at the clouds, moving over me, and daydream, all kinds
of things."[2] Malcolm, who says he was about eight or nine when he began
to visit Hector's Hill, had already found similar contemplative moments
working in his little garden. He recalled that after he had carefully tended to

it, he would often lie down on his back between the rows, "and I would gaze up in the blue sky at the clouds moving and think all kinds of things."

Like many children, Malcolm was sensitive and meditative. But as an adult he attributed these events of reflection under the daytime sky, as well as other reflective moments in later life, with a religious significance. Indeed, though Malcolm would refer to his reflections as "daydreaming," he mentioned them specifically in the context of what he called "pre-visions."

Malcolm's youthful moments of meditation may have entailed more than simple childhood fantasy. In contemplation, both before and after his father's death, he began to feel the stirring of a certain sense of purpose in his life. His continuing fascination with the sky and clouds, though certainly a childlike characteristic, held for Malcolm a deeper meaning that he carried with him throughout life, and even sought to explain in the closing pages of his autobiography.

A religious education theorist has noted that when we "pass from early childhood into a stage of self-reflective consciousness, the religious mysteries of the universe recede." Malcolm's early years, as in the case of all young children, was likely "one of unending mystery and unalloyed wonder," where the divine seemed to be everywhere, manifested even in "daily miracles." His growing contemplative sense of himself seems to suggest, then, that young Malcolm had passed into the youthful stage of "self-reflective consciousness," and had begun to experience a more mature stage of religious development. "Religious" here suggests "those attitudes and activities that challenge the limits of experience," including even the things that one may not understand.

The particular religious nature of Malcolm's reflective "pre-visions" seems to be what some scholars call the "primal experience," one of a variety of unusual experiences that are fairly common. Primal experiences range from "occult" events and metaphysical phenomena to dreams, a sense of presence, and notions of destiny. They are often kept secret because secular society tends to deny that they are real. "And because primal experiences are unusual, medical and psychiatric establishments identify them as abnormal and classify the people who have them as disturbed or mentally ill."

Malcolm referred to these early childhood reflections as "personal memories," and when reviewing all of his "pre-vision" experiences since childhood, he stated that to speak to anyone about his personal notions of destiny "would have sounded crazy. Even I didn't have, myself, the slightest inkling."

Malcolm thus confessed that his first primal experiences challenged the limits of his own human life at the time, defying the very boundaries and definitions that were supposedly immovable and unchangeable. It was perhaps for this reason that he grasped for himself the identity of the "seventh child," which Malcolm's psychobiographers have aptly underscored, though their appreciation of its significance is bogged down in psycho-speculation.[3] As a traditional symbol of divinely endowed charismatic leadership, Malcolm's embrace of the "seventh child" self-image very likely expressed his own childhood primal experiences—experiences that nurtured within him a sense of destiny.

Researchers have noted that a significant number of people who have undergone primal experiences are people who have had minimal contact with churches and organized religions, prompting some to conclude that there exists a "pool of religiosity" that established religions have not tapped. This point may likewise be significant in considering Malcolm's religious background as a child.

It is important to note that despite Malcolm's assertion in his autobiography, and in other autobiographical statements, that his father was a Baptist preacher, the Little family was never given to traditional Baptist beliefs. It has already been noted that Earl Little spent a good deal of time in the church, and had occasion—as a Garveyite—to utilize the pulpit. No doubt he built his appeals upon the biblical text. However, the religious life-style of the home was, either before or after Earl's death, never given to denominationalism or traditional religiosity.

In Wilfred Little's memory, his mother Louise taught her children never to give themselves to any religion. She encouraged them to cultivate their own personal belief in God, and to establish their own private spirituality rather than submit to denominational divisiveness.[4] The religion of the Little household, then, was a kind of personal theism which was religiously and theologically eclectic:

Sometimes they'd have us read the Bible, and we'd talk about that. But my mother would always take us to different places. She'd take us to the Seventh Day Adventist [church], because she wanted us to be exposed to all these various things, because each of them had something she felt that we might want to hear and accept. . . . She'd take us to the Seventh Day Adventist [church], because she liked their dietary rules.[5]

Malcolm noted, in fact, that Louise Little had observed similar dietary rules in the family cooking, which excluded much of the "soul food" that his father Earl, "a real Georgia negro," loved so much. This harmonizes with

Malcolm's recollection of being brought to a virtually all-white Seventh Day Adventist church, where the people were kind but their food was seasoned blandly, and they themselves smelled different from black people.[6]

> She'd take us to the Jehovah's Witnesses, so we [could] hear them, because she liked the way they interpreted some of the things in regard to prophecy and things of that kind. She would take us to the Baptists—she even took us to the Church of God [in Christ], the ones that do all this jumping and shouting and hollering.[7]

Just as the Little family religion emphasized personal theism, it was also ecumenical—including not only mainline Christian churches, but also sectarian groups such as the Seventh Day Adventists and cultic or new religious movements such as the Jehovah's Witnesses. Growing up, Malcolm and his siblings were directed to follow the biblical Golden Rule and the Mosaic Ten Commandments, and to obey God without conforming to the doctrines of any one religion or denomination. It is possible, then, to consider the Little family's religious life to be very much a part of society's untapped "pool of religiosity." While the Littles were well exposed to denominational Christianity, to sects, and even cults, they remained independent, believing in God but largely remaining indifferent to established religious groups.

Louise Little, whose formative years in Grenada included significant exposure to the spiritual practices of the indigenous Caribs, was herself accustomed to primal experiences, as were a good many others in the Little family. The unique approach to theism characterized by Louise Little's personal religious teachings and experiences not only set the pace for her children's religious education, but it apparently shaped Malcolm and his siblings in ways that would prove significant for their later attraction to the Nation—at least in one major respect: "We never set Jesus apart from the other men who had divine inspiration," says Wilfred Little. When Malcolm spoke about visiting the black Christian church as a boy, he recalled that the animated worship and prayer of the church service was somewhat disturbing to him. But he added a most revealing insight: "Even at that young age, I just couldn't believe in the Christian concept of Jesus as someone divine. . . . I had very little respect for most people who represented religion."

Without understanding the religious education of the Little household and the major impact Malcolm's mother had on her children's religious life, Malcolm's stated disbelief in the divinity of Jesus and disrespect for clergymen might seem inappropriate for a boy who presented his father as a Baptist preacher. His comments are better understood when one takes into account that his family religion upheld Jesus only as a prophet and eschewed denomi-nationalism.

Understanding Malcolm's actual religious background will help the reader to be more critical in assessing Malcolm's later inclination to refer to his pre-Nation religious life as "Christian." For Malcolm's unusual religious orientation was Christian only in a very limited sense. Because he was reared in a community where most people were Christians, he was quite familiar with black Christianity, but his family's religion was eclectic and it was quite inexact for Malcolm to refer to himself later as having been "a brainwashed black Christian."[8]

As Malcolm approached adolescence, conditions in the Little home worsened. Louise was unable to find or keep employment. Maybe this was because she was not only black but also the widow of a controversial black man who in death may have been even more disparaged by both whites and blacks. According to Malcolm, it was even rumored that Earl Little had committed suicide—a rumor the life insurance people gladly seized upon. Welfare assistance brought some relief, but it also introduced intrusive, racist welfare agents into their home.

Louise Little, who was a capable, independent Garveyite, deeply resented the involvement of welfare agents in her domestic life. But Malcolm did not realize until later how important it was for his mother to maintain her pride, since pride "was just about all we had to preserve." However, by 1934, during the depth of the Great Depression, Malcolm's home life began visibly to fragment. Making every effort to keep her independence, Louise took in sewing and rented out garden space and even the dump that Earl had kept on the back of their property. She was fighting a losing battle, and it seems that her white neighbors made no significant effort to assist the fatherless Little family. Indeed, some may have been eager to see them leave. Wilfred recalled that somebody even shot their pet dog, just to give the Littles a "hard time."[9] This period became the first phase of Malcolm's wayward years, the tragic detour his life would take on the road to religious activism. Ironically, however, it would be this same tragic detour that would lead Malcolm Little into the first moment of conversion.

Poverty was an enemy of the Littles, but they faced yet another formidable foe. While the increasing scarcity of food and clothing pained Malcolm and his siblings, the psychological deterioration that was taking place inside the family proved to be an insurmountable barrier toward their recovery of a healthy family life. The Little family, once fundamentally independent as well as critical of the white man's system, were now at the mercy of the state.

Welfare agents responded to Louise Little's visible animosity toward them by using their official power to enter her home and interview the children. Malcolm felt later that this was their way of planting "seeds of division" in their minds. Like his younger sister Yvonne, Malcolm probably was thinking of his mother's angry words to the welfare agents: "You know what you're doing to me." Without a strong father, and with their mother under increased pressure, Malcolm and his siblings acted out their own frustrations by getting into mischief. This in turn brought increased pressure on Louise from the welfare people, who were apparently building a campaign to remove the seven Little children from their home and place them in foster care.

These welfare agents, whom Malcolm characterized as "vicious as vultures," verbally accused Louise of being "crazy" for refusing a black neighbor's gift of butchered pork, even though she had done so for religious reasons rather than pride. With virtually no alternatives left, and no apparent resources from which to draw provision for her family, Mrs. Little found herself under a great deal of stress. She briefly sought hope and respite in an intimate relationship with a man, but he soon backed away from the responsibility of her children. The breakup left Louise shocked, broken-hearted, and even more burdened.

When his mother began to show visible signs of mental and emotional decline, the "state people" placed Malcolm in the home of some black Christians named Gohannas. He seems to have found comfort in the stability of this foster home, but found the religious environment of the Gohannas's church to be quite "spooky," since it was that of the "sanctified Holy Rollers"—the black Pentecostal church: "The preachers and congregations jumped even higher and shouted even louder than the Baptists I had known. They sang at the top of their lungs, and swayed back and forth and cried and moaned and beat on tambourines and chanted."

Later, after Malcolm was transferred to a county-sponsored detention home in the largely white community of Mason, Michigan, he regularly had to attend a white church. He would later note that white people in that church "just sat and worshiped with words," while all the black people he had ever seen in church "threw their souls and bodies wholly into worship."[10]

Malcolm had been transferred to the detention home because his behavior had worsened; but in Mason he tried to turn over a new leaf. According to his own account, he was well liked by the all-white staff of the detention home and his white classmates. On weekends he was allowed to spend time with his siblings in Lansing, but at the same time he also developed an interest in Lansing's lively black bars and nightclubs—foreshadowing his imminent transformation into a creature of the urban underworld.

Malcolm's experience in Mason then became increasingly bitter for him, particularly after he spent the summer of 1940 in Boston with his older half-sister, Ella. Free to explore the black world of Boston, he discovered that the juke-box clubs and other night spots in Lansing were nothing compared to the night life of Boston's black neighborhood, Roxbury. "I couldn't have feigned indifference if I had tried," Malcolm said. He was not simply impressed by the flashy nightlife, but by the experience of being within a vast black population for the first time.

After summer vacation, Malcolm returned to Mason feeling "restless" and increasingly irritated by the unbridled, insulting, and insensitive racial remarks that were commonplace in his white surroundings. The racist comments of his teachers, especially one who had advised him to limit his career plans to carpentry since it was "a realistic goal for a nigger" rather than attempt to become a lawyer as he wished, were now more than Malcolm could bear. The chasm between the increasingly race-conscious Malcolm and his paternalistic white guardians became unbridgeable, and after the end of the eighth grade, he moved to Boston, to live under the care of his half-sister, Ella.

Ella had already made a great impression on Malcolm when she had visited him and the rest of her younger half-siblings in Lansing earlier. According to Malcolm, his father had boasted a great deal that Ella was a strong and capable woman, and that she also shared in his racial pride. Malcolm's first impression of her, which made a major impact on him, was that Ella "was the first really proud black woman" he had known. "She was plainly proud of her very dark skin," Malcolm said, adding that such pride was "unheard of among Negroes in those days," especially among the black people of Lansing.

From the beginning, when Malcolm first came to the busy streets of Boston's Roxbury section, he savored the night life of the black urban community. But Ella had bigger plans for him. She felt that her bright half-brother might prove to be a great lawyer, perhaps even a great, black Clarence Darrow.

To that end, Ella enrolled Malcolm in an all-boys' school in Boston. He later recalled that when he saw that there were no girls in the class, he walked out and never set foot in a school again. He was also not impressed with the "Hill Negroes" of Roxbury—the upwardly mobile blacks whom he considered snooty, pretentious, and out of touch with the mass of Boston's black population. To Ella's disappointment, Malcolm preferred the "town ghetto section" which, to Malcolm, "seemed to hold a natural lure."[11]

Malcolm quickly made his way into the clubs, pool halls, bars, and dance halls of Roxbury. He also began to experiment with alcohol, tobacco, marijuana, and gambling. He adapted easily to the life of the streets, and began to dress in the popular ghetto "zoot suits" worn by young black men. These were brightly colored outfits with pants that were unusually wide at the knee and cut very narrow at the bottom; the accompanying jackets were long, pinched at the waistline, and flared out at the bottom. With these outlandish suits, young men donned feathered, broad-brimmed hats and sported gold-plated chains for the final touch. And invariably, the style necessitated that the men "conk" their hair.

Malcolm's first exposure to the "conk" style was when he came to Boston. He later recalled that, at the time, he couldn't stop marveling at how straight and shiny—and how much like a white person's hair—a black person's hair could become with this styling process. Along with his zoot suit, the new Malcolm Little also sported, quite proudly, a new conk.

Later, as a spokesman for the Nation and writing in his autobiography, Malcolm emphasized that the "conk" was a tragic aspect of his youthful waywardness, his "first really big step toward self-degradation." By conking his hair he had "joined the multitude" of African Americans who were "brainwashed into believing" the superiority of whites, even to the point that they would "even violate and mutilate their God-created bodies to try to look 'pretty' by white standards." For Malcolm, this hairstyle, which could be attained only by the painful application of a lye and starch mixture, thus became the ultimate shame.

It is possible, however, that in retrospect Malcolm simplified the complex issue of black hair style—especially for the sake of the Nation. He noted that many among the "upper class" and entertainment circles of the black community engaged in this "self-defacing" hair-straightening process. But in speaking of the "conk," one African American essayist has noted that black men who were most inclined toward integration and assimilation "*seldom if ever have processed hair.* Indeed they have always been the major opponents of the process." The essayist concluded that Malcolm, in his own self-reflective commentary, was trying to "politicalize" the conk. To the contrary, the conk worn by Malcolm and his streetwise peers was no imitation of whiteness, but was actually a "Negro-idiom" that was directly influenced by the wavy-haired Latin "dandy" rather than the straight hair of the pale-faced "Anglo-Saxon of the power elite." Many blacks wearing the conk were either in show business or identified with blacks "in the world of show business— which, of course, includes stylish prizefight promoters, gamblers, pimps, racketeers, and so on. For most Negroes the process goes with certain manners in clothes, speech, music, and even movement, which are anything but ofay oriented."[12] To be sure, Malcolm's days on the streets of Boston's Roxbury, just as his activities in New York City's Harlem section, were never "ofay"—white—oriented. Malcolm Little was not pursuing the ways of white people, nor was he seeking their love. Quite to the contrary, he was perhaps reveling in the images of the black vanguard of the urban underworld and the stylish, "hip" masculinity of black entertainers, musicians, and pimps.

Once Malcolm had embraced the teachings of Elijah Muhammad and committed himself to the Fard-Muhammad dialectic of the black thesis and the white antithesis, he must have felt compelled to impute to his former life an absolute race shame that reflected none of its more human characteristics, exceptions, or ambivalences. It is possible, then, that young Malcolm Little, zoot suit and all, was not fleeing his Garveyite roots as much as he was naively looking in the wrong place for the kind of success and recognition that his personal sense of destiny seemed to promise.

Malcolm's closest friend in his Roxbury days, the musician Malcolm Jarvis, recalled that Malcolm always sought out the company of celebrities, and "always wanted to be next to famous and notorious people"—especially singers, musicians, and entertainers. According to Jarvis, Malcolm was seeking a sense of self-importance. "These feelings that he had about importance and being somebody in the world took place long before he landed in prison."

To many it might have seemed that Malcolm was seeking vicarious glory by associating with celebrities. But Jarvis seems to have realized that Malcolm's quest for recognition was deeply rooted in his life. Perhaps Malcolm, still immature and lacking in moral strength, had sought the importance he believed to be his destiny by pursuing the more earthy subculture of the hustler moving on the fringes of the entertainment world.

Malcolm apparently had an aversion to what he perceived to be pretensions of the up-and-coming blacks of Lansing and Boston. He disliked them for their posturing in imitation of their white patrons and supervisors, and considered them as "status-symbol-oriented." No doubt this was not only Malcolm's impression, but part of his political legacy as a Garveyite child, whose parents surely found these pretend "successful" blacks to be among their worst critics.

It is possible that Malcolm, in choosing to become wayward, had sought the only sincere approach he thought was left for him. When he was later asked by a reporter what he had been before he was a black nationalist,

Malcolm responded, "I was a bum. I was a misfit. I was an outcast. I was a black man in America."[13] Malcolm's statement must be understood as a self-analysis refracted through the lens of Mr. Muhammad's Nation. Nevertheless, it is likely that, as an adventuresome teenager, Malcolm chose the "honesty" of open rebellion against the status quo over playing a hypocritical role to please the enemies of his parents and their black cause.

On a return visit to Lansing, probably when he was well adapted to the hustling life of the streets, Malcolm recalled the words of an elderly black Christian woman, which he received as a bittersweet salute: "Malcolm, there's one thing I like about you. You're no good, but you don't try to hide it. You are not a hypocrite." Malcolm knew that he was bad, but for himself, even as a delinquent youth, hypocrisy was the unpardonable sin. If there is a deeper meaning behind Malcolm's reference to hypocrisy, however, it is perhaps related to the motivation behind writing the autobiography itself. His eagerness to highlight the religious hypocrisy of white and black "Christians" was very much a function of his role as chief advocate and propagandist of the Nation. This is particularly key to understanding his comments about Christianity and Christians in his autobiography.

Malcolm inevitably found that life on the street was not without its own brand of pretensions. However, he was not pretending to be white, nor was he likely to be as oblivious to the black struggle as he depicts himself in his autobiography. One must remember that most of *The Autobiography of Malcolm X* was written with Malcolm's consent and cooperation for the express purpose of enhancing and uplifting Elijah Muhammad and the Nation. It is therefore both a brilliant demonstration of Malcolm's ability to propagandize on behalf of the Nation, and a tribute to his unmatchable devotion to Elijah Muhammad.

Malcolm expressed his religious motivation to Alex Haley from the onset of the project: "I think my life story may help people to appreciate better how Mr. Muhammad salvages black people." It was therefore expedient, if not altogether necessary, for Malcolm to portray himself—prior to his involvement in the Nation—not only as a "sinner" but as Christian with a minimal amount of race-consciousness. In truth, however, Malcolm Little was never really a Christian, and he was probably always—at least to some degree—a race critic. In fact, when Malcolm was running the streets of Boston, he showed interest in the black cause by attending community forums at St. Mark's Congregational Church, together with some of his teenage peers. "There were a lot of rough young fellows who used to come to the meetings and Malcolm Little was one of them," Rev. Samuel Laviscount, the pastor of St. Mark's recalled. "He was a pretty fine young chap, but he was misguided." Yet as misguided as the streetwise young Malcolm may have been, he was evidently enough of a "race man" to ask a guest speaker from Scandinavia about the treatment of blacks in his country.[14]

In another incident, a somewhat more dramatic moment, Malcolm and his friends were gathered at a Boston nightspot called "Wally's Paradise" when a white policeman was attempting to remove an intoxicated black woman from the premises. When the woman, who had stumbled to the floor, resisted the officer, he got rough and began to pull her out by her hair. Malcolm sprang to her defense, telling the policeman he had a gun. "Take your hands off that woman!" Malcolm yelled. "If she were your mother or your sister, you wouldn't manhandle her like that." The policeman, intimidated by Malcolm and the surrounding crowd of angry people, retreated to call for backup. Malcolm quickly squired the woman into a cab and paid her fare. Then, in a moment, Malcolm, his friend Malcolm Jarvis, and another associate sped off in their own car.[15]

This incident raises an interesting point, again with reference to the purpose behind the writing of *The Autobiography of Malcolm X*. If Malcolm deliberately overlooked this heroic moment in recounting his pre-Nation days, it may be that he did so because it did not fit the scenario he was constructing—that is, the story of a young man too bogged down in the muck and the mire of "the white man's Christian world" to save himself, let alone stand up on behalf of black people. Malcolm the autobiographer wished to impute to Elijah Muhammad, not just his own moral reformation, but also his zeal for the black struggle. In fact, though, Malcolm's zeal was not Mr. Muhammad's doing.

Though Malcolm's life-style may have morally declined as he descended into the life of ghetto hustling, his race-consciousness remained intact. "I turned into a complete atheist," Malcolm would later recall of his days on the streets.[16] This atheism was more practical than philosophical, convenient as it was to his emerging criminal life-style. Even so, it would prove to be fleeting. On the other hand, he never tried to shed his black consciousness: it was already too much a part of him.

# 5

## Wayward Youth

*It was while I was a Christian that I was evil.*

Malcolm was never the seasoned underworld figure he liked to portray, and those following his lead probably embellished his story as well. While his autobiography concentrates a great deal on his wayward years, it is important to note that Malcolm was interested in characterizing his pre-Nation life in the most sensational terms in order to better enhance Elijah Muhammad's redemptive claims.

This is not to suggest that Malcolm did not know crime and debauchery. However, by his late teens, he was operating only "on the fringes of the Harlem underworld" and not at the center. "Malcolm," writes his first biographer, "may at times have exaggerated his past in the retelling—may have added a few bills to his bankroll, a few employees to his private staff, a few degrees extra to the prestige of his clientele and to his own status in the world of the Harlem hustle." Malcolm had no police record in New York City, "not even a traffic ticket." Early on, journalists made attempts to find out more about his criminal career. The sheer lack of information about him on the streets seems significant; one elderly racketeer who did remember the youthful Malcolm Little said that "he never got nowhere." [1]

"Nowhere" does not suggest that Malcolm was lying about the depths of his degradation. It does suggest, however, that his particular role in the urban underworld was that of the common hustler—not gangster, vice lord, or even mob lieutenant. As a hustler, Malcolm learned to bounce back and forth between legitimate and illegitimate means of acquiring money. In Boston, as later in Harlem, young Malcolm the hustler worked both part-time and full-time jobs, though never for very long. And while he was working these legitimate jobs, or "slaves," as they were called, Malcolm and his hustling peers were frequently involved in a variety of illicit activities as well.

One journalist described the urban hustler as a person who manages to earn the financial rewards supposedly enjoyed only by the "God loving, hard working, white middle class." In doing so, the hustler violates all of the middle-class laws, and does so "with a glee that informs the white middle class precisely where they can shove their value system." To be sure, this description could easily describe hustlers of any hue. However, as far as urban black hustlers are concerned—social irresponsibility and spiritual weakness notwithstanding—the racial situation cannot be ignored.

This same journalist knew Malcolm X and felt he was a brilliant man with great potential. "He didn't want to make it; he wanted to outwit it." This was undoubtedly true to a large extent. Malcolm later admitted that he had taken the easy way out in becoming a hustler, dropping out of school as he did: "I just gave up," he told an interviewer. But with a young man who believed he had the capability to be a good lawyer, it is hard to know just how much of his criminality was surrender to the seductive powers of the underworld, and how much was submission to the powers-that-be. Toward the end of his life, Malcolm told an interviewer: "They didn't have too many Negro doctors or lawyers, especially where I grew up. . . . They didn't even have any Negro firemen when I was a youth. When I was a youth, the only thing you could dream about becoming was a good waiter or a good busboy or a good shoeshine man. I mean, that's the American dream." [2] Ironically, it was only later, when Malcolm began to attack the "American dream" head-on instead of trying to escape from it, that he gained the attention of the New York City Police Department. While he was still a young hustler, the son of Earl and Louise Little was planted like a seed in the darkness of the urban underworld. When he finally began to blossom, it was the "Islamic dream" of Elijah Muhammad that he would embrace wholeheartedly.

Malcolm wrote that from his early days in Lansing, he had wanted to see Harlem, New York City's great center of black life and culture. Later on, when he lived in Boston, he would hear stories about "the Big Apple" from black musicians, merchant marines, and hustlers who had already visited the city. For Malcolm, however, Harlem was not just "the Big Apple," the glamorous haven for black musicians, celebrities, and hustlers. Harlem was also the heartbeat of Africa-in-America. For Malcolm, making the trip to Harlem was a kind of Garveyite pilgrimage, a way of reaffirming his belief in the black gospel that had been preached by his parents. "In fact," Malcolm reflected, "my father had described Harlem with pride, and showed us pictures of the huge parades by the Harlem followers of Marcus Garvey."

When Garvey was reigning in Harlem, it was still a young black metropolis. According to James Weldon Johnson, before Harlem was transformed into a center for New York City's black population, most African Americans in Manhattan had lived around West 53rd Street. While the housing was good, the growing population had turned the private homes into apartments in order to maximize housing availability.

By the early 1900s, however, blacks were looking for even better housing, and one black real estate businessman in particular, Philip Payton, began to focus on Harlem—which was a white neighborhood. Payton made his initial move into Harlem by persuading white landlords to allow some black tenants to move into a few newly built, vacant apartments that were considered undesirable by whites because of their uptown location. With this achieved, Payton began to expand his real estate goals, and more black tenants moved into Harlem. Once a trend was established, the white residents countered with restrictions enacted through specially devised realty organizations. But the black move had gained enough impetus to persevere despite resistance from whites, who called the influx an "invasion." Whites began to move out. With the outbreak of World War I, the need for black laborers drew increasing numbers of migrants to Harlem from the South, and Harlem became permanently black. By the time Marcus Garvey arrived there in 1916, it was a ripe, black fruit, ready for him to pick.

When Malcolm arrived in New York City, eager to explore Harlem, it was not the glorious black Mecca it had been at the time of Garvey, or during the 1920s, when black painters, sculptors, poets, novelists and other creative individuals joined together in an artistic outpouring that was a self-announced cultural renaissance. When Malcolm arrived, probably in the summer of 1941, black New York in general was still recovering from the pangs of the Depression.

Only five years before, a terrible human explosion had occurred in Harlem because of the pent-up resentments and frustrations of the unemployed. Millions of dollars worth of property was destroyed, and a commission was set up by state and local government to deal with the problems of unemployment and housing. By this time, the housing shortage in Harlem had become acute, since heavy migration from the South and from the Caribbean had caused the population to swell.

As World War II was exploding on the European continent, factories in the United States received huge contracts to produce military equipment but refused to hire black workers. Pressure from black organizations like the Brotherhood of Sleeping Car Porters, the National Association for the Advancement of Colored People (NAACP), and the National Urban League eventually resulted in the issue of Executive Order 8802, which banned discrimination in industries holding government contracts. At the same time, these black organizations were fighting segregation in the armed services as well.[3]

Malcolm's ticket to Harlem came through a job he obtained on the New Haven Railroad, which ran along the eastern seaboard between Boston and Washington, D.C. He worked on the kitchen staff, serving food to passengers. However, for Malcolm, the job was only a way to reach Harlem. His employment record shows that he worked for the railroad three different times between 1941 and 1943, being discharged for insubordination at least once. One dining car waiter who worked with Malcolm later recalled: "At that time Malcolm's energy was not directed toward hard work. He was wild. He had only an eighth-grade education. I could have predicted he would eventually get into trouble."

Malcolm had discovered on one of his first jobs in Boston, working as a shoeshine in a dance hall, that "all you had to do was give white people a show and they'd buy anything you offered them." He found that, similarly, when he was selling sandwiches and other refreshments to white passengers, if he entertained and played up to them he would make plenty of sales. However, Malcolm apparently began to tire of "Uncle Tomming," as he called it. It seems, in fact, that the more familiar he became with Harlem and its environment, the less inclined he was to patronize white passengers.

Though Malcolm claimed to have had a politically "sterile mind" at that time, it is probably the case that being in Harlem increasingly sharpened his race-consciousness, just as his initial trip to Boston had done when he was still an adolescent living in Lansing. Thus, while he was seemingly oblivious to the message of the black Communists hawking copies of the *Daily Worker* in Harlem, he was not blind to the politics of race in the United States. His attitude toward white passengers became flip, and he began to flaunt himself as "an uncouth, wild young Negro," most likely to annoy the white passengers. "I'd even curse the customers," Malcolm later admitted. Malcolm had a particular dislike for white servicemen, for whom he would save his foulest language and sarcasm.

"It was inevitable that I was going to be fired sooner or later," Malcolm said, and eventually "an angry letter" from a passenger did get him fired. And though Malcolm was only about sixteen years old, he knew that because of his height he could again easily pass for an adult and acquire another job in the busy wartime economy. What really mattered to him was that he was in Harlem—which he described as being both "Seventh Heaven" and a narcotic for him.[4]

In between his legitimate jobs, Malcolm was exploring the money-making possibilities of hustling. His autobiography gives vivid descriptions of accomplished hustlers, pimps, houses of prostitution, drug dealers, and other seamy sides of the Harlem underworld. Malcolm portrays himself as both a drug dealer and a "steerer"—the intermediary between prostitutes and their clients. However, while he illegally earned dollars playing these roles, he also became adept at gleaning financial support from women whose confidence he won.

At one woman's home, Malcolm would sit around and read "everything from Nick Carter thrillers to the Holy Bible"—an ironic glimpse that suggests that Malcolm was not entirely as "illiterate" as he would later portray his youth when representing the Nation: "I was a very wayward criminal, backward, illiterate, uneducated-type of person until I heard the teachings of the Honorable Elijah Muhammad."

Malcolm the hustler was not yet driven to scouring through volumes on philosophy, history, and religion, as he would later in prison. Discouraged and without motivation, Malcolm's intellectual flame was reduced to a flicker. His interest in the Bible was still an ineffective spark; his immaturity and lack of discipline kept his reading diet limited to what he would later call "cowboy books." However, with his Garveyite background, his mother's good education and religious eclecticism, his religiously experienced notions of destiny, and his academic success in junior high school, Malcolm could never have been languishing in the kind of ignorance that typified the lives of the pushers, pimps, hustlers, and prostitutes with whom he associated. Malcolm himself acknowledged that the average hustler and criminal was "too uneducated to write a letter. I have known many slick, sharp-looking hustlers, who would have you think they had an interest in Wall Street; privately, they would get someone else to read a letter if they received one."[5]

Malcolm's old friend, Clarence Atkins, has noted that in Harlem "a lot of guys, street guys, fancied themselves as pimps . . . they would try to find a girl or two or three that they could play on, for whatever benefits." Malcolm was, after all, hustling. And according to Atkins, because Malcolm was tall, handsome, and red-complexioned—and sporting a long, reddish conk—he could easily draw women into his lure. His relationships with women in this period of his life could not have been those of a normal teenager simply because his life was not that of a normal teenager. Malcolm was living a life that pretended manhood, one that tragically disavowed any sense of commitment except to one's own gratification: "He was just wild, man," Atkins continued, "he didn't give a shit about nothing." Malcolm's treatment of women, like the rest of his life at this time, was completely self-serving and impulsive. "Whatever he thought was the thing for him to do at that particular time, that's what he would do."

In *The Autobiography of Malcolm X* this is perhaps no more clear than in Malcolm's relationship with a white Bostonian whom he identifies as "Sophia." His relationship with her had begun before he had taken the railroad job, and it continued while he was commuting back and forth from Boston to New York City, and even after he moved to Harlem. When Malcolm told her how excited he was about New York, Sophia, a Negrophile who probably shared similar sentiments, told Malcolm he would never be satisfied anywhere but in New York. "She was right," Malcolm recalled.

In Harlem, Sophia, who was actually an Armenian American named Bea Caragulian, became Malcolm's status symbol, just as she had been in Boston's black nightspots.[6] The fact that Bea married a white man in the midst of her interracial relationship only verified for Malcolm what he had been told about "the black man and white woman psychology":

The white woman wanted to be comfortable, she wanted to be looked upon with favor by her own kind, but she also wanted to have her pleasure. So some of them just married a white man for convenience and security, and kept right on going with a Negro.[7]

"It wasn't that they were necessarily in love with the Negro, but they were in love with lust—particularly 'taboo' lust," according to Malcolm.

Malcolm was introduced to "the black man and white woman psychology" by his friend and associate "Sammy the Pimp," whose real name was Sammy McKnight. Sammy, who figures as a major character in Malcolm's autobiography, apparently employed an interracial team of prostitutes. Thus, when later under the influence of the Nation, Malcolm found ample evidence in his own experience with white women to propound Muhammad's teaching that white people were naturally immoral: "I got my first schooling about the cesspool morals of the white man from the best possible source, from his own women."

Even more, Malcolm saw that Harlem was the white man's "sin-den" and "fleshpot," where black flesh was marketed for the satisfaction of whites. Moving in and through this "black-white nether world," Malcolm saw how race and sex mixed with business, and how the customers who could afford to pay for the use of black flesh were considered above repute within that netherworld. Malcolm had apparently been aware of the dynamics of interracial sex since his youth in Lansing, but in Harlem he saw those dynamics translated into a business. It is no wonder that Elijah Muhammad's ban on interracial relations—especially intermarriage—would later appeal to Malcolm.

Undoubtedly, Malcolm's experience in the interracial sex market had convinced him of what Hernton calls "the sexualization of racism" in the United States. He inevitably came to believe that it was impossible for whites and blacks to respect each other as long as they interacted along the lines of the racial-sexual exploitation that has historically been a part of the white man's social order, ever since the days of slavery. Further, in looking back over these experiences in Harlem, Malcolm said he became suspicious of any white person who was "anxious to hang around Negroes, or to hang around in Negro communities." This reminiscence probably included Sophia, who Malcolm said "still came to New York whenever I called her."

As a hustler, therefore, Malcolm apparently involved himself in behavior in which he allowed himself to be sexually exploited. This degradation has been much used by those who have wanted to reduce Malcolm's masculinity to a fragile facade, or to appropriate him as a gay hero. In either case, however, there is only one source of alleged proof that Malcolm's hustler activity included homosexual behavior—and even here it is acknowledged that such encounters were both infrequent and financially motivated.[8]

These shabby, self-serving attempts to homosexualize Malcolm have tended to negate his genuine religious growth and transformation in his later life. Those who knew Malcolm well deny any youthful homosexuality on his part, yet he still owned up to the fact that his life in the streets had been degrading. In 1964, reflecting on his youth, Malcolm told one journalist: "I was a human zombie. My mind and my soul were in chains." To another, Malcolm declared: "Moving through the streets of Harlem . . . I disregarded religion completely."[9]

Malcolm the hustler's definition of atheism was not philosophical. While he would continue to identify himself as an atheist, it was only later that he realized that genuine atheism, like religious thought itself, required some sort of intellectual "framework." His atheism consisted of a fundamental disregard for the moral principles he had heard expounded by whites and blacks alike, especially those he perceived as religious hypocrites—such as the Sunday morning evangelists, whom he saw only as hustlers "peddling Jesus." At one point Malcolm noted how his half-sister Ella "couldn't believe how atheist, how uncouth" he had become while in Harlem. No one, then, should doubt the reality of Malcolm's moral and spiritual lapse.

While he would later exaggerate certain aspects of that lapse and perhaps omit others from his autobiography, Malcolm's story is still not primarily that of a black rebel fighting against an evil white empire. Though a major theme of threading through Malcolm's life was certainly white racism and his response to it, the Nation stood to benefit from this way of modeling his life story. This interpretation, which was expressed in his determination to Christianize and whiten all of his former sins was, of necessity, the influence of Elijah Muhammad upon Malcolm's story.

The real story of Malcolm X is actually a conversion story. Indeed, it is a double conversion story, not unlike that of St. Augustine, who escaped from "abominable things" and the moral "havoc of disruption." Augustine, like Malcolm Little, escaped moral degradation only to enter the redemption of a cult in which the chains of moral abomination were traded for the chains of religious bondage. In like manner, both eventually found religious freedom outside their respective cults.

By the early 1940s, Malcolm Little was known as "Detroit Red," a street-wise young hustler who despite his height and good looks had to be differentiated from two other red-complexioned Harlemites with whom he shared the streets. The first was a professional armed robber who hailed from St. Louis and was thus tagged "St. Louis Red." The other, a friend of Malcolm's, was from Chicago, and bore the appropriate name, "Chicago Red." Malcolm preferred to identify himself by the best-known city of his home state, Detroit,[10] rather than his hometown of Lansing.

"Chicago Red," whose real name was John Elroy Sanford, had come to Harlem several years before Malcolm. Sanford, who had come from Chicago via Philadelphia, was a natural-born comic who left home with hopes of attaining show business fame. Probably not long after Malcolm arrived in Harlem, the two met in a pool hall and struck up a warm friendship. As it turned out, the two red-complexioned youths worked in a famous Harlem eatery called "Jimmy's Chicken Shack," where Malcolm waited on tables, and Sanford was, in Malcolm's words, "the funniest dishwasher on this earth." When times got tough and they were without money during cold weather, the two glory-seeking youths slept on a Harlem rooftop, using as much newspaper as they could find for insulation and warmth. Years later, after Detroit Red had become the nationally famous Muslim, Minister Malcolm X, he would briefly be reunited with his old friend Chicago Red, who had succeeded in the world of comedy as Redd Foxx.

According to Foxx, in his Harlem days Detroit Red was not given to "talking" the "stuff" of black nationalism and the white devil anthropology. However, according to Clarence Atkins, who perhaps knew Malcolm better, having likewise met him at Jimmy's Chicken Shack, Malcolm made time in their youthful discussions—which usually revolved around jazz music—to talk about his Garveyite background: "He would talk often about how his father used to get brutalized and beat up on the corner selling Marcus Garvey's paper and he would talk a lot about *Garvey's concepts in terms of how they could benefit us as a people.*"

Atkins also remembered that Malcolm often rehashed the eighth-grade incident in which his racist teacher had tried to discourage him becoming a lawyer. "You know . . . that had to have some kind of impact on his thinking for him to be constantly speaking on this in our presence," Atkins concluded. In fact, despite Malcolm's indifference to the political activism of Harlem's prominent black organizations in those days, "He was always political, even in the midst of all that street hustling and everything else he was doing, he was political."

In contrast, however, Atkins did not recall, even once, his friend Detroit Red speaking either good or ill about the church. Malcolm had truly shunned religion—he could not envision, as he would later, that there existed an undeniable connection between religious faith and the liberation of blacks. It seems, at best, that Malcolm saw religion as part of the world from which he was trying to escape. At worst, he thought religion was for whites—and for black people who had resigned themselves to living submissively in the white man's world. Malcolm's appreciation for Garvey and the black nationalism of the UNIA was genuine, but he seems to have been oblivious to Garvey's black Christianity, which had perhaps been lost in the array of Louise Little's religious eclecticism.

Later, in a loyal attempt to enhance Elijah Muhammad's claim of influence upon him, Malcolm X minimized his youthful black consciousness both in his own autobiographical portrayal and in interviews with reporters and journalists. Maybe also out of loyalty to Elijah Muhammad, Malcolm X tended to attribute his own youthful immorality to Christianity rather than to the practical atheism he had personally chosen to follow. Thus, in a 1960 interview, a smiling Malcolm X declared, "It was while I was a Christian that I was evil."[11]

"He had no regard for law and order and the system and government— none of that," Atkins said of Malcolm's days in Harlem. This is consistent with Malcolm's autobiographical image. There was apparently no line of demarcation between legal and illegal in his money-making activities. Just as easily as Malcolm waited on tables in Harlem or peddled sandwiches on trains running from New England to Florida, he peddled marijuana and directed "clients" into brothels.

In fact, according to his brother Wilfred, young Malcolm would "go out to California or wherever they would send him and come back with two of the biggest suitcases you ever saw, full of that stuff . . . marijuana pressed into bricks, you know . . . but they would pay him a thousand dollars a trip." A close Boston friend also remembers Malcolm arriving from New York City, where he obviously had a connection, often returning home with marijuana sewed into the lining of his heavy overcoat. "Sometimes he had as much as a quarter to a half a pound of it, and then he would package it up himself, roll it up into joints and sell them for a dollar apiece."

When Malcolm could not make money in independent endeavors, he might get temporary work, as he did at Jimmy's Chicken Shack in Harlem. He claims to have worked there briefly as a waiter, but Clarence Atkins suggested that Malcolm's affiliation with the restaurant was far more exten- sive—perhaps reflecting Malcolm's dependency in those days: "He was flunking for Jimmy . . . doing anything, like washing dishes, mopping floors, or whatever, you know . . . because he could eat, and Jimmy had a place upstairs over the place where he could sleep." Malcolm's prison file confirms that he worked at the popular Harlem restaurant for about two years, from 1942 through 1944, after which he returned to Boston. Rather than empha- sizing his more extended, and perhaps humbling, dependency on Jimmy's Chicken Shack, it is interesting that Malcolm focused heavily on his job as a waiter at Small's Paradise, a famous Harlem nightspot.

Malcolm admitted that he did not work very long at Small's, and that he lost his job after he attempted to steer a customer to a prostitute—and the customer turned out to be a vice officer. However, Malcolm made Small's Paradise the centerpiece of his street schooling—the place where sophisti- cated, big-time hustlers taught him about a more urbane level of professional crime. It is not clear if Malcolm worked at Small's steadily or shifted between it and other jobs, both legal and otherwise.[12] In any case, it is certain that he spent a great deal of time there.

For a while, Malcolm worked for a "downtown Jew," a nightclub entrepreneur whom he called "Hymie." According to Malcolm, he and Hymie got along pretty well, and Hymie was sympathetic to the black struggle in a racist society. For Hymie, Malcolm processed and delivered bootleg alcohol until the operation fell through. He wrote in his autobiography that he thought his Jewish boss had been killed under mysterious circumstances. However, it seems Hymie, whose real name was Abe Goldstein, was still alive by the time Malcolm was imprisoned in 1946. Goldstein remembered his young black assistant as being "a bit unstable and neurotic but under proper guidance, a good boy." Unfortunately, Goldstein had not been willing or able to give young Malcolm such proper guidance.

Another time, Malcolm created his own traveling drug dealership by using his old railroad employee I.D. to gain access to the train. With a large supply of marijuana, Malcolm moved throughout the East Coast, catering especially to the peripatetic jazz bands. He apparently enjoyed associating with these musicians, not only because he was a jazz enthusiast himself but because he undoubtedly hungered for the kind of public recognition they received. One senses a hint of pleasure in Malcolm's recollection that he was sometimes mobbed by jazz fans along with the band members. Even more, Malcolm enjoyed the success of his novel line of work: "Nobody had ever heard of a traveling reefer peddler."

Malcolm's evolution into an outlaw was steady, though, as Clarence Atkins said, "I'm sure that he was never no big time racketeer or thug." He dabbled in gambling, numbers, "little cons—little confidence games on people." Otherwise, he and his friend Sammy "Pretty Boy" McKnight would periodically burglarize one of Harlem's popular nightspots, such as LaFamille, and then divide the spoils. Through Sammy in particular, Malcolm seems to have customized his criminality. As Malcolm's closest friend in Harlem, it was apparently Sammy who encouraged him to specialize in peddling marijuana, as well as to snort cocaine—especially before committing armed robbery. In any case, according to Atkins, Sammy's apartment was probably the closest thing to a traditional home that Malcolm had in Harlem.

Atkins recalled that Malcolm and his associates would regularly gather at Sammy's apartment, often in a spontaneous "communion gathering," where Sammy would cook and where they would relax and smoke marijuana. This was perhaps the only family Malcolm knew when he was a hustler in

Harlem. Typically, while some ate and fell asleep on the couch, or listened to the latest bebop records of Charlie Parker and Dizzy Gillespie, others frequently swapped their girlfriends for sexual relations. "Sammy would cook and we had music," Atkins recalled, "and there were always girls, always." It was probably one of the few secure moments at a time when Malcolm's life was otherwise essentially a continuous, and sometimes dangerous, street contest of "liberties and chances." "It was a time," Clarence Atkins recalled, "when you did whatever it was necessary for you to do in order to persevere. And that's all he did, was what he had to do at that time to persevere."[13]

Key to that perseverance, for Malcolm, was minimizing or avoiding altogether the necessity of a full-time job, a jail sentence, or a term of service in the military. He had been able to keep full-time employment to a minimum by hustling and moving from job to job. He was also able to avoid going to jail. But in 1943 Malcolm received "Uncle Sam's greetings," which came to him in Harlem by way of his sister Ella in Boston. He was determined not to serve in the military—particularly not in wartime.

Malcolm agreed with his friend Shorty, and many other "ghetto Negroes," who objected to serving in the wartime military: "Whitey owns everything. He wants us to go and bleed for him? Let him fight." So when his draft notice came, Malcolm was determined to find a way not to serve. In his autobiography, he explained how he began to hustle extensively in the hope that his reputation would render him *persona non grata* in the eyes of the draft board. Malcolm, assuming that Harlem was filled with black army intelligence agents, began to make a public spectacle of himself—hoping to get their attention; he began "noising around" that he was a Japanese sympathizer and deliberately acted "high and crazy" in public places.

On the day of his review, Malcolm appeared at Local Board #59 in Manhattan "costumed like an actor," wearing a garish zoot suit, yellow knob-toe shoes, and his hair frizzled into a "reddish bush of conk." His account suggests that he tried to come across as a kind of lunatic, "'Harlem jigaboo' archetype," knowing that he would either horrify or amuse the whites into thinking he was unfit for military duty. He saved his best performance for the psychiatrist, who Malcolm said had tried his best to remain objective and professional throughout his review.[14]

This may have been Malcolm's best hustle: he evaded and toyed with the psychiatrist's questions, all the while jerking around as if preoccupied by the belief that he was being observed from outside the room. "Suddenly," Malcolm recounted, "I sprang up and peeped under both doors, the one I'd entered and another that probably was a closet." He continued: "And then I bent and whispered fast in his ear. 'Daddy-o, now you and me, we're from up North here, so don't you tell nobody . . . I want to get sent down South. Organize them nigger soldiers, you dig? Steal us some guns, and kill up crackers!' "[15] He was immediately dismissed, and later received his 4-F disqualification card in the mail.

The FBI report of the interview verifies Malcolm's success in hustling the psychiatrist at the draft board. It does not contain the picturesque description of Malcolm's review outlined in his autobiography, but it does reflect Malcolm's intent: "Subject was rejected for military service in 1943 for mental reasons at which time they were found to be psychopathic personality inadequate, sexual perversion and psychiatric rejection." Malcolm's performance apparently included aspects that he did not mention in his own account, including references to sexual perversion. For Malcolm, however, the goal was to avoid military induction at any cost.

According to Malcolm, he left Harlem in 1945 because he tired of living under the threats of criminals and police officers alike. Although there are some variations of Malcolm's account of this time,[16] there is agreement that Malcolm left Harlem at a time of crisis. His associate Clarence Atkins suggests that while Malcolm may have been facing dismal circumstances, he and his friends gathered together on the night of his departure from Harlem. He recalled that none of Malcolm's Harlem friends wanted him to leave, leading Atkins to suspect that Malcolm was not in the kind of danger he portrayed in his autobiography.

[Malcolm] may very well have been in danger—I don't think he was in danger of getting killed; he might have been in danger in terms of him getting hurt . . . he may have been in danger, but I don't think so. This much I know: the severity of the circumstance was not enough for us in that gathering to want to encourage him to get out of town. Because it was unanimous—except the girl ["Sophia"], and Jarvis ["Shorty"], because Jarvis lived in Boston."[17]

Probably persuaded by his Boston friends as much as by his bad luck in Harlem, Malcolm decided to return to Boston with his white woman and Jarvis. Perhaps high on drugs, he talked incessantly throughout the whole trip. His criminal career in Harlem ended, as it would also end in Boston— quite ingloriously, even by criminal standards. However, the next time Malcolm Little would come to Harlem, things would be different.

# 6

## Crime, Imprisonment, and Redemption

*Into the ocean of blackness where I was . . .*

"Looking back, I think I really was at least slightly out of my mind," Malcolm would say later regarding his life on the streets. Returning to Boston did not, in itself, bring any great change in his life. After a month of "laying dead," as Malcolm called it, his restlessness returned; his excessive use of cocaine and his white girlfriend's faithful supply of money did not calm him, or keep him from looking for new hustles. He turned to gambling, and then formed a burglary ring.

Malcolm said in his autobiography that he thought of burglary because he felt it would provide extra money for both himself and his friend Shorty. He recalled that the formation of the burglary ring took a great deal of care and planning—based on what he had learned in Harlem "from some of the pros." He not only included Shorty but Shorty's half-Italian, half-black friend, Rudy. Also, Malcolm noted that Sophia and her younger sister also joined the burglary ring. The white women, according to Malcolm, acted as advance agents, entering unsuspecting households under false pretexts while scouting for the best targets and providing a layout sketch of the homes. "We quickly got it down to a science," Malcolm concluded of his last venture as an outlaw.

In fact, much of Malcolm's account seems to be fictitious. It is true that Sophia—Bea—was involved, along with her younger sister, Joyce. Another Armenian American woman, Kora Marderosian, whom Malcolm did not mention in his autobiography, also joined in. Another gangster appears to have been "Rudy," an African American actually named Francis E. Brown, also known as "Sonny." Shorty—Malcolm Jarvis—also participated, though not in the first two burglaries.

According to Malcolm's extensive statement to the police, it was Brown—and not he, who had devised the whole burglary scheme, though Malcolm brought along the three white women, who never left their car while the burglaries took place. Their burglary operation was hardly down to a science—essentially Brown did the breaking in, then let Malcolm and Jarvis into the homes while the women waited outside. Most of the stolen goods were not sold to a fence in exchange for cash, as Malcolm claimed, but were actually kept. Even when Malcolm and his fellow burglars forayed into New York City on December 16, 1945, they sold only enough of the stolen goods to cover their expenses. They were not as efficient at their craft as Malcolm claimed in his autobiography, just as they were not as experienced or seasoned. His burglary ring seems to have emerged by accident—and in the same manner, it came to an end.

According to Malcolm's autobiographical account, he was arrested after he brought an expensive stolen watch into a repair shop. The official record corroborates Malcolm's claim on this point—he had accidentally broken an expensive watch and brought it to a Roxbury jeweler for repairs. What he did not say was that he had carelessly given another stolen watch to a relative for Christmas; the relative sold it to a jeweler who suspected it was stolen and informed the police. Thus, the police already had a lead on the stolen merchandise when Malcolm brought the watch in for repair. When he returned to pick it up on January 12, 1946, he was immediately arrested. The arresting detectives promised Malcolm, who was carrying a weapon, that they would drop the gun charges if he named his accomplices. Fundamentally a hustler with no loyalty except to himself, Malcolm turned in all of his partners, who, except for the elusive Brown, were apprehended by the police.

Since Malcolm and Jarvis could not afford to pay the ten thousand dollar bail set by the court, they were literally caged inside the courtroom during their trial on February 27, 1946. Both pleaded guilty and were sentenced to the Massachusetts State Prison for eight to ten years. Since Malcolm had committed crimes both in Middlesex and in Norfolk counties he had two different trials. The trial he recounted in his autobiography was the first, which took place on February 27, 1946, in Middlesex County Court. He was sentenced to four concurrent eight- to ten-year terms. The second trial, in Norfolk County Superior Court, took place on April 10, 1946. Here he was given three concurrent six- to eight-year sentences.

In 1946 Malcolm was not guaranteed a defense attorney by the state of Massachusetts, so he had none. Sitting inside their cage on a wooden bench, the young black men quickly realized that they were on trial for more than burglary. Their involvement with three white women had angered spectators, attorneys, and courtroom officers, and indeed some of the spectators made blatantly racist remarks. When Malcolm commented to one of the attorneys that they seemed to be on trial for having been with white women, he was scolded outright: "You had no business with white girls!" Years later, Malcolm told a journalist: "When the judge sentenced me, he told me, 'This will teach you to stay away from white girls.' I took him at his word." [1]

Malcolm served about seven years of an eight- to ten-year sentence in three different Massachusetts state prison facilities. At first he was sent to Charlestown State Prison, less than five miles from the rented room at Harvard Square where many of the stolen goods had been stashed. According to Malcolm, Charlestown Prison was an archaic facility, built in 1805 and modeled after the Bastille. "In the dirty, cramped cell, I could lie on my cot and touch both walls," he recalled. These small cells had no running water, and inmates had only covered pails for toilets. The old facility, which lay just across the Charles River from Boston, was plagued by rodents, white lice, and the continuous stench of human excrement.

Malcolm was now a "fish"—a new inmate. His autobiographical description of himself as a newly incarcerated youth—like his description of himself as a skilled burglar—was exaggerated. However, no one should doubt that Malcolm was "physically miserable and as evil-tempered as a snake," as he chose to describe himself. Yet it appears that his dramatic characterization of himself as an unyielding convict who preferred to pay for his aggressive acts of rebellion in solitary confinement is a fabrication. He may have paced "like a caged leopard, viciously cursing aloud," but his prison record suggests he did so in his own small cell, not in solitary confinement. As one biographer has pointed out, if Malcolm had been such an aggressive inmate, hardened by solitary confinement, he would not have been allowed to transfer to a less restrictive facility after one year at Charlestown.

Nevertheless, Malcolm Little was clearly miserable and bitter in such bleak and filthy surroundings. His animosity and rebellion may have been acted out, but not aggressively. He continued to pursue his former pastime of getting high, sometimes by purchasing nutmeg (which, in the right quantity, would produce a "high" comparable to the use of marijuana), and sometimes by obtaining drugs that were smuggled in and sold by correction officers. In addition, in his various jobs he proved to be a poor worker. His record shows that at best he was considered cooperative, but more often he was evaluated as "lazy" and "not inclined to do any work." One foreman noted that Malcolm received his work assignments "seemingly in silent disgust." He may also have rebelled in a more subtle way by giving exaggerated, false, and misleading information to various interviewers.

There is certainly no evidence that Malcolm verbally abused the prison psychologist, as he claimed in his autobiography. His interview for the State Prison Psychometric Report, for instance, notes that his cooperation, attention, effort, and emotional stability were good. Still, he was unwilling to tell his interviewer, on March 8, 1946, about his family background. He claimed that his parents had been missionaries and that his mother was a white Scot whose marriage to a black man resulted in racist opposition in the various desirable white neighborhoods where they had lived.[2] Whether he hoped to win favor by such descriptions or simply wanted to keep his Garveyite parents a secret is unknown. His first interviewer sensed he was being "calculating and cautious" and observed that he "has fatalistic views, is moody, cynical, and has a sardonic smile which seems to be affected because of his sensitiveness to his color. To offset this he seems to assume a nonchalant, complacent, superior attitude."

Malcolm's approach toward his interviewers, far from being explosive and vulgar, was played out in low-key rebellion. He exhibited a hustler's indifference toward authority, laced with a kind of sarcasm that was probably as much an expression of racial contempt as it was a disguise for his actual anxieties. "I've been heading here a long time," he coolly assured his interviewer. Malcolm also claimed that if he had known he was going to receive an eight- to ten-year sentence he would have gone in for armed robbery instead of burglary. His interviewer concluded that Malcolm was "worldly-wily and amoral."

Malcolm likewise sought to cultivate the "amoral" impression among his fellow inmates. He acted out some of this demeanor in his cynicism toward religion which, in Charlestown Prison, seems to have blossomed into a militantly "antireligious attitude." Considering himself "beyond atheism," Malcolm now took special pride in his flamboyant irreverence toward God and the Bible, soon earning him the nickname "Satan" among his peers.[3] Imprisoned and with nowhere to go, Malcolm may have been making his last stand against the religious sensitivity that haunted him deep inside.

"As an atheist," Malcolm would later tell a British interviewer, "my atheism was a rejection of all that I had heard about religion up to that point." He continued that such religion "didn't follow what, to me, was a logical pattern. Plus, all of those who belonged to one of these different religions, I got to know them intimately and personally and I didn't see anybody living according to the religion that they were talking about, so it lost its appeal for me."[4] This analysis of his own atheism is very revealing. First, he noted that the religions he had observed until the time of his imprisonment did not seem to follow a "logical pattern." In all probability Malcolm's reference to "different religions" suggests only the various Christian denominations to which he had been exposed throughout his life, especially during his childhood. There is no evidence that he got to know any non-Christian religions "intimately and personally"—except perhaps the cult of the Jehovah's Witnesses, which is, however, still much like fundamentalist Christianity in many respects.

Malcolm's contention was probably that *Christian* groups did not follow a "logical pattern," and he probably alluded to issues both of theology and practice. The Christian belief in the divinity of Jesus was never acceptable to him—and certainly not logical. The notion of any man being a divine incarnation was as absurd to him as it had been to his mother and siblings. In addition, he must have found hypocrisy in the Christian denominations' inability to integrate theology into the lives of people beyond a "Sunday morning" experience. His concept of religion, as he revealed in the same 1964 interview, wasn't limited "just to praying, [and] things of that sort, but my concept of religion was that which included every aspect of one's life—economic, political, and social."

Malcolm's idea of religion was heavily influenced by the kind of politically sensitive religion he had known in his family as a boy. Although he became rebellious and turned to a life of crime and debauchery, he nevertheless carried with him the deep conviction that religion must be wholistic. If religion did not address the political, social, and economic needs that had been so central to the lives of his parents, then it was not worth embracing. In essence, then, it seems Malcolm felt that any religion that did not truly benefit people, especially black people, was not logical, and thus not believable. Finally, Malcolm also noted that his observations of religious people themselves undermined any appeal that religion might have had for him.

It is no surprise, then, that Malcolm did not happily receive his first letter from home, which came from his older brother Philbert, who had become involved in a fundamentalist "holiness" church in Detroit. Philbert's promise that the church was going to pray for him only served to antagonize Malcolm. "I scrawled him a reply I'm ashamed to think of today," Malcolm later recalled. Even after he would become a deeply religious man, Malcolm could never tolerate a religion that used prayer as a substitute for action.

In the Nation, Malcolm invariably portrayed his intellectual growth and transformation to be the direct result of his conversion to the teachings of Elijah Muhammad. In 1959, for instance, he told a journalist, "All I have learned has been from the Islamic influence of Mr. Muhammad." In an interview with Alex Haley for *Playboy* several years later, Malcolm declared, "Whatever I am that is good, it is through what I have been taught by Mr. Muhammad." This was, however, the rhetoric of religious loyalty.[5]

To be sure, Elijah Muhammad greatly influenced Malcolm, but Muhammad cannot be credited with investing in Malcolm either his native intellect or his intellectual rebirth while in prison. Even Malcolm's own autobiographical account inadvertently reveals that before Malcolm had even heard of Elijah Muhammad he had already begun the metamorphosis of intellect that would turn him into a stunning speaker, debater, and apologist for the Nation. And key to this metamorphosis was another inmate whom Malcolm met at Charlestown State Prison.

In his autobiography, Malcolm referred to this inmate only as "Bimbi," whom he met in 1947. Like Malcolm, Bimbi was a tall, light-skinned African American with a reddish complexion. He was a seasoned burglar, and it is possible that it was actually Bimbi's expertise in burglary that is described in Malcolm's autobiography as part of his own career. Nevertheless, it was not his competence in crime that impressed young Malcolm about Bimbi. Rather, according to Malcolm, "Bimbi had always taken charge of any conversation he was in," and "he was the first man I had ever seen command total respect . . . with his words."

Because Bimbi was so widely read and knowledgeable, he kept a respectful following of inmates—as well as a few correction officers—who listened to him expound on a variety of topics. The respect Bimbi commanded was stunning to Malcolm, especially in a prison society where vulgarity and insult were common: "Nobody cursed Bimbi." But what really drew Malcolm to Bimbi was something far deeper: "What made me seek his friendship was when I heard him discuss religion." Bimbi had not yet said much to Malcolm, whose street atheist role was still largely based on his "vicious cursing attacks on God."

Malcolm knew that Bimbi was an atheist, too. Yet Bimbi's atheism was cool, confident, and was expressed intellectually—a trait that had always impressed Malcolm, even when he was a small boy attending Garveyite meetings with his father. Not surprisingly, he broached the discussion of religion with Bimbi—whose real name was John Elton Bembry—the very first time they spoke. Bembry recalled that one day, while he and another inmate were playing dominoes in the prison yard, Malcolm bumped into him yet continued walking without saying a word. He returned in a short time, staring at Bembry, apologizing, then blurting out: "Do you believe in God? God the father, God the son, God the Holy Ghost, and all that crap?"

It is apparent that Malcolm felt tension over the fact that Bembry, whom he greatly admired, had already handled the topic of theology with confidence and assurance. Tension was created precisely because Malcolm's own "antireligious" thinking was probably never as atheistic as he had thought it to be. Indeed, it appears that Malcolm's "Satan" facade had actually begun to crumble—ironically in the face of a genuine atheist.

Bembry's atheism was self-assured and reasoned; Malcolm's atheism was only anger, contempt, and rebellion. Bembry's atheism was a confident abandonment of all forms of theism, including Christianity; Malcolm's was only a street-hardened contempt for the Christian church and its members. Bembry had, as Malcolm said, "a framework" for his atheism; Malcolm's had no intellectual or philosophical framework because, it seems, Malcolm actually believed in God enough to fight him. Malcolm's desperate outburst before Bembry in the prison yard revealed his own anxiety over the nature and existence of God. Apparently Malcolm was not attracted to Bembry's atheism, but he was certainly stimulated by it. Deep inside, Malcolm may even have been bothered by it. In any case, Bembry's influence on Malcolm has been greatly underestimated, probably because of the Nation's more popular legend of Malcolm's prison education that is expounded in his autobiography. On closer examination, it becomes clear that two important facts have been overlooked in order to maintain the Nation's legend.

First, while Malcolm entered prison intellectually underdeveloped, he was never illiterate, nor was he academically stranded at a basic level of learning. According to the results of a test he took in the first few months of his incarceration, his reading ability was evaluated as "good" and his arithmetical ability (even though he seems to have disliked math) was "high average." It is also significant that both his abstract reasoning and his "range of information" skills were rated "superior." It is obvious, then, that despite Malcolm's claim that "the streets had erased everything I'd ever learned in school," he was exaggerating. He probably meant only that his English and writing skills in particular had suffered.[6]

Second, and equally important, Malcolm's process of self-instruction and intellectual discipline was already underway when he met the Nation in prison. Elijah Muhammad gave him a higher, perhaps more rigorous motivation for learning, but in reality it was the Nation that benefited from Malcolm's personal intellectual revolution. According to Malcolm, it was Bembry's influence that was fundamental: "He started me reading myself; in fact, his influence turned me from reading what you might call cowboy books, which was my diet at that time, into a higher level of reading."

Even in his autobiography Malcolm notes that Bembry, along with Malcolm's eldest sister Hilda, urged him to take academic courses through the prison education program. Taking this advice, Malcolm completed a university extension course in Plain English Part I, Elementary German, and Elementary Latin, Parts I–IV, scoring "with excellent marks" in the latter two language courses. He also began to order and read books of interest to him during that first year of prison. "After about a year, I guess, I could write a decent and legible letter," Malcolm said. However, his now legendary fascination with etymology and linguistics was already blossoming, and his personal life of study—still unguided and without purpose—had been quite successfully realized long before his exposure to Elijah Muhammad.

Still, Malcolm was hardly interested in the notion of personal reformation. Bimbi's good influence did not preclude or even discourage Malcolm from engaging in small hustles among his fellow prisoners, such as "cigarette and money bets on ball games." He maintained his tough, cynical, and moody manner—especially in the presence of prison authorities, one of whom noted that Malcolm's "tenet of racial injustices looms largely in his mind." Despite the awakening of Malcolm's intellectual life, he still lacked moral purpose. He had probably abandoned his brand of atheism for no other reason than out of embarrassment before the superior intellectual atheism of Bimbi. But Malcolm was miserable in prison, and his supervisors feared that incarceration would only harden him. "Prognosis is poor," the same official wrote of Malcolm, concluding that "his present 'hard' attitude will no doubt increase in bitterness; the possibility of amelioration through a good marriage being precluded by this incarceration. Seeking positive guidance, the picture for the future is not hopeful as seen at this time."[7]

Malcolm remained at Massachusetts State Prison for about one year. His first year of prison was not as dramatically rebellious as he chose to portray in his autobiography. But there is little doubt that he felt unhappy, restless, and without purpose, and that his attitude and behavior were reflected in his cynical and fatalistic comments. During this time, however, his siblings continued to show their love and concern for their incarcerated brother, who was actually on the dramatic road to conversion.

Malcolm was transferred to Concord Reformatory in January 1947, and remained there fourteen months. It was not the transfer he had requested, and he continued to maintain his indifference to life, expressing it especially by his unwillingness to work. But he was told that if he kept his record clean, he could reapply for transfer to another facility. In 1948, while still at Concord, he received another enthusiastic letter from his brother, Philbert. This time, however, Philbert was not writing on behalf of a "holiness" Christian church; but rather, he explained that he had discovered "the natural religion for the black man." Malcolm's response was even harsher than to Philbert's first religious letter—"although in improved English."

Malcolm did not realize at the time that Philbert was writing not only for himself, but on behalf of the entire family, which had already joined Muhammad's organization. They had entered the Nation following the lead of Wilfred, the eldest sibling, who had joined up in 1947. Given their upbringing as religious eclectics, none of Malcolm's siblings were given to joining religious movements—with the exception of Philbert, who Malcolm said "was forever joining something." However, whatever it was that attracted Wilfred and the others to Muhammad's teaching, it eventually drew in Philbert as well. No doubt they were attracted to the Nation because it was a black movement. According to Wilfred, "It was a program designed to help black people. And they had the best program going."

At the family's request, Malcolm's younger brother Reginald wrote a nonreligious letter, but with an irresistible challenge: "Malcolm, don't eat any more pork, and don't smoke any more cigarettes. I'll show you how to get out of prison." Malcolm accepted this challenge, but apparently only because it held out the mysterious hope of getting out of prison. Still, the family's plan to induct Malcolm into the Nation was forestalled. Wilfred and the others knew that Malcolm's letters would be read by the prison censor, so they temporarily avoided extensive discussion about the Nation in the mail, though they did not abandon their intention of inducting Malcolm into Muhammad's organization. Wilfred in particular knew that his family's unique background and Garveyite orientation would make all of them assets to this black-oriented movement, including Malcolm: "It would be something easy for him to adopt, because it fit the philosophy we had grown up under." Wilfred was also certain that Malcolm would benefit from the Nation's discipline once he was a free man.[8]

Meanwhile, Ella was trying to arrange for another prison transfer for Malcolm, even as Malcolm himself wrote a letter to the official in charge of transfers to the Norfolk Prison Colony. The letter shows that Malcolm's race consciousness and his desire for education were already a vital part of his thinking:

My sole purpose for wanting to go to Norfolk was the educational facilities that aren't in these other institutions. If I had completed my education I never would have been in prison today. I'm serving ten years for burglary on my first offense—my first crime. That doesn't hurt so because, being a Negroe [sic], I'm used to heavier punishment than usual. But, I have long ago realized my mistakes and cannot see how an educated man would break into other peoples' houses.[9]

It is clear that Malcolm's interest in further education was already a part of his life, even before he converted to Muhammad's Islam:

Since my confinement I've already received a diploma in Elementary English through the State Correspondence Courses. I'm very much dissatisfied, though. There are many things that I would like to learn that would be of use to me when I regain my freedom. . . . All I'm asking you for is a chance to ammend [sic] my mistakes. Then, if I fail, I have no one to hate but myself.[10]

Through the assistance of Shag Taylor, a Roxbury ward boss, Ella succeeded in securing Malcolm's transfer from Concord Reformatory to Norfolk Prison Colony at the end of March 1948.

Norfolk Prison Colony served as the ideal place for Malcolm's conversion to come to fullness. Here the environment was dramatically different with its program of "experimental rehabilitation." Open for less than two decades when Malcolm arrived, the facility was spacious, suburban, and fairly modern—and it had walls instead of prison bars. It was an intermediate-security facility housing only "well-behaved transfers." Malcolm said Norfolk had a high number of inmates who sought out "intellectual" activities instead of the usual prison pastimes of graft, gossip, and perversion. Crucial to Malcolm's development, however, was the fact that Norfolk gave its inmates private quarters and made an extensively stocked library available to them.

In Norfolk, Malcolm was visited by his younger brother, Reginald, whose trip from Michigan was sponsored by Wilfred in order to expose Malcolm to the teachings they preferred not to send by letter. Malcolm's family felt that Reginald was best able to introduce Muhammad's Islam to him: "He had been on the streets with Malcolm for a short time and so he knew Malcolm, and he knew things Malcolm had been involved in and all, so he knew how to talk Malcolm's language."

Malcolm said later that Reginald knew how his mind operated, and therefore came with an effective approach—one that contained no religious rhetoric. Wilfred agreed: "If he had went to him talking religion, he never would have got to him." Instead, Reginald appealed to Malcolm's experience with white people, reminding him over and over again that none of the whites he had encountered over the years had ever shown any genuine interest in his welfare. Malcolm thus counted his experiences with whites, from his youth in Michigan until now, and found that he could not deny Reginald's insistence that "the white man is the devil." Reginald's appeal was strongly geared toward black interest as well; for his point was to show Malcolm that not only had whites used him personally, but they had used him often to exploit his own people. He was cornered by Reginald's streetwise observations: he could not deny that the white man was the devil, and that he himself had been the "devil's imp" while he believed he had been hustling for himself.[11]

According to Malcolm's recollection, however, Reginald's proselytizing was not without its theological aspects. While it was true that he based his persuasive case largely on Malcolm's own experience of white racism and corruption, Reginald did express some of Muhammad's theological teachings as well. Noting the terminology of the Masons, Reginald told Malcolm that white people had only "thirty-three degrees of knowledge"—in comparison with Allah, God, who had 360 degrees, "the sum total of knowledge." To top this off, Reginald announced, "God is a man."

Malcolm was, according to his own admission, confused by Reginald's new doctrines. At first he could not accept the suggestion that all whites are devils. And while he did not say so, it must have been equally difficult for him to believe that God, Allah, was a man. This was, after all, what the Little family had rejected in Christianity all along. Malcolm himself had never believed that Jesus was divine; now, his own family was trying to convince him that God had in fact appeared in the form of another man. Thus Malcolm was not able to embrace these teachings immediately.

Malcolm does not mention in his autobiography that, even before Reginald visited him, he had already become interested in religious ideas, and had even begun his own comparative religious studies. True to the religious eclecticism of his family, "Malcolm pored through the books on Buddhism, Hinduism, Islam, and Christianity" that were in abundance in the Norfolk prison library. He even contacted the Watchtower Bible and Tract Society seeking Bible-study assistance from the Jehovah's Witnesses. For an extended time, their representatives visited him regularly, one of them remembering his particular interest in Jesus and in some similarities between Jesus and Islam's prophet Muhammad.

It is interesting to note that Malcolm turned to the Watchtower Bible and Tract Society for theological guidance rather than to a mainline Protestant, Evangelical or even Fundamentalist Christian Bible study association. Certainly, there was no lack of orthodox Christian Bible-study correspondence programs. It would seem that he turned to the Jehovah's Witnesses because he was drawing on his own religious background. As noted earlier, Malcolm's mother had found certain aspects of the Jehovah's Witnesses' doctrine of great interest and had exposed her children to their meetings as much as she had exposed them to Christian groups. However, true to his religious roots, Malcolm was not won over by them: he was apparently only interested in availing himself of their survey of biblical literature. At the same time, he was also interested in Islam and the Prophet Muhammad, and his Jehovah's Witnesses tutor no doubt found this quite disturbing. His conclusion that Malcolm was feeding a great ego probably suggests something of his failure to indoctrinate Malcolm.

Reginald apparently stayed in the area so he could make a number of return visits, then finally left Malcolm "rocking with some of the first serious thoughts I had ever had in my life"—particularly regarding the lost "Asiatic" identity of the black man and the imminent and divinely ordained downfall of the white man. After Reginald's visit, Malcolm's siblings stepped up their correspondence with him, knowing that by now he had gained enough understanding so they could urge him to accept Muhammad's teachings.

While Malcolm was in Norfolk Prison Colony, he was also visited by his elder sister, Hilda, who came to solidify Reginald's work. She introduced him specifically to the Fard-Muhammad tale, "Yacub's History," which essentially stated that a black genius had invented the devilish white race as the result of a centuries-long genetic "grafting" project. Black people were the "originals," the superior race who were predestined to be oppressed for six thousand years by the "bleached white" devil race that had been grafted from them. However, the "originals" were then to be freed by "the greatest and mightiest God who appeared on the earth . . . Master W. D. Fard." Fard, as Hilda explained it to Malcolm, had an interracial identity that allowed him to lead black people while also moving secretly among the devils in order to understand and judge them. Hilda explained how Fard had come to the black community in 1931 and was revealed as Allah in the flesh. By the time Hilda was done explaining these teachings, Malcolm was stunned.

Heeding Hilda's suggestion, Malcolm began to correspond with Elijah Muhammad in Chicago. He was undoubtedly won over by Elijah's personal response and the apparent concern he showed by sending him generous monetary gifts. His family continued to write, and now they advised him to pray facing the East. Malcolm found it difficult to pray, especially since it required that he bend his knees, but he eventually did so, though with hesitation at first: "When finally I was able to make myself stay down—I didn't know what to say to Allah."

It seems that initially Malcolm's conversion was prompted more out of personal need than religious belief. He wrote that at first he had stopped eating pork and smoking cigarettes, as Reginald had advised him, because he was looking for a way out of prison. However, personal crises often motivate people to search for a new meaning system to explain their condition and afford peace. Still, it is clear that Malcolm genuinely embraced the teachings of Elijah Muhammad as he became more exposed to them—especially the black-and-white logic of the Nation's philosophy. Like his brother Wilfred, Malcolm was probably drawn to it because it was a religion for black people only.

People join cults and new religions when they are offered a social base that affirms their identities. In Malcolm's case, the Nation appealed to his personal motives and goals, allowing him to reorder his life on a number of levels while—for the first time—fusing his personal religious sense with his black consciousness.[12] The Nation's social base was not only appealing to Malcolm, but it was quite familiar, since Muhammad's teachings, like Garvey's ideas, were fundamentally designed to affirm the black identity. It seems that Malcolm found his raison d'être in the Nation—something that simultaneously required moral reform and mission, giving him both a new purpose and a new goal in life.

Conversion to another religion invariably allows believers to see the world in a new way—reinterpreting their lives in light of the newly adopted religious tradition. "Suddenly the convert's world has changed. It is shaped by a new outlook, dominated by new goals." This was Malcolm's experience, who marveled at how swiftly his earlier "thinking pattern slid away . . . like snow off a roof." He recalled that it was as if "someone else I knew of had lived by hustling and crime. I would be startled to catch myself thinking in a remote way of my earlier self as another person."

Malcolm's life and his goals had certainly changed by now. His first inclination was to activism, yet as an inmate he could only write letters. He wrote them regularly not only to his family and to Muhammad, but began an evangelistic letter writing campaign in an attempt to reach his friends who were still on the street. The many letters Malcolm wrote not only gave him practice in writing but also prompted him to continue his studies.

In order to enhance his writing, Malcolm would study the dictionary intensely so that he could seize for himself the same kind of "stock of knowledge" he had admired in Bimbi. He began a regular and fervent program of reading, with its goal being the betterment of Muhammad's movement: "I took special pains to hunt in the library for books that would inform me on details about black history." Malcolm thus embarked on his studies in a new and revitalized way, thereby enhancing his new religious worldview.

Malcolm's new sense of mission required that he overcome his reading and writing inadequacies and provided him with intellectual exercise. His commitment to Elijah Muhammad's teachings helped him formulate a curriculum for study that closely resembled formal academic training, and probably surpassed the undergraduate level in intensity if not in content. However, whatever Malcolm read, he did so with the intent of affirming the teachings of Elijah Muhammad. He studied world history, African and African-American history, ancient history, Eastern and Western philosophy, genetics and anthropology, the literary classics of Shakespeare and Milton, linguistics, religious literature, and many other scholarly works. "As I see it today," Malcolm said in retrospect, "the ability to read awoke inside me some long dormant craving to be mentally alive."

Malcolm noted that two other aspects of his self-education at Norfolk were critical in his religious development as well. The first was his deliberate effort to obtain disciples for Muhammad in the prison. "I began to catch every chance I could to recruit for Mr. Muhammad." This included verbal presentations as well as handwritten copies of letters he had sent to other people. The second aspect was Malcolm's involvement in the prison's weekly debating competition, where he attempted to advance his "Islamic" doctrines; but since the topics were varied and prearranged, and the positions apparently assigned, he benefited more from the experience of having to learn how to prepare for and engage in debates. He found debating "exhilarating."[13]

As far as these debates are concerned, Malcolm was in the right place at Norfolk Prison Colony. Since its opening in 1927, Norfolk emphasized prisoner education. Besides the academic and vocational courses and the library available to the inmates, the debating program was a popular feature. Many inmates participated in the program, and the debates themselves were popular, generally filling the prison theater's capacity of 250–300 seats.

In one debate in which Malcolm participated about the abolition of capital punishment, he took the position that the death penalty is ineffective as a deterrent to murder. "The whole history of penology is a refutation of the deterrence theory," declared Malcolm, "yet this theory, that murder by the state can repress murder by individuals, is the eternal war cry for the retention of Capital Punishment."

Malcolm's argument showed a considerable amount of research in penological studies. Quoting some experts, he hoped to buttress his conclusion that fear of death would not, in itself, keep men from committing murder. To illustrate his point, he emphasized that men condemned to death must be closely watched in order to prevent them from committing suicide. "It is also a well-known fact," added Malcolm—probably with a smile—"that pickpockets in England would ply their trade with great success at the execution of one of their members." Malcolm admitted that the death penalty might be a deterrent for murderers who kill with the belief that they are immune because of "influence," but actual deterrence could result only from mandatory death penalties, near perfect detective forces, scrupulous officials, unbiased juries, and stern pardoning power. "These unobtainables would result in such a large number of executions," Malcolm concluded, "that the defenders of the death penalty would stand aghast."

Malcolm said that as a hustler "in the streets," being a public speaker "never would have crossed my mind." He had undoubtedly craved fame and success, but it was not until his conversion that he began to understand that his able mind and his love of public speaking could have a far more glorious purpose: the black struggle. "And if there was any way in the world, I'd work into my speech the devilishness of the white man."[14]

Malcolm's conversion was not complete, however. He had submitted to the wishes of his family first, and then he came to embrace the teachings of Muhammad on his own. The conversion gave him a sense of renewal and a new meaning and purpose to his life; his self-education was empowered and directed by that new purpose. Yet the greatest test of his conversion did not occur until he faced the despair and frustration of Reginald's falling out with Elijah Muhammad and the Nation.

It started when Reginald came to visit Malcolm in Norfolk. Malcolm had apparently launched into an enthusiastic discussion when he was suddenly cut short by Reginald. Reginald began "to speak ill" of Elijah Muhammad, making some negative comments that Malcolm left unrecorded. (Were Reginald's criticisms a foretaste of the terrible revelations Malcolm X would receive regarding Mr. Muhammad, many years later?) "It caught me totally unprepared. It threw me into a state of confusion," Malcolm said. Reginald was, after all his "blood brother" and the one who had first convinced him of the truth of Muhammad's teachings. Now, Reginald was speaking against Elijah Muhammad's Islam, which, Malcolm said, "meant more to me than anything I had ever known in my life."

Malcolm then learned that Reginald had been suspended from the Nation because of repeated sexual encounters with a female member of the organization. "When Reginald left," Malcolm recalled, "I was in torment." Malcolm, who already enjoyed a serious correspondence with Elijah Muhammad, took up his pen to write a letter of intercession, "trying to defend my brother, appealing for him." Malcolm said that after he posted the letter, he began to pray to Allah. "I don't think anyone ever prayed more sincerely to Allah. I prayed for some kind of relief from my confusion."

The next night, recalled Malcolm, as he lay awake on his bed, his small, private cell was suddenly shared with the apparition of an Asiatic-looking man in a dark suit. Malcolm stared at the man, who was seated, and after a few moments the strange visitor vanished.

Not long afterward, Elijah Muhammad wrote back to Malcolm about Reginald's fall from grace. What struck Malcolm most about the letter was that Muhammad turned the issue back on Malcolm himself: "If you once believed in the truth, and now you are beginning to doubt the truth, you didn't believe the truth in the first place. What could make you doubt the truth other than your own weak self?" This cut him deeply. Malcolm realized that Elijah Muhammad had decided to use this occasion as a test for his faith. He would either have to submit to Muhammad's judgments and consign his brother to a spiritual wasteland, or be considered faithless himself. Malcolm came to a decision, choosing his newfound faith over Reginald: "All of the influence that my brother had wielded over me was broken. From that day on, as far as I am concerned, everything that my brother Reginald has done is wrong."

Apparently Reginald persisted in visiting Malcolm, and with each visit Malcolm saw that his brother's appearance and behavior were degenerating. He became dirty and shabby-looking: "I could see him on the way down." He would tolerate Reginald, but with apparent coldness. Eventually, Malcolm began to attribute Reginald's obvious mental and emotional decline to the workings of Allah. Muhammad taught that deviants from the Nation would be punished by Allah himself, who would turn the minds "of any defectors into a turmoil."

Years later, as Reginald's mental illness became more acute, Malcolm X was even more persuaded that his brother was suffering divine punishment. Jeremiah Shabazz, one of Malcolm's closest Nation associates and fellow ministers, recalled driving through Detroit with Malcolm sometime in the mid-1950s. At one point, Malcolm spotted his brother, who was standing nearby: he stopped the car and beckoned Reginald to come over to them. Shabazz did not know this was Malcolm's brother, and it was clear to him that the man's speech was bizarre. Afterward, Malcolm told Shabazz that the man was his brother Reginald, and that he had fallen under divine chastisement for opposing "the Messenger."

With his brother's eventual institutionalization, Malcolm rationalized that Reginald had been Allah's sovereignly appointed instrument for his own conversion. From the perspective of the Nation, Malcolm saw Reginald only "as a bait, as a minnow to reach into the ocean of blackness where I was, to save me." Writing these words as the most fervent follower of Elijah Muhammad, he concluded, "I cannot understand it any other way." He would later come to see his brother's mental and emotional decline differently, but as a new convert to the Nation, Malcolm was obliged to consider his brother an apostate under divine judgment. Malcolm was now truly and completely devoted to the Nation, which had "changed his whole world."

In writing his autobiography, Malcolm thus placed the "pre-vision" of the Asiatic-looking man in the context of the crisis over his brother Reginald. The apparition of the mysterious man came the night after Malcolm first sought to intercede on Reginald's behalf. This memory remained lucid and disturbing until later, when he would come to believe that he had discovered the identity of the apparition.

Malcolm X of the Nation felt certain that his "pre-vision" had been of "W. D. Fard, the Messiah," the one he believed had appointed Elijah Muhammad as leader of the Nation. However, this was neither Malcolm's original nor independent assessment of the image. At the time the apparition occurred, he did not attach any particular meaning to it—and certainly he had not applied to it any direct relationship to the Nation itself. However, once his conversion to the Nation was complete, and he had been fully baptized into an unyielding faith in Elijah Muhammad, the Nation supplied Malcolm with the meaning of the Asiatic-looking man.

Cults and new religions characteristically give "convincing theological interpretation" to individual primal experiences. Malcolm's encounter with the mysterious man in his prison cell was—to Malcolm—a spiritually generic experience at the time it occurred, as are most primal experiences. Like Malcolm's childhood sense of destiny, at which he hinted in the closing pages of his autobiography, the "pre-vision" of the Asiatic man had no objective interpretation. It merely was. The Nation provided Malcolm with an interpretation of the "pre-vision" that not only satisfied his own questions about its meaning, but also affirmed the ideology of the organization. The belief that the apparition was W. D. Fard therefore affirmed Malcolm's embrace of the new mythology—at the expense of his relationship with his brother Reginald.

In 1964, Malcolm himself would be expelled from the Nation, branded as an apostate under the judgment of Allah—just as his brother Reginald had been in those early days of conversion. Malcolm would eventually renounce Muhammad's form of Islam and experience another, very different, conversion. But in his second conversion Malcolm never offered a new interpretation of the prison pre-vision of the Asiatic-looking man. Indeed, the pre-vision remains perhaps the outstanding religious mystery of *The Autobiography of Malcolm X*, and it ultimately regains its original identity as a primal experience in the autobiography. Having been left unexplained, the Asiatic-looking man still sits—quite mysteriously—in the gap between Malcolm's two conversion experiences.

Malcolm would eventually recant all that he had taught on behalf of Elijah Muhammad, and he would renounce the Nation as a religion that in no way related to traditional Islam. He and Alex Haley would even write a kind of disclaimer into the autobiography pertaining to Reginald's mental decline: "I came to believe that it wasn't a divine chastisement upon Reginald, but the pain he felt when his own family totally rejected him for Elijah Muhammad." This, however, was something Malcolm would not realize for many years to come.

While he was a fervent disciple of Elijah Muhammad, Malcolm committed himself completely to the Nation and its leader. Indeed, as new religions go, Malcolm became the prototype of the committed follower who sacrificed, invested, and surrendered his personal time, energy, and life-style to his cult. From such commitment Malcolm would find meaning, purpose, and identity, and his complete conformity to the Nation only served to enhance his level of commitment to Muhammad.[15]

# 7

## Early Ministry

*I am a citizen of Asia.*

Malcolm remained at Norfolk Prison Colony until March 1950, when he transferred back to Charlestown State Prison, where he was first incarcerated. According to Malcolm, his transfer back to Charlestown occurred because the Norfolk Prison Colony administration wanted him out of there. The official reason was that he had refused a standard inoculation, but Malcolm believed that the prison officials were upset with him for his promulgation of Muhammad's teachings. Though he was transferred for rejecting the inoculation, it seems that he was quite aware of the consequences of his refusal. It is likely that he wanted to put himself into the position of doing missionary work in Charlestown, as his brother Wilfred has noted.[1]

Malcolm hinted at a degree of persecution at Norfolk, and it is probable that prison officials were concerned about his spreading the message of the Nation. The transfer summary report that followed Malcolm back to Charlestown mentioned that his "correspondence was mostly concerning the Moslem faith and beliefs and his dislike for the white race." Malcolm also pointed out that at Norfolk a book he had cited in public debate regarding the wickedness of the white race "disappeared from the prison library." Of course, this act may have been undertaken not by an official but by an antagonistic white inmate who resented Malcolm's public diatribes. Regardless, the incident suggests that Malcolm had become known, not only for his debating skills, but also for his controversial "Muslim" teachings. Malcolm remained in Charlestown State Prison from March 23, 1950, until August 7, 1952. It appears that he built up a small following during that time, and at least two of the inmates—one of them his old friend Malcolm Jarvis—chose to follow Malcolm from Norfolk to Charlestown as well.

Though he was only unofficially active in Muhammad's service, Malcolm's career as the rising star of the Nation began while he was still incarcerated, and particularly during this last leg of his prison experience. He evidenced many of the same characteristics of his later involvement in the Nation, and when he later left prison, he entered immediately into the service of the movement as an evangelist.

Malcolm appears to have kept up his correspondence and his prison crusade to advance Muhammad's teachings. He may have presented his teachings with a "general air of importance," though his identification with the character of Jesus noted in one biography is an exaggeration. That Malcolm wrote to one of his friends, saying that Jesus was going to return in the flesh someday, more likely suggests theological confusion than messianic delusion. He may have been alluding to the expected return of W. D. Fard, the Nation's "Christ." However, given his religious eclecticism, it is also possible Malcolm had appropriated a doctrine from the Jehovah's Witnesses.[2]

In his autobiographical account, Malcolm shortened his second term at Charlestown, referring to it as his "last year in prison," even though he was actually there for over twice that long. His account of this period is also quite brief, hinting only that he had "less maneuverability" there. The only autobiographical vignette Malcolm provided took place during a Bible study conducted by a visiting seminarian. According to Malcolm, he challenged the young white professor regarding the skin color of the historical Jesus.

Very shortly after Malcolm's return to Charlestown he apparently succeeded in converting the younger brother of one of the men who had transferred with him. The two brothers, Osborne and Leroy Thaxton, along with Malcolm Jarvis and Malcolm Little, were the prison's first Muslims. In April, only a month into their stay at Charlestown, Malcolm and his small following demanded a menu that allowed them to adhere to Muhammad's dietary restrictions, and prison cells that faced east, toward Mecca. The warden at first refused but, after Malcolm threatened to appeal to the Egyptian consul, granted their second request for cells facing east.[3]

The local press picked up the story about their demands for religious freedom, describing Malcolm and his cobelievers as wearing beards and mustaches and declaring piously that Allah "will help us and protect us from evil." Giving only brief coverage, the *Boston Herald* treated the matter lightheartedly, jesting that there was no truth to an additional report "that several other convicts had proclaimed themselves fetish worshippers and demanded hacksaws in their cells." While the press may not have taken these new "Moslems" seriously, the men were quite earnest about their role as Muhammad's disciples—particularly Malcolm.

Not surprisingly, Malcolm failed to make mention of this minor victory in Charlestown Prison in his autobiography. It seems likely that he disregarded the whole affair because it would have made him appear more influential than his autobiographical purpose required and might undercut the suspenseful development of his "salvation" story. Just as it benefited Muhammad's image for Malcolm to picture himself as an illiterate but sophisticated criminal, it was important to his story that his own development as a leader climax under the very wing of Muhammad himself—which would undoubtedly have marked the end of the story in its original conceptualization. But with Malcolm's departure from the Nation in 1964, his autobiography was suddenly extended, and the theme of Mr. Muhammad's saving power was swallowed up by another, more credible conversion story.

Malcolm, and probably his three fellow Muslims also, did not violate Muhammad's dietary restrictions, even though the prison did not respect their refusal to eat pork. The cooks, upon discovering that the bearded black "Moslems" would not eat pork, frequently harassed Malcolm by serving his food with utensils that had been used to handle pork. Consequently, for the better part of his second stay at Charlestown, Malcolm's diet consisted mainly of bread and cheese.[4]

Malcolm was outspoken and rigorous not only with regard to his own circumstances, but he supported other Muslims with equal fervor. This is readily apparent in several letters he wrote to the prison's commissioner. In the first of these letters, dated April 18, 1950, Malcolm wrote Commissioner MacDowell on behalf of a Muslim who was being held in solitary confinement at the Norfolk Prison Colony. The letter, which Malcolm headed "In the Name of Allah, the All-Wise[,] True and Living God" and "in the Name of His Holy Apostle . . . the Honorable Mr. Elijah Mohammed," is filled with the cultic language of light and darkness, guilt and wrath, and the pilgrimage east toward truth: "The more-informed persons of this occidental world Travel all of their lives toward the East, Craving the Light that they do not now have. The more of this Light they 'obtain,' the more *Just* they become."[5] However, Malcolm's appeal was not without the threat of Divine judgment:

One who is well-Traveled will not in this *Most Crucial Day* sow unjust seeds by wrongfully persecuting a man of Allah simply because he Faces the East to Pray. *Today* if one sows unjust seeds one will reap them *Today* . . . because all Travelers have reached their Final Goal, and This Day they must Face the Only Judge: He Who Creates all Light.[6]

The Muslim in solitary confinement, Malcolm maintained, was held there for four months "for reasons that flow from the warped minds of biased men whose ignorance has filled their hearts with racial and religious prejudice." In this letter there was no mention of whites being devils, and in fact Malcolm closed the letter by admonishing the commissioner to "let your Conscience Be Your Guide." Still, Malcolm warned the commissioner that when one goes against conscience, "one is only assisting in and hastening one's own self-destruction."[7]

Two months later, Malcolm wrote another letter to Commissioner Mac-Dowell, again introduced "In the Name of Allah" and "His True Servant and Holy Apostle, the Honorable Prophet Elijah Mohammed." In this letter, Malcolm complained that one of the "illiterate" Muslims at Charlestown was prohibited by a certain prison official from being placed in a literacy workshop with his own brother. That prison official had rejected the Muslim brothers' request, Malcolm declared, "yet, the homosexual perverts in here can get job-changes whenever they wish to change or acquire new 'husbands.' You figure that one out!" By setting up the Muslims, who he said had "never broken any regulations of this institution" unlike the homosexuals in the facility, Malcolm was attempting to underscore the moral inequity of the circumstances.

Likewise, Malcolm noted that the Muslims were prohibited from purchasing books by J. A. Rogers, the black historian: "Is it actually against the 'law' for a Black man to read about himself? (let me laugh!)." He charged the deputy at Charlestown with lying and "speaking unwisely of things that are beyond his knowledge and over his head," and with discussing the followers of Muhammad with white inmates, "an act that increases racial tension and ill-feeling."

Malcolm then presented a not-so-veiled warning: "We would prefer outright segregation where we would be together, to ourselves, and have Peace permanently . . . because if it becomes the Will of Allah for Peace to cease,

*Peace will cease!"* Believing that the commissioner was likely a Mason, or that he had associates who were part of the Masonic lodge, Malcolm hinted that he would, "to a degree," understand Islam. "If this humble, but most sincere, message is beyond your comprehension, get one of the devils who has acquired *his maximum* of Light (33°) and he will surely understand it."

In another letter Malcolm made a similar allusion, this time to the highest position in the Masonic lodge, by stating that water "at the 32° level is frozen, cold and *lifeless.*" In so doing, Malcolm reiterated Muhammad's absolute rejection of the Masons, and his teaching that the Masonic order possessed limited but damnable insight into the whole truth of Islam.[8]

In December 1950, Charlestown's deputy warden apparently prohibited Malcolm and the other Muslims from getting out of their beds to face east in prayer after curfew hour. In another letter to the commissioner, Malcolm complained that the sudden enforcement of the curfew "smells fishy!" He also challenged that it was "an open attack upon our religious rights," and reminded the commissioner that "the 'constitution' of this land is 'suppose' to guarntee [sic] these Rights to *all* men."

Interestingly, Malcolm also invoked an international authority, just as he had done when threatening to alert the Egyptian consul. However, instead of appealing to a single Islamic nation, Malcolm spoke of "the *Whole Body* of Islam." Reminding the commissioner that the United States was currently in crisis (the Korean War was in progress), he said that the "ultimate outcome" of the "plight" of the United States depended "solely upon her success in convincing The People of the East that she is truly seeking *Peace.*" It is very likely that Malcolm's willingness to hold "the present international situation" over the head of the commissioner was not something he learned from Muhammad, but was an influence of his Garveyite background.

It would be characteristic of Malcolm's later messages, both within and out of the Nation, to speak of the African American's place in the "Dark World" and in the Muslim world. Likewise, he would emphasize the important role of black nationalists, even though they were only a militant minority within a minority community. He liked to compare the black nationalists to the wick in a powder keg, suggesting that their small number should not be mistaken for little influence within the black community. Thus, in one of his earliest prison letters, Malcolm reminded the commissioner that the fire that consumed Rome was started "by a minute and most remote *spark*" and that the tragic Chicago fire "was set off by the resentful 'kick' of a lowly, domesticated farm animal."[9]

Commissioner MacDowell was hardly impressed. He wrote to Malcolm's warden at Charlestown, asking him to tell Malcolm that the Muslims must adhere to the prison's rules just like the Christians. Even though prison officials had some concerns about Malcolm and undoubtedly kept him under surveillance, his lengthy, dramatic, and symbol-laden letters failed to evoke the response he wanted. It is possible that Malcolm's fervor was partly responsible for the psychiatric examination he underwent in May 1951, in which the doctor's report concluded: "He claims to be a Mohammedan, but his conversation expresses a confused jumble of ideas which make little sense."

The last dated letter by Malcolm on file was to Commissioner Grossman, who was apparently the successor to Commissioner MacDowell. The letter, written on June 6, 1951, ironically included a request to be transferred back to Norfolk Prison Colony, citing its more balanced atmosphere and his own "clean" prison record. In language the commissioner probably didn't understand, Malcolm stated that he had not yet "acquired a living knowledge," but that he could "walk in perfect accord with all rules governing Norfolk." Writing with cultic allusion, Malcolm now seemed to admit that he had erred in refusing to take the required inoculation while at Norfolk. He did not apologize and claimed his refusal was due to a sincere mistake made as a fervent convert to Islam: "When experience is the only available Teacher one must suffer many set-backs."

Malcolm's reasons for wanting to be transferred back to Norfolk are not clear. He may have felt that his evangelistic efforts were too marginalized, or he may simply have begun to miss the more intellectually stimulating environment at Norfolk. In any case, Malcolm's request was apparently refused. He spent the last fourteen months of his term at Charlestown and was paroled on August 7, 1952.[10]

In July 1952, Malcolm's eldest brother Wilfred was able to obtain the permission of the Massachusetts Department of Corrections to have Malcolm's parole transferred to the state of Michigan. Even though Wilfred was already supporting a wife, two young children, and his younger brother, Wesley, he consented to take responsibility for Malcolm as well. Apparently the family had decided that Malcolm would be better off in Michigan than if he stayed in Boston. With the thirty dollars he received from the prison officials, plus the money given him by his elder sister Hilda who met him at his release, Malcolm bought new eyeglasses, a suitcase, and a wristwatch. He later realized that those three purchases gave him the basic equipment he would need for the new life ahead of him.

Malcolm moved in with Wilfred and his wife Ruth, who had recently purchased a five-room frame house in Inkster, Michigan. Wilfred found a job for Malcolm at the Cut Rate Department Store on Oakland Avenue in Detroit, where he was hired as a porter and was promised a forty dollar per week salary. At first he experienced some setbacks due to health problems. Wilfred, Ruth, and even the parole officer noted that he was pale, anemic-looking, and weak because of his poor diet in prison; in addition, he had a nagging problem with hemorrhoids that eventually required hospitalization.

Even after surgery Malcolm had a difficult time regaining strength; when he found a better-paying job at the Lincoln-Mercury plant in January 1953, he was soon fired because he was not strong enough to keep up with his assembly-line position. Understandably, Malcolm avoided discussing these health problems in his autobiography, instead claiming to have quit the Lincoln-Mercury plant to pursue a full-time ministry for the Nation. Malcolm wanted to work full time for Mr. Muhammad, but the road to full-time ministry was apparently a bit more rocky than he wished to share with his readers.[11]

At first Malcolm's parole officer suspected him of "malingering," but he soon found it to be "obvious by his physical appearance that he was actually ill." The officer's report shows not only a sympathetic view of Malcolm's condition, but it reveals the sincerity with which Malcolm was attempting to follow his commitment to Muhammad. "So far he has shown no inclinations to return to his former pattern of living. He does not appear to have any associates outside of the family and has been developing an interest in church activities." The reference to "church activities" by the parole officer reflects Malcolm's busy new life, which was undoubtedly guided by Wilfred, who made sure Malcolm "got involved to the extent that he didn't get a chance to get too much with anybody else."

Wilfred was at first concerned that Malcolm would be lured back into the streets, especially because Malcolm's honest wage was only a fraction of what he could make illegally. He knew that Malcolm was frustrated by working all week for only forty dollars. "You know what?" Malcolm would declare to his brother in frustration. "I could have breakfast with you this morning, and come back and meet you for lunch and have more money than this!" Nevertheless, Malcolm did not resort to his old ways of crime. He remained loyal to Muhammad and began to build his first relationships within the local temple, known as "Temple No. 1"—the first temple founded by Elijah Muhammad after the disappearance of Fard. Malcolm's parole officer concluded in February 1953 that "prognosis in this case appears favorable at the present time." Malcolm was successfully discharged from parole by the state of Massachusetts on May 4, 1953.[12]

Early in 1953 Malcolm's health had improved enough to get another job, at the Gar Wood Factory in Wayne, Michigan. One day he was pulled off his job by an FBI agent, who informed him that he had failed to register for the Korean War draft. Malcolm said later that he acted as if he thought being an ex-offender disqualified him from the draft. He was told to register immediately if he wanted to avoid prosecution and another jail term. Since this was just before his completion of parole, Malcolm quickly reported to the draft board. It seems that Malcolm's failure to register for the draft was deliberate, however. His negligence may actually have been an expression of allegiance to Elijah Muhammad and the Nation, which had been persecuted during World War II for refusing draft registration.

The initial questionnaire Malcolm filled out apparently contained a section for seminarians and others studying for the ministry where they were to list the name of their church and school. In this section Malcolm claimed to be a student studying at the University of Islam in Chicago, under the direction of the Temple of Islam. In the section on citizenship, Malcolm found the sentence, "I am a citizen of —— ," and filled in "Asia." Beside the statement that inquired whether he had filed "a Declaration of Intention to Become a Citizen of the United States" he replied negatively. The questionnaire also asked if he had "any physical or mental condition" which, in his opinion, merited disqualification from military service. Malcolm answered "Yes," and explained that his "mental attitude and outlook in general regarding war and religion" merited disqualification.

In addition, Malcolm filled out a "Special Form for Conscientious Objectors," stating his belief in a supreme being. When asked to describe the basis of his claim for conscientious objector status, Malcolm wrote: "Allah is God, not of one particular people or race, but of *All the Worlds*, thus forming All Peoples and Nations into *One Universal Brotherhood*, and Brother definitely should seek peace with Brother, not war."

In answering where he received his training and acquired his convictions, Malcolm answered that "Allah guided me off the road of wickedness onto this path of Righteousness while I was yet in prison and all praise is due to Allah alone. There is no God besides Him." Aside from noting that Muslims fight only in self-defense and seek peace as "the way of righteousness," Malcolm submitted as evidence of the consistency of his convictions the fact that after accepting Islam in prison, "I taught it there for nearly four years, under the worst conditions and against the most severe opposition and ridicule imaginable and shall *forever* do so!! (with Allah's permission)." When asked to identify and give the location of his religious guide, Malcolm did not mention Elijah Muhammad at all, but wrote: "Allah the Divine Supreme Being, who resides at the Holy City of Mecca, in Arabia."[13]

In his autobiography, Malcolm recalls that his answers aroused the concern of several "older devils," who further cross-examined him about his beliefs and asked him if he actually understood the concept of conscientious objection to military service. He said he responded that his conscience made him object to fighting on behalf of white people when they treated black people as they did in the United States. Malcolm also mentions that they directed him to take a physical examination, but he does not note that he failed it, once again, on May 25, 1953.

Malcolm not only refused to take the blood test for religious reasons, but he may also have acted as he did before the New York City draft board a decade earlier, when he had failed the physical exam the first time. The psychiatric diagnosis concluded that Malcolm had an "asocial personality with paranoid trends (prepsychotic paranoid schizophrenia)." Likewise, Malcolm denied that he was a member of any religious sect or organization, and insisted the "religion of Islam is not a sect or organization for it was never *organized*. It has always been!! Its origin is with Allah. It is Peace. It springs forth from Peace and its return unto Peace." According to Malcolm, he never heard from the draft board again, except when he was sent a classification card in 1960.[14]

Malcolm had succeeded twice in convincing draft board officials to exclude him from service classification. The first time, he only had the desire to stay out of the army—whatever act he had put on was purely self-serving. But then, as a follower of Elijah Muhammad, he considered himself an "Asiatic" and not a citizen of the United States. While he did not readily offer Muhammad's name, it does not appear that he was attempting to be secretive, for he did acknowledge his affiliation with the local Nation branch. Rather, it seems that Malcolm's unorthodox answers were sincere and—like his prison letters—demonstrated his genuine desire to follow along "the path of Righteousness." Now free of any further obligations to the state, Malcolm embarked upon that path. He would follow it faithfully for the next twelve years of his life, and in the process, carry the message of "Islam" farther than even Elijah Muhammad had ever imagined.

# 8

## Evangelism and
## Nation-Building

*Indeed we are living in a great day.*

"Malcolm was always a very energetic person," Wilfred Little recalled. "He had an exceptional amount of mental energy, so when he came to the Movement, he had a lot to offer—more than what had been realized." While Malcolm had read much in books in prison, in his new freedom he turned to studying the realities of racial oppression in his own surroundings. Some of these realities were most evident in the first department store where he worked, where he saw firsthand that poor black urbanites often had no alternative but to buy the cheaply manufactured and highly priced products made available to them by white retailers: "I would see clumsy, work-hardened, calloused hands scrawling and scratching signatures on the contract, agreeing to highway-robbery interest rates in the fine print that never was read."

Malcolm's mind and energies focused on the social and economic condition of his people: "Now I watched brothers entwining themselves in the economic clutches of the white man who went home every night with another bag of the money drained out of the ghetto." He likewise observed the status and condition of the Nation itself, embracing Fard's vision of a black nation within an oppressive white one. As he became more and more angered at the situation of blacks in the United States, he became increasingly comfortable in the company of the Nation.

Malcolm recalled that Detroit's Temple No. 1 was located not far from a slaughterhouse. The sounds of squealing hogs emanated into the temple during services—a vivid reminder to Malcolm that he and his people were truly lost in the "wilderness of North America," where blacks ate unclean meat in an unclean land. Experiences such as this made him all the more impressed with his encounters of the Muslims: "I had never dreamed of anything like that atmosphere among black people who had learned to be proud they were black, who had learned to love other black people instead of being jealous and suspicious."[1] Much later, he would learn that they were not all that free of jealousy and suspicion. Still, they were proud black people who embraced a black god and did not hesitate to hold the white man accountable for his racial sins. This kind of religion was custom-made for an inspired scion of the Garveyite tradition.

In early August 1952 Malcolm requested permission from his parole officer to leave Michigan to visit Chicago later that month to meet Elijah Muhammad. Permission was granted, and Malcolm went to Chicago on the Sunday before Labor Day, riding in a small caravan of cars with other Muslims from Temple No. 1 for a joint meeting with Temple No. 2. Malcolm recalled later that the eagerness and excitement he felt that day as he journeyed to meet Elijah Muhammad was never again duplicated in his life: "I experienced tinglings up my spine."

Malcolm quickly noted that the combined attendance of the Detroit and Chicago temples was only about two hundred. Though another eight temples comprised the movement, its total membership at this time was only about four hundred. Encouraged by Elijah Muhammad's tableside declaration that the Detroit temple should have "thousands" of members and that the movement should be recruiting young people, Malcolm immediately began to give thought to how the Nation could be expanded. "I made up my mind," Malcolm said later, "that we were going to follow that advice."[2]

The first phase of Malcolm's ministry was marked by aggressive evangelization in the Detroit area. He made it "his particular mission" to expand the Nation, beginning with Temple No. 1. "And that's what he started doing," Wilfred Little recalled, "he started the others to working with him in going out into the community and bringing people in to hear the teachings . . . [and] those would go out and bring in some more and they just kept expanding."

Malcolm recruited in the very places he would have gone to himself as a street-wandering youth. Temple No. 1 gathered a motley array of refugees from bars, poolrooms, and street corners who would soon be transformed into proud, disciplined "Asiatic" Muslims. In his days of glory in Detroit's ghetto, the mysterious W. D. Fard had preferred to go into black homes to recruit followers; but by going into Detroit's spiritual wastelands to "fish" for new black souls, Malcolm had now outdone even the founder of the Nation. In a relatively short time, the roster of Temple No. 1 would grow threefold from what it had been in the summer of 1952.

Malcolm's ardent commitment to evangelism quickly won the attention of both the more conservative local Muslim minister as well as Elijah Muhammad himself, who encouraged and praised him for his great potential. In response to such glowing recognition, Malcolm planted his religious roots with Muhammad. "I worshiped him," he later recalled. In this same period, Malcolm officially applied for his Nation surname, "X." Like the other Muslims, he believed Muhammad when he was told that he would bear his "X" until Fard, "God Himself," would return and give holy names to each of his followers.

In the opportunities that he was given to speak in the temple, Malcolm would launch invectives against "Christianity and the horrors of slavery." By the summer of 1953 his zealous work earned him a promotion in Temple No. 1 to assistant minister. His sermons from that period formed the standard of his later approach on behalf of the Nation. One FBI source, for instance, claims that Malcolm told his audience that no black person was a real citizen of the United States, and that the need for government legislation such as the Bill of Rights and "the Fair Employment System" only underscored this point. In another meeting, Malcolm complained that the recent arrival of thirty thousand Hungarian refugees would only take more jobs from black Americans. Noting the horrendous treatment of the American Indian by the white man, he declared: "The white man screams equality in his Constitution, but speaks with a forked tongue in that he does not mean that for the black man."[3]

Malcolm soon began to eye the regions beyond Detroit as a mission field ripe for harvest. "It had become clear to me that Mr. Muhammad needed ministers to spread his teachings," he recalled later. A natural-born missionary, he strove to stretch the boundaries of the established, more conservative Nation clergy. "He more or less made his own niche," Wilfred Little remembered. "Nothing was done to hinder him . . . what they wanted was numbers and wanted people, and he was doing this on his own. So they just stepped back and let him take over and do it because he was doing better than anybody else."

As Malcolm expanded his work for the Nation into other areas, he was also able to expand the organization's base and strengthen its traditional infrastructure. To avoid creating tension and jealousy in the minds of the older ministers, Malcolm included the conservative ministers in his campaign and carried on "revival"-type meetings in the established temples, which served to increase attendance and membership. As a result, most of the ministers were glad to have this new evangelist in the movement, and he was welcomed to their areas. Later in life, Malcolm would speak of emulating the evangelistic method of Billy Graham, the Fundamentalist Christian preacher, as he sought to spread word of his independent political program. But Malcolm had already employed similar techniques in an ecclesiastical sense much earlier.

At the same time, of course, Malcolm was breaking new ground in membership recruitment. When he went into a black community where no Nation congregation existed, he would contact individuals who he thought might be interested in his message. Once he won an ally, that person's home became the first phase of a new Nation temple. Much like Fard had done in Detroit, Malcolm built up these house meetings until rented facilities could be secured.[4] Unlike Fard, however, Malcolm's overall ministerial style never lost its fundamental concern for bringing in the down and out from the streets.

By the mid-1950s, Malcolm's work had extended to a number of major cities, some of which, such as Boston, had no previously established Nation temples. In 1955, one FBI source reported from Chicago, the Nation's headquarters, that "brother Malcolm appeared to be enjoying" Elijah Muhammad's confidence, "and seemed to have had a free hand in the movement in general." To be sure, Malcolm had no liberties that were not first granted by Elijah Muhammad, with whom he was in continual contact for advice and instruction. But his success was as much a tribute to his own energy, skills, and modern approach as it was to Muhammad's insights into human resource management. Malcolm, after all, did not know the basics of the movement as did Elijah Muhammad.

This critical change within the Nation could not have been wrought without Malcolm's youthful zeal, complete dedication, and fervent, tireless efforts in many urban settings. Nevertheless, everything Malcolm said and did, "politically and theologically, was approved by the Messenger," Elijah Muhammad. Years later, even when their relationship would sour and Malcolm would speak of Elijah Muhammad with bitter disillusionment, he would not negate the mutuality of their success: "I was going downhill until he picked me up, but the more I think of it, we picked each other up."

Malcolm's first success at starting a temple was probably his most glorious, since it was in the city of Boston. "He knew the lay of the land," Wilfred recalled, and this included his old Roxbury haunts. Ironically, it seems that Malcolm was not very successful in winning over his former peers, some of whom he dismissed as being too "brainwashed" to accept Islam. According to Malcolm, the Boston congregation, Temple No. 11, was reasonably established by March 1954.[5]

After the success in Boston Elijah Muhammad directed Malcolm to move to Philadelphia to begin another temple organization program. With monies that had been wisely invested by Malcolm and Edward Jones, another Muslim, a suitable temple facility was secured; they were reimbursed by Elijah Muhammad later. Within three months, Temple No. 12 was established with an adequate number of new members. Malcolm was undoubtedly a rigorous recruiter and pastor. According to one FBI source, he told his new congregation that the Nation was not a club but an actual nation growing out of a nation.

Jeremiah Shabazz, one of the founders of the Nation temple in Philadelphia and a close ministerial associate, recalled that one of Malcolm X's first words were of his pre-vision of the Asiatic-looking man. "The way he laid it out," Shabazz said, "we all believed him—I believed him, and everybody else believed he had had such an experience." Shabazz remembered that the apparition really seemed to have "upset" Malcolm, especially since at the time he did not know who the Asiatic-looking man was.

However great these successes at temple organization may have been for Malcolm, his greatest single endeavor for the Nation was still before him. With the Philadelphia congregation established, Muhammad now ordered Malcolm to assume the pastorate of the Nation temple in New York City. Temple No. 7 was only a small band of Harlem "Asiatics" meeting in a storefront temple when Malcolm arrived in June 1954. He said that even in Harlem, the Nation was relatively unknown.[6] But that would change shortly.

Malcolm's new position in Temple No. 7 did not dampen his overall organizational activities. By his own accounting in the spring of 1955, he was responsible for the temples in Boston, Philadelphia, and Springfield, Massachusetts, while pastoring the New York congregation; he was likewise supervising the teaching of Muslims in a variety of other missionary endeavors on behalf of the Nation.

Malcolm found that work in New York City required a more sophisticated method of outreach than he had used elsewhere. New York was already inundated with a variety of black-oriented groups, particularly black nationalists. And worse, the city's black population seemed to be indifferent to modern-day activists and organizations: they had seen men as great as Garvey rise and fall, and many lesser lights had come and gone as well. Harlem had worn down many leaders and organizations, "less out of malevolence or envy or even its deep corroded cynicism than out of despair."[7]

To overcome both the competition and the indifference of Harlem's population to his message, Malcolm developed a new method of aggressive evangelism. The first step was the preparation of leaflets, which Malcolm and a handful of his parishioners passed out on street corners. Second, they went "fishing" for new members among the fringes of black nationalists, and outside the many small, store-front Christian churches of Harlem. Malcolm noticed that whereas the black nationalists tended to have male followings, the churches were attended mostly by females. His skillfully enhanced version of Muhammad's religio-political gospel apparently began to catch on as he and his small band of Muslims continued to fish.

Like Marcus Garvey before him, Malcolm X told his Harlem audiences that Jesus Christ was a black man. However, Malcolm's version of Muhammad's gospel shocked Harlem's Christian and Christian-oriented listeners as they heard the young minister declare that the black Jesus, killed by whites, was still dead and buried in Jerusalem. He assured his congregation and Christian guests in Temple No. 7 that Jesus could not return and save the black man; only Elijah Muhammad could save them. In another presentation which he called, "Who the Earth Belongs to," Malcolm condemned the "mysteries" falsely taught to black Christians, especially the notion of life after death. Heaven, Malcolm told his listeners, was in Mecca, not in the sky. The white man, whom Malcolm characterized by the Nation's belief as devil and "skunk of the planet earth," had thoroughly deceived black Christians into thinking they had no claim to this earth, when in reality the earth belonged to black people.

Malcolm was particularly adept at blending the rhetoric of the Nation with biblical texts. In the first years of his ministry, neither Malcolm nor the rest of the Nation had paid much attention to the Qur'an's text and message. He even told his audiences that President Eisenhower was a "modern Pharaoh" who was oppressing the black nation, and he declared that the popular Twenty-Third Psalm ("The Lord is my Shepherd") referred to Allah (Fard), and to Muhammad, the shepherd of his flock.

In his Philadelphia appearances, Malcolm's speeches were no less dramatic and controversial in regard to biblical doctrine. At one meeting, he affirmed Muhammad's doctrine that whites were the devil and the source of all sin by declaring: "You are not to blame for the evilness you have committed, because you have had the author of sin to follow for the past four hundred years, and he has taught you that white makes him supreme."

Regarding the origins of white people as wicked mutants of the original black race, Malcolm concluded: "These people were made from us, and they have all the wickedness. This is why the Bible says they are devils." Just as Malcolm reiterated Muhammad's doctrine of the inferior, reprobate white race, he likewise echoed Muhammad's claim that "Asiatic" people were superior: "All wisdom comes from the root of civilization which is in the East, where our forefathers came from. Here black men were the wisest of all people on the planet earth. . . . Here the soil was rich and black." While socially discerning, Malcolm's doctrines could be extremely color-bound: "Everything on the earth that is good is dark. . . . Black soil is richest and if God made man from the earth, he too must have been dark like you and I."

And as zealously as Malcolm struck out at the white race and Christianity in his sermons, there is no doubt that he was as rigorous in enforcing the conservative moral strictures of the Nation among his followers, as shown in an FBI account of Malcolm's admonition not to eat pork: "The devil breeds filth. They eat the filthiest of animals. The pig. The black man is afflicted with the white man's illnesses and diseases. And even now we eat the pig and bring more filth upon ourselves."

Malcolm said in his autobiography that, noting the need to "offer something special" for the women whom he hoped to "fish," he emphasized the black man's responsibility to the black woman. The black man's duty, as Malcolm proclaimed it, was to shelter, protect, and respect the black woman as the ultimate act of defying white oppression.[8] This dictum became key to Malcolm's Nation messages, echoing the sentiments and teachings of Elijah Muhammad, whose view of women was less than egalitarian by contemporary Western standards:

The only thing that is different is that we are a little better than her in the power of our creation. We have more powerful brains than she because we were made to rule. She is a helpmate. . . . We must treat them right and honor them. Then they will learn to honor you and they will produce you a little baby who will honor you.[9]

Malcolm did not yet realize that such seemingly honest sentiments belied Mr. Muhammad's well-concealed sexual abuses of women.

Malcolm gave many moral warnings to his Philadelphia Muslim brothers. At one meeting he urged them not to find themselves alone in a house with a woman, "or you will lose your reward. She will tempt you, but you must be strong." At another meeting, he spoke on the topic "Hell hath no fury like a woman scorned" before an especially large audience. He preached that since the time of Eve, women had led men into evil, and that because of sex, men had been reduced to the slaves of women. These women who ruled by sex, Malcolm declared, were like serpents—sneaky, weak, and wicked. Drawing his texts from the biblical books of Proverbs, Job, and Genesis, Malcolm offered proof that woman will be the undoing of man unless she takes her proper place as the modest, homebound helpmate of her husband. He was especially hard on women domestic workers employed in white households; these black women, he contended, abandoned their families to care for whites and were invariably reduced to "imps and tools" of the devil.

Malcolm propounded Muhammad's eschatological teachings just as faithfully as any of the Nation's other official doctrines, albeit with a bit more fire and brimstone. Speaking of the end of the white man's world, he promised his Temple No. 7 audience that the devils' heads would roll in the streets of New York City, and that their blood would flow in the gutters. And before the Philadelphia congregation, he gave a detailed description of the downfall of the United States. Airplanes would first drop pamphlets in Arabic and English, warning blacks "to get on to their own kind at once" (by this time the Nation would already have been evacuated from North America). Next, an ear-piercing trumpet would sound, driving men insane and causing pregnant women to give birth. Finally, Allah (Fard) would return in an airplane and light a match, setting an inextinguishable fire that would consume the white man's world.

This airplane was undoubtedly the "mother plane" that had been a part of the Nation's eschatology for decades. In the 1950s, however, when modern science began to look toward space exploration and science fiction films featured "outer space" themes, the Nation began to present a "mothership" instead, built by wise men from the East and containing a host of smaller spacecrafts—just as the traditional mother plane was said to have carried within it a host of smaller planes. According to Malcolm, this gigantic spaceship was hovering over the earth, ready to descend and attack the United States upon command by Elijah Muhammad. The attack had been delayed for the time being to give Elijah Muhammad a chance to get his followers out of North America.[10]

As an honored guest in Chicago's Temple No. 2, Malcolm comfortably ridiculed biblical teachings. In particular, he challenged the doctrine of an afterlife as an interpolation by the white man to enslave black people. FBI sources noted that on one occasion, Malcolm preached for over an hour against Christianity, reminding his listeners that when he himself was a Christian he had committed many crimes.

In another meeting before the same congregation, he discussed the cruelties that had been forced on pregnant black women in slavery, and, according to one FBI source, he talked about killing white babies by bashing in their heads. Malcolm admitted this sounded cruel, but that the only way to clear the weeds from the field was to uproot them. His prescribed racial infanticide was only a vengeful fantasy to be sure; but he had probably found a precedent for it in biblical texts and in the slave revolt of Nat Turner, whose makeshift army of liberators had killed infants and children as well as slavemasters.

Knowledge about the Nation in New York City was all but limited to the black community, even three years after Malcolm had arrived in Harlem. Besides the FBI, which already had the movement (and Malcolm) under surveillance, probably the only whites who were at all aware of the existence of the Nation were local law enforcement officials and a few scattered journalists or religious leaders who paid attention to the black press and, for a variety of reasons, maintained an interest in the black community.

On a national basis, the Nation had an unimportant place on the country's social and political landscape. In this era, when the civil rights movement focused national attention on the South, even those African Americans who had become aware of the Nation apparently did not regard it with much interest. In 1956, a column by Elijah Muhammad entitled "Mr. Muhammad Speaks" began to appear in the nationally distributed *Pittsburgh Courier*, the most prominent black publication of the era.

Early on, letters to the editor about Muhammad's column reflected frustration over his teachings. One Christian reader commented: " 'Mr. Muhammad Speaks' chilled me. . . . It is true that the white man's religion is nothing to be desired, which I, from day to day, avoid. I worship God in truth and in spirit."[11] Muhammad was not without his write-in supporters, however, though it seems that many of them were his own followers. Meanwhile, a good number of black Christian pastors, laypeople, and even some traditional Muslims wrote in to express their concerns about the strange new teachings of the Nation.

A particularly interesting letter of complaint to the *Courier* was written by a high school principal in Inkster, Michigan. In his letter, the man complained that the "Muhammad Speaks" column was "misleading as to fact and history," and "wholly undesirable for consumption of high school students." The letter obviously struck too close to home for Malcolm X, for it not only cast aspersions on the nature of Muhammad's message, but came from a town close to Malcolm's racially troubled childhood home. He lashed back at the letter writer as one "who professes to be principal of Inkster High School," declaring: "This man is the principal of a high school and, as such, is in position to poison the minds of our fast-awakening oncoming generation with his long outdated 'tomism'."

Malcolm either knew or assumed that this principal was African American, and accordingly accused him of being an "Uncle Tom"—a black man whose attitude and behavior were subservient to and even favored white supremacy: "He says he believes in freedom of speech as long as it doesn't interfere with the dignity and rights of others. How can a black man speak truth today without upsetting the white man's dignity?"[12] Perhaps because Muhammad and Malcolm X continued their forthright assault on whites, Muhammad's column seems to have increased in popularity. The Nation usually received a good deal of attention in the *Courier* as well as in other black newspapers such as the *New York Amsterdam News*.

One of the least recognized contributions of Malcolm X to the Nation's organizational development is his writing. In his autobiography, Malcolm described his efforts to start the Nation's own publication, *Muhammad Speaks*, but he didn't mention that the Nation launched a number of other publication ventures as well. In particular, he was the editor of the short-lived *Messenger Magazine*, which, along with several other publications, became a financial failure. It was Malcolm X himself who ordered their demise. In addition, Malcolm had contributed to *The Moslem World & The U.S.A.*, and he wrote a column entitled "God's Angry Men" that was syndicated to the *New York Amsterdam News*, the *Los Angeles Herald-Dispatch*, and the *Westchester [N.Y.] Observer*, all of them African-American newspapers. He does mention some of this newspaper activity in his autobiography, but his comments are made in passing and do not convey the extent of his journalistic contributions to the Nation.

Malcolm's columns are characteristically marked by his use of capital letters for emphasis and by his frequent quotation from the Bible. As in his sermons, he used biblical verses to reinforce the claim that Elijah Muhammad was a modern-day prophet sent from God to deliver black people from the bondage of white society and religion.[13] In one installment of "God's Angry Men," Malcolm interpreted the wonder of Elijah Muhammad's divine mission this way:

To save His Chosen People from this lake of fire, God would raise one of OUR OWN KIND from our very midst . . . a man like Moses (Deut. 18:18), whose job and mission would be to show us the way to FREEDOM and SALVATION. This MAN OF GOD would not be seeking to INTEGRATE us with the slavemaster. . . .This man like Moses, just as ancient Moses did, would condemn the modern Pharaoh's religion (Christianity), his plurality of gods (TRINITY), and his SLAVE EMPIRE (America). This Modern Moses would not teach his long enslaved people to love their enemies (the wicked white race who had enslaved them), but would ask OUR GOD, the GOD of our foreparents, to destroy this wicked white race and the Slave Empire with plagues of cancer, polio, heart diseases, air[,] auto and train DISASTERS . . . floods, droughts, earthquakes, tornadoes and HURRICANES.[14]

Malcolm's invocation of divine judgment upon the white race may have been extreme, but it was entirely consistent with the biblical image of an elect people awaiting deliverance from God. He would in time become infamous for openly delighting in such catastrophes when they did occur. But his sentiments were not so much mean-spirited as they were an expression of his cultic commitment to the apocalyptic vision of Elijah Muhammad—which included rejecting Christianity as polytheistic, even though the Nation itself celebrated a divine incarnation in W. D. Fard.

In Harlem, the Muslims became better known than when Malcolm had first arrived in the summer of 1954. His intellect and personality brought new dimensions to the city's Muslims, as they did to the entire Nation. His well-honed organizational abilities quickly provided Temple No. 7 with a new lease on life. On November 14, 1955, Malcolm obtained a business certificate for the "Temple #7 Luncheonette," a new Nation restaurant that would prove to be an important meeting place and successful business venture for New York's Muslims.

Rather than allow the temple to become just another "storefront church" in Harlem, Malcolm established its legal presence in the community by filing a certificate of incorporation for the state, city and county of New York on May 11, 1956. Along with two other members he is noted on the certificate as an "elected Trustee" of "Muhammad's Temple of Islam," the purpose of which was primarily to "provide a suitable place of worship for its members and others in accordance with the Islamic Faith." Temple No. 7 was undergoing expansion in Harlem just as Muhammad's followers were increasing nationwide.

According to Malcolm, he was "directly involved" with the founding of three more temples through 1955: Temple No. 13 in Springfield, Massachusetts, which was begun with the assistance of Osborne Thaxton, whom Malcolm had converted while in prison; Temple No. 14 in Hartford, Connecticut; and Temple No. 15 in Atlanta, Georgia.[15] Malcolm had achieved a virtual organizational omnipresence that allowed him to pastor more than one temple, visit or plant others, launch new endeavors and programs, confer with Muhammad and fellow ministers, as well as maintain a correspondence with Muslims over their individual concerns.

In one letter to a prison inmate who Malcolm felt was "blessed with much free time," he wrote as if reflecting on his own years of prison study, urging the man to "take every opportunity to learn all that you can, in all fields of science, and about people in all walks of life . . . for in the immediate future you will be given ample opportunity to utilize your skills to your advantage and for the uplifting of our own kind." His words also reflect his own busy life as the new energizing force of the Nation: "Your letter reached me in the midst of my travels, and this is my first chance to answer." There is, in fact, a kind of eschatological burden in Malcolm's excitement: "Indeed we are living in a great day. Many of the things we once thought we'd never live to see are shaping up before our very eyes right now. A New World Order is in the making, and it is up to us to prepare ourselves that we may be qualified to take our rightful place in it." It appears, then, that Malcolm believed the era of the black man's liberation and independence would dawn shortly, according to the millennial notions of the Nation. Before closing the letter as "Your brother and Servant Minister," Malcolm added—in capital letters: "ISLAM IS ON THE MARCH."

One might argue that Malcolm's final advice to the imprisoned Muslim to "study hard where you are. Train your mind to think, weigh things well and analize [sic] them for yourself"[16] reflected Muhammad's philosophy. But it seems more likely that this counsel came as a result of Malcolm's own development and philosophy.

In fact, the intellectual independence that Malcolm espoused would ultimately conflict with the cultic parochialism on which the Nation depended. As long as Malcolm's love for critical analysis did not rival his faith in Elijah Muhammad, such encouragement would benefit the movement and go a long way toward enhancing Muhammad's prestige. However, a free-thinking, studious, and analytical minister could not forever feel at home in Mr. Muhammad's Nation.

# 9

## From Harlem to the Dark World

*The only uniform that I shall wear is . . . this black skin of mine.*

Malcolm X and his Muslim parishioners made a startling appearance in the public eye of New York City in April 1957, after one of the Temple No. 7 members was seriously wounded in a confrontation with policemen in Harlem. Malcolm related the event in his autobiography, noting that two Muslims had interrupted a police action during which two white officers were violently breaking up a sidewalk argument. When the policemen told a gathering group of spectators to disperse, the Muslims refused. According to Malcolm, the police then brutally attacked Brother Johnson X (Hinton) with a nightstick, leaving him with a serious head injury. Rather than being rushed to the hospital for medical attention, the wounded Muslim was brought to Harlem's 28th Precinct by the police. When he began to pray in his jail cell the police beat him again.

Not surprisingly, in his autobiography Malcolm somewhat minimized his role in the dramatic series of events that rapidly unfolded after the beating of Johnson X. He noted that the police at the 28th Precinct at first denied that they had the badly wounded Muslim in custody; he also noted that members of Temple No. 7 and other enraged members of the Harlem community had lined up outside the police station and, under Malcolm's orders, refused to leave until their brother Muslim was given medical attention. Nevertheless, Malcolm did not explain the entire episode fully, nor did he reflect just how central he had been to the whole affair.

In fact, Malcolm was the major figure in two emergency meetings with the police department. The first meeting took place on the night of the incident, when Malcolm met with several high-level representatives of the New York City Police Department. The emergency meeting was held in the office of James Hicks, the editor of the *New York Amsterdam News*, who was asked to mediate. According to Hicks, the police officials initially tried to intimidate Malcolm, telling him that they would not beg him to ask his followers outside of the Precinct building to disperse.

However, Malcolm called their bluff, walking out of the meeting without saying a word. The police officials were forced to ask him to return to the meeting, and thereafter found themselves humbled before a righteously indignant Malcolm X. "Nobody got down on his knees. But they bowed," one historian concluded of the incident. In effect, Malcolm scored a moral and psychological victory over the police, and they would not soon forget it. He demanded to see Johnson X and requested that he receive medical attention if necessary. The police complied.[1]

Johnson X was in critical condition. The beating he received by the police resulted in multiple lacerations of the skull, a contusion of the brain, and a bloodclot that necessitated hospitalization. When Malcolm was finally able to have him moved from his cell to Harlem Hospital for treatment, the crowd of Muslims moved from the police station in an orderly fashion, followed by a swelling crowd of black nationalists and other Harlemites not affiliated with the Nation. Hicks estimated that the crowd grew to about two thousand people in front of the hospital. Already frustrated and concerned, the police department became alarmed and pressed all available officers in the department into service under the direct command of the chief inspector.

Johnson X was treated and released into the custody of the police, who returned him to the 28th Precinct. Malcolm's account gives the impression that this was the climax of the event, but actually it continued further into the night. Followed by his Muslim disciples and the thousands of other Harlemites who had gathered at the hospital, Malcolm went back to the precinct, marching along 125th Street, the main thoroughfare in Harlem. Malcolm and an attorney then discussed bail for Johnson X and the two other Muslims involved in the incident.

Meanwhile, outside the precinct building, the crowd had grown to several thousand. While they remained peaceful, Hicks recalled, the sight of orderly

Muslim men and women, lined along both sides of the street for a full block and in several rows, was intimidating to the police, who were keeping a nervous watch from inside. Suddenly Malcolm came outside, raised his arm, and gave a signal. "And it was eerie, because these people just faded into the night. It was the most orderly movement of four thousand to five thousand people I've ever seen in my life—they just simply disappeared—right before our eyes." The chief inspector, who was standing next to Hicks at that moment, said aloud, "This is too much power for one man to have." Remembering that statement, Hicks commented, "He meant one black man. I'll never forget that."[2]

In his autobiography, Malcolm stated that the Johnson X case undoubtedly resulted in a new awareness of the Nation on the part of the N.Y.P.D. The police, Malcolm wrote, "pulled out and carefully studied the files on the Nation of Islam, and appraised us with new eyes." Malcolm was right, though it would have been equally correct to say the police department was appraising *Malcolm X* with new eyes.

The police department now took great interest in Malcolm X in particular, outside of any other knowledge they may have had of the Nation itself. While Johnson X was still recuperating in the hospital, the N.Y.P.D. began a desperate search for information on Malcolm X from sources outside the city. On May 15, 1957, the chief inspector sent out a barrage of letters to police and prison officials inquiring about Malcolm's background.

These "Urgent Report" requests were sent to the commissioner of the Detroit Police Department, the Michigan Parole Commission, and the police departments of Lansing, Michigan, and Dedham and Milton, Massachusetts—all locations where Malcolm had been indicted for criminal activities as a youth. Additional requests were sent to the superintendents of the Concord Reformatory and the Charlestown State Prison in Massachusetts. The letters solicited full reports about Malcolm, complete with photographs "and full details of contents of your files." The recipients were directed to telegraph collect to the police commissioner of New York City for immediate acknowledgment, and to send all materials by special delivery air mail.

Certainly, then, this was a turning point for the Muslims in New York City, and for Malcolm X in particular. It is not an exaggeration to say that after the Johnson X case, Malcolm began to develop into the most watched—and probably the most disturbing—black leader in New York City in the eyes of law enforcement officials. He became a major focus of the N.Y.P.D.'s surveillance program, the Bureau of Special Services (BOSS).

Even though all the Muslims involved in the Johnson X case were acquitted, the N.Y.P.D. still attempted to win a grand jury indictment against Johnson X seven months later. After a grand jury summarily dismissed the charge that Johnson X had been disorderly and resisted arrest, this second legal victory for the Muslims paved the way for the Nation to file a half-million dollar suit against the N.Y.P.D.[3] In addition, Malcolm further wounded the pride of the police department by dispatching a challenging telegram to Police Commissioner Stephen P. Kennedy.

"Members of Muhammad's Temple of Islam here in Harlem are greatly disturbed," Malcolm began. He noted that the philosophy of the Nation was to obey and respect law enforcement officers and that Muslims were ideal citizens who refrained from vice and criminality. He then boldly charged that Johnson X had been "the victim of one of the most savage beatings ever inflicted upon an innocent human being since the days of slavery" by "two white sadistic policemen of the 28th Precinct." Furthermore, he pointed out that he had been in a meeting with his attorneys and deputy commissioners from the police department on April 29, 1957 (three days after the incident), and that these police representatives "promised us that an immediate and complete investigation would take place and that justice would be done" with regard to the "unwarranted acts of criminal brutality by these demented white members of the police department."[4]

As he had done in his prison letters, Malcolm appealed to the supposed international solidarity the Nation enjoyed with the Islamic world. He stated that when Johnson X had been beaten in his jail cell while attempting to pray to Allah, his brutalizers "showed contempt not only for his dark skin but also for his God and the religion of Islam. This outrageously inhuman act," Malcolm declared, "incenses not only our fellow citizens of the Harlem area, but also ignites great concern in the hearts of 600 million sons and daughters of Allah throughout the Moslem world, which stretches from the China Seas [sic] to the shores of West Africa." These sentiments were clearly not those of Elijah Muhammad. Malcolm's native Garveyite internationalism and his own growing affinity for the Islamic world (which he yet knew only through personal contacts) were gradually emerging and becoming more and more a part of his black-oriented appeal.

Malcolm reminded the commissioner that Johnson X's abusers had vainly attempted to "justify" their crime by charging him with resisting arrest, but that the grand jury had nevertheless established his innocence. "You must realize," Malcolm challenged, "that their heartless acts were without just cause, and criminally wrong. . . . Therefore we respectfully trust that the confidence imposed in the promise of your representatives will not be shaken by your allowing these prejudiced white men, disguised as police officers, who are responsible for this inhuman act of brutal savagery, to remain on active duty."[5]

One of the deputy commissioners, Walter Arm, told the *Amsterdam News* that an investigation would still be carried out, based on the findings of the grand jury. However, according to a Muslim publication, as late as 1960 several police investigations had been conducted, with no satisfactory results. Nevertheless, in his autobiography, Malcolm happily reported that Johnson X was eventually awarded $70,000, "the largest police brutality judgment that New York City has ever paid."

One of Malcolm's leading biographers believes that both federal and local law enforcement officials who dealt with Malcolm carried on a kind of "schizoid fight" with him. "The funny thing was that they liked him— liked him personally, that is, even when they abhorred his politics." One anonymous senior official in the N.Y.P.D. even went so far as to admit "If I were a Negro, I'd follow Malcolm. . . . But I'm not a Negro. I'm not going to follow him, I'm going to fight him." Whether the actions of law enforcement officials were schizoid or not, Malcolm X was considered an enemy, and the police carried on a surveillance campaign that would relentlessly haunt him throughout his life.[6]

The New York City Police Department was not alone in its interest in Malcolm and the Nation. The federal government had been watching Muhammad and his Muslims since the World War II era, when both leader and followers had served time in jail rather than register for the draft. In fact, in 1957, the same year of the Johnson X case, the FBI had begun wiretap surveillance of Elijah Muhammad's Chicago residence. The FBI's concern over the Nation and its surveillance war against Elijah Muhammad, Malcolm, and other Muslims formed the basis of its later COINTELPRO (Counter Intelligence Program) operation against "black nationalist hate groups" in 1967–68. COINTELPRO had been operative since the 1950s, but it targeted Communist and left-wing groups and did not yet think of black nationalist movements as posing danger to national security.

It was undoubtedly Malcolm's fanciful claim, while in prison that he was a Communist that first caught the attention of the FBI. In a letter dated June 29, 1950, he wrote: "I have always been a Communist. I have tried to enlist in the Japanese Army, last war, now they will never draft or accept me in the U.S. Army. Everyone has said . . . [']Malcolm is crazy['] so it isn't hard to convince people that I am." Perhaps Malcolm wrote this in the hope of avoiding the draft upon his release from prison; regardless, the statement attracted the attention of the FBI—which never stopped observing Malcolm thereafter. Malcolm's main file, in the central office of the FBI consists of over two thousand pages; in addition, field offices in other cities kept their own files on Malcolm and the Nation, and the one in the New York office is especially large. There is also evidence that the FBI cooperated with and drew information from the BOSS program of the New York City Police Department. (BOSS also cooperated with other metropolitan police departments in surveillance of the Nation.)

Malcolm was thus caught in a broad net of government surveillance— constantly tracked, targeted, and tagged as a subversive. One FBI agent noted in an August 1960 memo that while he was conducting a drive-by "spot surveillance" of Malcolm's neighborhood, he was apparently caught in the act by Malcolm, who eyed him intensely as he drove down the block and turned the corner. The agent recommended that a different car be used in any future surveillance of Malcolm's home.[7] Considering the breadth and depth of the government's surveillance program, this incident was fairly insignificant, but it reflects Malcolm's awareness of surveillance and suggests his refusal to be intimidated by it.

Malcolm's influence was growing in dimensions that transcended geography. The Johnson X case had won him the esteem of the Harlem community as much as it garnered the sobering attention of the police. According to FBI sources, Malcolm wielded a great deal of influence in the movement and was probably the "Number Two Man" after Elijah Muhammad. Malcolm recalled in his autobiography that from time to time he was "chastised"— gently scolded—by Muhammad for pushing the members harder than they could bear.

Still, Elijah Muhammad's reprimands were made as if to a favored son; in return, Malcolm guarded Elijah Muhammad zealously. When he was away from Muhammad, whether on the road or teaching in one of the established temples, "Malcolm's thinking was defined by his total commitment to Elijah Muhammad," and he fervently protected the Nation's interests as if they were his own father's legacy. When beside him in Chicago, Malcolm guarded him with equal fervor. For example, when one unidentified phone caller tried to reach Muhammad at home in the hope of arranging a meeting, Malcolm intercepted the inquiry, putting the caller off bluntly: "*We* are too busy."[8]

One source in particular claimed that Malcolm's influence was so great that he was able to convince Elijah Muhammad to accept and adopt teachings that were formerly "contrary to the teachings of the [Nation of Islam]." He offered as an example the fact that Malcolm apparently got Elijah

Muhammad to grant his ministers permission to use Muslim-styled surnames instead of the standard "X" (Malcolm's was Shabazz, which was the "family name of the Nation itself). While the source was sure that Malcolm was still "genuinely convinced" of Elijah Muhammad's divine apostleship, this person nevertheless maintained that Malcolm was asserting himself in new ways: "[Malcolm] has become less dependent on Muhammad and seems to make many small day to day decisions on his own, on which he previously had consulted Muhammad."

It appears, however, that Malcolm's scope of concern in the Nation was not restricted to "small" decisions only. In 1957, one FBI source in Detroit noted that Malcolm X was lobbying to have his brother, Wilfred X, installed as the new minister of Detroit's Temple No. 1. According to the same report, while he was carrying on a successful two-week speaking engagement there, Malcolm openly expressed dissatisfaction to Muhammad over the inefficiency of the minister of Temple No. 1. Further, it was likely that Malcolm X himself fed victorious reports of those Detroit meetings back to Harlem's *New York Amsterdam News*—probably in the hope of encouraging his own parishioners and further glorifying the Nation before the black community. In fact, the *Amsterdam News* noted that Malcolm "directed the progress of the Detroit Moslems" for two months during 1957, probably before the new minister, Wilfred X, had been installed.[9]

As Malcolm recounted, by late 1958 he exhausted himself "trying to be everywhere at once, trying to help the Nation to keep growing." He did not mention that his exhausting schedule had already landed him in Manhattan's Sydenham Hospital from October 30 to November 2, 1957. Apparently Malcolm—who loathed having to sleep even several hours a day—had pushed himself to the point of what he feared was a coronary condition. But he only had an inflammation around the ribs—an apparent sign of stress and exhaustion that required him to take several days of rest in the hospital.

True to form, the day after he was released, on November 3, Malcolm rushed up to Boston for the dedication of the new Nation temple. By the end of the month, he had spoken in Washington, D.C., at a Nation banquet and then flown to the West Coast for a rigorous round of preaching. As long as he believed in Muhammad, it seems, Malcolm X was indefatigable.[10]

With his increased fame in the Nation, Malcolm began to diversify his influence in the movement, both locally and nationally. As the Nation continued to expand, Malcolm was not only intricately involved with every new temple that was founded, but he became virtually an extension of Mr. Muhammad himself. Thus, speaking before a Muslim audience in Troy,

New York, in 1957, he introduced himself as a "traveling emissary to teach the truth regarding the religion of Islam."

Malcolm had undoubtedly seized the role of Muhammad's "traveling emissary" long before he announced it as such. Moving from city to city, he sought to introduce the Nation to local black communities both by organizing and presiding over special programs. Sometimes these programs were somewhat different from his speaking engagements at the temples; they were both public relations and evangelistic endeavors carefully designed to attract a broader range of the Africentric members of the community.

One such event was hosted by Malcolm X in Newark, New Jersey, early in 1955. The affair was labeled "Brotherhood of Our Own," and he used the parishioners from New York's Temple No. 7 as the hosting staff. In another special event in 1957, Malcolm and the Newark Nation minister hosted a dinner commemorating the Muslim feast of Ramadan. The FBI informant who attended recalled that Malcolm would give orders to the Newark minister "in a very emphatic manner."

A year after Malcolm had gone down to Atlanta for the founding of a new Nation temple, he returned there as Elijah Muhammad's representative in the "First Southern Goodwill Tour of the Brotherhood of Islam," which began on August 25, 1956. One FBI informant who carefully observed the program noted that Malcolm made everything appear like "clock-work." According to the *Pittsburgh Courier* the program was no small effort on the part of the Nation. Apparently seven Nation ministers attended with representatives from various temples—including newly established ones such as those in Baltimore, Atlantic City, and Lansing.

The convention meeting of the "Goodwill Tour" took place in the main auditorium of an African Methodist Episcopal (Zion) church in Atlanta, and Malcolm presided as Muhammad's representative. "We are not here to judge," Malcolm declared from a borrowed Christian pulpit, "but to teach; not to divide, but to unite." According to a sympathetic Eastern Muslim journalist, the tour resembled an invasion, since it was designed to penetrate a traditional Christian stronghold. The same writer noted that as a result of the tour, the Atlanta Temple doubled its membership.[11]

Not all of Malcolm's missions were so glorious; some of the fields where he fervently sowed seeds for Muhammad did not yield a satisfactory harvest. For example, in 1958, Malcolm was assigned for two months to the West Coast to do what one FBI source called "promotion work" for the Nation. He was based in Los Angeles, where he had founded Temple No. 27 about a year earlier. In Normandie Hall, a rented facility, Malcolm pummeled away at the United States and Christianity. Pointing to a U.S. flag in the room, Malcolm declared, "This represents our enemy." He then pointed to a photo of a lynched black man and—still imputing the flag—concluded: "As you know, this is all we ever got from it." At the surface, such dramatic and controversial presentations seemed to evoke an enthusiastic response from the attendants; an FBI source concluded that Malcolm's speeches were so rousing that audiences gave quite liberally in the collections. Still, some of the older Nation members expressed some concern over Malcolm's "inflammatory" comments. Though Malcolm was generally well received, he personally felt the results of his emotion-packed preaching were substandard. In one of his last sermons before returning to the East Coast, he seemed visibly annoyed, according to an FBI observer, and openly lamented that his Los Angeles endeavor was not very successful—that he had found it to be one of the hardest cities in which to win converts.

Not all of Malcolm's missions were planned in advance, nor were they necessarily pleasant in the challenges they offered. One FBI source claimed that Malcolm was not only active in policy making in the Nation, but he had clearly assumed the role of "trouble shooter." He was thus weighed down with a variety of problems, including the bureaucratic duty of fund-raising— or finding other ways of directing members' money into the central treasury of the Nation. In his own New York temple, Malcolm advised parishioners who had $400 to $500 to send it directly to Elijah Muhammad, who would invest it for them. Another time he informed the membership they were being taxed at 3 percent for a central fund supposedly set aside to build new temples.

Invariably, Nation constituents would ask Malcolm in public what the position of the movement was in regard to draft registration and military service. No doubt aware that FBI informants were in his audience, Malcolm still showed support for those who decided not to join up, though he carefully told his listeners that this was an individual decision. As for himself, Malcolm declared, pointing to his own face: "I'll tell them and any other white man's government that the only uniform that I shall wear is this one here, this black skin of mine."

Malcolm could be just as blunt with his own followers as he was in the face of anonymous FBI informants. In the case of one temple where Malcolm was authorized to take command, his first act was immediately to dismiss all the officers appointed by the previous minister. He also wielded an iron rod when it came to "church discipline." He firmly suspended members for ninety-day periods for various ethical and organizational violations, and even excommunicated one member of Temple No. 7 "for harboring beliefs" against Nation doctrines and for threatening and slandering him. So fervent was Malcolm in administering this ecclesiastical punishment that he even removed one of his closest assistants who had not immediately reported these problems to him. He is said to have antagonized another member, who happened to be an officer in Chicago's Temple No. 2, to the point that the man eventually left the movement. According to one source, Malcolm had taunted and threatened him for not having succeeded in converting his wife to "Islam." [12]

As the Nation continued to grow, incidents of conflict similar to the Johnson X case began to occur in different parts of the country. Just before its annual convention in Chicago in February 1957, Malcolm X received a call for emergency assistance from some Muslims in Alabama who had clashed with local police. The conflict occurred when two Muslim women, en route to the convention, chose to sit in a "whites only" bench at the Flomaton, Alabama, station of the L & N Railroad. Railroad officials immediately called a local sheriff to come and remove the women from their seat, and the women cooperated. However, the two women were accompanied by two male companions who were less prone to yield in the face of injustice. When the sheriff demanded to see their "papers" and pulled his gun from its holster, the two Muslim men struck back. Beaten somewhat badly, the sheriff scurried into his office, locked the door, and called for reinforcements. The two Muslim men were eventually arrested and charged with battery with intent to kill.

Though he must have been in the midst of convention preparations, Malcolm flew south, apparently equipped with the necessary monies to cover legal expenses for the Muslims. According to one report, the county solicitor told Malcolm that upon learning the two men were Muslims and not "our boys," he warned his officers to leave them alone, fining the two Muslims $226 each, which one renowned black journalist considered "an unbelievably light sentence." Speaking of the incident later before the Boston congregation, Malcolm said that the Muslims in Flomaton had disarmed and beaten the policeman "with the help of Allah." [13]

Another incident involving Malcolm's intervention occurred much closer to home. While he was away in Boston on May 14, 1958, two police officers attempted to gain entry into the two-story, two-family residence which Malcolm and his new wife, Betty, shared with some other Muslims in the Corona (Queens) area of New York City. [14] The pretext of the police visit was to speak with someone who, according to the Muslim women present, did not reside at the house. However, the police officers persisted by attempting to gain entry and were forcefully shut out. The officers purportedly left, then returned with a third officer, and violently forced their way into the house through another door.

The Muslims, most of them women, fought back furiously against the police, who fired their guns through the door and into the house. Even though two of the officers were badly wounded, they went on a rampage through the entire building, bursting through all the inner residences, and forcing the women and children into the street, where they were arrested. By the time Malcolm was alerted and was able to return home, a Muslim demonstration had formed outside of the 114th Precinct building. Malcolm was able to break off the demonstration, gain bail for the release of most of the arrested Muslims, and immediately initiate legal action. Ultimately, all the Muslims involved were exonerated,[15] and Malcolm, ever more conscious of global issues, declared that the United States government did not need "to look to 'foreign instigation' to see why America is so hated abroad, but should look right here in America where the Gestapo tactics of the white police who patrol Negro neighborhoods are similar to those used by 'occupation forces' when the conquering armies take over and enter into 'occupied territories.' " This time, however, Malcolm's global references apparently had some substance. The *Courier* noted in passing that representatives of African-Asian nations had "besieged the Moslems for details of the case."[16]

It is true that Malcolm believed that the Nation "offered a community and a value system which bestowed meaning upon his life as a *human being* and upon blacks as an *African* people." It was in Malcolm's blood to speak of Africa and Africans, given his awareness of the Garveyite tradition. On August 1, 1957, he took time out of a nationwide tour to appear as the sensational guest speaker at a Marcus Garvey Day Celebration, sponsored by the United African Nationalist Movement—a Harlem-based organization that was, for all intents and purposes, the Nation's competitor.

Still, Malcolm had to conform to the rhetoric as well as to the ideology of Elijah Muhammad and W. D. Fard, which spoke of black people as being "black" and "Asiatic," but not as "African." About a week after he spoke at the Marcus Garvey Day Celebration in Harlem, he lectured the Muslims of the Boston Temple that, in fact, they were "Asiatic black Muslims, owners and makers of everything, father of all civilization."[17] It seems that Malcolm had one eye on Chicago, and the other eye on Africa. However, unlike Elijah Muhammad, who apparently had never held serious aspirations to reach eastward, by the mid-to-late 1950s Malcolm spoke more and more about the "Dark World," which seems to have been an inclusive phrase that could please the Nation's Asiatic leanings while serving as a vehicle for Malcolm's own Garveyite orientation.

In his rousing sermons, Malcolm sought to tap into the revolutionary current that was pulsing through men and women of color worldwide. Unlike Elijah Muhammad, whose provincial war cry was "to get on to your own kind" (meaning an exclusive black American community), Malcolm wanted his listeners to take their cue from "the fast-awakening dark nations, who are tossing off the yoke of white imperialism," and to begin to see themselves as a key part of the Dark World.

Black people, declared Malcolm, were now "in a most unique and strategic position," which he compared to the scriptural characterizations of Daniel in Babylonian captivity and Joseph in Egyptian bondage—slaves who ultimately possessed a divine advantage over their oppressors:[18] "We affect both foreign and domestic policy."

The majority of earth's people are non-white (Africans and Asians). Today they are beginning to realize that this white man can not [sic] love or treat them any better than he (in sincerity) can love or treat us. Thus we become the yardstick by which all dark nations of earth can measure the real attitude of the white public here in America, as well as the attitude of her president.[19]

It is very unlikely that Malcolm drew the notion of black Americans being a "yardstick" from the conservative, monocultural worldview of Elijah Muhammad. However, he seemed to believe that Muhammad's work was "of equal importance to the entire dark world," and could help "our own kind the world over." To emphasize Elijah Muhammad's importance, Malcolm cited a biblical text from the Hebrew prophet, Malachi: "Behold, I am going to send you Elijah the prophet before the coming of the great and terrible day of the Lord. And he will restore the hearts of the fathers to their children, and the hearts of the children to their fathers, lest I come and smite the land with a curse (5:6)." His use of Malachi's "Elijah the prophet" text was no innovation on his part; Muhammad and his Muslims had already appropriated it as one of their central proof-texts prior to Malcolm's entry into the Nation. What was unique about Malcolm's usage was its new international application to the Dark World. "Our people of the East must learn to see that our fight is theirs and their fight is ours," Malcolm concluded. In short, Elijah Muhammad was to be the divine link between the fathers of the Dark World and their black children lost in the wilderness of North America.

Malcolm was reaching, perhaps groping at first, toward a world where men and women of color were the norm, and where a black man could find strength in numbers. Rather than see the Nation as a minority group within a minority community, Malcolm's view of the Nation spiraled outward in ever-growing circles of dark humanity. While lecturing in Muhammad's small, urban temple or writing in his little attic study in Queens, Malcolm saw himself, by virtue of race and religion, as standing behind a global podium, summoning the attention of the Dark World:

O, dark nations of the East, know this: there are over seventeen million of us here in America who are being awakened by the Honorable Elijah Muhammad. Though we have long been as "dead," we know today that we are your long lost brothers. We have been a dead (enslaved) nation, though we outnumber many of you who are recognized as free nations.[20]

Malcolm continued by saying to his imaginary Dark World audience that if numerical strength were the "yardstick for nationhood we would have long ago out-qualified many of you." However, according to Malcolm, Elijah Muhammad was now "qualifying" his people in the United States by supplying them with the "missing basic factors"—intellectual, spiritual, and economic independence.

Where all others who tried have failed, Messenger Muhammad is putting us as a nation back on the path toward home. . . soon we shall be making efforts to unite ourselves with you. We have been told by Almighty Allah that we must return to our own kind. Therefore, O brothers of the East . . . do not reject us or turn your backs upon us, lest you incur the wrath of Our Savior, Almighty God Allah. We must return to our own kind.[21]

It had been Elijah Muhammad's aspiration to be saved, in some vague and remote sense, out of "the wilderness of North America." However, Malcolm—invoking the curse of Fard himself—was attempting to build a genuine bridge from West to East out of the fragments and strands of Muhammad's cultic doctrines. Unlike Elijah Muhammad, Malcolm X was truly looking eastward.

This is undoubtedly why Malcolm made sure he was on hand to greet two Indonesian leaders who came to see Harlem in July 1957 and were welcomed by Harlem's leading clergyman and politician, Adam Clayton Powell, Jr. Powell, who had been the only African American to attend the Afro-Asian Bandung Conference in 1955, had invited these leaders to come and see Harlem for themselves. In a public reception, Malcolm welcomed the Eastern visitors on behalf of Elijah Muhammad, and commended Powell for showing "great wisdom and foresight" in inviting them. Malcolm continued: "The 90 million Moslems in Indonesia are only a small part of the 600 million more in other parts of the Dark World, Asia and Africa." Again, Malcolm linked African Americans with the Dark World vis-à-vis Islam: "We here in America were of the Moslem world before being brought into slavery, and today with the entire dark world awakening, our Moslem brothers in the East have a great interest in our welfare."

In another event, a "feast" held by the Nation in the same month, Malcolm invited many "notables from the Moslem World," including two United Nations representatives, the Syrian envoy, and the attaché of the Egyptian delegation. In his welcoming address, he sounded the same theme of "the unifying powers of Islam" bringing together all the Muslims of the world. "In fact," Malcolm declared, "Islam is the greatest unifying force in the Dark World today. The unity of 600 Million Moslems from the China Sea to the shores of West Africa, is a force and a factor that has long been recognized by the major powers of the world."[22]

This was the same theme Malcolm had used seven years earlier to threaten prison officials in Massachusetts, and the police commissioner of New York City only several months before. But now Malcolm was turning the idea of the Nation's place in the Islamic world into an appeal—directing it to the Dark World itself: "We are calling upon our 600 Million Moslem Brothers of the East to support Messenger Elijah Muhammad in this great work, that he may resurrect the so-called Negroes here in America from their graves of ignorance."[23] Malcolm was clearly calling for the attention of the Muslim world as a whole, whether Asiatic or African. Though he undoubtedly supported African independence, he was not yet in a position to emphasize the essential Africanism of blacks in the United States.

Still, Malcolm was watching Africa. When he was in Detroit in the fall of 1957, giving a talk, the finance minister from Ghana, who was visiting the United States, was mistaken for an African American in a restaurant in Dover, Delaware. The Ghanaian official, K. A. Gbedemah, was shocked when he was snubbed by both a white waitress and the restaurant manager because he was black; he immediately lodged a complaint with the U.S. State Department. Malcolm found it interesting that, shortly afterward, President Eisenhower personally apologized to Gbedemah and invited him to the White House for breakfast. Malcolm pointed out to the Detroit Muslims that the incident proved that "foreign black people" are not mistreated; only black people with "the slavemaster's name" were abused in the United States.[24]

Undoubtedly, Malcolm was looking eastward for the sake of the Nation, and he envisioned that such an international affiliation with the dark Muslim world would obligate whites, by reason of embarrassment or fear, to practice racial justice. At the same time, he believed that if the African American community could be "raised from the grave" of the Christian Negro mentality, it might also become a vital factor in swaying the policies of the United States in favor of the Dark World. In a very real sense, this was an adaptation of the Garveyite notion that an independent Africa and a politically and economically unified black America could be mutually beneficial to all blacks worldwide. However, Malcolm was also carrying the burden of Islam—and Elijah Muhammad's Islam, no less.

Ironically, by reaching toward the Dark World and its Islamic faith, Malcolm initiated a new phase in the evolution of his own religious and political understanding. By inviting the attention of Asians and Africans and seeking a bond with the Islamic community worldwide, Malcolm exposed himself to greater realizations that would, in time, force him to move beyond the borders of the Nation. At first, he would attempt to bring the movement and its leader along with him in this new direction. However, the further he moved toward the East, the more he found that the borders of the Nation, like Elijah Muhammad himself, were rigidly cultic. Malcolm would eventually discover that no one in Mecca ever heard of W. D. Fard.

# PART THREE

# The Second Moment

*When, on the day he conquered Mecca, the Apostle of God*
*appeared before the Ka'bah, he found the idols arrayed*
*around it. Thereupon he started to pierce their eyes with the*
*point of his arrow saying, "Truth is come and falsehood is*
*vanished. Verily, falsehood is a thing that vanisheth."*
     *—Hishâm Ibn Al-Kalbî,* The Book of the Idols,
       *commenting on Sûrah XVII: 81, Qur'an*

In the spring of 1964, Malcolm X found himself moving along in a vibrant human stream of pilgrims, a multicolored, multicultured mass of travelers who seemed to move as a single body and whose only purpose it was to worship the One God in absolute unity. This was the Hajj, the pilgrimage made (if possible) by all true Muslims to Mecca, the holiest of all holy sites in the Islamic world.

Dressed in the humble and mandatory outfit of the pilgrim, Malcolm wore two white towels wrapped around his body. The *rida* was wrapped at the neck and shoulders, leaving bare his right shoulder and arm; the *izar* was folded around his loins. The only other essentials were the *na'l*, a plain pair of sandals, and a simple belt and bag for carrying money and personal items. Along with myriad other pilgrims dressed the same way, Malcolm had circumambulated the ancient black stone house, the *Ka'ba*, seven times— and, unable to touch it, or even draw close to it because of the great crowd, Malcolm cried out, "Takbir!" ("God is great!") Guarded by his *mutawaf* (the pilgrim's guide) from the great circular flow of humanity around the Ka'ba, Malcolm prostrated himself and prayed two Muslim prayers, called *rak'as*. He then drank water from the well of Zem Zem and ran between the ancient hills called Safa and Marwa, where Muslims believe Hagar, the concubine of Abraham, sought water for Ishmael, her son. As Malcolm recalled his pilgrimage, he also traveled on foot from sunrise until noon, reaching Mount Arafat, where he and others prayed and chanted until sunset. With hands lifted, the black pilgrim declared: "There is no God but Allah. He has no partner. His are authority and praise. Good emanates from Him, and He has power over all things." Finally, Malcolm, following the ancient tradition, threw seven stones at the devil.[1]

In the immediate aftermath of Malcolm's Hajj experience, he penned numerous letters and postcards to family, friends, and associates in the United States, sharing his experiences. However, what was central to all of Malcolm's excited communications was the unity and brotherhood he witnessed among this international body of believers:

There were tens of thousands of pilgrims, from all over the world. They were of all colors, from blue-eyed blonds to black-skinned Africans. But we were all participating in the same ritual, displaying a spirit of unity and brotherhood that my experiences in America had led me to believe never could exist between the white and the non-white.[2]

This was a far cry from the taunting and merciless voice that had become a finely honed weapon in the service of the Nation. It was certainly unusual for Malcolm to speak of "blue-eyed blonds" without also speaking of "devils"; but it was even more unusual for him to speak of whites and non-whites cooperating, in any sense of the word, in "unity and brotherhood."

Typically, as his story has been told and retold—beginning with *The Autobiography of Malcolm X*—the Hajj marked the beginning of a new phase in Malcolm's life. As the story goes, he came to Mecca as Malcolm X, still carrying the scent of Elijah Muhammad's fire, and left as "El Hajj Malik El Shabazz," the pilgrim who has suddenly awakened to the real possibility of racial reconciliation. There is, of course, validity in seeing Malcolm X in contrast to El Hajj Malik, for Malcolm's pilgrimage did mark a turning point in his life and career. However, the drama of the Hajj was hardly the beginning of this great change in Malcolm's life; indeed, it might be more appropriately considered the end of his second conversion.

Malcolm did not come to Mecca in 1964 without any knowledge of traditional Islam; his familiarity with the religion of the prophet Muhammad dated back many years, even to his days in the Massachusetts state prison facilities. He had met real Muslims all along the way in his dramatic postprison sojourn, and the farther he traveled in carrying the message of the Nation, the more he seemed to be confronted by the reality of Elijah Muhammad's questionable form of Islam. But Malcolm X was a true believer in Elijah Muhammad, and his religious confidence was more than sufficient compensation for all the other dubious aspects of the Nation's doctrine.

This religious security was reinforced by Malcolm's central organizational position in the movement and the satisfaction he gained in working on behalf of his black people—this quest was virtually his birthright as a Garveyite offspring. Yet, ironically, Malcolm's Garveyite spirit gave him a predisposition toward some kind of black internationalism, and the more he groped for such a perspective, the more he was forced to handle genuine Islam.

For the better part of his career as Elijah Muhammad's chief spokesman, it was one of Malcolm's greatest feats to prove that the Islam of the Nation and the Islam of Mecca were of the same letter and spirit. Inevitably, such a cultic crusade drew him closer and closer to Islam, very likely creating religious tensions within him that he was constrained to face alone. As long as Malcolm X remained on the devoted vanguard of the Nation's advancing campaign he either would not or could not see the problematic nature of Elijah Muhammad's Islam.

When, in late 1963, Malcolm fell from grace in the Nation, his second conversion truly began. Like his first conversion, he did not immediately embrace his newfound faith. The sojourn that culminated in the Hajj led him downward, as if on some anguished, Dantean path that first descended into torment before ascending to paradise. Cast out of Muhammad's kingdom, Malcolm had to undergo a process of separation before he could completely embrace traditional Islam. He had to break all religious ties to Elijah Muhammad—redefining every essential doctrine of his faith, from the nature of Allah to the nature of the devil.

All the more dramatic, then, was the final ritual of Malcolm's Hajj, when he picked seven stones to cast at an invisible devil. With each stone cast, the last cultic threads that bound Malcolm to Elijah Muhammad were finally severed. For twelve years of his public life, he had hurled words like stones at the "devil" white man whom he could see. Now, in Mecca, he hurled real stones at a devil whom he could not see. In so doing, he had emerged from the cultic netherworld into the sunlight of a genuine religion.

The Hajj marks the second moment in the religious sojourn of Malcolm X. Like the first moment, this second religious moment is dramatic and powerful. However, the latter not only succeeds the former, but also supersedes it—not only in the literary flow of Malcolm's autobiography, but especially in his religious experience.

In many ways El Hajj (or Hajji) Malik Shabazz is identical to Malcolm X. Popular commentaries on Malcolm's life tend to distort the significance of the Hajj with regard to his social and political understanding of the United States. That many assume Malcolm X took the name Malik Shabazz after making the Hajj may symbolize the frequent biographical misinterpretation of Malcolm X as well. Actually, Malcolm had already used the name Malik Shabazz while still in the Nation; he became El Hajj Malik once he made the sacred pilgrimage and converted to Sunni Islam. Likewise, Malcolm X did not become a "new man," nor did he ever impugn his former analysis of racism in the United States after going to Mecca. The Hajj did not turn Malcolm into an integrationist or a liberal.

Nevertheless, the Hajj profoundly influenced Malcolm's entire worldview—socially, politically and religiously. Finally free from the Nation, he was able to cast aside cultic racial ideas and adopt a kind of theistic humanism. In a very real sense, the Hajj influenced Malcolm X by changing his view of humanity without undermining his view of race. An awareness of this influence requires an understanding of Malcolm's earlier encounters with traditional Islam, and his apologetic attempts to defend the integrity of the Nation against its Muslim critics. Finally, understanding how and why Malcolm was eventually able to break with the Nation will allow the reader to realize the fullness of the second religious moment.

# 10

## The Making of an Emissary

*Africa is the land of the future.*

While the Nation had been steadily growing in popularity within the African American community, it was not until 1959 that the mass of whites in the United States became aware of the movement. Unfortunately, when the white public did learn of its existence, it was in the most sensational and astonishing terms that the media could create.

Since white society has always chosen to be fundamentally unfamiliar with black culture, the revelation of such an organization as the Nation was all the more shocking to whites, though it disturbed a good many blacks as well, albeit for different reasons. Without being aware of the state of the urban black community, and lacking an understanding of the history of black separatism in the United States, most whites were jolted by the extensive film and press coverage of Mr. Muhammad's Muslims.

Malcolm X, the most eloquent and capable spokesman of the movement, invariably caught the media's attention. In this sudden notoriety ushered in by probing journalists and newscasters, Malcolm X was more than capable of making an effective presentation on behalf of Muhammad and the Nation. And the Nation itself, as the white man's new nemesis, became both popular and disreputable. The gravity with which the media handled the Muslims put them in a position of social importance they had never known; in some sense, they became a far more "legitimate" alternative to many blacks than they would have been without such notoriety.

Along with this new awareness of the urban Muslims, there came an array of criticism of the movement—social, political, and religious. Most of the criticism centered around the movement's view of "race relations." In the midst of the civil rights era, what most rattled the public was the bold contempt Muhammad and his organization had toward integration. The country as a whole was increasingly concerned about the end of southern segregation, and most northern whites were unified in their opposition to *de jure* segregation in the United States as a whole. However, whites in the United States were not prepared for such blatant rejection of integration and Christianity—both of which the Nation insisted would be inseparably damned in the coming kingdom of Allah.

In July 1959, two television journalists collaborated on a story that was destined to bring the Nation—and Malcolm X—to the attention of a horrified white public. Mike Wallace, who was at that time the producer of *News Beat* on New York's WNTA-TV, presented five one-half hour installments of a program entitled, "The Hate That Hate Produced." Being white himself, Wallace was not able to gain access to the Nation; however, the black journalist Louis Lomax was able to secure permission from Elijah Muhammad (through Malcolm X) to film the documentary, which included an interview with Malcolm X himself.

In one episode, Lomax interviewed Malcolm, asking him about the Nation's notion of the devil. At the point when Malcolm calmly informed Lomax that the serpent of Eden was not a real snake, the interview reached its desired racial climax:

*Lomax:* It was not a real serpent. . . . What was it?
*Malcolm:* But as you know the Bible is written in symbols, parables and this serpent or snake is the symbol that is used to hide the real identity of the one that this actually was.
*Lomax:* Well, who was it?
*Malcolm:* The white man.[1]

In his autobiography, Malcolm complained that the documentary had been quite deliberately turned into "a kaleidoscope of 'shocker' images," edited in a way to frighten the public. Taking the lead of Wallace and Lomax, the print media immediately took up the same theme. Within several weeks of the Wallace/Lomax documentary, *U.S. News & World Report* and *Time* magazines both featured alarming, sensational accounts of these strange new Muslims and their doctrine.

The Nation responded immediately by barring Mike Wallace and all other white journalists from attending a huge Muslim rally the same month in New York City's St. Nicholas Arena, in which Elijah Muhammad appeared (Louis Lomax was admitted to the meeting and apparently developed a working relationship with the Muslims thereafter). In the rally, Muhammad charged that Mike Wallace was trying to split up the Nation and was afraid of the Muslim message. "Does he classify the truth as Hate?" Muhammad declared rhetorically. "No enemy wants to see the so-called American Negro free and united. He wants to use you as a tool." In another New York rally in July at Harlem's Rockland Palace, Wallace Muhammad charged that *Time* was purposely twisting his father's words "to make him sound as if he is plotting for the Muslims to overthrow the government." [2]

The continuing growth of sensationalized stories in newspapers and magazines often put Malcolm on the firing line. Consequently, he increasingly distinguished himself as an apologist for the Nation's racial stance, meting out his fiery diatribes as much against black civil rights and integrationist leaders as against white critics. Although Malcolm complained that his words were usually slanted and twisted by the press, his defense of the Nation's position on race was thorough, clear, and consistent. Considerably less attention was paid to Malcolm's position as a religious apologist.

In the same New York rally where the Nation had banned white journalists and reporters, Elijah Muhammad boldly asserted that he was "backed by 500 million people, who are lifting their voices to Allah five times a day." [3] This boast became the crux of a fierce debate between the Nation and a variety of nonaffiliated Muslims, both black American and Eastern. Elijah Muhammad's claim of support from the Islamic world was not his own brainchild, though he had continued Fard's teaching that blacks in the United States were linked to the people of Mecca. However, the notion that the Nation was kin to the world body of Islam was Malcolm's idea, and for this he was willing to fight tooth-and-nail against those who claimed otherwise.

Before he made the Hajj in 1964, Malcolm X had had significant contact with traditional Muslims. Indeed, it seems to be the case that—given the Nation's peculiar doctrines—he was aware of the differences between Eastern Islam and Muhammad's religion all along. He noted in his autobiography that his first encounter with traditional Islam came while he was in prison. He recalled that "a member of the orthodox Muslim movement" in the Boston area had come to visit him, though he did not mention in which facility the visit had taken place. The Muslim who had visited him was named Abdul Hameed, and Hameed had taken enough interest in Malcolm to send him authentic Muslim prayers in the Arabic language. Malcolm noted that, at the time, he memorized all the prayers phonetically.

One biographer has noted that Malcolm was visited by a Muslim while he was incarcerated at Norfolk Prison Colony. It is possible that this Muslim was Abdul Hameed, though he is known in this account only by the pseudonym "Omar Khalil." Khalil greatly impressed Malcolm, but apparently not enough to win Malcolm over to Eastern Islam. That Khalil was not able to draw Malcolm away from Muhammad's Islam is not surprising. He had already embraced the black tenets of "the Lost Found Nation of Islam"— tenets that spoke more directly to Malcolm than the Eastern version—in his language and in terms that were more immediately relevant to him. Yet there may have been still another reason why Malcolm did not accept his visitor's form of Islam.

Khalil was apparently a member of a Muslim sect called the Ahmadiyya, which was not a traditional form of Islam, either. Actually, the Ahmadiyya were a late-nineteenth-century development in the Muslim world, referred to by one scholar as an Indian "syncretist movement" that arose in an era when modern Islam was giving birth to new sects worldwide. The Ahmadiyya were named for Azrat Mirza Ghulam Ahmad (1835–1908) of Qadian, who preached a pacifist gospel. Ahmad also perceived himself as the bearer of a revelation that would help Muslims reinterpret the Qur'an to suit their needs. Needless to say, by naming himself a prophet, Ahmad and his followers exposed themselves to persecution from traditional Muslims and carried the stigma of heresy with them into the twentieth century. Unlike Christianity, which leaves the door open to new prophets after the advent of Christ, traditional Muslims recognize no prophet after Muhammad.[4]

Apart from the distinctive claims of the movement's founder, the Ahmadiyya were quite faithful to the traditional reading of the Qur'an. Indeed, after the movement had split into two rival branches in 1914, one of them, the Lahoris, endeavored to be completely reconciled to traditional Sunni Islam by deemphasizing the claims of Ahmad. However, both branches distinguished the Ahmadiyya throughout the entire Muslim world by becoming zealous missionaries. Though a minority within their own Indian/Pakistani Muslim world, the Ahmadiyya engaged in extensive proselytization programs in India, England, Africa, and the United States.

Malcolm did not identify his visitor, Abdul Hameed, as being a member of this movement. Yet it is quite likely that he was an Ahmadiyya missionary, even though Malcolm identified him as being "orthodox"—a term he probably used to distinguish Hameed's teachings from those of the Nation. This adds weight to the possibility that Malcolm's Hameed and "Khalil" were one and the same missionary visitor.

Many of the Ahmadiyya's converts in the United States were urban African Americans—especially in Chicago, where the first Ahmadiyya missionary began his work in 1925. In the early days of their presence in the United States, they had even interacted with the UNIA and converted some of Marcus Garvey's followers. They expanded their conversion endeavors to many urban centers in the United States, including Boston,[5] where Malcolm was incarcerated.

Ahmadiyya teachings and publications usually served to advance knowledge of the Qur'an and Islamic culture, and to discredit the integrity of the Bible and the Christian message. The Ahmadiyya emphasized racial equality as well, which was of particular interest to black converts. Undoubtedly all of this would have been of interest to Malcolm though he was probably more inclined to borrow from the Ahmadiyya selectively—as his mother had taught him to borrow from a variety of Christian denominations and sects without accepting any of them totally. Malcolm had already embraced W. D. Fard as his Savior, and it seems likely that an Indian messiah named Ahmad would have held little interest for him.

As a minister for the Nation in New York City, one of Malcolm's most distinctive allies was, in fact, a Pakistani Muslim missionary/entrepreneur named Abdul Basit Naeem, who had apparently made his base of operations in nearby Brooklyn. In the mid-1950s he published *The Moslem World & The U.S.A.*, a magazine that was increasingly focused on the Nation, both as news and as a market for distribution. Naeem was a representative of the Islamic organization Jam'iat-ul-Falah, which sought to advance the Islamic cause as well as to mobilize support of various Muslim nationalist movements such as the Algerian independence movement and the nationalization policies of Egypt's President Nasser.

Naeem's support of Muhammad must have placed him in an awkward position among the other Eastern Muslims in the United States, but the Pakistani missionary seems to have been undaunted to walk in the shadow of heresy by associating with Mr. Muhammad and his Muslims. In fact, Naeem hoped to see an eventual commitment to traditional Islam on the part of Elijah Muhammad. However, it is quite likely that Naeem's enthusiasm for the Nation was otherwise motivated as well: Certainly he enjoyed serving as a kind of Muslim consultant to the Nation. He was highly instrumental in helping Malcolm to achieve his first great step toward the Islamic world—his visit to the Middle East and Africa in 1959.[6]

According to Malcolm's autobiography, by the late 1950s certain "African and Asian personages" had made "private" expressions of admiration and encouragement to the Nation and its leader. Somewhat modestly he added that sometimes "the messages had been sent through me." As a result of these expressions of admiration and interest that flowed between the Muslim world and the Nation, Malcolm emerged as the logical candidate to visit the Middle East and Africa as "Mr. Muhammad's emissary." It seems to be the case, in fact, that Malcolm's position as emissary was well cultivated on his part. To be sure, his interest in the Dark World had already grown from prison cell and platform rhetoric to genuine contact with African and Asian leaders, particularly through his United Nations connections in New York City.

However, though Malcolm admitted that he was the liaison through whom African and Asian leaders contacted Elijah Muhammad, he did not mention in his autobiography that he was also the catalyst for official messages of support to these leaders on behalf of the Nation. Two significant messages, in fact, preceded Malcolm's 1959 trip abroad, and both bear his own definite imprint, though they were sent in the name of Elijah Muhammad. The first, in March 1957, was a cable that Malcolm probably submitted for publication in a salutary supplement in the *Pittsburgh Courier* honoring the newly independent West African country of Ghana. The other communication to the Dark World was a cable sent on December 31, 1957, to representatives attending the Afro-Asian Solidarity Conference in Cairo, which was presided over (and largely funded) by Egyptian president Gamal Abdel Nasser.[7]

Of course, none of this suggests that Malcolm X acted unilaterally in sending these greetings. No doubt he took care to gain Muhammad's approval for both the initiatives and their contents. Still, it seems likely that it was Malcolm's own dream to build such bridges into Africa and Asia; Muhammad merely benefited from Malcolm's zealous advances into the Islamic world.

As it turned out, President William V. S. Tubman of Liberia and President Nasser of Egypt sent greetings to Elijah Muhammad during the Nation's 1959 convention in Chicago, essentially reciprocating with messages of unity and solidarity. Indeed, three months after Nasser's greeting to the Nation's

1959 national convention, his government issued a direct invitation to Elijah Muhammad to come and visit the Muslim world. According to Naeem, the New York-based Muslim missionary (who was interviewed, apparently by a BOSS agent), Elijah Muhammad flew him to Chicago especially to discuss the Egyptian invitation.

When Elijah Muhammad apparently determined to send Malcolm X as his advance man in July 1959, Malcolm himself received assurances from the Egyptian attaché to the United Nations, Ahmad Zaki El Borai, that both the government and people of Egypt would receive him with cordiality. Naeem was sure that the Nation had paid Malcolm's plane fare; however, Borai was present to see Malcolm X off at the airport—undoubtedly foreshadowing the kind of politically propitious reception that awaited him in Egypt. The FBI was likewise apprised of Malcolm's trip to Egypt, and one of their informants in particular noted that, apparently, "intense cooperation" existed between the Nation and its Middle Eastern friends—though the informant was not sure if the "cooperation" included Arab finances.[8]

Once in Egypt, Malcolm X was greeted by government officials who, according to Naeem, had him "constantly in hand." In addition, he was introduced to "prominent people" and was hosted after his arrival by a professor from the University of Cairo. Malcolm was given "considerable time" by President Nasser's leading representative, Anwar El Sadat, and was cordially received by the religious authorities of Al Azhar, the leading Islamic university.

Naeem's interviewer expressed the belief that Malcolm's positive reception by the Egyptian government and other dignitaries revealed that President Nasser attached importance to black nationalists in the United States, perceiving them as a potential "minority pressure group," and therefore he went out of his way to "flatter them." Indeed, the interviewer concluded, there was certainly very little religious rhetoric in the bridges that Nasser was building with the Nation. Nasser's diplomats were generally disinterested in religion, wanting to entertain Malcolm X and Elijah Muhammad for purely political reasons.

It is no coincidence that Naeem himself—Muhammad's ready Muslim consultant and ally—worked with an African American travel agent named Hilton Hill in New York City as a consultant in recruiting other "Negro Nationalist" types interested in touring the Afro-Asian world. A supporter of Nasser, Naeem obviously saw both the political and economic benefits involved in pointing African Americans eastward.

If Nasser's representatives had political concerns in mind, Malcolm X had his own organizational agenda as well. In private, he later admitted to Naeem that at first he had apprehensions about the kind of reception he would receive from the Egyptian Muslims, given the fact that Muhammad's "Islamic" practices were hardly traditional. In addition, Malcolm had to deal with the anxieties of his own lack of familiarity with traditional Muslim worship, ritual, and theology.

Malcolm confessed to Naeem that he was extremely embarrassed during his stay in Egypt because he was obligated to go through the five daily Muslim prayers in Arabic with insufficient knowledge of the language and only a sketchy notion of the ritual itself. Naeem concluded that Malcolm was observant and thought "he got by" by "mumbling" through the prayer ritual.

Malcolm was undoubtedly relieved to find that his Muslim hosts took the Nation virtually at face value. Apparently, most were simply unaware of the peculiar teachings of Muhammad's movement, which Naeem identified to his interviewer as "Elijah's blasphemy"—a somewhat hypocritical remark, given Naeem's otherwise flagrant support of the Nation. It was the opinion, at least of Naeem's interviewer, that some of the traditional Muslims (probably referring to those resident in the United States) who were familiar with these "pseudo-Moslem sects" regarded the Nation and other black "Muslim" groups with suspicion. "The devout are shocked by the illiteracy and cheap pagentry [sic] and the disregard for the dogma of the Koran."

Fortunately for Malcolm X and Elijah Muhammad—who made the trip eastward late in 1959—their politically astute hosts were willing to "close their eyes to the ridiculous dogma deviations" of the Nation. Malcolm would later recount to his New York parishioners that his Arab hosts had received him kindly, but wanted to know why he, being a Muslim, couldn't speak Arabic. He said he explained this was because he had been kidnapped for four hundred years, and was robbed of both his true language and religion.[9]

Malcolm succeeded at selling himself to the Egyptians as a true Muslim with religious and cultural deficiencies; his proficiency at justifying the gap between Muhammad's Islam and Sunni Islam was, to some extent, arguably rooted in historic racism. However, the moral strength from which Malcolm made his appeal was certainly dependent upon his own sincere belief that African Americans actually were African Muslims scattered in the West. Unlike Mr. Muhammad, who had—for most of his ministry—never encouraged his followers to study the Qur'an, nor to travel to the Muslim East, Malcolm arrived in Egypt as a self-proclaimed "fellow African coming back to his real home and a Moslem, eager to pray at the seat of the one true religion!"

However, Malcolm's sincerity and zeal for the Afro-Asian world, and his great respect for the Muslim world in general, were supplemented by his ability to convey to sympathetic Arabs the agonies of racism in the United States. He showed his hosts pictures of Nation gatherings and emphasized to them the arrogant injustice of white Christians in the United States. "The Egyptians loved it," Naeem concluded in his interview.[10]

Still, if Malcolm had hoped to enhance the Nation's relations with the dark Muslim world, he had an even greater desire to use his trip to excite, stimulate, and engender Afro-Asian and Muslim pride in his black brothers and sisters at home. Hoping to broadcast his sentiments to as many African Americans as possible, Malcolm corresponded with both the *Pittsburgh Courier* and the *New York Amsterdam News*. One *Courier* columnist reported that he received a personal letter from Malcolm X, declaring that he was "spellbound, amazed, and eternally proud" of his African heritage as he stood in the shadows of the great Sphinx and the pyramids of Egypt. In the presence of such ancient splendor, Malcolm said, he was "beholding the wisdom and strength of our forefathers depicted in these magnificent structures."

Of course, Malcolm did not stay in Egypt the whole time. After spending about nine days in Cairo, and then falling ill with dysentery (which waylaid him for an additional two days), Malcolm was able to visit Saudi Arabia. From Saudi, he returned to the African continent, visiting Khartoum, Sudan, Kano, Nigeria, and the much-lauded nation of Ghana. Throughout his trip, Malcolm continued to write to the black American press. In his room at the Kandarah Palace Hotel in Saudi, he wrote: "The people of Arabia are just like our people in America in facial appearance. They are of many differing shades, ranging from regal black to rich brown, but none are white. It is a safe postulation to say that 99 per cent of them would be jim-crowed in the United States of America." Furthermore, he announced: "There is no color prejudice among Moslems, for Islam teaches that all mortals are equal and brothers. Whereas the white Christians in the Western world teach this same thing without practicing it."[11]

Malcolm's assertions that none of the Saudis were white and that Eastern Muslims practiced no color prejudice is, at the very least, a curious pairing of racial notions. Neither assertion was absolutely true, particularly the claim that no Saudis were white—a claim Malcolm himself would eventually negate when finally making Hajj in 1964. That Malcolm's religious commitment to Elijah Muhammad might prohibit him from seeing white skin in Saudi Arabia is somewhat easier to comprehend than is the awkwardness of his other assertion.

In declaring that the Muslim world holds all "mortals" as equals, Malcolm was staring directly into the face of the very revelation that would characterize his later conversion to Sunni Islam. Standing in the Muslim world in 1959, Malcolm was actually saying that race and color do not matter in Islam; he was asserting that humanity, and not the Nation's black-white dogma, was the basis of commonality in the religion of Allah. However, humanity, as Malcolm viewed it through the eyes of "the Lost Found Nation," was dark, and only dark. Thus, when he spoke of humanity, equality, and brotherhood, Malcolm's words always included the inevitable footnote that such truths could not be applicable, nor even possible, in the white Christian world.

The major themes of Malcolm's communications to the black press, however, were essentially Garveyite. First, they entailed the presentation of a new vision of the African continent that would grant African Americans a sense of pride and unity:

Africa is the land of the future . . . definitely the land of tomorrow, and the African is the man of tomorrow. Only yesterday, America was the New World, a world with a future—but now, we suddenly realize Africa is the New World—the world with the brightest future—a future in which the so-called Negroes are destined to play a key role.[12]

He concluded that his travel had granted him "an even broader vista of 'things yet to come' "—things which Malcolm felt only enhanced the "vital role being played by Mr. Elijah Muhammad and his work among our people in America."

The other Garveyite aspect of Malcolm's message was to show the vital corollary to African American interest in the destiny of Africa: Africa's interest in the condition of African Americans. Writing to the *New York Amsterdam News* Malcolm noted that recent racial incidents occurring in the city of New York itself had not escaped the attention of concerned African people: "Racial troubles in New York occupied prominent space on the front pages here and in other parts of Africa yesterday. Everyone here seems aware of America's color problems."[13]

In his letter, Malcolm portrayed Africans as being "more concerned with the plight of their brothers in America than in their own conditions" since they were dependent on foreign economic and technical assistance for their own industrial development:

Thus, Africans consider American's [*sic*] treatment of Black Americans a good yard-stick [by] which they can measure the sincerity of America's offer of assistance here, and many young Africans are openly stating that what America practices at home does not coincide with what she preaches abroad, and are thus suspicious of her overtures here.[14]

He reiterated the same essential message in writing to the *Courier*, adding that "having long suffered European exploitation at the hands of whites, all Africans are suspicious of the white man's motives when he extends the 'helping hand.' "

Malcolm emphasized that there were growing "hordes of intelligent Africans" who found flagrant racism in the United States "difficult to understand" given the country's "loudly boasted" claims of equality. The African American plight, which was particularly the burden of underdeveloped and heavily taxed and conscripted ghetto dwellers "and other social imprisonments," could not be obscured from the African's vision by the "veil of global diplomatic art" the United States was attempting to place between the East and the West. Malcolm wanted his people, as well as white society in the United States, to know for certain that "the all-seeing-eye of the African masses is upon America."

The only regret Malcolm openly expressed about his 1959 trip abroad was that it was disrupted by the extreme discomfort of dysentery and extremely hot weather "beneath a pitiless sun." He announced that he would both put off going to Mecca, as well as a visit to the northeast African nations of Eritrea and Ethiopia, lamenting, "I should have felt the pulse of as many of the African masses as possible before returning to the United States."

Malcolm's first sojourn into the Dark World may have aroused other regrets. To be sure, his exposure to the authentic Muslim faith did not shatter his commitment to Muhammad; if anything, it became a means by which he could better enhance the Muslim façade of the movement back in the United States. Still, upon returning home, Malcolm urged Elijah Muhammad to study Arabic before making the trip abroad himself.

Malcolm and Muhammad knew—as Wilfred Little later recalled—that "what they were teaching at the time was not really in line with orthodox Islam." The trip to the Afro-Asian world undoubtedly disturbed Malcolm, as all cultists may be disturbed when their cosmological skies are darkened by the threatening clouds of orthodoxy. Wilfred Little remembered that Malcolm and Muhammad "were becoming more and more aware" of these clouds blowing from the East, "and they were trying to figure out how to deal with it." Of course, this problem remained subterranean once Malcolm's feet were back on North American soil. Speaking at a rally in honor of Muhammad's appearance at New York City's St. Nicholas Arena on July 26, 1959, Malcolm assured the audience that he was well accepted in Egypt and Africa because he was a Muslim. [15]

# 11

## Religious Apologist

*We are properly called "Muslims"!*

Both Elijah Muhammad and Malcolm X would undoubtedly have preferred that the issue of the Nation's Islamic integrity not be discussed. However, the Muslim door they had sought to enter opened two ways: the more Malcolm X influenced the Nation toward a broad identification with the Muslim world, the more he unintentionally subjected the movement and its leader to religious analyses and criticism.

A discerning observer has noted that "Malcolm X was a strong advocate of the internationalization of the Nation of Islam. Elijah Muhammad never was." And while Muhammad "may have wanted the legitimacy of orthodoxy, the possibility of his black nation losing its identity in the vast configuration of international Islam was a notion he never entertained seriously." In a real sense, then, the relationship between Elijah Muhammad and Malcolm X, no matter how close and mutually edifying, could not escape the inevitable crisis of separation. Malcolm X was fundamentally an internationalist, both in his political and in his religious orientation; Elijah Muhammad was parochial, and he saw his trip to the Middle East, and any contact with the Islamic world in general, only as a means of gaining recognition as a legitimate leader within the United States. This is perhaps exemplified by the fact that the Nation's temples were renamed "mosques" only after Muhammad's trip abroad at the beginning of 1960.

Elijah Muhammad's visit to the Muslim world was relatively successful. Like Malcolm X, Elijah Muhammad used the black American press to announce the warm receptions he had received in Turkey, Egypt, and Saudi Arabia. In the Los Angeles *Herald-Dispatch*, Muhammad declared that he was recognized and backed by the Muslim world, and that they had asked him to make the Hajj to Mecca, to which he traveled with two of his sons. Meanwhile, back in the United States, Malcolm X happily declared that Muhammad's legitimate standing as a Muslim was clear since "those who are not orthodox do not go to Mecca."[1]

In *Salaam*, one of the movement's several ill-fated publications, Elijah Muhammad portrayed his visit to Mecca in more detail, recounting (as Malcolm would later describe his Hajj) the sacred routine of his pilgrimage. Still echoing Fard's cultic descriptions, Muhammad spoke of Mecca as "the only city on our planet that is divinely protected." Equally true to cultic form, Muhammad spoke of the Black Stone of the Ka'ba in biblical allusion, calling it "that prophetic sign . . . that the builders rejected." He had apparently gone through the entire routine of the pilgrimage and remained deeply impressed with the "thousands of sincere worshippers of God, His religion, and Muhammad, His prophet." This was ironic, however, considering that when the Nation's membership spoke of Allah and his messenger, they were talking about W. D. Fard and Elijah Muhammad.

Neither Elijah Muhammad's trip to the Middle East nor his pilgrimage succeeded at silencing his critics, however. In fact, shortly after Malcolm returned from his Afro-Asian tour, the first big wave of Muslim opposition rose against the Nation. Muhammad had had Muslim critics before—some of whom occasionally expressed their frustrations over his column in the *Pittsburgh Courier*.

"Let us fervently pray," wrote one Algerian Muslim, "that the readers of The Courier will not confuse the sect of Muhammad with that of true Islam. Islam does not preach hate, it does not preach racism, it only calls for love, peace and understanding." Another angry Muslim reader railed that Elijah Muhammad "twists the Koran around to fit his hate teachings," calling him "a rabble-rousing race hater" who was "anti-Allah." Yet these were lone voices, and they were virtually drowned out by a good many more African American followers of Elijah Muhammad who consistently praised their leader in the black press.

At that time, as a Nigerian scholar recognized, the black urban community had a variety of self-styled Muslim spiritual leaders and foreign Muslim missionaries vying for influence—all claiming to be purveyors of authentic Islam. This has undoubtedly been a common occurrence since the days of Noble Drew Ali and W. D. Fard; however, as Elijah Muhammad's move ment had been empowered by Malcolm X and had begun to swell to unprecedented proportions in "Muslim" terms, these various Muslim leaders tended to unite in opposition to the Nation.[2] The most successful voices of opposition within the community were mostly those who could raise doctrinal criticisms without endangering their own positions.

In this regard, the most outspoken was a Caribbean-born black leader named Talib Dawud, who headed a small Muslim organization based in Philadelphia and New York, "Moslem Brotherhood of America, Inc.," which was founded in 1950. Dawud's organization was affiliated with the Ahmadiyya movement in the United States for a while, but became disassociated from it in 1958 after Dawud became opposed to a white Muslim holding office in the movement. Dawud was apparently as anti-integrationist and opposed to Christianity as Muhammad, though his sentiments were conventionally Muslim rather than cultic. Like Muhammad, Dawud had traveled to Mecca and had also interacted with leaders from the Afro-Asian world.

Dawud's opposition to the Nation first exploded in August 1959, in between Malcolm's and Muhammad's visits to the Middle East. The main instrument of attack was the Chicago-based black newspaper *New Crusader*, which was virtually "bought over" by Dawud in order to provide a forum for his front-page assaults. These front-page assaults ran somewhat frequently between August 1959 and March 1960 and targeted Muhammad's incarnational theology, his denial of a future, bodily resurrection, and his followers' failure to adhere to proper Muslim prayer rituals. Even more devastating, Dawud published a never-before-seen photograph of W. D. Fard in the *New Crusader*, with a headline proclaiming, "White Man Is God For Cult Of Islam."[3] The effect of the print war initiated by Dawud rippled through the rest of the black press.

What further glamorized this offensive was that Dawud—himself a former jazz musician—enjoyed the support of his wife, Dakota Staton, the popular jazz and R&B singer, and Ahmad Jamal, the brilliant jazz pianist. In fact, when the mainstream press first broke the news about the Nation to the white public, Jamal had sent a telegram of protest to *Time* magazine, lamenting that it was an "unfortunate coincidence" to be referred to as a Moslem in the same issue that featured a story about Elijah Muhammad.

"Muhammad['s] movement is rejected by peace-loving and law-abiding true Moslems," Jamal concluded. *"Time* readers should differentiate in justice to true Moslems in U.S."

In one interview, Dakota Staton, whose Muslim name was Aliyah Rabia Dawud, called the Nation "an aberration" and insisted she was part of worldwide Islam, a religion that "favors no particular race." Dawud's attacks also included flagrant attempts to discredit or deny the Nation's links to the Muslim world—particularly in regard to the overseas visits of Malcolm X and Elijah Muhammad. Dawud claimed, in fact, that both men had been denied entry into Mecca because they were not considered true Muslims. He apparently did everything else in his power to discredit the Nation, including making anti-Muhammad pronouncements to Muslim officials based in the United States and claiming that the Nation was working in cooperation with members of the KKK.

At first, Dawud's assault was not met with rigorous retaliation. In particular, Malcolm X's voice was strangely silent in the black press, even in the New York City area—which suggests that Elijah Muhammad possibly sought to keep a low profile with his initial response. However, when Dawud ran his *New Crusader* exposé on Fard being a white man, the Nation in Chicago and New York attempted to purchase and destroy as many copies of the paper as possible. Writing in the *Pittsburgh Courier* and other black papers, Elijah Muhammad claimed that his own moral character was superior to that of Dawud and Staton—especially characterizing the latter as an immoral nightclub singer.

Unfortunately, events turned ugly when New York Nation members were snubbed in a Harlem reception for the visiting president of Guinea, Sekou Toure. The snub came when Malcolm X and his parishioners were blocked from participating in the welcoming program of the hosting organization, the United African Nationalist Movement. Evidently the movement's director, James Lawson, was allied with Dawud and his followers and shared a similarly critical view of Muhammad's teachings. Malcolm X, whose internationalist sentiments on behalf of the Nation were undoubtedly crushed by the snub, became bitter. A battle of harsh charges and countercharges resulted, and Dawud and an associate were attacked by acid throwers who apparently were members of the Nation.[4]

Dawud's belligerence seems to have quieted temporarily, particularly after the *New Crusader* and James Lawson both disassociated themselves from his campaign. In fact, Dawud's collaboration with the *New Crusader* came to an abrupt halt in March 1960, when the Chicago-based newspaper did an about-face and began to collaborate with its neighbor, Elijah Muhammad. Lawson's move away from Dawud was possibly a maneuver of political expediency, since Malcolm X's black nationalist platform was steadily growing in popularity among black New Yorkers.

However, in the summer of 1962, the black press noted new aggression on the part of Dawud and Staton. In a Chicago press conference, the Muslim couple declared that Elijah Muhammad and his followers were "frauds," and that the Nation had done great damage to Staton's career since, being a Muslim, she was wrongly associated with the Nation by the press.

To underscore this, Staton announced she was filing a suit against Elijah Muhammad, seeking injunctive relief against any future claim on his part to being a Muslim. To support their case, a white Republican senator, Arthur Gottschalk—a bitter critic of the Nation—affirmed Staton's charge, claiming that he himself had wrongly discriminated against all Muslims because of Muhammad's spurious Muslim claims. In the interview, Staton added that besides her husband being attacked by acid throwers in New York City, phone threats and a "bomb incident" had occurred in Philadelphia.

While the legal action proved to have no teeth, it was at least carried through. A "Complaint for Injunction" was filed in the District Court of the United States for the Eastern District of Pennsylvania, requesting that Elijah Muhammad and the Nation "be enjoined from professing to be spiritual leaders of the Muslim Faith and the Islamic Religion." The complaint did not call for the Nation to stop its teachings, but only to refrain from calling them Islamic teachings.[5]

In immediate retaliation, Muhammad banned two of Dawud's Islamic associates from attending a Nation rally at the Philadelphia Arena in June 1962. What made their public rejection particularly offensive was that Muhammad permitted two hundred whites into the rally's segregated seating area. As to the complaint, Malcolm X mocked the legal act as a "publicity stunt" that sounded so ridiculous that "I have to get ridiculous in order to answer it." Malcolm charged that Staton's career had digressed for other reasons and that this was only an attempt on her part to "get back into the lime light." Scoffing at the possibility of answering Staton's accusation, Malcolm compared her complaints to the barking of a dog at the moon.

When Malcolm's hometown newspaper, the *New York Amsterdam News*, featured Staton's comments about Elijah Muhammad, Malcolm lashed out harshly. Rather than having her career hurt by a false association with Muhammad, Malcolm declared, Staton's reputation had declined because she had criticized him. "Ever since she changed her 'tunes' and started singing against Mr. Muhammad, her popularity has been on the downturn." Referring to her as a "hip swinging, blues singing" entertainer, Malcolm made light of Staton's religious integrity. "Even the non-Muslim public knows," Malcolm concluded, "that no Muslim sister who follows Mr. Muhammad would think of singing sexy songs, half-naked in a night-club where people are getting drunk and expect people to respect her as an 'example' of religious piety."

Turning on Dawud himself, Malcolm claimed that Staton was trying to help her husband's failing career as a Muslim leader by attacking Elijah Muhammad. "In other words," Malcolm mocked bitterly, "all of Dawud's combined followers can fit into the front seat of his station wagon." Apparently Talib Dawud's aspirations to prove the illegitimacy of Muhammad's Islam never amounted to much, particularly as far as the black community was concerned. As C. Eric Lincoln noted, "the aegis of orthodox Islam means little in America's black ghettos."

Since Dawud never enjoyed organizational strength in the black community, his vehement attacks against Elijah Muhammad probably only served to alienate him from Islamic-oriented African Americans. Furthermore, being both an avowed opponent of Christianity and a Caribbean, Dawud very likely found himself an outsider with regard to black religious life in the United States. Malcolm X was probably correct in surmising that Dakota Staton, being a renowned African American singer, offered Dawud some access to a potential popularity base within the black community. However, even Staton's fame in the community could not empower Dawud sufficiently. Elijah Muhammad even played somewhat on Dawud's Caribbean background, as one scholar noted, "suggesting the antagonism between American Negroes and West Indians."[6]

In contrast to his vehement opposition of Dawud and his small organization, Abdul Basit Naeem treated the Nation quite warmly. In fact, the Nation enjoyed what might be called a mutually beneficial relationship with the Pakistani Muslim missionary/entrepreneur. According to Naeem, he became aware of the Nation in 1948 while residing in Chicago and finally established contact with Elijah Muhammad, sometime in the mid-1950s, through Shaykh Jamil Diab. Diab, a Palestinian who taught Arabic in the University of Islam for Temple No. 2 in Chicago, would eventually turn against the Nation.

Naeem immediately took up the cause of Elijah Muhammad in his *Moslem World & The U.S.A.*, and gave the Nation priority coverage throughout 1956, arousing a good many criticisms from Muslim readers not affiliated with the Nation. Naeem appealed to his critics that the Nation was inseparable from the "over-all picture of Islamic affairs in America," and thus merited news coverage. Furthermore, Naeem said that despite the racial characteristics of Elijah Muhammad's teachings, the Nation "enabled more Americans to form acquaintance with Islam than the efforts of all other individuals seeking converts to Islam here put together."

Naeem acknowledged that Islam's advancement in the largely Christianized United States would be highly problematic, given certain of its theological and ethical prescriptions. He concluded that being interested in the advancement of Islam, "we would rather see an all-black Moslem community in America than none at all." Consequently, *The Moslem World & The U.S.A.* began to look like a Nation publication, and Malcolm X and Elijah Muhammad frequently appeared in its pages, giving the impression that the Nation was being mainstreamed into the American Muslim community. Indeed, it seems that Naeem was doing his best to create such an impression.

Attending the Nation's annual convention in 1957 as an honored guest, Naeem declared before the assembly that Elijah Muhammad was a leader "whose teachings and messages are just about the only way I can now see of bringing the so-called Negroes into, or shall I say 'back into,' the fold of Islam en masse." Naeem lauded Muhammad as being "one of the greatest Moslems of our day" and praised him for his exceptional success at bringing blacks into Islam. In an audacious and patronizing gesture, Naeem even conferred the title of "Ameer Maulana" (Chief Religious Leader) upon Elijah Muhammad and called for a two-minute standing ovation.

Abdul Basit Naeem not only enjoyed these great opportunities to advance his political and economic special interests through the support of the Nation, but he also seemed more willing to overlook Muhammad's problematic doctrines than other Muslims. In fact, Naeem comfortably reiterated Elijah Muhammad's begging notion that Islam had to be significantly altered to fit the particular plight of African Americans: "You cannot use the same medicine to treat altogether different diseases."[7]

Besides using one issue of *The Moslem World & The U.S.A.* to publish an assortment of Elijah Muhammad's teachings, Naeem wrote a laudatory foreword for the Nation's publication *The Supreme Wisdom*, which was essentially a compendium of the same teachings. "I consider the difference between Islam of the East and teachings of Mr. Elijah Muhammad to be of relatively minor importance *at this time*," Naeem wrote, "because these are not related to the SPIRIT of Islam, which, I am sure, is completely shared by *all* of us."

In other words, Naeem was suggesting that Elijah Muhammad should be given time to make adjustments, religiously speaking; there was great potential in the Nation, and all that was needed was time and patience on the part of the Nation's true Muslim friends. Naeem apparently believed that Elijah Muhammad would come into a more sound and complete understanding of Islam—in the meantime, a near-Muslim was better than a black Christian. The same sentiments, however, were not shared by the Ahmadiyya missionaries who were competing for black support in the United States.

The director of Ahmadiyya headquarters in Chicago, Nur Al-Islam, was not antagonistic toward the Nation's leader, but was hardly supportive in his analysis: "Muhammad is a self-appointed Messenger of Allah. He teaches nationalism. Places emphasis upon economic, political and social independence. Religion for him is the last thing. It is a tool for these goals."

Nur Al-Islam recognized that Elijah Muhammad had gained a lot of African American followers as a result of his nationalistic philosophy. In contrast, Al-Islam noted that the Ahmadiyya was "strictly a religious group." A minimalist in his appreciation of the Nation, Al-Islam admitted that "Elijah has done a lot for his followers particularly by making them become self-respecting and proud of themselves. . . . He has at least made many aware of the fact that there is such a religion as Islam." Thus, despite their different affiliations, Nur Al-Islam and Abdul Basit Naeem—both foreign-born missionaries—recognized the opportunity for Islam that had been created by the work of Elijah Muhammad in the black community.

Unlike Nur Al-Islam, however, another African-American member of the Ahmadiyya had no appreciation at all for Muhammad's efforts. Adib Nuruddin, a Chicago follower of Nur Al-Islam, lashed out at Elijah Muhammad as a "race-hating, scheming, cynical and power hungry fanatic" who used the "disguise of religion" to perpetrate "a most dangerous cult" among African Americans. Theologically speaking, Nuruddin accused Elijah Muhammad of giving African Americans a doctrine that was vague, unintelligible, unverifiable, and contrary to both nature and common sense. "The doctrine is not profound or sublime; on the contrary, it is embodied with crude absurdities and trivial nonsense." With regard to Muhammad's historical explanations, Nuruddin found them equally ridiculous: "The facts of history, like the letters of the alphabet, can be arranged so as to mean anything. Therefore, since our history has been falsified, Mr. Muhammad feels that he is entitled to give us an even larger falsification."[8]

Another foreign-born Ahmadiyya showed no restraint in criticism of Elijah Muhammad. Abdul Ghafoor Soofi, whom the Baltimore *Afro-American* called the "head missionary" of the Ahmadiyya in the United States, was quite blunt in his dislike of the Nation: "I think from what I read about the movement . . . we have nothing in common with them. Islam for them is a label to focus the attention of the Muslim world and to enlist their sympathies in their hate campaign." In another interview, Soofi told black reporters in Detroit that if Elijah Muhammad refrained from calling his teachings "Islam," he would do a great service to himself and the truth. Still, even in Soofi's clear repudiation of Elijah Muhammad's "hate element," there was a ring of sympathy for the Nation's "campaign against white supremacy": "We cannot support colonialism, nor do we approve of attempts to perpetuate white supremacy or domination anywhere."

Ironically, even the most harsh criticisms, like those expressed by Adib Nuruddin, only proved to serve as a catalyst to further cohesion for the simple followers of Elijah Muhammad.[9] Like Talib Dawud's appeals to orthodoxy, neither mild nor zealous criticism from the Ahmadiyya seemed to have much of an impact on the Nation itself. And while the Ahmadiyya missionaries were well aware of the problems inherent in Elijah Muhammad's teachings, ultimately their overall challenge to the Nation was ambiguous. Unable to either beat or join Muhammad, and given their own controversial standing in Islam, the Ahmadiyya perhaps settled for an uneven détente with the Nation.

One of the Nation's most ardent Eastern Muslim critics and competitors was the Palestinian teacher, Shaykh Jamil Shakir Diab. For an extended period, beginning in 1948 when he migrated to the United States, Diab was employed by Elijah Muhammad and served as principal and teacher at the Nation's University of Islam in Chicago. Even though he was a Muslim, he was not permitted to join the Nation. Still, the arrangement apparently brought him good remuneration. In time Diab took it upon himself to expose his Nation students to the real Islamic doctrine, which ended his teaching appointment.

Diab told one interviewer that the Nation could not be evaluated by the usual criteria applied when evaluating Islam, and he characterized Muhammad's movement as controversial, aggressive, and propagandistic "at the expense of Islam." With regard to the Nation's racial doctrines, Diab concluded that the "very cornerstone of Islam, universal brotherhood of man, black as well as white, has been turned into hatred by them."

A leader with his own interracial Muslim flock in Chicago, Diab did not venture to attack the Nation. Instead, he heavily emphasized that a major factor in Islam was that it transcended race and did not "herd human beings" according to a "barbaric" racial basis. "[T]here are no such creatures as white or black Muslims," Diab concluded, "all are as one, under Allah." [10]

Malcolm X spent a great deal of time in his autobiography recounting the verbal battles into which he was drawn in defense of Elijah Muhammad and the Nation. He provided many examples of the kinds of social and political accusations and rhetoric that the Nation had to counteract, and he noted that black Christian ministers were often antagonists of the Nation. Yet he said very little about the criticism to which the Nation was subjected by Eastern Muslims. However, Malcolm did make at least one allusion to the debate surrounding the Nation's religious integrity when he quoted a black critic's charge that the followers of Muhammad were "[r]idiculous pretenders to the ancient Islamic doctrine."

The press generally preferred to concentrate on the Nation's identity as a "black supremacist" group rather than its religious nature as a Muslim organization. However, some journalists were perceptive. In an interview with Malcolm X, one of them did take note of Malcolm's belief that the "Black Muslim movement" was "an authentic offshoot of Islam." Malcolm X also proclaimed that "the Messenger" had made "the pilgrimage to the inner shrine at Mecca," and he had not gone to Mecca himself because he didn't want to visit there ahead of Mr. Muhammad. The journalist remained somewhat skeptical about Malcolm's explanation, and pointed out that the Islamic presence in the United States lacked the kind of ecclesiastical hierarchy that might issue an ultimate judgment about the Nation's religious integrity.

Such skepticism also surfaced in the writings of other journalists who wanted to do more than sensationalize stories on the movement. One noted, for example, that "the religion of the American Muslims seems to be a peculiar mixture of orthodox Mohammedanism and the personal prejudices of Elijah Muhammad." Another concluded that, in comparison to traditional Islam in Mecca, "the real heresy of the American Muslims is their disavowal of the principle of racial equality. However, Elijah visited Mecca last year and was received by Muslim leaders." This journalist, however, was apparently bothered by a contradictory undercurrent he sensed between the Nation and other Islamic groups—notwithstanding the assured claims of the Nation's leading spokesman: "Malcolm X asserts that the trip settled the legitimacy of the American movement. But the 75,000 orthodox Muslims in the United States continue to refuse to recognize the new group." [11]

Overall, it appears that the Nation had fallen prey to the sensationalized commentary of the media, which invariably traveled the low road toward educating the public about matters relating to African Americans in general. With the release of C. Eric Lincoln's scholarly assessment of the Nation, *The Black Muslims in America* (1961), the media found an even more exploitable opportunity. Lincoln had coined the "Black Muslim" term, probably because it helped to distinguish Muhammad's followers from other Muslim groups. The appellation was quickly appropriated by the media and it became loaded with inflammatory and sensationalized journalistic baggage. Rather than using "Black Muslims" in a scholarly sense that Lincoln had intended, the media exploited the term to enhance the kind of "black supremacist threat" stories that had first arisen after the Wallace/Lomax documentary in 1959.

The term "Black Muslims" disturbed Elijah Muhammad and Malcolm particularly because it polarized them from the Islamic world—something that Lincoln himself had not intended. As Elijah Muhammad's chief spokesman, Malcolm recalled:

I tried for at least two years to kill off that "*Black* Muslims." Every newspaper and magazine writer and microphone I got close to: "No! We are black *people* here in America. Our *religion* is Islam. We are properly called 'Muslims'!" But that "Black Muslims" name never got dislodged. [12]

The Nation's leadership was understandably perturbed with Lincoln for inventing such an irreversible problem. Consequently, Malcolm X was quoted as saying that Lincoln was "just a Christian preacher from Atlanta . . . who wanted to make some money, so he wrote a book and called it 'Black Muslims in America.' " All of the Nation's efforts, including the two trips to the Muslim world, seemed to have been lost in the explosion of "Black Muslim" rhetoric. To no avail, Malcolm X spent the rest of his career in the Nation declaring that "we are not even Black Muslims . . . we are black people who are Muslims because we have accepted the religion of Islam." [13]

An apparent side-effect of "Black Muslims" was that it aggravated preexisting tensions between the Nation and other Muslims in the United States. If there had been apathy or even sympathy on the part of Eastern Muslims with regard to the Nation, the tide now seemed to be turning. Attacks by Muslims of the Dark World became regular and perhaps more probing than ever before—inevitably placing Malcolm X in an even more precarious position as the Nation's chief apologist.

For instance, when a Sudanese Muslim student at the University of Pennsylvania complained to the *Pittsburgh Courier* that Elijah Muhammad's pilgrimage to Mecca was probably a farce since he had not gone in the proper season,[14] Malcolm retaliated. Recalling that he had visited the Sudan in 1959, Malcolm noted how impressed he had been with the piety and hospitality of all African Muslims. He concluded quite firmly that this critical Sudanese student could not be a real Muslim, let alone a Muslim from Sudan. "No real Muslim will ever attack another Muslim just to gain the friendship of Christians," Malcolm chided. In effect, Malcolm had totally sidestepped the student's perceptive (and significant) complaint by launching a religiously garbed character assault in response:

This man can't be a real Muslim. He probably is an American Negro who is a Christian, but is posing as a Muslim just to lend "authenticity" to his attacks upon Messenger Elijah Muhammad. How can we tell? If real Muslims have difference[s] they settle their differences in private, but never to the public delight of Jews and Christians.[15]

Even though the writer declared himself to be a Muslim and an admirer of the anti-Christian Talib Dawud, Malcolm apprised him of the Qur'anic prohibition against making Christian and Jewish friends—forcing the analytical spotlight, quite unfairly, back on the Sudanese student.[16]

This modus operandi was not new, either to Malcolm X or the Nation. The Nation's first manifestation had been fundamentally grounded on W. D. Fard's gainsaying, fault-finding arguments that based cult integrity solely on the sins of the orthodox. Likewise, an observer in Elijah Muhammad's earlier days noted how the "Messenger of Allah" had also derided Christians and Jews. This tendency to infer "evidence by ridicule" was Elijah Muhammad's "essential tactic" in putting off the more probing, critical questions of the Nation's orthodox opponents.[17] Now, with the rise of Muslim opposition in the early 1960s, Malcolm X took up Muhammad's cudgel of derision and became quite skilled at knocking about any Muslim who dared to suggest the Nation was anything less than an authentic Islamic organization.

When the *New York Amsterdam News* featured the religious critique of a Muslim scholar from Afghanistan who questioned Elijah Muhammad's authenticity as the Messenger, Malcolm responded with a written sneer, calling the Muslim's criticisms "amusing" and placing references to him as a scholar in quotation marks. Discounting the relevance of authorities on Muslims, Malcolm claimed that "if all the Muslim 'scholars' in the East were to come to America at the same time and put forth their efforts for the purpose of spreading the Religion of Islam among the white Americans, Allah's name would still be unknown among these Western Infidels." He instead turned to Elijah Muhammad's alleged astounding success at turning "hundreds-of-thousands of the so-called Negroes" toward Mecca in prayer. He recalled his own experiences in the East, reminding the scholar that the Eastern Muslims he had met never criticized Elijah Muhammad—especially since "there is too much for them to do in their own country that is yet undone, despite the fact that they claim to have been 'true' Muslims for almost fourteen centuries."

Not letting up, Malcolm continued by lauding Elijah Muhammad's high conversion success rate as a sign of Allah's favor, and then accused the Muslim scholar of allowing "Christian enemies of Islam put words in his mouth" that could be used to denigrate a Muslim leader. Skillfully shifting his attention to the Muslim world, Malcolm then reminded the scholar that Algerian Muslims had separated from the French, Arabic Muslims had separated from the Israelis, and Pakistani Muslims had separated from the Hindus. How, then, Malcolm challenged the scholar, could any Muslim consider Elijah Muhammad a teacher of race hatred?

Finally, Malcolm closed his attack by citing two favorite Qur'anic texts—one that speaks against friendship with Jews and Christians, and another that Malcolm read with an eye toward the eschatological destruction of the white race: "The day when the trumpet is blown; and we shall gather the guilty, blue-eyed, on that day." [18] No doubt this many-pronged attack from Malcolm had legitimate points and revealed that he had an early awareness of the real incongruities of the Muslim world. Nevertheless, his counterattack was made according to the letter and spirit of the Nation.

When a historian of Islam wrote a revealing piece in the *New York Times Magazine* that contrasted traditional Islam with Elijah Muhammad's Nation, Malcolm was again compelled to make a counterattack. "Islam is essentially democratic and egalitarian," the scholar had written. But the "Black Muslims" did not claim to be orthodox, nor were their teachings in line with the teachings of Islam. "They preach race hatred and claim that God is black and that it is the destiny of the black race to inherit the earth."

Several weeks later, Malcolm's retort appeared in the same publication's letter section. He labeled the scholar's work "a frantic effort to bring division" between the "rapidly growing" Nation and "our Muslim brothers in the East." This writer, declared Malcolm, had "skillfully twisted many half-truths" to prove that Muhammad was not a sincere Muslim. Malcolm dispensed with any further epithets, and launched into a scriptural tour de force instead, citing several verses from the Qur'an, including his two favorites about nonalignment with Jews and Christians and the eschatological destruction of the "guilty BLUE-EYED" (which he placed in upper case for emphasis).

Since the historian had criticized the Nation's teaching that the black man was the original man, Malcolm also cited the Qur'anic verse: "Surely We created man of sounding clay, of BLACK MUD fashioned into shape." Malcolm concluded by daring the scholar to ask his "orthodox Muslim friends" to explain how Elijah Muhammad's teachings conflict with these pertinent passages of the Holy Qur'an.

The editors of the *New York Times Magazine* did not allow Malcolm to get in the last word, however. The scholar's rebuttal to Malcolm X was included in the same issue, and it called particular attention to Malcolm's quotation of the Muhammad Ali English translation of the "guilty, blue-eyed" text from the Qur'an. He noted that the original text read differently ("and [the sinners'] eyes shall become dim with terror"), and that it contained no reference to the white race whatsoever. Then the scholar concluded that, according to the Qur'an, "All sinners, not only blue-eyed ones, are implicated in the judgment." As if to put Malcolm X to silence, he concluded that "the essential nature of Islam, like the essential nature of Hebraism and Christianity, is pacific, tolerant and charitable. The Black Muslims, by their own accounting, are neither pacific, nor tolerant, nor charitable."[19]

Malcolm would probably not have admitted it at the time, but he clearly lost this round—and not only because the scholar was allowed the last word. His ability to defend the Nation by means of scholarly, reasoned, and religiously sound argument was inadequate. His limitations were not based on any lack of understanding or exposure to Islam on his part, though. Quite the contrary—if Malcolm X could not effectively defend the Nation against such penetrating criticisms it was because he was too bound up in Muhammad's cultic straitjacket.

For a long time, Malcolm's commitment to Elijah Muhammad had obligated him to defend the Nation's doctrines, even when the logic of his defense seemed absurd. It seems that Malcolm X was finding it increasingly difficult to make a firm case for Elijah Muhammad's Islamic integrity. This is probably why, sometime in the early 1960s, Malcolm began to make statements that suggested he was beginning to move away, ever so subtly, from Muhammad's exclusive religious claim on his mind and soul. This gradual departure became particularly apparent in Malcolm's mounting interviews and activities outside the guarded realm of the Nation.

# 12

## Foreshadowing Mecca — Between Cult and Orthodoxy

*Islam is a religion of brotherhood in which color is not recognized.*

At the end of March 1963, Malcolm X appeared on a late-night television program, *The Ben Hunter Show*, in Los Angeles, California. The talk show featured a group of panelists that included the black journalist Louis Lomax, who had first introduced the Nation to television viewers in 1959. On this occasion Malcolm X did not immediatcly invoke "The Honorable Elijah Muhammad" when he was asked about being a Muslim— something quite uncharacteristic of his other media interviews. Instead, Malcolm X declared: "One becomes a Muslim only by accepting the religion of Islam, which means belief in one God, Allah. Christians call him Christ, Jews call him Jehovah. Many people have many different names but he is the creator of the universe." Malcolm noted further that becoming a Muslim entailed submitting oneself to God, praying, fasting, being charitable, brotherhood, and having respect for authority and other people.[1]

There are two significant aspects to Malcolm's statement here. First, he emphasized the traditional view of the submitted life according to Islam rather than the central tenets of Elijah Muhammad's black religion of separation. Second, Malcolm equated Allah with the divinity of Christianity and Judaism, claiming that only the names for God are different. Indeed, by adding that "many people have many different names" for Allah, he was appealing to an ecumenism that was irreconcilable to Muhammad's black cult theology. Indeed, such ecumenism may even have echoed the personal theism of Louise Little and the religious flexibility Malcolm had learned at her feet. Certainly, it was a far cry from Elijah Muhammad's doctrine of a black incarnated God named W. D. Fard.

Malcolm did, however, address the teachings of Elijah Muhammad on the show, including the notion that whites are devils. But his case sounded somewhat hollow, as if he believed in "the Messenger" but not the message:

The Honorable Elijah Muhammad teaches us that God taught him that the white race is a race of devils and what a white person should do if he is not a devil is prove it. As far as I'm concerned the history of the white race as it has been taught to us by the Honorable Elijah Muhammad is pretty strong evidence against that particular race. [2]

Malcolm's words give the impression that he was relaying a message that he did not personally own, religiously speaking. What he did convey were *the claims* of Elijah Muhammad, not actual revelation—only "pretty strong evidence." He concluded: "Now, if they are not devils, all I say is that they should prove they are not and I'll go back and tell Mr. Muhammad that perhaps he might be wrong." [3]

Malcolm did not actually say that Muhammad was wrong; he was still unable to make such a suggestion. However, his words clearly left the door open to the idea that Elijah Muhammad's teachings were not above the scrutiny of human reason. In the eyes of the true believer, revelation is not subject to tests and proofs. It seems that now Malcolm X himself had begun to test Muhammad's doctrines against his own understanding of Islam.

Louis Lomax left the television studio with Malcolm X after the show in the early hours of the morning, and later recalled an incident that occurred as they walked toward their car with another Nation official. In the parking lot "a number of Arab students from UCLA literally surrounded Malcolm. They had seen the program and were visibly angered by Malcolm's 'white devil' utterances."

The students, who Lomax recalled were white by appearance, flatly accused Malcolm of preaching a false doctrine. "Malcolm attempted to counter by saying that it was necessary for him to take the 'white devil' approach in order to 'wake up the deaf, dumb, and blind American Negro.' " According to Lomax, however, the Arab students angrily rejected any such explanation, and Malcolm—visibly disturbed by their rejection—"stalked" away from the students and got into the car with his companions, apparently saying nothing more about the incident.

A similar event had also occurred when Malcolm was speaking at the University of Michigan on January 23, 1963. During his presentation he had a similar encounter with an Eastern Muslim during a question-and-answer period. When the Muslim in the audience identified himself as white, Malcolm immediately insisted he was not white. When the man persisted by asking him if the Nation would accept a white Muslim, Malcolm dodged the question by saying that it would be a waste of time trying to convert whites after Eastern Muslims had failed to do so and, further, that Mr. Muhammad's concern was for black people.

When the Muslim still persisted, Malcolm declared: "We are brothers," noting that during his stay in Egypt he "felt the spirit of brotherhood." However, rather than carry that admission to its logical conclusion, Malcolm triumphantly shifted the attention back on the Eastern Muslims in the United States instead: "But an Egyptian who comes to America should realize the problem confronted by Black people in this country. And when you see us being chased by a dog, the best thing for you to do is wait until the dog stops chasing us and then ask us some questions. Especially when you should have come a long time ago and helped your little brothers whip the dog." Though Malcolm was skillfully able to disarm this Muslim critic in public, he was not as successful in the confrontation with the Arab students outside the television studio. As Lomax noted, their firm rejection of his presentation deeply disturbed Malcolm X, who genuinely believed in Muslim solidarity.

Malcolm admitted in his autobiography that increased exposure to students and other sympathetic whites had moved him to alter the Nation's presentation slightly. Speaking to his audiences in the early 1960s, he began to declare: "Unless we call one white man, by name, a 'devil,' we are not speaking of any *individual* white man. We are speaking of the *collective* white man's *historical* record." It would seem that criticism, especially the increasing hostility of Muslims toward Nation doctrines, had begun to weigh heavily upon the shoulders of Malcolm X, who had to deal with this burden while Elijah Muhammad remained sequestered in his Chicago mansion or his winter home in Phoenix, Arizona.

It is interesting to note how critical the attitudes of Eastern Muslims had become toward the Nation in the wake of the media's "Black Muslim" craze. Ahmad Kamal, an official in a traditional Muslim humanitarian organization called Jami'at al-Islam commented: "Elijah Poole's teachings, his dogma and doctrine of hatred, are utterly non-Muslim. It is anti-Muslim. We feel a great compassion for all Negroes who have been duped by the Black Muslims."

In 1963, journalists began to take more note of the fact that the "Black Muslims" had been rejected by traditional Muslims in the United States, including the Federation of Islamic Associations in the United States and Canada. In an article published in Chicago's black *Daily Defender*, Ahmad Kamal further sharpened his attack upon the Nation. Calling Elijah Muhammad's doctrines "satanic" and referring to him as Elijah Poole, Kamal declared that blacks had a "new burden to bear," since the leader of the Nation had "taught his listeners that in following him they are guided by a living prophet and that they are Black Muslims. He is going to have much to answer for." Another journalist observed that the legitimacy of the Nation as a Muslim organization was still a matter open to debate, though certain Muslim scholars had expressed "negative opinions on the question."[4]

As to Malcolm X's position, the debate was still raging. In most ways, he persisted in his normal role as the purveyor of Muhammad's diatribes against whites and Christianity. Despite his vigorous words against white religion, however, Malcolm's inclination toward traditional Islam was becoming more apparent. For instance, when he appeared on a Chicago television program called *At Random* on March 3, 1963, he defended the "white devil" epithet of the Nation—but did so strictly on the basis of behavior, not biology. Indeed, Malcolm cited Muhammad—but not Elijah Muhammad. "Well, sir, in the Koran, in the teachings of Muhammad in Arabia 1400 years ago, he said you judge a man by his conscious behavior or by his intentions . . . which means that anyone who intentionally or consciously carries into practice the attributes or characteristics of the devil is a devil."

In a Washington, D.C., radio interview in May 1963, Malcolm seemed at first to be conveying the standard racial-religious line of the Nation. Islam, he declared, "is the very nature of which the black man was created." As the black man's religion, he said further, Islam alone could teach blacks the truth about themselves and would "automatically" include black people who gained knowledge about their "cultural pasts." Not only did Islam best suit black people, according to Malcolm X, but it had "a spiritual power within it that automatically makes the man turn toward God, have respect for one God, the oneness of God, [and the] unity of God."[5]

Malcolm's references to Islam turned toward orthodoxy at this point, however. Reminding the radio audience that the "people in the Muslim world don't regard a man according to the color of his skin," Malcolm seemed to be hinting at a more conciliatory approach: "When you are a Muslim, you don't look at the color of a man's skin . . . whether he is black, red, *white* or green or something like that; when you are a Muslim you look at the man *and judge him according to his conscious behavior*." This was certainly not the voice of Elijah Muhammad speaking through Malcolm X. "And many people in this country think we are against the white man because he is white," Malcolm concluded. "No, as a Muslim we don't look at the color of a man's skin; we are against the white man because of what he has done to the black man."[6]

As early as 1959, when he was in the Middle East, Malcolm had declared to the black press that in the Islamic world, humans are not judged according to their color. However, he flatly denied that Saudi Arabians could be white—suggesting that Muslim fraternity was essentially a black brotherhood. But now, in 1963, he included whites in the Muslim family and further claimed that no white man was judged according to his color—only by his deeds. This was, for all intents and purposes, *the same declaration* Malcolm would make in Mecca one year later, after being ousted from the Nation.

The extent to which Malcolm was apparently experiencing the fragmentation of his cultic worldview is quite dramatically illustrated in this radio interview, especially so since his words reflect how desperately he was groping for traditional Islam within the confining straitjacket of Muhammad's organization. It might be risky to make much of Malcolm's every word, but his awkward switch from first person singular to first person plural in the comment above seems significant: "As *a Muslim, we* don't look at the color of a man's skin." Was Malcolm X now longing to express his own religious thoughts, independent of Elijah Muhammad—so much so that he nearly confessed to holding orthodox convictions over the radio?

The real issue, then, was how long Malcolm could continue parroting Muhammad's doctrines and live with his own growing need to express his religious, social, and political independence. Political historians have already noted that in the 1960s Malcolm X was moving steadily toward a progressive, activist stance that could not ultimately be reconciled to the nonpolitical, sectarian nature of the Nation,[7] but few have adequately appreciated the religious corollary to the same crisis in Malcolm X's career in the Nation. Just as he was increasingly confronted by those who criticized the Nation for its nonactivism, he was likewise frustrated by the cultic chasm that prevented him from stepping up to the religious highground of orthodox Islam.

Still, 1963—Malcolm's last year in the Nation—was essentially characterized by his stubborn devotion to Muhammad's teachings, which he lauded as "our only solution." Similarly, Malcolm did not spare the Nation's Muslim critics—his best defense being the charge that Eastern Muslims had not promoted Islam as successfully as had Elijah Muhammad. Whatever fluctuations of faith and doctrinal conviction Malcolm experienced, he continued to make cultic warnings to his audiences, as he did on a Cleveland television show: "all Scripture," according to Elijah Muhammad, had predicted the fall of the European world after six thousand years of unjust rule.

Committed above all to Elijah Muhammad, Malcolm continued to sing his praises: "I was in prison in Massachusetts when I began to study the teachings of Muhammad. I had committed a crime. It was his teaching that saved me. This is when my life changed." However, Malcolm could not hide altogether that his life was still changing and that he would have preferred to proclaim a form of Islam that was not so much a black religion for black people exclusively, but a religion for all people.

"We are not Black Muslims," Malcolm preached to the students of Michigan State University, "we are Muslims. Islam is a religion of brotherhood in which color is not recognized."[8] In retrospect, it seems certain that Malcolm X already believed that Islam could make brothers of all men—even when those men were black and white. However, he was still loyal to Elijah Muhammad and could not stop believing in the man who had reached into his prison cell to save him in 1948. It was Elijah Muhammad himself who stood between Malcolm X and orthodoxy, not the teachings of the Nation.

Malcolm's first political biographer recognized that Malcolm "stretched the bounds of Muhammad's doctrine to the limit, and sometimes beyond. He introduced new elements into the movement, not only of style but of ideology."[9] Indeed, every significant study on the Nation discusses the central importance of Malcolm X to the development of Elijah Muhammad's organization, but there is considerably less appreciation for the religious elements he contributed and on the movement's impact on him as a religious man. This may be because generally the Nation was not recognized as a religious organization. This oversight is clearly the most common weakness in historical appraisals of the movement. In the rare cases when religiously sensitive analyses have been made, they usually lend Elijah Muhammad and his Muslims a legitimacy that does not clarify the movement's cultic nature and its ramifications.

For example, one religious study of Malcolm X and Martin Luther King, Jr., reflects such misunderstanding by viewing Malcolm X and the Nation only through black liberation theology, which judges the depth of religious commitment by one's dedication to justice. In "using the liberation activity of human beings as the lens through which one sees God," both Martin Luther King, Jr., and Malcolm X are seen as deeply religious persons. Malcolm X, like Dr. King, was deeply religious, but seeing him mainly as a black liberation activist tends to keep his theological and experiential religious views in the background. The important distinction between orthodoxy and cult (or new religion) is consequently overlooked.

For instance, liberation theology may observe great continuity between Dr. King's "personal vision of God" and Malcolm's prison vision of a man he took to be W. D. Fard. In such a perspective, the striking similarity of the two religious experiences are due chiefly to the black leaders' common grounding in the African American religious experience. While this perspective is valid, it does not provide sufficient criteria for evaluating the differences between King's and Malcolm's religious experiences—let alone the differences between Malcolm's religious life during and after his involvement in the Nation.[10] Similarly, one can say that the Nation was "specifically designed to address the spiritual, social, economic, and political needs of the black underclass"—in contrast to Euro-American Christianity, which was designed to fit the needs and desires of white racism.[11] This may be true insofar as liberation theology addresses the social and political aspects of religion. But insofar as theology and experience are concerned this analysis only creates further questions.

The black counterpart to Euro-American Christianity in the United States is, after all, African American Christianity—not cultic black "Islam." Indeed, the religious differences between African American Christianity and the Nation itself are profound and irreconcilable. Yet these differences, as in the case of Malcolm X, can be discerned only when religious orthodoxy and heresy are factored into the black religious experience as well. Thus, while liberation theology correctly maintains that the Nation provided a distinctly black religion, the abiding question remains: what kind of religion was it?

The need for such clarification is apparent when the leading black liberation theologian states that Malcolm X made a religious distinction between Elijah Muhammad as a "divine man" and Allah—in contrast to other Nation members, who revered Elijah Muhammad to the point of worship. Likewise, this analysis concludes that Malcolm X revered "the religion of Islam" above Elijah Muhammad, and was therefore able to "develop his own thinking about God." To verify this distinction, the same scholar notes an incident of reflection from *The Autobiography of Malcolm X*, pertaining to Malcolm's speech before the Harvard Law School Forum in Cambridge,

Massachusetts, on March 24, 1961. In this reflective moment at Harvard, Malcolm expressed awe at the great distance that Allah had brought him from his former life of sin, and he acknowledged that his reverence for Islam was even greater than his reverence for Muhammad.[12] In his autobiography, however, Malcolm wrote that his religious devotion to Elijah Muhammad was, in fact, tantamount to worship:

My adoration of Mr. Muhammad grew, in the sense of the Latin root word *adorare*. It means much more than our "adoration" or "adore." It means that my worship of him was so awesome that he was the first man whom I had ever feared—not fear such as of a man with a gun, but the fear such as one has of the power of the sun.[13]

Even granting that this unusual devotion is descriptive of Malcolm's earlier commitment to Elijah Muhammad and that it began to wane by 1961, the analysis of liberation theology still does not sufficiently explain the nature of Malcolm's religious experience—just as it does not sufficiently explain the kind of religious movement that could engender such an experience. Certainly, Malcolm's differing conceptions of Allah during and after his involvement in the Nation are not clarified. How did Malcolm perceive Allah? At the time Malcolm spoke at Harvard in 1961, did Elijah Muhammad's influence extend to Malcolm's understanding of Allah's nature, and did that understanding conform to the Qur'an?

In fact, as late as June 1963—less than a year before he would make Hajj as a Sunni Muslim—Malcolm X was arguing for a theological understanding of Allah that was distinctly Muhammad's own cultic formula. Malcolm X appeared on a New York City radio talk show, *Program P.M.*, in June 1963, which involved answering telephone questions. During the program, Malcolm broached the topic of divine nature and recalled that during his 1959 trip some Eastern Muslims had criticized him for holding to Muhammad's teaching that W. D. Fard was Allah incarnate. Malcolm explained:

My answer to them was that how could they believe that Allah is all powerful enough to create a universe—put a sun in the universe, many stars, and the planet upon which you and I live, plus all else that goes with it, showing that He's all powerful, all wise, all everything, and then doubt His power or ability to manifest Himself in the flesh.[14]

Malcolm further proclaimed that Muslim, Christian, and Jewish theology all agreed that God would "manifest Himself at the end of time" and bring an end to the "wicked world," replacing it with a "righteous kingdom."

Malcolm also appeared on a Norfolk, Virginia, late-night radio program in August 1963. Here Malcolm likewise told his radio audience that W. D. Fard's coming was in fulfillment of the prophecies of "Jewish theology," as well as the Islamic expectation of a coming "Mahdi" from the East. In fact, Malcolm X referred to W. D. Fard as "the Son of Man," a biblical title implying a divine-messianic nature, in both Hebrew and Christian scripture.[15]

In both cases, Malcolm appealed to Allah's power and sovereignty, and to messianic expectation, in order to justify the Nation's belief that W. D. Fard was Allah-in-the-flesh. This was hardly an Islamic notion of God and could just has easily have characterized a Christian's defense of the divine incarnation in Jesus Christ. How then may Malcolm's conception of Allah be perceived? Certainly, he was already heavily inclined toward orthodox Islam by 1963. How, then, could he have made—in Muslim terms—such a heretical appeal on behalf of Fard's divinity? Liberation theology's emphasis on black religion is inadequate without understanding Malcolm's relationship to Elijah Muhammad in cultic terms. If it is understood that, by 1962–63, Malcolm was experiencing the birth pangs of a new conversion and that his faith was constantly fluctuating between belief in Muhammad and belief in orthodox Islam, then a religious explanation may adequately account for these apparent conflicts within his statements.

Contrary to the idea that Malcolm X escaped the Nation's fanatical devotion to Elijah Muhammad, it seems that Malcolm's faith actually personified the most deeply entrenched cult devotion. Some Muslims, such as Malcolm's brother Wilfred, had joined the movement because the Nation had a good program for blacks; others joined because they believed in Elijah Muhammad's doctrine. But Malcolm's abiding commitment to the Nation had solidified at the point of his belief in Muhammad himself. As religion goes, Malcolm could jettison Muhammad's teachings, or shuffle them about in true cultic fashion, all without losing faith; but he could not easily surrender his faith in Muhammad.

When C. Eric Lincoln's *Black Muslims* was first revised and updated in the early 1970s, Elijah Muhammad was still alive, and the movement still endured. Only with Muhammad's death in 1975 did the Nation cease to exist as it had for the better part of four decades. In fact, when Warith (Wallace) Muhammad took his father's place as the new leader of the Nation, the movement converted to Sunni Islam. With Elijah Muhammad gone, the Nation's doors were opened to all true Muslims, black and white, and its heresies were purged in submission to the teachings of the Qur'an.[16]

Early on, Lincoln had observed the Nation's relationship to the Muslim world, and discerned that the bridges built by Afro-Asian Muslim leaders between themselves and the Nation were done so primarily out of political interest. Speaking of Elijah's pilgrimage in December 1959, Lincoln concluded that Elijah Muhammad could not have been admitted to Mecca without being sponsored by "powerful friends abroad." Even more, Elijah Muhammad's doctrines seemed, to Lincoln, to have disqualified the Nation from receiving religious sponsorship. Indeed, the Muslim leaders of the East considered taking the chance of inviting Muhammad to Mecca because the "political possibilities" outweighed the "religious risk." [17]

As it turned out, however, it is not clear that the "religious risk" was as great as it seemed, just as the pilgrimage itself was not what Muhammad and Malcolm made it seem to their adoring followers back home in the United States. As one critical young Sudanese student had discerned—much to Malcolm's dismay—Elijah Muhammad had not actually made Hajj. He had certainly gone to Mecca as an honored guest, but in Islamic standards Mr. Muhammad's pilgrimage to Mecca could did not prove his orthodoxy, regardless of the claims he and Malcolm X made afterwards.

In reality, by Islamic standards, as Malcolm himself would later reveal, Elijah only made *Omra*—a visit to Mecca, "outside of the *Hajj season*." [18] This explains not only why Malcolm lashed out so harshly at the Sudanese student who raised suspicions about Muhammad's pilgrimage, but it reveals the cultic intentions of the Nation's leadership in making Muhammad's pilgrimage more than it really was. The leaders of the Muslim East, especially those of Egypt, had apparently courted Muhammad in the hope that their friendship would win a pro-Arab voice in the black community, and possibly be an Islamic inroad as well.

For these gains they were willing to send an eminent leader like Mahmoud Youssef Shawarbi, a Cairo University professor, to flatter the Nation as a Muslim organization with a great mission. "We need you here to help bring the great truths of our faith to this country," Shawarbi proclaimed at a 1960 Nation rally. It may be that Shawarbi was thinking politically when he told the Nation that their role in the United States was to build up "understanding between the U.S. and Africa." [19] Regardless of what contacts were made between the Nation and the Muslim world, and despite the advantages Muhammad could claim in his pilgrimage, the Nation did not yield to the influence of the outside Muslim world—since Elijah Muhammad apparently had his own agenda.

Indeed, in retrospect, Malcolm X admitted that Elijah Muhammad had little sympathy for either the African or the Arab worlds—which leaves us to conclude that whatever investment Eastern Muslim leaders had made in the Nation had returned them nothing, either politically or religiously. "Muhammad does not want orthodoxy," Lincoln concluded of Muhammad's flirtation with the East. "Paradoxy will do."[20]

Despite its great value as a classic study of Malcolm X and the Nation, in the *Black Muslims* Lincoln has overestimated the religious legitimacy of the movement—even in his revised version he suggests that the Nation could lay claim to being a legitimate Islamic sect. In so doing, *Black Muslims* dissents from Milton Yinger's 1957 study that had classified the Nation as a cult. To justify this dissent, Lincoln maintains that the Nation was not a localized and isolated sect, and that it would probably endure after Elijah Muhammad's death. Lincoln predicted that the Nation's membership, which he estimated at between fifty and one hundred thousand, would be able to "draw upon the vast prestige and power of international Islam" in its defense. Lincoln reasoned that the Nation might be accepted even as "deviates," because of the need for Islam to "fit local conditions."

To buttress his argument, he cites the Ahmadiyya movement as an example of Islam's toleration and acceptance of "deviates." However, this thesis cannot be sustained, either by closer study or in the facts of history, and the older analysis of the Nation as a cult then stands all the more firm. In fact, the Nation's membership seems never to have been greater than twenty-five thousand at its peak in 1959–60, followed by a rapid decline by 1962. Furthermore, the Nation as it was defined and guided by Elijah Muhammad was never accepted by the Muslim world. Unlike the Ahmadiyya sect, the Nation remained beyond the pale of Islam, both theologically and geographically.

The greatest deficiency of *Black Muslims*, however, is its affirmation of Elijah Muhammad's cultic claim that Islam had to be rendered doctrinally deviant in order to become relevant to African Americans. In so doing, *Black Muslims* reinforces Elijah Muhammad's condescending remark, for instance, that *he* would not blame the Muslim world if they differed with the Nation over "certain interpretations."[21]

A true cult, Elijah Muhammad's Nation was a "tight communal group" united by an "unconventional religion" in tension with the rest of society. While the Nation was apparently in tension with white society, it was also at odds with the Muslim and Christian religious communities. The difference in the Nation's reactions to Islam and to Christianity had to do with how

Elijah Muhammad identified these tensions. As their unquestioned leader, his perception of how these tensions related to his notion of salvation defined how the Nation would react to them.[22]

In the case of Islam, the tensions felt by Muhammad and his Muslims were real but manageable. Consequently, the aggression of the Nation toward Islam was passive. Malcolm's barbed comments about certain Eastern Muslims notwithstanding, the threat posed by the Nation to traditional Islam was difficult to discern since it came wrapped in a cloak of Muslim unity. Yet inherent in Muhammad's claim "to cut the cloak to fit the cloth" was a rejection of the cultural forms of orthodox Islam, and its theological essence as well.[23]

# 13

## Fame and Fury

*You're having trouble because the devil is on the rampage!*

When he was asked about social equality for blacks on the WCBS radio program, *Let's Find Out*, Malcolm X decried the notion of racial equality based on white standards. "The white man is not the yardstick by which equality is measured." The yardstick, Malcolm maintained, was Elijah Muhammad's program of moral uplift, not the notion of achieving civil rights. He boasted of his Muslim rejection of the black status quo, and did so in a manner that was bound to keep even his black admirers at arm's length: "I deny my name and my background because I don't know enough about it. My skin is light, but I'm black inside. Most Negroes are white inside. That's what the American society has taught them. They are white Negroes."[1]

Even with all this spite, Malcolm X was increasingly drawn into the very realms he most readily assaulted. His rising public stature as a skilled debater and self-made intellect brought invitations to college and university campuses, often sponsored by black or racially mixed student organizations that were branches of civil rights groups. Ironically, Malcolm's growing popularity, which he fully exploited for the benefit of Elijah Muhammad, fueled his own transformation as well as the resentment of the Nation's leaders toward him, culminating in his falling-out with Muhammad at the end of 1963.

While Malcolm was enjoying popularity as the media nemesis of both whites and blacks involved in the civil rights movement, he found himself facing a two-sided war that grew in intensity in 1962–63. First, the Nation was targeted by the police, the press, and the judicial system. Physical attacks on Nation members in various cities were followed by legal indictments and press coverage that put the Muslim movement, especially Malcolm X himself, constantly on the defensive.

Second, the more publicity Malcolm enjoyed as the Nation's representative and defender, the more he began to experience the resentment and opposition of Muhammad's family, which sought to undermine his national influence in the movement. It is a testimony to Malcolm's deep religious commitment to Elijah Muhammad that these crises weakened but did not in themselves shatter his confidence in his leader. However, with his imminent fall from grace, Malcolm's views were sufficiently challenged, forcing him to break the chains of religious servitude.

Malcolm's popularity as a campus speaker had started as early as 1960, and before long he was well on his way to becoming one of the most popular personalities on the university speaking circuit. In the beginning, the very announcement of Malcolm's campus appearances created controversy. For example, his scheduled appearance at the University of California at Berkeley in May 1961 was canceled by the school's administration, purportedly because the university generally prohibited any kind of political or sectarian "influence." Malcolm X criticized the administration by pointing out that they apparently had less respect for their students than did the administrations of Harvard, Yale, Columbia, and Brown universities, where he had already spoken.

Ultimately, Malcolm's voice was not silenced. Not only did the Nation sponsor a well-attended rally at San Francisco's Fillmore Auditorium that same week, but Malcolm was given a hearing at the local YMCA hall on the University of California campus. The audience, which was predominately white, enthusiastically received Malcolm's speech—especially when he noted that the ban only underscored that "the older generation" was "trying to protect its system from young ideas." The fact that the Christian evangelist Billy Graham had recently spoken on campus was not a point that went unnoticed, either by Malcolm, the students, or the local chapter of the American Civil Liberties Union.[2]

At New York University's Heights campus in the Bronx, Malcolm spoke as an invited guest of the Department of Sociology in February 1962. "We don't have any confidence in the white man," Malcolm declared before an all-white student assembly. "I am not a white man. I am not a western man. I was brought here by your forefathers. We are the lost found [N]ation of Islam. We were kidnapped from our Islamic culture by slave traders 400 years ago." Calling African Americans a "lost people," Malcolm accused the white man of robbing "all human characteristics" from us for over three hundred years in slavery. Of the postemancipation period, Malcolm continued that the white man "turned us loose and brainwashed us with his own religion, [and] his own culture."

As usual, Malcolm also chastened black integrationists and their leaders in the civil rights movement as being "black on the outside, white on the inside." James De Metro, who covered the event for the student newspaper recalled that after the speech a student who was apparently neither black nor Muslim used the Qur'an in an attempt to justify integration on the basis of love and unity. Malcolm undoubtedly shot back with his favorite Qur'anic texts that reinforced a doctrine of separation between Muslims and Christians, and the imminent judgment of the "guilty blue-eyed."

In a presentation at the University of Chicago, Malcolm debated a representative of the Congress On Racial Equality (CORE), arguing with regard to blacks and whites that it was "impossible for the two of us to live side by side and have peace." When his opponent argued that integration was the "natural by-product" of black people's search for dignity, Malcolm charged that black integrationists had already spent $100,000 trying to integrate public facilities, when that money would have been better spent creating black-owned businesses and facilities for their own community. Besides, Malcolm concluded, the number of pro-integration blacks was really a minority within the overall black community.

Interestingly, a University of Chicago student who interviewed Malcolm X found him to be "intelligent, articulate, and extremely pleasant," quite in contrast to his media image. Although the student concluded that Malcolm maintained "an overly violent hatred" of whites, and that the Nation's "extremism" did not promote the best image, the young journalist felt that the Muslims were "totally non-violent" and that the Nation's leadership was "friendly and interested in convincing white people of their view point."

Controversy over Malcolm's appearances was not limited to predominately white campuses, however. In fact, Malcolm had been prevented from speaking at the most renowned black campus in the country, Howard University, in February 1961. The invitation he had to appear before the campus NAACP chapter was suddenly reneged when the administration explained that the event had not been cleared by the student activities office. When the students persisted and obtained use of an off-campus church for Malcolm's appearance, an NAACP official intervened and canceled the invitation, claiming the church was too small to house the event.[3]

The cancelation apparently did not bother Malcolm, probably because he knew that the incident would only spark more interest in the Nation among black students. In a letter to Elijah Muhammad, in fact, Malcolm took a most ironic approach to explain the cancelation: "We really threw a 'stone of stumbling' onto the Howard University campus because they are all divided and arguing now, and it places us in an even better position to pour 'boiling water' on them when we get there."

Malcolm X actually did get to Howard University later that year, appearing in a debate with integrationist leader Bayard Rustin—which was apparently the only acceptable platform that the university would grant a representative of the Nation. When the campus debate took place, Malcolm stole the show from the eloquent, scholarly Rustin—despite the political limitations of his appeal for separate land and his mockery of "20th Century Uncle Toms with top hats and doctoral degrees." Rustin, who later seems to have exaggerated his good rapport with Malcolm X, recalled that the administration at Howard University was fearful of offending the Congress by allowing Malcolm to appear—particularly because Howard's charter grew out of the Freedman's Bureau, which allocated financial support directly from Congress itself.

In the same letter that Malcolm wrote to Muhammad, he stated his enthusiasm for the "young generation" and his apparent desire to prove to Muhammad that the campus experiment was worthwhile. Noting that it was the students who were "arguing that *you* should be given the right to be heard," Malcolm assured Muhammad that they were "more sympathetic toward *you* than toward anyone else." Malcolm was patronizing him, of course, for it was not to Elijah Muhammad that the students were drawn, nor could they have been attracted to the aging leader and his lackluster oratory.

As Malcolm later admitted, Elijah Muhammad had never been enthusiastic about these campus appearances, and apparently Malcolm felt compelled to justify them to his leader. Nevertheless, he said he did not immediately realize that this negativity was based on envy, which Muhammad felt because he himself did not possess such intellectual prowess and oratorical charisma. However, Elijah Muhammad apparently controlled his envy for the sake of the respectability Malcolm was gleaning for the Nation through

1. After "electrifying" his Harlem audience the year before, Malcolm X was invited back to speak before the 1958 Marcus Garvey Day celebration. By this time Malcolm had already become a local legend as a leader in the Harlem community, a newspaper columnist, and a traveling speaker for the Nation of Islam. (Anonymous photographer, Photographs and Prints Division, Schomburg Center for Research in Black Culture, New York Public Library, Astor, Lenox, and Tilden Foundations.)

2. "I worshiped him." Malcolm X with Elijah Muhammad in 1958 when Muhammad visited New York City to address an overflow audience at Harlem's Park Palace. Photo by Austin Hansen.

3. "I could *feel* Mr. Muhammad's *power*," Malcolm later recalled of "the Messenger's" appearances before the Nation. Mr. Muhammad speaking at the Park Palace as Malcolm and other Nation dignitaries listen intently. Seated at Malcolm's right is Wallace Muhammad, who eventually succeeded his father as leader of the Nation and led the movement into traditional Islam. Photo by Austin Hansen.

4. Malcolm attending the opening of Abdul Basit Naeem's "Shalimar International Travel Service" ca. 1962 in New York, along with some Muslim dignitaries from the "Dark World." Naeem (*far left*, wearing astrakhan hat), a Pakistani Muslim, was a longtime supporter and ad hoc consultant to the Nation of Islam. (Photo by Robert Haggins. All rights reserved, copyright © 1983 by Robert L. Haggins.)

5. *Above*: On January 11, 1963, a demonstration was held by the Nation of Islam at Manhattan's Criminal Court building under the direction of Malcolm X. The demonstration was provoked by the arrest of two New York Muslims on Christmas Day 1962, and other incidents reflecting police hostility toward the "Black Muslims." (Photo by Robert Haggins. All rights reserved, copyright © 1983 by Robert L. Haggins.)

6. *Right*: At the demonstration scene, Malcolm X confers with Muslim associates from Mosque No. 7, Benjamin 2X *(left)* and Captain of the Fruit of Islam, Joseph X *(right*, facing Malcolm), along with the minister of the Nation of Islam mosque in Newark, New Jersey, James X *(center)*. (Photo by Robert Haggins. All rights reserved, copyright © 1983 by Robert L. Haggins.)

## America has become a Police-state for 20 Million Negroes

Here in the State of New York the Republican Administration of Governor Nelson Rockefeller and Senator Kenneth Keating is practicing criminal hypocrisy by attacking Mississippi's Ross Barnett and others in an effort to pose as a "friend" of the Negro . . . while at the same time right here in New York State they are waging a relentless campaign of harassment, inhuman persecution, and unlawful prosecution of all Negroes who want to reform themselves and live a clean Muslim life by practicing the religion of Islam and by following the spiritual guidance of the Honorable Elijah Muhammad.

Millions of dollars have been spent with public relations experts by political hypocrites to make Negroes think Rockefeller and Keating are white "liberals," and are friends of the Negro.

Negroes aren't fooled that easily today. Mr. Muhammad is opening the eyes of our people too fast for these "political tricksters" to put one over so easily as they once did. We see Mississippi's Ross Barnett and Arkansas's Orville Faubus as the vicious wolves that they are, who aren't cunning enough to hide their dog-like hate for Negroes . . .

But these awakened Negroes today, also see Rockefeller and Keating and the other phony so-called liberals here in the North for exactly what they are too. We see them as white FOXES: sly, tricky, deceitful, and cunning enough to pose as "friends" of the Negro.

But whites should never again think Negroes are still dumb enough to think the Northern Fox is any better or any different in MOTIVE than the Southern Wolf!

Both the Southern Wolf and the Northern Fox are of the CANINE family. BOTH ARE DOGS!!! They differ only in strategy, but their appetite and their intention is the same. They both have the same motive and objective when it comes to halting and victimizing defenseless Negroes.

Senator Kenneth Keating is using Cuba to distract attention from what is taking place in Rochester, New York; his own home town. Keating is crying for Castro's blood to keep you from seeing the blood of the Negroes in the Rochester area that is on his own hands.

How can Keating talk about Cuba when Negroes in Rochester, New York are living under the terror of a police-state. Real gestapo-type tactics are used daily to terrorize the Negro Community, suppressing their civil rights, their human rights . . . and even in Keating's home city of Rochester the gestapo-like police have invaded and broken up religious services that were being conducted there by the local minister.

In Rochester, police dogs are used to keep Negroes off the street, to keep Negroes from congregating, and to keep Negroes from uniting. Even more recently, the police in Rochester used their vicious dogs to invade and break up religious services that were being conducted there by the local minister.

To climax their reign of terror, last Friday a Rochester grand jury returned a secret indictment ordering the immediate arrest of 16 of the Negroes who attended the religious services at the time the Rochester gestapo broke into the religious services with their police dogs.

Thirteen of these innocent Negroes, including the local Muslim minister, were arrested, handcuffed, and jailed last Friday . . . and charged with 3rd degree assault and inciting to riot, simply because these innocent Negroes manifested open indignation at the gestapo-like manner in which the police disrupted their religious services.

Hitler's gestapo in Nazi-Germany did the same thing to the Jews, and now here in New York Governor Nelson Rockefeller sits silently by while HIS police use the same police-state methods to terrorize and suppress the Negro Communities of his state.

At this very moment thirteen innocent Negroes are in jail in Keating's home town. They have not eaten one bite since their arrest last Friday. They are not on a hunger strike . . . they are fasting and praying to ALLAH for His Divine Help, for His Divine Intervention.

We must let them know they are not alone. We must let them know that Harlem is with them. We must let them know that the whole Dark World is with them.

We must let the white man know that we will all go to jail today for what we believe. We will all fight for what we believe. We will all die for what we believe . . . but we must also let him know that we don't endorse the foolish philosophy of "turning the other cheek" . . . if we must die, we will not die alone!

We demand Justice or Death!!!!

---

8. A flier/poster advertising an "African Bazaar" sponsored by Mosque No. 7 in Harlem, featuring Malcolm X as keynote speaker. The poster, like the event itself, demonstrates the strong Africentric influence injected into the Nation of Islam by Malcolm X. (Flier from the BOSS files.)

7. A flier prepared by Malcolm X for the January 1963 demonstration. In it Malcolm charged that police had attacked the civil, human, and religious rights of African Americans. Characteristically, Malcolm identified the struggle of the Muslims with "the whole Dark World."

**AFRICAN BAZAAR**
SPONSORED BY THE
**MUSLIMS**
AT
**369th ARMORY**
Cor. 142nd Street and 5th Avenue, New York City
**SAT. SEPT. 21, 1963**
12 NOON TILL MIDNIGHT
EXHIBITS • DISPLAYS • BARGAINS GALORE

FEATURED SPEAKER **MALCOLM X**

ENTERTAINMENT BY
**OLATUNJI** AND HIS AFRICAN DRUMMERS
**DINIZULU** AND HIS AFRICAN DANCERS
Also Many Top Entertainers of Stage, Screen, Radio & T.V.

SUBSCRIPTION $2.00
FOR TICKETS AND BOOTH INFORMATION:
Shabazz Restaurant, 113 Lenox Ave. — MO 3-9772 — Manhattan
Muhammad Speaks News Office, 113 Lenox Ave. — AC 2-6522 — Manhattan
Shabazz Foods, 1892 Fulton St. — PR 1-9110 — Brooklyn
Shabazz Restaurant, 105-05 Northern Boulevard — TW 9-9635 — Long Island

🐾 JOIN THE MUSLIM BUS CARAVAN 🐾
TO HEAR:
**MESSENGER ELIJAH MUHAMMAD**
IN PHILADELPHIA
Subject: "SEPARATION OR DEATH"
SUNDAY, SEPTEMBER 29, 1963 - 2:00 P.M.
At the PHILADELPHIA ARENA, 46th and Market Street
BUS FARE ROUND TRIP - $3.75
Buses will leave from Manhattan at 8:00 A.M. from MUHAMMAD'S MOSQUE, 102 W. 116th St. (Cor. Lenox Ave.)
Buses will arrive back in New York City About 10 P.M. Sunday Night
FOR TICKETS AND INFORMATION:
SHABAZZ RESTAURANT, 113 Lenox Ave., Manhattan - MO 3-9772      SHABAZZ GROCERIES, 1892 Fulton Street, Brooklyn - PR 1-9110
MUHAMMAD SPEAKS News Office, 113 Lenox Ave., Manhattan - AC 2-6522 SHABAZZ RESTAURANT, 105-05 Northern Blvd., Long Island - TW 9-9635

---

9. "In The Middle," cartoon by Melvin Tapley, appeared in Harlem's *New York Amsterdam News* on March 14, 1964, and is quite significant for its grasp of the tensions that undoubtedly characterized Malcolm's first weeks as an independent but self-proclaimed loyalist to Elijah Muhammad, just prior to the Hajj. Note the contrasting political fist and minister's heavenward gesture. ("In The Middle" used by permission of Melvin Tarpley.)

**In The Middle**

10. Shaykh Ahmed Hassoun is introduced by Muslim Mosque, Inc., official, James Shabazz, on December 13, 1964, at an OAAU rally at New York's Audubon Ballroom. The elderly Muslim teacher was sent to the United States to assist the Muslim Mosque, Inc., in teaching Islam after Malcolm's second trip abroad in 1964. (Photo by Robert Haggins. All rights reserved, copyright © 1983 by Robert L. Haggins.)

11. At the meeting of the OAAU on December 13, 1964, the featured guest speaker was Abdul Rahman Muhammad Babu, one of the revolutionary leaders from the newly independent African nation of Tanzania. Babu *(right)* is seen here rising to greet Malcolm X and Shaykh Hassoun on the stage of the Audubon, a scene that reflects that Malcolm was equally comfortable with religion and revolution. (Photo by Robert Haggins. All rights reserved, copyright © 1983 by Robert L. Haggins.)

these campus appearances. "Brother Malcolm, I want you to become well known," Muhammad had formerly counseled his popular young lieutenant. "Because if you are well known, it will make *me* better known." However, there is little doubt that Malcolm's successes on the battlefield were a threat to Elijah Muhammad's traditional image within his own court as "the intellectual of the movement."[4]

For his part, Malcolm X said he enjoyed the campus audiences the best, except for black audiences. He found students to be "usually objective and always alive and searching" in their thinking. Benjamin Karim, who accompanied Malcolm to many campus meetings, recalled that "most students, black and white, received his message openly, and after a lecture would crowd around him, asking him all kinds of questions." Karim always believed the students were not only impressed by Malcolm, but that they really liked him.

Robert Little, who was a college student when Malcolm first started making his campus appearances, recalled that he attended a good many meetings, observing his famous brother in action. "He almost never pitched religion," Robert reminisced. However, when Malcolm did discuss it he generally encouraged students to reevaluate their religious assumptions critically. It was "a much higher-level pitch. . . . He went for the rational man— you know, the intellectual thought process."

Undoubtedly, Malcolm X enjoyed such meetings, even with the many white students he encountered—something that Alex Haley also observed: "I saw Malcolm X too many times exhilarated in after-lecture give-and-take with predominately white student bodies at colleges and universities to ever believe that he nurtured at his core any blanket white-hatred." Malcolm's accessibility to white students was no act, despite the isolated incident he recalled in his autobiography in which a white student, whom he turned away at the Muslim Luncheonette, fled Harlem in tears. When Joan Durham, another white student, decided to do her senior thesis on the Nation, she found Minister Malcolm X more than willing to sit for an extensive interview with her when she was home in New York City on Christmas vacation.[5]

Another young person, Charles Keil, was a student at Yale University who heard about Malcolm X from a black friend and came to Harlem repeatedly for sessions with him at the Muslim Luncheonette. "I told people at the time that far from feeling threatened or uncomfortable across the table from Malcolm, I felt clear and relieved of the burden of having to play a role or a game . . . the general feeling was of basic equality." Keil was set at ease by Malcolm's "pervasive sense of humor," and found that his "direct and forceful" manner of speaking to the issues set him at ease, and dispelled any need for what he calls "'race relations' etiquette."

Keil got to know Malcolm pretty well, and admired him a great deal. He particularly recalled that Malcolm used his gifts to emphasize Muhammad's words, "like a skillful interpreter deals with a great text, showing off the best parts." However, Keil also believed that Malcolm "was hiding behind Muhammad's Muslim correct line at times rather than thinking everything through for himself." What Keil recalled most dramatically, however, was the first time he saw Malcolm X within the context of a Nation meeting—a rally in New York City in which Elijah Muhammad appeared. Keil noted that Malcolm was warmly applauded; but when Muhammad appeared at the podium the rafters shook with the applause and roar of the crowd: "It suddenly became clear to me that Elijah Muhammad was a charismatic leader, full of magical power for his people, a little man saying great things to them, while Malcolm was one of many lieutenants . . . not the leader inside his movement that I had thought he was."[6] What Keil expressed, at least in part, was the disparity he recognized between the world of the Nation and the world outside. In the outside world, Malcolm X moved as Muhammad's awesome representative. Speaking, debating, conferring, and sitting for interviews, Malcolm's brilliance belied the actual deficiencies and aberrations of the Nation and its leader. However, inside the Nation, which was its own world—as is usually the case with cults—no charisma could be tolerated except that of the leader himself.

The cult leader, no matter how irrational it may seem to the outsider, is the supplier of existence to those who believe in him. This was no truer than for Malcolm X himself, who admitted to having been intensely consumed with the doctrines, ways, and wisdom of Elijah Muhammad, and who preached: "You can be around this man and never *dream* from his actions the power and authority he has." Indeed, Malcolm X claimed that at times he could actually feel emanations of power from Muhammad, particularly when the latter sat on stage, beatifically enthroned before his assembled Muslims. To the faithful, Elijah Muhammad was the charismatic center around which a whole new world was coming into being. "To us," Malcolm said, "the Nation of Islam was Mr. Muhammad. What bonded us into the best organization black Americans ever had was every Muslim's devout regard for Mr. Muhammad as black America's moral, mental, and spiritual reformer."

In this light it is easier to understand why Malcolm X, fighting the

Nation's battles on the outside, was indifferent to any harsh or critical statements made about him. However, when some uncharitable word was spoken against Muhammad, Malcolm noted, "I would grow furious." It is likewise clear why Malcolm's agony at his break with Muhammad would be great—finding in the midst of his warfare that neither the Nation nor its leader was able to return the love and devotion he had so fervently offered them.[7]

Though the Nation attained its peak of popularity within the African American community by 1960, the movement gradually began to lose steam immediately thereafter. Not surprisingly, the black press, which found itself in competition with Muhammad's successful weekly, gloated over the turning tide of popularity. James Hicks, the editor of the *Amsterdam News*, claimed that they had broken with Muhammad "because he was so out of line with everything we thought"—though ideology had not prevented them from having at one time published Muhammad's column.

It is likely that the *Amsterdam News* and other major black papers had begun to reconsider Muhammad. However, the point remains that *Muhammad Speaks* had established itself as competition, and the black press may have begun to minimize the Nation as much out of resentment as out of awareness of Muhammad's restrictive politics. By 1963, other black newspapers, such as Cleveland's *Call & Post*, were reporting that the Nation was faced with "growing disenchantment among the masses they would lead to a black man's utopia." This disenchantment, the article continued, not only reflected the organizational inadequacies of the Nation in the face of opposition but also its religion, which the writer characterized as "an intellectual wasteland."[8]

This is not to suggest, of course, that Muhammad's Muslims stopped making news in both the black or the white press; his columns did not altogether disappear from the pages of the black press, either. For Malcolm, however, admitting to the decline of the Nation was unthinkable. He perceived the Nation's role in the black struggle as being distinct from the civil rights organizations, which he viewed primarily as competition. "He viewed the Nation as a religio-political organization, the one that was best suited for achieving freedom, justice, and equality for blacks in America." Malcolm told one Norfolk, Virginia, radio audience in 1963 that the Nation followed Master Farrad [Fard] Muhammad, "our Messiah. He is the [S]on of [M]an, not a spirit. He was born for searching out the Biblical lost sheep. Muslims cannot be equated with civil rights groups. We are a religious group seeking the right to practice our religion."

Malcolm maintained in interviews throughout the country that this religion, "the divine solution" offered by Fard through Elijah Muhammad, still attracted black people. And while he had to admit indirectly that the Nation was not the mass movement it was once said to be, Malcolm alluded to its grassroots influence in the African American community nationwide. "There is some Muslim in a whole lot of Negroes," Malcolm told one white journalist; in an interview with a black journalist, Malcolm teased, "The most important part of the keg of dynamite is the fuse. Give me the fuse anytime."

However, in his own mind, Malcolm X was convinced that the Nation could enhance its public image if it would only become more action oriented. "I thought privately that we should have amended, or relaxed, our general non-engagement policy," he later admitted. And if one charge haunted Malcolm X the most, it was that the Nation was a "talk-only" organization. Such criticism was often leveled by civil rights activists who recognized the Muslims as being perpetually on the sidelines of the struggle but never in the battle itself. While this charge was probably wearing away at Malcolm's armor of devotion to the Nation, he was quite skillful at playing it down, as he did in an interview at the University of California at Berkeley in 1963, when he said black civil rights activists were "foolish" to get "involved with an enemy." Whatever came upon them, Malcolm concluded, was their business, and was not a concern of the Nation.[9]

Malcolm was not only evading a discussion about general noninvolvement, but he was also trying to avoid having to explain why the Nation had failed to respond with force when its own members were physically attacked. Between 1962 and 1963, several incidents took place in which white policemen made bold assaults on the Nation. These attacks seem to have been deliberate and malicious strikes at the Nation itself, and they were probably designed to either provoke or intimidate the whole movement. Furthermore, in earlier clashes between individual Muslims and law enforcement officers, the cases generally ended either in détente or with the Nation winning huge monetary awards in court. In the police assaults of 1962–63, however, insult was added to injury by the indictment of Nation members as well.

These events occurred against the backdrop of other anti-Nation incidents in 1962–63, including a failed attempt on the part of a Southern congressman to turn the Nation over to a House on Un-American Activities Committee investigation.[10] In addition, Malcolm was blocked from participation in a rally of the Southern Christian Leadership Conference (SCLC) that was held to protest an incident in Los Angeles. Further, the Nation was receiving a new wave of acerbic media criticism as other legal problems arose across the country involving Nation members. "You wonder why you're having trouble in this country," Malcolm exclaimed in a Harlem rally. "You're having trouble because the devil is on the rampage! A blue-eyed devil is on the rampage . . . and you haven't got sense enough to know how to handle him!"[11] With all of these burdens weighing upon him, Malcolm was understandably concerned for the welfare of the Nation; but other burdens were developing as well.

During this critical period Marc Crawford, a freelance journalist, sought out Malcolm X for an interview. Crawford and another African American journalist were finally able to track down Malcolm in Chicago, at Mosque No. 2. Crawford, who had not met Malcolm before, figured that his best ploy for obtaining an exclusive interview would be to remind him of the looming congressional investigation and to advise that Malcolm would do well to talk to the press beforehand. "I kept hammering away, and painting the ugliest of scenarios about what would befall him," he said.

However, instead of showing consternation, as Crawford had hoped, Malcolm merely turned around and walked to the window, standing there for a couple of minutes, saying nothing—only looking out at the birds that were perched, singing in the trees. Suddenly, Malcolm turned to Crawford and said, "Sir, I do not believe even a bird can fly unless Allah wills it so. Good afternoon gentlemen." Though his ploy had crumbled before the firmness of Malcolm's faith, Crawford recalled that he was struck by Malcolm's serenity: "I was won over by his calm."

Crawford and Malcolm X became friends after this initial encounter, but the young journalist still puzzled over the fact that such a bright man could "accept so thin a porridge of ideology" as was offered by Elijah Muhammad. Yet, it was hard to refute Malcolm's charge, Crawford admitted. "He did not temporize. His commitment was whole. There were no angles—which was part of his undoing . . . Malcolm threatened people in the Movement."[12]

Undoubtedly Malcolm's troubles within the Nation did not begin with direct resistance from Elijah Muhammad. While Muhammad was probably envious of Malcolm's growing popularity as well as his ability to dynamically communicate the Nation's message, there was still an undeniable affection between the elder and his young lieutenant that would not be easily undermined. After all, while Muhammad had created a cultic world of redemption for Malcolm, the latter had refurbished that world in ways the leader of the Nation had never anticipated. "And Malcolm just made a whole new world for [Elijah Muhammad]. He started bringing in money," Wilfred Little recalled. "[M]oney started coming in from all over the country . . . into headquarters, and for the first time they were finding themselves without a problem as far as finances were concerned."

Not only did Malcolm upgrade the movement, but he had personally taken it upon himself to elevate Elijah Muhammad's family by providing them remunerative positions in and through the Nation. Malcolm X recounted in his autobiography that by putting on "a special drive" he had raised money that funded new business endeavors for Elijah Muhammad's children, or that allowed them to earn professional salaries by working in the Nation itself. In the process, Herbert Muhammad received the editorship of *Muhammad Speaks* and moved the newspaper's offices permanently to Chicago. "I felt that I should work for Mr. Muhammad's family as sincerely as I worked for him," Malcolm concluded. Betty Shabazz later recalled that "Malcolm used to say that one of the worst things to do is to give an ignorant man power"—but he never applied this rule to Elijah Muhammad's family, she concluded.

Nevertheless, for his deeds of devotion, Elijah Muhammad praised Malcolm, even in public, such as in the Nation's 1962 convention, when he declared: "Minister Malcolm is a much better speaker than I am, and I'm blessed to have such an assistant." At a Nation rally in Milwaukee, Wisconsin, Muhammad boasted that anywhere he went Malcolm would also be found. "He will go everywhere—North, South, East or West, to China if I say go to China, he will go there. So I thank Allah for my Brother Minister Malcolm." [13]

Apparently Elijah Muhammad was not exaggerating. In early 1961, in fact, Malcolm was sent South, though the distance he traveled—figuratively speaking—was much further than China. On January 28, 1961, Malcolm and Jeremiah Shabazz, the Nation's minister in Atlanta, met with representatives of the KKK. It seems that Elijah Muhammad had agreed to establish clandestine communication with the white racist organization, since the latter were interested in making land available to the Nation for settlement. As Malcolm X later revealed, the KKK thought that land would make the Muslim program appear more attractive to African Americans in general, and hoped the Nation's consequent success would weaken the influence of the integrationist movement. According to Malcolm's account, the secret alliance—despite an earlier exchange of polemical letters between Klan chief J. B. Stoner and Elijah Muhammad—provided for a kind of mutual nonaggression pact between the two organizations. [14] Malcolm was undoubtedly disturbed by having been sent to represent the Nation in this southern summit; he said later that Elijah Muhammad never again sent him South, and reiterated that he never went South anymore after that incident.

That Malcolm never again went South on behalf of the Nation may suggest that he had protested the secret meeting to Elijah Muhammad afterwards. However, it may also reflect one aspect of Malcolm's growing internal conflict with the Nation—a maturing realization that the movement was evolving into something he could not justify, even with regard to his religious faith in Elijah Muhammad. As Malcolm recalled, it was in the early 1960s that he first began to hear "chance negative remarks," "veiled implications," and "other little evidences" of the burgeoning resentment toward him in the Nation. However, Malcolm X drew strength and assurance from his belief that Muhammad was supporting him. Indeed, Elijah Muhammad himself had "prophesied" to Malcolm that such jealousies would develop.

At the same time, Malcolm X began to note that *Muhammad Speaks* no longer made mention of him, even when he had conducted significant programs that were vital to the Nation; he also began to experience what he called "a chilly reaction" from Muhammad's Chicago officials. Malcolm's knee-jerk response was an understandable resentment. Yet even these natural sentiments were overpowered by his devotion to Muhammad, which forced him to repent his self-perceived "weakness" and look beyond these criticisms toward the greater good of the Nation.

This greater good, which has been called the "plausibility structure" of cults in general, is really the social base of affirmation for its members—allowing for suspension of all doubts. Like other cults, the Nation's plausibility structure was its religious base—and this was firmly centered in Elijah Muhammad. As a minister of the Nation, Malcolm X had enforced sanctions against other members for expressing opposition to Muhammad. Malcolm had gone so far as to sever relations with his own brother Reginald, whom he even turned away from the door of the Temple No. 7 Luncheonette in New York.

However, cult sanctions may also be internalized by the individual in the form of self-criticism and imputed to one's personal defects or weaknesses. Not surprisingly, then, Malcolm loyally imposed the charge of "weakness" upon himself and then sought to accommodate Muhammad and his supporters by taking every measure to deemphasize his own role in the Nation. Consequently, even the FBI noted that Malcolm canceled a university speaking engagement in October 1962, due to "throat trouble," and apparently postponed further engagements. Malcolm also declined major news interviews out of concern for jealousies within the Nation.[15]

The jealousy and envy of his peers and the Nation's officials was not a new occurrence, however. As early as June 1961, Wallace Muhammad, who was no enemy of Malcolm, told a colleague at a large Nation rally in Washington, D.C.: "Malcolm is on the mountain now, and it's made of ice and meltin' fast." But Malcolm was not insensitive to the heat of envy that emanated from his peers and from Chicago headquarters. This is why he would often give out photographs of Elijah Muhammad instead of his own, and he was known to become publicly indignant when reporters and journalists addressed him as Muhammad's "Number Two Man."

Writing in his own defense, Malcolm declared: "I have called up reporters and radio and television newscasters long-distance and asked them never to use that phrasing again, explaining to them: '*All* Muslims are number two—after Mr. Muhammad.' " Malcolm was not exaggerating. Louis Lomax, who had once been the Nation's journalistic gadfly, remembered Malcolm's emotional response to an *Amsterdam News* article that had suggested that only a "minor" difference existed between the roles of Muhammad and Malcolm in the movement: "It's a lie. . . . There is no such thing as a 'minor' difference with the Messenger. Any difference with him is *major*. . . . I am his slave, his servant, his son. He is the leader, the only spokesman." Malcolm did not limit these expressions to private protest, either. Appearing on a panel discussion show with journalist George Schuyler and the popular writer James Baldwin, he was introduced by the host as the Nation's "Number Two Man." At his first opportunity to speak, Malcolm denied that he held any such position in the Nation.[16]

Even Elijah Muhammad, who was doubtlessly being harangued by his family for indulging his young lieutenant, found Malcolm's attempts at self-abnegation somewhat extreme. As late as 1963, when Malcolm's opponents within the Nation had become actively committed to destroying his influence, FBI telephone surveillance recorded Elijah's almost fatherly doting over the fact that Malcolm was, in fact, his "right arm." There was no need for him to resist the appellation of "Number Two Man," Elijah assured Malcolm in another conversation, since no one was "more next to him" anyway. However, Malcolm would have none of these kindly assurances; he insisted that the press used the "Number Two" title only to create division.[17]

In 1963, Malcolm X was an important figure in the media—as much as on the campus speaking circuit. However desperately he tried to keep Elijah

Muhammad in the spotlight, the reality was that any reference to the "Black Muslims" was usually associated with Malcolm. It was Malcolm X, and not Elijah Muhammad, who made news. In May 1963, for instance, Malcolm moved to Washington, D.C., to promote and lead the Nation's mosque in that city while a new minister was being selected. His arrival in the capital made headlines, as did his sharp criticism of President Kennedy—who he said had the wrong motivation with regard to civil rights.

Speaking of the president's recent meeting with some white newspaper editors from Alabama, Malcolm declared that Kennedy had "urged a change not because it is right but because the world is watching this country . . . he did not open his mouth in defense of the Negroes." Indeed, the *Washington Post* noted that an "informed source" at the same meeting recounted that the president had specifically held up the "Black Muslims" as an example of the new "extremism" among black leaders—a jab that very likely caught Malcolm's attention. In turn, Kennedy was perhaps stung by Malcolm's well-publicized criticism—though the president's response seems to have been low-key. In speaking to the press about the controversy his administration had faced regarding the proposed TFX fighter plane, Kennedy slipped in a comment about Malcolm's presence in Washington: "We have had an interesting six months . . . with TFX and now we are going to have his brother Malcolm for the next six."[18]

Malcolm, however, probably found it difficult to keep a low profile, not only because the media would not allow him to do so, but because he was changing steadily into his own man. Benjamin Karim, the assistant minister at Mosque No. 7 in New York, recalled that "Malcolm was beginning to feel the limitations of Mr. Muhammad's teachings and the restraints of the [Nation]. Malcolm's intellect had begun to outgrow [Nation] doctrine . . . and he had to move where his mind took him." It is interesting that Malcolm told a journalist in the early 1960s that his extreme religious ardor had begun to wane after he came out of prison. In fact, this was more likely an expression of Malcolm's feelings at the time of the interview. Contrary to his claim, every evidence of his exhaustive labors, fervent preaching, and rapturous writings on behalf of Muhammad suggests the post-prison Malcolm was the Nation's preeminent religious zealot.

In the early 1960s, however, Malcolm became steadily disenchanted with his religious life. In the midst of what he perceived as an ongoing assault by the police and the government upon the movement, Malcolm X was increasingly frustrated by the Nation's lack of involvement in the struggles of African

Americans. As much as he had begun to outgrow the cultic religion of the Nation, Malcolm had also begun to outgrow the narrow limits of Elijah Muhammad's escapist political method.[19]

Key to Malcolm's disenchantment were attacks by police, the first being a violent invasion of the Nation's Los Angeles mosque in the spring of 1962. Equally disappointing to Malcolm was the passive and ineffectual manner in which Muhammad responded. The incident erupted after the Los Angeles police apparently incited an altercation with two Muslims on the street; however, backup units went directly to the mosque, interrupting a service. The unarmed Muslims in the mosque fought the intruders but were shot down; among the fallen, one Muslim died and another was permanently disabled. Worse, these Muslims were indicted and found guilty (in 1963), while the police were entirely exonerated.[20]

Upon receiving word of the attack, Malcolm wept. The Los Angeles mosque was one he had founded, and the dead Muslim was an old friend. Canceling a speaking engagement, he immediately flew out to Los Angeles to preside over the funeral—probably expecting, as the other Muslims certainly did, to receive some plan of action from Elijah Muhammad. Instead, the Muslims were told, "Hold fast to Islam." The only subsequent campaign launched by Mr. Muhammad was a new drive for sales of *Muhammad Speaks*.

As Malcolm X saw it, the net result was a loss of respect for the Nation among the black masses—a telling bruise on the face of a movement that always claimed it believed in self-defense. To his closest followers in the New York mosque, Malcolm complained: "We spout our militant revolutionary rhetoric and we preach Armageddon . . . but when our own brothers are brutalized or killed, we do nothing. . . . We just sit on our hands." Though Malcolm's hands were restrained by the Nation, he nevertheless retaliated— his warfare being limited to angry words, which he spewed out at every opportunity throughout the following year against the "gestapo tactics that are practiced in Nazi America against Black people."[21]

It seems that the Los Angeles incident actually marked the beginning of a new nationwide attitude of law enforcement militancy toward the Nation. While police brutality was always a factor of life for urban blacks, especially in Los Angeles, one may assume that this incident was critically observed by—if not modeled for—other major city governments and constabularies throughout the nation, especially those with large black populations. The Los Angeles Police Department boasted about its superior intelligence program, and Chief of Police Parker—no friend of the black community—

openly declared his liaison with individuals and police officers in every major city in the country.

While Malcolm X was still dealing with the aftermath of the Los Angeles incident, two crises occurred in New York State. On Christmas Day 1962, two Muslims selling *Muhammad Speaks* papers at Times Square in New York City were arrested when they scuffled with a policeman who had harassed them unnecessarily. Before their trial could even open, police in Rochester, New York, attempted to invade the Nation's mosque on January 6, 1963. The Rochester incident, which ended with the arrests and indictment of sixteen Muslims, was apparently initiated by a bogus call to the police about a gunman in the Muslims' building. In Rochester, Malcolm X warned reporters that their city "may be a precedent-setting city for police hostility toward Muslims." However, Malcolm was probably aware that the precedent had already been set.

The arrests in New York City and Rochester prompted Malcolm to organize demonstrations, the first of which took place outside City Hall in New York after the two Muslim newspaper salesmen were found guilty on January 11, 1963. Malcolm likewise sent telegrams of protest to both Mayor Wagner and Police Commissioner Murphy of New York, and to Manhattan District Attorney Frank Hogan. During the protest at City Hall, Malcolm and the Muslims passed out a flier declaring, "America has become a Police-state for 20 Million Negroes." The flier accused New York's Governor Rockefeller and Senator Keating of "waging a relentless campaign of harassment, inhuman persecution, and unlawful prosecution" of the Muslims. The flier also referred to the disruption of Muslim services in the Rochester mosque as "gestapo-like," and bore in its challenge to black people Malcolm's own inimitable signature: "We must let [the Rochester Muslims] know they are not alone. We must let them know that Harlem is with them. We must let them know that *the whole Dark World is with them.*" [22]

Malcolm struck back with a second wave of protests the following month, leading a contingent of 230 Muslims in a Times Square demonstration on February 13, 1963—which was itself an act of defiance, since there was a general ban on demonstrations at Times Square. When the police warned him in advance about the ban, Malcolm said he was only going to exercise his rights as a citizen to walk at Times Square, and anyone who wanted to follow him had the same right. Asked why he insisted on this move, Malcolm responded that he expected to be the next Muslim minister to be subpoenaed, as ministers had been in several other cities. On February 16, 1963, Malcolm sent a telegram to Attorney General Robert F. Kennedy, protesting invasion of the Nation's religious services by police. Malcolm warned that an "explosive current is building up in the Negro community against these police-state conditions." He further demanded an immediate investigation by the government, and charged that New York State had "become worse than Mississippi, and the city of Rochester has become worse than Oxford and Jackson, Mississippi combined."[23]

A year after the Los Angeles incident Malcolm was still catching the fall-out of resentment from the media over a particularly disturbing speech he had given in that city during the aftermath of the attack. Sometime after the attack, an airplane carrying mostly passengers from the United States had crashed in France, killing all on board. As it turned out, over one hundred of the crash victims were whites from the state of Georgia who were apparently considered some of the leading representatives of the southern artistic community. Malcolm had actually predicted divine retaliation before the crash had even occurred; he immediately interpreted the plane crash as God's retributive justice—especially after a Los Angeles coroner's inquest had ruled in favor of the police in the incident there.[24]

What particularly galled the press was that Malcolm had seized upon the crash during a Nation rally in Los Angeles, and he openly reveled in what he joyfully welcomed as God's defense of the Muslims. "I got a wire from God today," Malcolm proclaimed amid the laughter of his audience. "[S]omebody came and told me that he really had answered our prayers over in France. He dropped an airplane out of the sky with over 120 white people on it because the Muslims believe in an eye for an eye and a tooth for a tooth (cheering and applause)."[25] One writer has noted that Malcolm had danced on the graves of these crash victims, figuratively speaking, probably for lack of any other form of "satisfying retaliation." Thus, Malcolm declared: "We call on our God. He gets rid of 120 of them in one whop. But thanks to God, or Jehovah or Allah, we will continue to pray and we hope that every day another plane falls out of the sky."

What the media overlooked, however, was that Malcolm's comments about the plane crash were actually quite consistent with the theological premises of the Nation, which taught its members they were a divinely chosen people struggling for freedom from a "modern day Pharaoh" in the "wilderness of North America." As disturbing as the celebration over the crash may have been, Malcolm X was actually posturing consistently with the kind of elation the chosen people of the Bible expressed over the destruction of their enemies.

Indeed, in a later interview, Malcolm directly compared the plane crash to the "hand of God" drowning the armies of Pharaoh in the Red Sea, pointing out that the Hebrews also rejoiced at the deaths of the Egyptians. "Instead of God letting Moses weep and moan over Pharaoh's destruction he told Moses, 'Don't you weep and don't you moan, that's Pharaoh and his entire army that's being drowned.' " Malcolm was actually quoting a black Christian spiritual instead of the Bible or the Qur'an, but his point was nevertheless compatible with the Nation's theological self-definition.

His critics, of course, could only hear Malcolm's words through the ear of modern liberal and ecumenical religious ideas. Dr. Ralph Bunche, an African American serving as Under-Secretary of the United Nations, quickly dismissed Malcolm X as having a "depraved mind"; and the chasm that had already developed between the Muslims and an alliance of ninety Los Angeles clergymen was undoubtedly widened even more after Malcolm's exultation was publicized.

Neither Muhammad nor the Nation apparently found the controversial statement to be offensive, and Muhammad himself later attributed the plane crash to "Allah's doing." Malcolm himself continued to proclaim God's judgment in the incident throughout the following year. In a Nation rally in Harlem he declared that the black divinity made white people's planes and trains crash, and their boats and submarines sink to the bottom of the ocean. "That's a good God. He remembers your enemies," Malcolm concluded. On the late-night television program the *Ben Hunter Show*, also broadcast in Los Angeles, Malcolm appeared in March 1963 and told the host that when the crash occurred he did not think it was a coincidence that most of the victims were from Georgia. Malcolm pointed out, as he did many other times, that Billy Graham had referred to the plane crash as an act of God. "In fact," Malcolm concluded, "I still believe that it is an act of God and I thank God for it."

In the summer of 1963, over a year after the controversial plane crash statement, Malcolm was still defending himself. As a guest on Barry Farber's New York City radio talk show, Malcolm parried his host's criticisms, declaring, "You act like I made that plane crash!" When Farber suggested that his Muslim guest seemed happy about the disaster, Malcolm responded, "I was thankful that God brought some white people out of the sky and dashed them to pieces on this earth." Farber, by now enraged, reminded Malcolm that shortly after the plane crash in France, another plane had crashed while carrying Indonesian Muslims to Saudi Arabia. Farber asked Malcolm if this was also the hand of God. Malcolm responded, "Everything that falls out of the sky today is the hand of God."

Malcolm had made his point clear—whether or not Farber and his radio audience could accept it. As far as Malcolm X was concerned, the prophesied judgment of God was falling on white people for their past and present sins against the black man. "All these scriptures are catching up with the white man today. All the chickens are coming home to roost," he concluded.[26] In retrospect, it is interesting that Malcolm X would speak of mortals plummeting downward according to divine will. His own descent from the cultic Muslim sky of the Nation was imminent. By invoking the proverbial chickens of judgment, Malcolm ironically seems to have been rehearsing his own tragic fall.

# 14

## Banished from the Nation

*I am, and always will be a Muslim.*

Malcolm's wife, Betty Shabazz, has said that her husband preached to others that Elijah Muhammad was morally infallible. Indeed, according to Malcolm's reasoning, "Allah had gone into [Elijah Muhammad], taken his heart out, overhauled and cleansed it, and then put it back in so he could do no wrong." However, she has also said that Malcolm was aware of Elijah Muhammad's moral weaknesses for a long time before he would admit to them, perhaps because he was afraid it would ruin the Nation. According to Betty Shabazz, when Malcolm was willing finally to acknowledge that Elijah Muhammad was contradicting his own moral teachings, he also began to remember things he had been told about "the Messenger"—things "that he had forgotten (or just put out of his mind)."

The things he remembered, specifically, were rumors and comments about Elijah Muhammad's sexual immorality. Malcolm said he had heard these rumors as early as 1955 but his "depth of faith" in Muhammad's holiness was so great as to prevent him from listening to them, let alone believe that they were true. Malcolm said that as evidence of Muhammad's repeated adulteries began to pile up in late 1962, he would feign ignorance rather than deal with the problem head on. Shabazz recalled that Malcolm phoned her one day after having seen three young women with young children who were fathered by Muhammad. At the time, the young mothers had apparently sought out Muhammad for assistance, only to be turned away. "The foundation of my life seems to be coming apart," Malcolm lamented to his wife. He had found in Elijah Muhammad a moral and spiritual model, a symbol of reform, and he held onto this perception as if his life depended on it.[1]

For this reason, Malcolm apparently ignored the pressing gravity of Muhammad's sin and hypocrisy. He had, after all, built up Elijah Muhammad as a cult leader; his first inclination was to join Muhammad in camouflaging these sins by adjusting his own teachings. At this point, Malcolm was already predisposed toward making his messages more political and social, as evidenced generally in his maturing years in the Nation. However, the nightmare of Muhammad's sins "only accelerated the pace" of Malcolm's drive toward a black nationalism unshrouded by religious garb. Perceiving that the Nation no longer had a moral foundation in their leader, Malcolm X began to talk to Muslim audiences about social, political, and current events rather than matters of religion and morality.

"I can't describe the torments I went through," Malcolm later recalled of those days in 1963 when he found Muhammad's sins had become impossible to ignore. In his own thoughts he saw Muhammad's sexual misconduct as a betrayal of the Nation, especially since the young women who were victimized were from within the movement—and had been officially excommunicated from the cult by Muhammad himself. According to his own account, however, Malcolm's first inclination was to search for a scriptural "bridge" that would traverse the gaping chasm of Muhammad's sins by justifying them according to biblical and Qur'anic "prophecy."

Malcolm had often selected scriptures from the Bible in order to establish Muhammad as a "divine man"; now he desperately scoured its pages to find "prophetic symbols" that could redeem both Muhammad's reputation as well as his own faith in Muhammad, such as accounts of adultery and incest among biblical characters. Still, as Marc Crawford recalled, Malcolm had been the one who actually recruited these promising young women from throughout the Nation, sending them to Muhammad's bosom with the assurance they would be given career and educational opportunities. Part of Malcolm's sense of betrayal, then, was his own feeling of accountability to these young women, their families, and the trust of the Nation on a whole. "He had that sense of responsibility for what he did . . . Malcolm did not walk over people."[2]

By April 1963 Malcolm decided that he had to address the issue personally and flew to Phoenix, Arizona, to meet Muhammad in his winter home. Malcolm told Muhammad what he had heard about the young women, and that he had found biblical and Qur'anic passages that might be used, "if it became necessary," to present the sexual affairs as "the fulfillment of prophecy." Muhammad, who stood otherwise without excuse, immediately blessed Malcolm's submission to the "prophetic fulfillment" notion, at the same time praising him for his "good understanding" of prophecy and "spiritual things."

It was undoubtedly a shabby redemption, but Malcolm returned to New York and forced himself to remain quiet—hoping that Muhammad would put his sins aside for good. Unfortunately, in October 1963 Wallace Muhammad told Malcolm "that this thing was as bad as it ever was," since the elder Muhammad continued his sexual misconduct.

Had Malcolm chosen to remain as quiet as the rest of the informed leadership had been (for reasons either of fear or indifference), his enemies in the Nation would not have gained an advantage. However, he now apparently felt obliged to come to Muhammad's defense and therefore quietly informed other Nation ministers about the new "prophetic" strategy to explain Muhammad's illicit sexual liaisons. Not surprisingly, some of them already knew of Muhammad's affairs, including Louis X [Farrakhan], the minister of the Nation's Boston mosque.

In fact, it was Louis X who deliberately told Muhammad about Malcolm's words to the East Coast ministers. Louis X had already shown himself to be a fastidious guardian of Muhammad's public image—possibly because he himself was envious of Malcolm's close rapport with "the Messenger." An FBI source had noted in 1959 that during a visit to the main office of the *Pittsburgh Courier*, Louis X had visibly chafed when he was asked about the imminence of Malcolm's assumption of leadership. In fact, Malcolm's young colleague fumed—complaining that the *Courier* gave Malcolm X too much coverage and did not give priority to Muhammad. Now Malcolm had provided his enemies in the Nation with the justification they needed to remove him for good. "Hating me was going to become the cause for people of shattered faith to rally around," he concluded quite correctly. [3]

Malcolm gave his opponents in the movement a critical opportunity to attack him after a speech he made in New York City on December 1, 1963—an event that would prove to be his last address on behalf of the Nation. In a prophetic-styled presentation, he repeatedly criticized the recently assassinated President John F. Kennedy, prompting questions from white reporters about the assassination. Against Muhammad's direct order to all of his ministers to remain silent on the Kennedy assassination, Malcolm spoke of it as a prophetic judgment on the United States, as a "case of the chickens coming home to roost."

To be sure, Malcolm's spontaneous comment was a direct contradiction of Muhammad's orders. However, it appears to have been an inevitable expression of his developing independence of thought, and perhaps an aspect of his religious desperation—an act that showed his languishing faith in Elijah Muhammad.

Even though Malcolm later sensed within himself that his act was "part of Divine prophecy," he could hardly have been prepared for the agonizing separation that lay ahead. He was immediately silenced by Elijah Muhammad, ostensibly for a period of ninety days. At first, Malcolm held high hopes of being restored to active ministry; but as weeks turned into months, he began to see, as Wilfred Little recalled, that "it didn't appear that there was any intention of him coming back at all—it was as if he was gradually being banished." And Malcolm himself would later admit, "I was just wasting away."[4]

After having been silenced, Malcolm learned that the entire Nation had been informed that he would be restored when he had "completely submitted." Malcolm, who had completely submitted from the first moment, now felt himself helplessly falling into the depths of despair. When the reality of his vulnerable position began to set in, he found himself desperately struggling to find his way back.

Unable to speak or teach, Malcolm buried himself in his copious notes of Muhammad's table talk. Thus, Mosque No. 7 carried a pleasant little announcement in its regular newsletter stating that while Minister Malcolm was "benefitting from the rest he is getting," he was secretly working on a publishable manuscript tentatively entitled, "The Messenger's Dinner Conversation."[5]

Malcolm also began to send to Elijah Muhammad what would become a long string of letters, humbly begging for reinstatement. One such letter, written somtime between December 1963 and early January 1964, began with Malcolm's appeal to Muhammad that a major reason that others wanted them to split apart was "because they know Allah has blessed me to be your best representative as well as your best defender. The only ones here who may think I'm against you are the ones that are not really with you themselves. This is a dangerous position to be in, because it only adds division upon division." In this letter, Malcolm compared himself with the biblical characters Isaac and Job, both of whom he presented as symbols of his own submission and vulnerability. Malcolm mentioned his notes on Muhammad's table talk, noting there was "both hope and life in your words." He promised that he could turn these notes into a powerful book to further advance the Nation—if only Muhammad would "have mercy" and restore him to the ministry.[6]

This letter, like Malcolm's other letters, seemed to have no effect—and may not even have reached Muhammad, considering that his family and officials in Chicago were determined completely to undermine Malcolm X. In doing so, Malcolm was not granted the open hearing before the Nation constituency that he desired; instead, only a closed hearing was held in January 1964. The outcome portended badly for Malcolm, whose only opportunity for restoration required him to collude in the Nation's cover-up of Muhammad's sexual misbehavior.[7]

Malcolm apparently yielded at first to the suggestion that he deny what he had already related to the Nation's East Coast ministers as truth. No doubt desperate to redeem his broken relationship with Muhammad, Malcolm "confessed" to some Nation ministers that he had spread lies about their leader. This meant that he had to present himself as a liar and troublemaker; it also meant cooperating with Nation headquarters in covering up Elijah Muhammad's sins—at the expense of the young women in question. Thus, despite his intentions, Malcolm's role in the Nation was discredited, and he found himself in an even worse role as persona non grata among the very clergy he had hoped to salvage on the Nation's behalf. Wilfred later recalled that his brother "was willing to tell a lie about a lie," a tactic Malcolm lived to regret. In his private thoughts he was staggered: "I was in a state of emotional shock. I was like someone who for twelve years had an inseparable, beautiful marriage—and then suddenly one morning at breakfast the marriage partner had thrust across the table some divorce papers."

Interestingly, Malcolm's choice of the marriage break-up allegory corresponds exactly to the "marital disengagement model" used in one scholarly analysis of those who left cults after having enjoyed deep commitments to them. "Love, sacrifice and devotion are linked together and expressed in strong emotional attachments, binding members to the group in ways that correspond to marital commitment." Those deeply involved in cults, like Malcolm X, must therefore be viewed within the "conceptual framework and language of commitment" as opposed to the more stereotypical assumptions of "brainwashing" that are associated with cults and new religions.

Malcolm's experience during the approximately three months of his silencing further exemplifies that breaking with a cult is the kind of disengagement that is often complicated, "emotionally disconcerting and often painful . . . characterized by high levels of difficulty and intensity, largely because prior commitment levels are relatively higher." Malcolm exhibited precisely such characteristics, ranging from shock and stress to what might be called overpowering episodes of sentimentality in which he became a captive audience to his own flood of memories—what he called "a parade of a thousand and one different scenes" of his active and committed life in the Nation.

Malcolm admitted that, as in a divorce between two formerly close people, he and the Nation were now "physically divorced"; but "to actually become *psychologically* divorced from each other," Malcolm concluded, "might take years." He did not limit his divorce allegory to autobiographical reflection. In both a telephone conversation and an interview with CBS newsman Mike Wallace, Malcolm spoke of his separation from Muhammad and the Nation in terms of a broken marriage.[8]

After the suspension period had expired and after he realized that Elijah Muhammad "was attempting to muzzle him," as Wallace Muhammad recalled, Malcolm went directly to Elijah Muhammad and demanded his reinstatement. "When my father remained adamant, Malcolm threatened to leave the organization. At this point my father put him out." In religious retrospect one might correctly welcome the ouster as a fortuitous escape, but the tragedy of this story is that Malcolm's departure from Muhammad's cult was both bitter and painful. However close he had been to moving away from the Nation's religious teachings, the point remains that Malcolm X was driven out of a religious body that was still his only redemption—and to a large extent, his masterpiece of organizational commitment as well. As he had wept over the slain Muslim brother in Los Angeles, Malcolm X now wept at the demise of his own life in Muhammad's world, and wondered what it would be like to remain a Muslim nevertheless.[9]

Like a man whose stable marriage had suddenly ended in divorce, Malcolm X approached his newfound independence with ambivalence. In the initial weeks of his official separation from the Nation, he seems to have longed both for reconciliation and autonomy. Though he wanted to remain loyal to Muhammad, Malcolm also yearned for an identification with orthodox Islam that would remain impossible as long as he stayed in the Nation.

Because no similar Islamic organizations existed for African Americans that also provided a social base, it is no surprise that Malcolm felt the need to start his own movement. Typically, those leaving cults adopt alternative structures in the transitional process after their previous commitments have been significantly disrupted. Further, defection from cults involves conceiving and selecting an alternative identity and worldview—a gradual process that, for a time, often leaves the person "floating" and possibly feeling disoriented.

In Malcolm's case, the founding of an independent Muslim organization, Muslim Mosque, Inc., served to satisfy his own religious needs—now in transition—as much as it provided a long-desired avenue for actual political involvement in the black struggle. In autobiographical reflection, Malcolm explained his rationale for the founding of the Muslim Mosque. He noted that he had gradually begun to realize his own independent leadership qualities, sensing his deep-rooted ties to the urban black community and his exceptional sensitivity to their dilemma. Malcolm thus concluded, "The organization I hoped to build would differ from the Nation of Islam in that it would embrace all faiths of black men, and it would carry into practice what the Nation of Islam had only preached."[10]

In contrast to Malcolm's bold new political stance, the earliest phase of the Muslim Mosque's religious existence is difficult to ascertain. Though he expressed a great deal of loyalty to Elijah Muhammad in the first weeks of his independence, he was clearly reaching for religious orthodoxy. Yet despite his proclamation that the Muslim Mosque would serve as a meeting place for blacks of all religious persuasions, it was still a Muslim organization—one that, at least superficially, claimed cohesion with the Nation. "I remain a Muslim," Malcolm said in his March 8, 1964, independence announcement.

After explaining that his new movement would be a thoroughly black nationalist organization, Malcolm stated: "I have reached the conclusion that I can best spread Mr. Muhammad's message by staying out of the Nation of Islam and continuing to work on my own among America's 22 million non-Muslim Negroes." The next day, he told a journalist: "Muhammad is the one who taught me everything I know, and the one who made me into whatever I am. I believe Allah has given him the best diagnosis of the ills that beset America's 22 million Negroes."[11]

On March 12, 1964, Malcolm held his first official press conference at New York City's Park Sheraton Hotel, declaring: "I am and always will be a Muslim. My religion is Islam. I still believe that Mr. Muhammad's analysis of the problem is the most realistic, and that his solution is the best one." He thus announced the formation of the Muslim Mosque, which he again said was for all blacks of all beliefs. As Malcolm explained further, the Muslim Mosque would provide "a religious base, and the spiritual force necessary" to deal with vices that undermined "the moral fiber of our community."[12]

However, his new organization faced two problems regarding its religious nature.

First, as a Muslim organization offering a "religious base" that was to be distinctly Islamic, the Muslim Mosque was hardly an inviting umbrella organization for blacks of other religious and philosophical persuasions. Malcolm's personal tendency to "embrace all faiths of black men" seems to have been a reemerging characteristic of his religiously eclectic upbringing. This tendency related somewhat awkwardly to the idea of a thoroughly Muslim organization—perhaps foreshadowing the tensions Malcolm would later face as an orthodox believer in the Muslim world. Second, Malcolm was at least claiming to create a loyal satellite organization for a movement that was religiously exclusive. As such, the function of the Muslim Mosque, no matter how good Malcolm's intentions were, would inevitably appear as a hostile invasion of the Nation.

On an individual level, Malcolm had the same problem as his Muslim Mosque, defining himself as the Nation's loyal outsider and Muhammad's "number one follower." "And since I love the Honorable Elijah Muhammad and what he is teaching," Malcolm told a Philadelphia radio audience, "I felt that I could better expedite his program and carry it into practice by keeping free and clear of those forces [of opposition] which I knew existed [within the Nation]."[13]

Unfortunately, Elijah Muhammad, who identified his program as "divine work," would not sanction any such notion. "Anyone who deviates from Islam is a hypocrite," Muhammad told a journalist. To the suggestion that Malcolm was still loyal to him, Muhammad responded that Malcolm had "no alternative but to remain with me—if he believes in the Divine Message that Allah has given to me to deliver to my people. He would not go after other groups who have not accepted Islam." These "other groups" to which Muhammad referred were the established civil rights groups, which Malcolm had now pledged he would support in the ambitious political activism and self-defense philosophy of the Muslim Mosque.

The issue of armed self-defense, however, became the particular obsession of the media and consequently clouded Malcolm's overall attempt at mainstreaming his new organization. At the same time, the self-defense issue invited the criticism of Elijah Muhammad—who took full advantage of Malcolm's purported "break," as well as his call to arms, to present himself as a benign but wounded leader. "My people are more adapted to peace . . . they believe in peaceful solutions," Muhammad declared. "I am stunned," he continued before the press, "I never dreamed this man would deviate from the Nation of Islam. Every one of the Muslims admired him. . . . What he has said makes it definite. He has deviated. Obedience is an important thing to us." As far as Malcolm's proposed program of self-defense, Muhammad concluded, "It is very silly to say such a thing, because where are they going to get guns and arms?"[14]

In his syndicated column, which ran in the *Gary Crusader*, Muhammad invoked the Qur'an in a warning against "imputing sin to Allah's Messengers." He then stated his case against Malcolm, charging that the latter had "disobeyed the Apostle of Allah" by refusing to keep quiet during the ninety-day period of silence. Muhammad declared that Malcolm refused to remain quiet, and instead spoke to the press, proving that he was "going for self." Referring to Malcolm's Muslim Mosque and his philosophy of self-defense, Muhammad concluded:

I am sorry for the poor fools who refuse to trust the God of the Hon. Elijah Muhammad, and follow Malcolm for self-victory. Malcolm says that he is going to set up a Mosque for himself and [his] followers. I am sure that Malcolm has not believed the Hon. Elijah Muhammad to be the Messenger of Allah. If he did, he would be afraid for his future.[15]

Contrary to Muhammad's words, however, Malcolm's faith in him *had* been complete. It was only Muhammad's persistence in covering his sins that dealt what Malcolm called the "major blow" to his childlike belief in "the Messenger of Allah." "That was how I first began to realize that I had believed in Mr. Muhammad more than he believed in himself," Malcolm would later write.

The first weeks of the Muslim Mosque were undoubtedly a novelty for Malcolm X, who perhaps found solace in his new political independence. Indeed, while Malcolm frequently identified himself to interviewers and audiences as a faithful Muslim, his messages were decidedly nonreligious— especially in comparison to his apocalyptically charged Nation preachments. The "divine message" of Elijah Muhammad was now replaced with what Malcolm called "the gospel of black nationalism," which proclaimed black people should be in control of their own communities, their own businesses, their own politics, and their own religion.[16]

In the Nation, Malcolm had fancied himself as playing the role of Aaron the spokesman to Elijah Muhammad's Moses;[17] but in his new independence, he looked elsewhere for a role model of leadership, ironically focusing his attention on the leading Christian evangelist, Billy Graham. However, it was actually Graham's method of conducting nondenominational Christian "crusades" that Malcolm wanted to model in the name of black nationalism: "Billy Graham comes in preaching the gospel of Christ, he evangelizes the gospel, he stirs everybody up, but he never tries to start a church . . . and in this way the church cooperates with him. So we're going to take a page from his book. Our gospel is black nationalism."[18]

Malcolm later recalled that it was at this point that he began to receive numerous requests to speak to various Christian clergymen, especially whites. When addressing these ministers, however, he did not play down his philosophy of self-defense nor his new role as the Billy Graham of black nationalism. Speaking before an interracial group of Methodist ministers in Brooklyn in April 1964, Malcolm declared: "I am taking my cue from methods used by Billy Graham to preach the gospel of Christ. I will preach the gospel of Black Nationalism to Negroes without asking them to join my organization, but rather urging them to go out and join any existing civil rights organization."[19]

Regarding whites, Malcolm X maintained that he held no confidence in either their morality or legality, but suggested they would respond intelligently to the racial issue if blacks first embraced a strong black nationalist, self-defense program. When a white minister asked Malcolm if he believed there were any "good white people," Malcolm responded: "I do not say there are no sincere white people, but rather that I haven't met any." Malcolm had clearly moved away from Elijah Muhammad's "white devil" anthropology, but he was yet unwilling to appear conciliatory—instead pleading a kind of racial agnosticism.

Malcolm's attitude toward Christianity may have appeared to be less acerbic now, though it was impossible to discern if any real change had occurred. Not long afterward, Malcolm addressed an interdenominational group of Christian ministers, one of whom asked him if his attitude toward the church had modified since his Nation days. Malcolm smiled and said, "I don't care what I said last year. That was last year. This is 1964."[20]

This was probably only an admission of political expediency, intended to promote the interaction of black Christian nationalists in Muslim Mosque programs. In fact, Malcolm X was no more interested in the cross in 1964 than he had been while in the Nation. His religious vision was aimed eastward, toward a holy world where dark people had long prayed to Allah, and where white men could only enter, as Malcolm would come to believe, in complete humility.

# 15

## The Pilgrim Convert

*I would spread the true message of Islam.*

"There was one further major preparation that I knew I needed," Malcolm recalled in his autobiography. "I'd had it in my mind for a long time—as a servant of Allah. But it would require money that I didn't have." That preparation was the Hajj, the pilgrimage to Mecca, the holiest city of the Muslim world. Malcolm noted that he took a plane to Boston, "turning again" to his elder half-sister, Ella Collins, whom he had often turned to as a youth. Malcolm recalled this particular visit, noting that despite the fact that he had made Ella angry with him at times as a wayward youth, she "never once really wavered from my corner." However, as Malcolm described this particular visit, a reader could not necessarily know why he had made the comment about angering his sister.

Indeed, it appears that Malcolm simplified the whole episode, portraying this visit as if his trip to Boston to see Ella were actually a fund-raising campaign. "I want to make the pilgrimage to Mecca," the autobiographical Malcolm declares to Ella, to which she replies, "How much do you need?" However, according to Ella Collins, Malcolm was not all that sure about going to Mecca, and her remembrance of the event seems in line with the agonies of separation from the Nation that were still tearing away at the inner life of her brother.

It is possible that Ella—in retrospect—might have wanted to take credit for Malcolm's legendary Hajj. Certainly, a number of people had actually urged him to make Hajj and thus enter the orthodox community of Islam. Nevertheless, her account otherwise rings true: "I was trying to get him to go to Mecca. He had put so much into the Nation. Sometimes I had to get abusive with him," Ella recalled. "We had to get down to the roots of things. I told him to never anticipate getting back to the Nation—he had risen too far above it." However, Malcolm apparently resisted that realization, and the two siblings argued into the night until Malcolm finally succumbed and wept. "You know," he told his older half-sister, "you're real mean to me." Ella, of course, felt it was necessary to be mean with Malcolm. Whether or not it was really necessary, it does appear that her brother finally left Boston with the inner resolve—and the finances—to make the Hajj.

As a "servant of Allah" still in the Nation, Malcolm X had often encountered Sunni Muslims and had taken a good deal of Muslim heat over his organization's religious teachings. But not all of these personal religious encounters were negative, and some of them undoubtedly contributed to his inner desire to reconcile himself and the Nation to Sunni Islam. Malcolm admitted that on a number of occasions, particularly when he was speaking at colleges or universities, he had met sympathetic foreign Muslims who felt he was sincere and urged him to gain further exposure to "what they always called 'true Islam.' " Malcolm "bridled" at such suggestions. While in the privacy of his own religious thoughts, he wondered: "If one was sincere in professing a religion, why should he balk at broadening his knowledge of that religion?"

Ironically, Muhammad's son Wallace held personal religious convictions that provided a model for Malcolm as much as they generated tension between him and his father. Malcolm noted that Wallace, whom he admired, also urged him to deepen his knowledge of Islam. It seems likely that Malcolm also carefully observed that Wallace's brother, Akbar Muhammad, had gone to Egypt to study at Al-Azhar University. Not only had Akbar gone to study in the heart of the Dark World, but he was converted to genuine Islam—though physical distance apparently minimized his influence on the Nation as an organization.[1]

However, Akbar was at least an indirect influence on Malcolm, since he had successfully traversed a religious chasm that Malcolm increasingly wished to cross. During a visit to the United States, Akbar made an appearance in a Nation rally in New York City on July 13, 1963. He delivered a stirring message of universal black unity—strongly admonishing the Nation to make a pronounced statement of its support of all black groups organized in the United States as well. Malcolm, who had hosted the rally, returned to the podium expressing both regret for having so long taken a critical approach toward other black organizations and his determination to seek unity thereafter. While the incident did not directly pertain to the issue of orthodoxy, it seems that Malcolm sensed in Akbar's example a religious integrity that personally challenged him.

Elijah Muhammad was challenged by Akbar, too. There was visible tension between the cultic patriarch and his orthodox son. Elijah Muhammad had apparently classified Akbar as a "hypocrite" from the time of the 1963 visit. Akbar would return again in late 1964 and openly denounce his father's religion as stifling and "home made." Akbar would also defend Malcolm X, who had by then followed him into orthodoxy.

Long before Malcolm could come to Mecca, however, Mecca seemed to have come to Malcolm. Most notable in this regard was the friendship that Malcolm formed with a Sudanese Muslim student named Ahmed Osman. Osman, who was studying at Dartmouth College, came to New York City to attend Mosque No. 7 services on a Sunday afternoon in 1962. Sitting in an audience of about five hundred people, Osman listened to Malcolm speak for about four hours, undoubtedly aggravated by what was being preached in the name of Islam. When the customary question-and-answer session was opened, Osman stood up to speak, challenging Malcolm that many of the Nation's statements and beliefs were contrary to Islam. Osman particularly challenged the "the claim of Elijah Muhammad that he is the Messenger of God and the interpretation of the race problem."

The crowd reacted negatively to the young Muslim student who boldly opposed the Nation's racial doctrines, but Malcolm asked them to allow Osman to finish his statement. Still, the point-counterpoint between Osman and Malcolm did not end on a conciliatory note. Osman recalled that the discussion was "heated" and he left the mosque "unsatisfied." Yet he could not help but feel "greatly impressed with Malcolm."

Unable to forget their encounter, Osman began an earnest letter-writing campaign, endeavoring to communicate "true Islam" to Malcolm; he likewise sent him literature published by the Islamic Centre in Geneva, Switzerland. Unlike his more heated confrontation at Mosque No. 7, Osman's sincere appeals were irresistible to Malcolm X, who by nature could not ignore reasonable, intelligent presentations. Malcolm responded to Osman's letters with appreciation and interest, and asked for more Islamic literature. He even began to ask Osman to provide explanations in Qur'anic exegesis. As their friendship solidified, Osman prodded Malcolm to make Hajj, knowing within himself that "a great change was unfolding" within the religious Malcolm X.[2]

As Malcolm recalled, when he did speak with sympathetic Muslim students they urged him to meet with Dr. Mahmoud Youssef Shawarbi, an eminent Egyptian Muslim scholar who, at the time, was residing in New York City and was the director of the Islamic Foundation. Malcolm admitted that while he was still in the Nation he more than once "resisted the impulse" to stop in and see Dr. Shawarbi. "Then one day Dr. Shawarbi and I were introduced by a newspaperman," Malcolm recalled.

Without proper background information, a reader might assume that Malcolm and Dr. Shawarbi were not acquainted. However, Malcolm had already known Shawarbi at least since the scholar had spoken at a special Nation function in November 1960. At the time, Shawarbi declared the confraternity of all Muslim groups, including the Nation. Expressing delight over Elijah Muhammad's trip to Mecca that same year, Shawarbi urged all of the Nation's members to make the same pilgrimage. However, the cooperation between the two men seems to have been minimized by Malcolm's inability to move closer to traditional Sunni Islam while in the service of Elijah Muhammad.

But now that Malcolm X was independent of Elijah Muhammad, he found himself free to deepen his knowledge of Sunni Islam, and reacquainted himself with Shawarbi in a series of instructional sessions during the first weeks of the Muslim Mosque's existence. Malcolm did not speak of these sessions in his autobiography, leaving his readers to think that after one meeting he no longer had contact with Shawarbi until he made preparations for the Hajj. This foreshortening may have been intentional because Malcolm wanted to emphasize the drama of his unfolding second conversion. Shawarbi recalled, in fact, that Malcolm came to him with the stated belief that he was already a Muslim who needed only to deepen his understanding of Islam.

In their quiet but momentous sessions together, Malcolm plied Shawarbi with questions about "real Islam"—while the latter sought to persuade Malcolm "to give up his racist ideas." Shawarbi pointed out to Malcolm that even in the Muslim world some Arabs think of themselves as special despite the egalitarian teachings of the Qur'an. In the end, Malcolm was persuaded, and not without great emotion. "I have no doubt of his sincerity," Shawarbi declared in an interview. "I could not help but be impressed by his desire to learn about Islam. Sometimes he would even cry while passages of the Holy Koran were being read."

As a result, Shawarbi urged him to make the Hajj—knowing full well that some of his own New York-based Muslim brethren objected, remaining suspicious of Malcolm's motivations. But Shawarbi believed in Malcolm's sincerity and he personally provided a letter of recommendation and a copy of *The Eternal Message of Muhammad*, a book written by an eminent citizen of Saudi Arabia. With his visa approved for the journey, Malcolm X left New York City on April 13, 1964, "quietly," as he put it, bound for the "Holy World" of Islam. [3]

"During the *hajj*," writes one observer, "the holy city of Mecca becomes an immense caldron of humanity, black, brown, yellow, and white." An ancient tradition and pillar of Islam, the Hajj draws approximately two million pilgrims, *Hajjis*, to Mecca every year during the month—Dhu'l-Hijja in the Islamic calendar. Muslims from every race and class come, stripping themselves of any outward sign of economic or social status, dressed in the humble and uniform attire of the Hajji.

The Hajj is "a profound statement of [the Hajji's] devotion to God, rejection of sin, and a celebration of the brotherhood of all Moslems." However, unlike the unifying religious rituals of other religions, the Hajj requires a very physical routine. By the time the Hajji has completed all the activities of the sacred event, he or she will have been transported (most en masse) on a 120-mile, six-day trip from Jedda to the holy sites and back again.

But if the Hajj is "one of the most potent unifying factors in the world of Islam," it has also functioned historically to develop a "suitable network of communications" between Muslim peoples and nations. As such, the Hajj provides an opportunity for economic, social, and intellectual exchange, which in turn has generated a sense among Muslims "of belonging to a single, vast whole." The equality of the Hajj is largely ritualistic—a point that can perhaps be demonstrated by the fact that Hajjis are accommodated in everything from luxury hotels to tents. Islam proclaims no socialist utopia on earth, only a unifying faith that mandates a universal Muslim family.

The Hajji not only advances physically toward Mecca, but also enters necessarily into a ritual state of consecration, *Ihram*. Entering Ihram not only requires the wearing of humble pilgrim attire, but also abstinence from many of the normal comforts and pleasures of life. The entire ritual, with its extensive itinerary of physical and spiritual activities, was observed by the Prophet Muhammad himself and is recorded in the Qur'an as a requirement of the faithful. For the individual Hajji, the Hajj is "a personal act following a personal decision and resulting in a series of wide-ranging personal experiences." And certainly among the 90,000 Hajjis who came to Jedda by air travel during the Hajj season of 1964, Malcolm's personal experiences may have been the most unusual.[4]

After spending "two happy days sightseeing in Cairo," Malcolm flew into Jedda, Saudi Arabia, with a group of Hajjis who had befriended him in Egypt. Once in Jedda, Malcolm was separated from his friends when his Muslim credentials were questioned by a passport inspector. "I never had been in such a jammed mass of people," Malcolm recalled, "but I never had felt more alone, and helpless, since I was a baby." Worse, Malcolm had arrived in Jedda on Friday, the day of prayer in the Muslim world—which meant his hearing before the *Mahgama Sharia*, the Hajj court, could not be held at least until the following day. Until his hearing, Malcolm was placed in a dormitory that housed "members of every race on earth," many of them still dressed in their native garb. "It was like pages out of the *National Geographic* magazine," Malcolm wrote enthusiastically.

Though free of the color barrier of the United States, Malcolm ironically found himself limited by language. None of the Hajjis in the dormitory spoke English, and Malcolm knew neither Arabic nor French, the *linguae franca* of the Eastern world: "I couldn't speak anybody's language. I was in bad shape." Although his fellow Hajjis were friendly, Malcolm knew that his awkwardness made him stand out, especially since he was so obviously unaccustomed to the Muslim prayer ritual. "Imagine," Malcolm mused, "being a Muslim minister, a leader in Elijah Muhammad's Nation of Islam, and not knowing the prayer ritual." He struggled to emulate the Muslim prayer posture, and when the time came to make the morning prayer, Malcolm recalled that the best he could do was mumble in imitation the prayers he heard being said in Arabic.[5]

Malcolm made a point of stating that his mumbling of prayers did not suggest levity on his part. "It was far from a joke with me." Still, many a reader might be struck by a sense of vanity in Malcolm's attempts, especially in a Western religious culture that has been permeated by the notion that prayer is, at its highest form, exclusively individualistic, private, and informal.

However, Muslim prayer differs from Western religious invocation because it is not essentially perceived as either petition or communication.

Rather, Muslim prayer is a ritual of acknowledgment of God's power. Further, communal prayer for the Muslim affirms the unity of all fellow believers. "Prayer is the celebrating of the unity of a great tribe held together by its submission to Allah and its obedience to his teachings." In a very real sense, then, Malcolm's prayers—while mumbled and frustrated by language—were entirely in synchrony with the Hajj as a religious event. "The purpose of prayer is not the same as the purpose of speech," echoes a voice from another great religious tradition. "The purpose of speech is to inform; the purpose of prayer is to partake."[6]

By the evening of the next day, Malcolm had still been unable to attain a hearing at the Hajj court. He recalled that he had just completed the "Sunset Prayer," *El Maghrib*, and was lying on a cot in his dormitory compartment—a kind of prison cell that restrained him from the freedom of the Hajj. It was an ironic spiritual rehearsal of that moment, many years before, when he lay on his bed in prison and suddenly became aware of the strange humanlike apparition. But now, what struck "out of the darkness" like "a sudden light" was no apparition but "a sudden thought." He remembered that in his possession was the book, *The Eternal Message of Muhammad*, that Shawarbi had given to him. In it was the telephone number of the author's son, who happened to live in Jedda. This was the turning point in Malcolm's Hajj experience.

The first hours of Malcolm's Hajj appeared to be a reenactment of his own personal spiritual journey: family, separation, alienation, and confinement. Now, as before, a blinding flash of light brought him liberation. However, the liberation he would experience in Mecca was not racial, but humanitarian; not parochial, but universal; not based on the strange vision of an unknown man, but on the redemptive vision of unity and brotherhood under one divine Creator.

Shortly after Malcolm's phone call, Dr. Omar Azzam, a tall white man with a European education and an important engineering position in Saudi, appeared at Malcolm's dormitory. In a matter of minutes, Malcolm's personal papers were retrieved and the two were chauffeured to the residence of the book's author, Abd al-Rahman Azzam. "My father will be so happy to meet you," Dr. Azzam assured Malcolm, who also learned he had been the object of the elder Azzam's interest for quite some time.

Malcolm met Abd al-Rahman Azzam at the Jedda Palace Hotel, where the latter was staying in his own suite. The suite, in fact, was turned over to Malcolm, who was overwhelmed by the hospitality of his Muslim hosts and the intervention of Allah. Malcolm dined with the Azzams, being deeply impressed by the elder Azzam, whose fatherly, scholarly wisdom and knowledge completely captivated him. Beyond all this, the Azzams spoke on Malcolm's behalf for his participation in the Hajj.

The next day, having rested in his luxurious hotel suite, Malcolm appeared before Shaykh Muhammad Harkon of the Hajj court. Malcolm recalled this experience somewhat idealistically, however. In his autobiographical record, Shaykh Harkon interviewed him and ruled in favor of his sincerity as a Muslim. However, according to Abd al-Rahman Azzam, a bit more persuasion was required in the hearing. Twice, in fact, the elder Azzam pleaded with Harkon: "The man says, *la ilaha illa Allahu*, 'There is no god but God,' and says he is a Muslim. What more do you want?" Harkon's apparent hesitancy in approving Malcolm's Hajj certificate was probably due to the fact that Harkon had met Malcolm in 1959 during his Middle East visit as Muhammad's emissary. According to Malcolm, the two had conversed over tea during that visit, and it is likely that Harkon now wanted to make sure that Malcolm was truly free from the spurious teachings of the Nation.

It is likely that Shaykh Harkon would have approved Malcolm's case based on the support of both Azzam and Shawarbi. However, it seems the judge could not argue when an additional message of support arrived—a missive sent from the ruler of Saudi Arabia, Prince Faisal, by way of his deputy chief of protocol, who immediately intervened on Malcolm's behalf. Intervention from the throne was not entirely miraculous, however; the son of Prince Faisal was married to Abd al-Rahman Azzam's daughter.[7] Malcolm's Hajj certificate was undoubtedly issued without further delays.

This diplomatic tour de force on his behalf did not astonish only Malcolm; the U.S. Embassy in Jedda was also quite aware of the incident. In a report about Malcolm's activities in Saudi, an embassy official later informed the State Department in Washington, D.C., that Malcolm's reception in Jedda "showed there was no doubt in the minds of the Saudi authorities as to his *bona fides* as a Muslim." Thus, when Malcolm would later tell a Chicago television audience that he had "no trouble" making the Hajj, he was not being dishonest—he was being modest.

The deputy chief of protocol, Muhammad Abdul Azziz Maged, thereafter provided an astonished Malcolm with his own private car in order to shuttle him around in fulfillment of Hajj requirements. With this privilege, Malcolm was able easily to complete the Hajj between April 19 and 24, including an Omra visit to the sacred grounds at Mecca proper and a visit to the city of Mina, twenty miles away.[8]

During his stay at Mina, in fact, Malcolm stood outside his hotel, amazed at the many kinds of people who, like him, had come to the "Holy World." Standing nearby him was another Hajji, Kasem Gulick, a member of the Turkish Parliament, who told Malcolm that the Hajj was indeed "an anthropologist's paradise." Malcolm said the Turk recognized him from news broadcasts and reports and was apparently quite surprised to find that the famous "Black Muslim" was on the Hajj.

Later that same day, Malcolm reached Mount Arafat, along with thousands of other Hajjis, where he spent the rest of the day praying under a tent on the mount. Malcolm sat there, absorbed by the tremendous diversity of peoples sharing the same shelter on the desert ascent. Of that experience, he later reflected that "present in that group was every shade—every shade, every complexion, there was every type of culture, there were Chinese, Indonesians; there were people from Afghanistan, Persia, there was one Russian and his wife, who were very white. There were [also] some Nigerians and Ghanaians." Malcolm was intensely moved by the realization of the great unity of the Hajj, especially exemplified by the Hajjis' sharing of nourishment, utensils, and even the space needed for prayer and sleep.[9]

Overwhelmed by the reality of this communion, it seems Malcolm reviewed his former life as Muhammad's representative, feeling regret for the role he had played in advancing the Nation's religion. "While I was on the top of Mount Arafat I swore to Allah that I would eliminate racism from the American Moslem movement. I swore that when I got back to America, I would spread the true message of Islam and rid its followers from any deviation."

"Deviation," of course, is roughly the Muslim equivalent of "heresy" in the Western theological tradition. The essence of Sunni Islam, however, is not found in mere doctrinal purity, nor in literal orthodoxy, but in loyalty to the Muslim community and its traditions. Deviation, therefore, is not so much an error as a breach of tradition—a social-religious offense more than a strictly theological one. Malcolm the Hajji now realized that at the heart of his deviation—and the deviation of the entire Nation—was their religious embrace of Elijah Muhammad himself. For as long as they held that Elijah Muhammad was Allah's last and greatest messenger, they would cut themselves off from the "Sunna"—the community of the faithful.

"There on a Holy World hilltop," Malcolm wrote—apparently of his meditations on Mount Arafat—"I realized how very dangerous it is for people to hold any human being in such esteem, especially to consider anyone some sort of 'divinely guided' and 'protected' person." Malcolm's supreme deviation, as he came to understand, was not his commitment to Muhammad's racialist doctrines but to Muhammad himself. Malcolm confessed his formerly "complete" belief in Elijah Muhammad as a *"divine leader"* and as a man who could neither make mistakes nor do wrong. As Abd al-Rahman Azzam noted, Malcolm X had been a man with a faith, "but it was faith in a man: Elijah Muhammad." Now, Malcolm was determined to set right his former deviation from Islam, not merely by correcting his own path, but by returning to the United States with the true message of the Prophet Muhammad.

There, on the same "Holy World hilltop," Malcolm later recalled that during the night, sleeping among his "brother pilgrims" under the great tent, he suddenly recalled his childhood experience of lying on the top of the grassy "Hector's Hill." Malcolm, now on the top of Mount Arafat, was able to correlate his satisfying new place in Islam with his most basic childhood meditations. The reawakening of these early thoughts, or "personal memories," may suggest more than simple recollection. Perhaps Malcolm, in recalling those memories, realized that his childhood preconceptions of himself—what he may have experienced as a sense of destiny—had been fulfilled. The strange path his life had taken—from childhood to troubled youth and prison, and then to the Nation—all seemed to fit together into the religious reality that had begun to unfold before him in Mecca.[10]

Malcolm was not content to wait until he returned to the United States to share his new knowledge of Islam. He immediately began a long stream of letters and postcards to friends, associates, and followers back home—all of the letters harmonizing on the theme of the unity of humanity under Islam and the genuine fellowship he had known with white Muslim Hajjis. To his friend James Farmer, the director of CORE, Malcolm wrote: "I've just visited the Holy City of Mecca where I've seen thousands of pilgrims of all colors worshipping together in perfect peace and brotherhood. It is a sight such as I've never seen in America. It was wonderful to behold."

To the journalist M. S. Handler, Malcolm wrote one of his most famous letters, declaring that he had eaten, slept, and prayed with "fellow Muslims whose skin was the whitest of white, whose eyes were the bluest of blue, and whose hair was the blondest of blond." The Hajj, proclaimed Malcolm X in words that would shortly make hot newsprint, "has forced me to 'rearrange' much of my own thought pattern, and to toss aside some of my previous conclusions."[11]

Apart from his own personal reevaluation of the white race and his euphoria over the spiritual kinship of the Hajj, Malcolm's letters to the press made clear his belief both in the possibility and even the necessity of a religiously guided racial reconciliation in the United States. "The immediate acceptance of the oneness of God," preached Malcolm, "is the only way out, the only way America can escape the inevitable destruction that every racist nation brings upon itself when it becomes too intoxicated with its own power to recognize the existence of a Spiritual Power greater than all of its military and nuclear might." [12] By recognizing the "Spiritual Power" of Allah, Malcolm contended, whites in the United States could redeem both themselves and their nation because an embrace of the oneness of God would guarantee their acceptance of the oneness of man. "America" could be spared the destruction of "the cancer of racism" by becoming acquainted with Islam, "a religion that has molded people of all colors into one vast family . . . [a religion] that leaps over all obstacles."

Malcolm noted that the white Muslims in the East were "much different from American whites," since Islam had removed "the 'white' from their mind." And since these white Muslims were so free from color prejudice, Malcolm said, it allowed him to "remove the 'Negro' " from his mind—with the result that all attitudes and behaviors had changed for the better. Malcolm believed that the United States could be saved from its suicidal path only if whites were freed from the nation's "insane obsession with racism." The best hope for whites in this regard was their own "younger generation," especially the students on campuses whose "young, less-hampered intellect" might allow them to "turn for spiritual salvation to the religion of Islam, and force the older generation of American whites to turn with them."

Malcolm recalled staying up into the night, copying letters with this theme especially addressed to colleagues in the Nation and to his own Muslim Mosque in Harlem. Malcolm knew that his new message of racial harmony in Islam would take especially his own followers by surprise. "You may be shocked by these words coming from me," Malcolm wrote to his "Muslim" supporters back home, "but I have always been a man who tries to face facts, and to accept the reality of life as new experiences and knowledge unfolds it." [13] Now, he was asking his followers to accept the possibility of a spiritual brotherhood that included whites, and a philosophy of black struggle that did not necessarily divorce itself from the redemption of the entire country.

Malcolm characterized himself to his followers as one who "always tried to face facts" and "accept the reality of life" as he gained more knowledge. However, as the critical reader of his autobiography may note, however sincerely Malcolm sought to face facts and accept reality, his previous religious commitment to Elijah Muhammad had greatly hindered or misdirected his personal religious and intellectual life.

Likewise, even though Malcolm X escaped the cultic deviations of Elijah Muhammad, his autobiography did not lose a religious agenda. Like Malcolm X himself, Malcolm's autobiography was converted to Sunni Islam. His account of the Hajj, while fundamentally honest, functions primarily as an evangelistic and apologetic self-witness. In so doing, however, it is likely that Malcolm idealized Muslims and the Muslim world in order to validate his newfound faith in Sunni Islam for his readers.

Certainly, Malcolm's autobiographical account of the Hajj does not leave the critical reader without certain questions. Of course, some skeptics may lightly dismiss Malcolm's entire conversion as a political act and suggests his Hajj was an international ploy to "refurbish his pocketbook." Such unwarranted and disingenuous interpretations aside, even Malcolm's admirers have sensed some problems in his Hajj account. Generally, these admiring critics have been those who write from a parochial black nationalist position and are therefore most concerned to challenge any notion that Malcolm's philosophy, both during and after the Hajj, was integrationist or socialist.

One such writer, despite his belief in the sincerity of Malcolm's religious conversion, emphasizes that the Hajj does not typify life in Muslim societies and that racism was historically a vital factor among Muslim Arabs. He further suggests that by enhancing his experience in Mecca, Malcolm may have been attempting to skillfully counter his negative image in the United States. A black nationalist Christian ally of Malcolm has likewise pointed out that Malcolm's autobiography has "an unintentional overemphasis on the change which took place in [Malcolm's] thinking in Mecca."[14] Elsewhere he speaks even more candidly about the difference between Malcolm's autobiography and Malcolm's real knowledge in relation to the Hajj:

Brother Malcolm knew history and he was guided by his interpretation of history. He interpreted the things that happened to him in terms of his knowledge and his understanding of the past. He would not have been taken in by what happened in Mecca. Brother Malcolm knew that the Arab Muslims had been the backbone of the slave trade.

Indeed, this black nationalist clergyman concludes that, in making the Hajj, Malcolm would not have been duped "by the window dressing in Mecca."[15]

# 16

## The Realities and Ideals
## of Witness

*I saw that people who looked alike drew together.*

It is essential to take note of an important background element
in Malcolm's religious story that reveals itself particularly in his conversion
to traditional Islam. Despite the great differences between the teachings of
the Nation and those of Sunni Islam, there appears to have been a kind of
"Muslim continuity" in Malcolm's thinking throughout his adult life, and
from the time of his prison conversion he had a definite sympathy for the
Islamic world. This orientation toward Islam not only buttressed his consum-
ing faith in Elijah Muhammad but propelled him toward the genuine Islamic religion when his faith in Muhammad collapsed.

His Muslim continuity surfaced, for instance, in an interview by Douglass
G. Bridson of the BBC in London in December 1964. When Bridson asked
Malcolm what had originally moved him from atheism into Islam, he spoke
primarily of his prison conversion to the Nation. This was no religious
contradiction, however, since Malcolm pointed out in the same interview
the "sharp contradiction" between the theologies of the Nation and Sunni
Islam. Still, Malcolm apparently sensed some Muslim continuity under-
girding his entire adult religious life: "But being in prison and then being
encouraged to read, and especially when I found the Islamic influence on

the African continent and positive contributions it had made to the development of various African cultures, I think that had a lot to do with me accepting the religion." Malcolm also underscored that since African Islamic societies present a "positive culture" to blacks living in a society such as the United States where Africa has been characteristically demeaned, one is "more inclined" to turn toward the "religious ingredient" of Islam.[1]

Not long after the Hajj, Malcolm was asked in another interview about his conversion to Islam. In his reply he described not the tutorials with Shawarbi or even the Hajj itself, but his conversion and reading experiences in prison. "And it was while I was serving a sentence in prison in the State of Massachusetts, that I first was exposed to the religion of Islam and I studied it and could see that it did for me what Christianity had failed to do."[2] Again, Malcolm stressed Africa as a factor contributing to his attraction to Islam:

Plus, besides, I read where on the African continent the predominant religion that existed at the time slavery was instituted, was the religion of Islam. It prevailed in that entire area. So I accepted it because I believed not only that it was the *right* religion, but also because of the historic part it played in the culture of the African continent.[3]

At other times in the post-Hajj period, Malcolm would likewise blur the distinction between the Nation and Sunni Islam.[4]

In essence, Malcolm's early attraction to Islam seems to have been Garveyite in nature. What apparently impressed young Malcolm about Islam was that it was a fundamental part of important African cultures—as it already was, in Malcolm's thinking, before the institution of slavery. This appears to be at the heart of Malcolm's Garveyite core: Islam was already a vibrant part of African cultures before the advent of the *European* slave trade in Africa. He undoubtedly knew that indigenous slavery had been institutionalized in Africa since antiquity, and that Muslim traders had carried vast numbers of Africans into slavery for centuries before the Europeans came. However, it was Europe's invasion, oppression, and exploitation of the African continent that concerned the Garvey movement—and Malcolm X.

As a young Nation minister, Malcolm had raised the issue of the Muslim slave trade in a 1956 letter to an incarcerated convert. In explaining to his correspondent that the white devils had undertaken a campaign to malign Islam as a "slavemaking religion," Malcolm brought his wit and imagination to bear in its defense. "History teaches us that slave[s] are used to do heavy industry . . . to make money for their masters. There are no heavy industries in Arabia, no cotton fields . . . what would a slave do there: Sift Sand?"

Of course, by equating "heavy industry" with the toils of the North American cotton fields, Malcolm was conveniently overlooking the diversity of labor that slaves of all colors undertook in the Muslim world. But Malcolm's Garveyite concern was to keep the burden of black people's dilemma on the shoulders of their modern-day enemies, who had colonized Africa and enslaved Africans worldwide.

In a 1960 radio debate with the integrationist leader Bayard Rustin, Malcolm was also selective in his use of African history. When Rustin suggested that the Nation was more a reaction against Christianity than a genuine Muslim religion, Malcolm defended the movement by equating it with the Islamic religion that blacks "were taken from four hundred years ago." To counter Malcolm's point, Rustin maintained that most of the Africans who were taken into American slavery came from regions of West Africa that had not yet been Islamized at the time of their removal. In response, Malcolm suggested that Rustin had been brainwashed by whites, and then invoked reference to the great Mali empire, a Muslim kingdom in fifteenth-century Guinea. While Malcolm was correct in citing this early Muslim empire in Africa, he was still very selective. Rustin attempted to point out, to no avail, that West Africa was never entirely Islamized, and in those areas where Islam emerged it did not do so until after the slave trade had begun.

Malcolm did not talk about his Muslim continuity only to Western journalists, whose exposure to Islam was minimal. In the summer of 1964 he told a reporter from the *Egyptian Gazette* that he had discovered Islam while in prison, and "with the discovery of Islam and Africa, had found a society I thought I could join." Even more explicit was Malcolm's interview published in the magazine *Minbar Al-Islam*. Here he noted that in prison he had read about Islam, Prophet Muhammad, and the military successes of Muslim forces against the European Crusaders. "This was the real reason of my adopting Islam. I began to think of the secret of Muslims' power. I was eager to find something full of strength and dignity until I discovered it in that religion."

These points suggest that Malcolm perceived Islam as intrinsically entwined with the positive aspects of African life and saw Muslim Africa as well as a brave and noble "society" in conflict with the white oppressor. Thus he preferred to focus on an apparent harmony between the Muslim and African worlds. This perception, which dominated Malcolm's thinking even after he left the Nation, impacted heavily on his religious presuppositions and, to a degree, left him unwilling openly to admit the racial sins and other short-comings of the Muslim world.

Anxious as he was to solidify his genuine commitment to Islam, Malcolm had nevertheless come to Mecca with a greater burden than most Hajjis. Like others who leave cults or new religions, Malcolm had to reformulate and select an alternative identity and worldview outside of the Nation. But fortunately he was not left entirely afloat. His Muslim continuity was not lost in the collapse of his faith in Elijah Muhammad—though it alone was not able to sustain him without being mediated by an organized religious group.

Sunni Islam, as a conservative religion, offered an avenue of resocialization that was appropriate for Malcolm because of his perception of Islam as the religion of the Dark World. Further, Islam did not restrict his intense religiosity but offered manageable terms in his religious commitment. Included in those terms was the permission, and even encouragement, to participate in activities that the Nation would have considered secular—in Malcolm's case, political action on behalf of African Americans.[5]

When Malcolm came to Mecca, then, his Hajj experience was already pregnant with the spirituality and insights he would later attribute to the pilgrimage itself. This is not to minimize the Hajj, of course. But the power of the Hajj—for Malcolm—seems to have been in its dramatic, physical, geographic, and collective qualities as a point of his religious reintegration into the world.

In those several weeks, from the time of his official "divorce" from the Nation until he arrived in Mecca, Malcolm's religious identity as "a servant of Allah" was incomplete—a serious problem since this was still a fundamental part of his own self-definition. It seems the euphoria he expressed in Mecca over the multicolored, multicultured commune of Hajjis was all the more pronounced because this was the "society" for which he had always longed, and in which he would now dwell as a political and religious leader.

The leading liberal interpretation of Malcolm's Hajj experience is that it was his "first real bath"—a baptismal cleansing of the Nation's doctrines. As such, it is considered a social self-immersion in the leveling democracy of the Hajj. Not surprisingly, the liberal analysis tends to stumble over the apparent inability of Malcolm X to accept white people in the United States, who "in Malcolm's sight . . . remained guilty of a collective and historic devilishness toward the blacks," standing guilty "until that millennial hour when they received Islam." This "millennial hour"—the possibility of whites in the United States accepting Islam and being saved from judgment—is therefore considered a "fantasy—the convert's starry dream of an entire nation now lost in sin being led to Allah by its own children."[6]

Of course there is a certain starry-eyed quality in Malcolm's words at the time of the Hajj—a quality that is likewise apparent in his autobiographical account of the Hajj. However, without understanding that the Hajj restored to Malcolm his full religious identity, reintegrating him into the heart of a vibrant, evangelistic religious community, this interpretation remains inadequate. The inclination to see Malcolm's newfound religious agenda as only fantasy indicates, perhaps, a certain philosophical myopia that may typify liberal commentaries on Malcolm's conversion.[7]

The dynamic of Malcolm's Hajj account, nevertheless, is not his plunge into democracy any more than it is a case of deception or naiveté. In analyzing the Hajj account, an Islamic scholar has noted that Malcolm's "heightened perceptions" as a black man from the United States enabled him "to see in the pilgrimage at Mecca a certain color pattern—though the belief which he had acquired and still cherished at that time prevented him from realizing the full implications of what he saw."[8] While this observation is perhaps more discerning of Malcolm's experience as a religious moment, it nevertheless leads to the questionable conclusion that Malcolm's faith in Islam had impaired his real vision of racial attitudes in the Muslim world— temporarily disabling his otherwise keen skills of social perception.

Of course this raises an important question regarding Malcolm's autobiographical Hajj observations. After his bountiful and explicit "brotherhood" descriptions of the Hajj, Malcolm suddenly mentions "a color pattern in the huge crowds," a pattern he began to observe among the Hajjis thereafter. "I saw that people who looked alike drew together and most of the time stayed together. This was entirely voluntary; there being no other reason for it. But Africans were with Africans. Pakistanis were with Pakistanis. And so on." Malcolm said that he made a mental note of this observation so that when he returned to the United States he could share it: "Where true brotherhood existed among all colors, where no one felt segregated, where there was no 'superiority' complex, no 'inferiority' complex—then voluntarily, naturally, people of the same kind felt drawn together by that which they had in common."[9]

Although one might agree that the Muslim world is no interracial paradise, it is inappropriate to consider Malcolm's observation as evidence of racial prejudice in the Muslim world. Indeed, a thorough religious interpretation must contend that Malcolm was not religiously blinded to racial prejudice, nor was his description of "color patterns" evidence that racism was practiced among the Hajjis.

The Hajjis were pilgrims from many different lands and cultures. Like Malcolm, most of them probably came to Mecca with few contacts among their fellow pilgrims. Likewise, most Hajjis were probably limited in their linguistic ability to cross into different cultures. The Hajjis' sense of belonging to a "single, vast whole" was not at all abrogated by Malcolm's "color pattern" observation. The glory of the Hajj seems to be its ritualistic collection of peoples, nations, and tongues—not the integration of individuals on a mass scale that one might assume in the West.

For his part, Malcolm X believed racial reconciliation between blacks and whites in the United States required that blacks *first* be united, fortified, and satisfied in their own sense of community. He understandably found in the sincere "color pattern" of the Hajjis a grounding principle for his own philosophy of racial reconciliation, which is implied in his own organization's statement: "We believe that our communities must be the sources of their own strength politically, economically, intellectually, and culturally in the struggle for human rights and human dignity." [10]

The proper interpretation of Malcolm's Hajj account, therefore, must be discerned from the standpoint of his religious agenda. Malcolm's desire was to advance Islam by means of self-witness. In so doing, he stylized his presentation of the sacred pilgrimage and his experiences as a Hajji. Yet this still leaves certain questions unanswered—particularly in regard to Malcolm's rapport with his white Muslim hosts.

One would not wish to belittle or doubt the enthusiasm, gratitude, and awe that Malcolm expressed at the overwhelming hospitality of his hosts. However honored and grateful he may have felt at the sudden intervention of dignitaries and rulers on his behalf, the point remains that Malcolm's Hajj was an elite tour entirely underwritten by men with an agenda of their own. [11] The fact that their agenda and Malcolm's agenda were complementary makes the Hajj account most interesting, especially at the points where those agendas overlap.

After being rescued by the Azzams from the anonymity and language barrier of the Hajji dormitory, and then finding himself lodged—free of charge—in a luxurious hotel room, Malcolm understandably prostrated himself in a prayer of gratitude. However, his autobiographical description of himself as being "speechless" at these unprecedented gestures of honor, and his running theological comments assuring the reader of Allah's intervention on his behalf, seem to serve the purpose of validating both the religious motivations of his hosts and his reaction to them.

Nothing in either of my two careers as a black man in America had served to give me any idealistic tendencies. My instincts automatically examine the reasons, the motives, of anyone who did anything they didn't have to do for me. Always in life, if it was any white person, I could see a selfish motive there. [12]

Malcolm further explained that the kindness of these elite Saudi Muslims could not have had an ulterior motive. Abd al-Rahman Azzam had nothing to gain from befriending him, he reasoned. Malcolm noted that he could offer nothing to his host that his host would need. In fact, Malcolm suggested that he might even have been a liability to the Azzams, given his negative "Black Muslim" image. Without money, power, or even a good reputation, Malcolm concluded, the Azzams had no motive except the pure, altruistic love of the true Muslim. "Ma sha'a-llah"—"It is as Allah has pleased," the unselfish host declared to the speechless Hajji Malcolm.

The Azzams were undoubtedly kind, and their hospitality must be seen as an example of Muslim generosity. However, Malcolm probably realized, but did not admit, that their actions were grounded in a definite purpose. Malcolm had neither money nor a formidable organizational base in the United States, but the Muslim cause needed neither of these. What Malcolm did have, however, was a brilliant gift of charismatic leadership, a genuine religious zeal, and a personal appeal to the black masses in the urban centers of the United States. "I hope you will become a great preacher of Islam in America," Shaykh Harkon counseled Malcolm at the Hajj court. We should not think the Azzams hoped for anything less. Malcolm's Muslim hosts have been properly tagged as leaders seeking religious opportunity, and possibly a foothold in the African American community.

Having been disappointed by Elijah Muhammad's empty flirtations with the Muslim world, some architects of the Islamic mission undoubtedly found in Malcolm X an exceedingly superior alternative. In fact, Malcolm did have a good deal to offer the Muslim world. His hosts knew how successful he had been in defending and advancing heretical Islam—including his skillful defusing of the black Christian church's influence in many cases. The degree to which these Muslim elites sought to assist Malcolm is very likely a good measurement of the urgency with which they were seeking a viable African American exponent of Islam.

Malcolm readily took up their offer, explicit or implicit as it was. He was now a true believer in Islam, and had long held that Islam was the authentic religion of Africa and Africans—including those who were stolen away from their motherland in slavery. Not surprisingly, Malcolm's analysis of racism was completely accommodated by his host in Jedda, who even encouraged a selective reading of history with a bit of propaganda. As Malcolm recounted it, Abd al-Rahman Azzam told him "the complexities of color, and the problems of color which exist in the Muslim world, exist only where, and to the extent that, that area of the Muslim world has been influenced by the

West." Malcolm's generous host concluded that any manifestation of color prejudice in the Muslim world "directly reflected the degree of Western influence."

To be sure, Azzam's analysis was simplistic at best. It has been well documented that color prejudice, and even Afriphobia, existed in the Muslim world independent of Western influence. Indeed, it has been likewise shown that such patterns were related, both directly and indirectly, to the enslavement of Africans by Muslim peoples. One writer, who considered Malcolm curiously "oblivious" to Muslim racial discrimination, has even noted that Saudi Arabia finally abolished slavery only three years before Malcolm's Hajj—leaving an estimated 250,000 black ex-slaves in the heart of the Muslim world.[13]

Of course, the issue here is not to attempt a moral competition between the Muslim world and the West, or between Islam and Christianity. As religious analyses go, the corrective directed to Malcolm X by an Islamic scholar in 1963 is worth repeating: "The essential nature of Islam, like the essential nature of Hebraism and Christianity, is pacific, tolerant and charitable."

Likewise, the issue is not to equalize the guilt of white peoples worldwide for the many abuses of Africa and its children. The fact remains that the West unleashed a centuries-long holocaust of enslavement, colonial exploitation, and brutality upon African peoples for which there is no historical equivalent among the whites of the Muslim world. "For nearly six centuries now," begins one Dark World history, "western Europe and its diaspora have been disturbing the peace of the world." Insofar as the African continent is concerned, the Muslim presence, however militant and expansive, never wreaked havoc as did the ostensible Christian presence. "There was indeed an Islamic colonialism," concedes one friend of the Muslim world, "but it was a relatively benign form of colonialism."[14]

Now we can return to the black nationalist assertion that Hajji Malcolm could not have been fooled by Saudi "window dressing." In December 1964, Malcolm appeared on the *Community Corner* radio broadcast in New York City, answering questions from the audience by telephone. When one caller specifically addressed the historic role of Arabs in the enslavement of blacks, Malcolm X responded: "I don't condone slavery, no matter who it's carried on by. . . . And I think that every power that has participated in slavery of any form on this earth, in history, has paid for it, except the United States."

Malcolm pointed out that both the Europeans and the Arabs had "lost their empires" while the United States had not. "She's the only one up till now who has yet to pay." Malcolm then quoted a rarely cited verse from the biblical book of Revelation (13:10) that speaks of captivity and the sword being returned upon those who practiced such evils on the innocent. Taking a poke at Christian preachers who taught pacifism, he said this passage was "the one the preacher thought didn't exist." Malcolm then concluded: "This is justice. So I don't think that any power can enslave a people and not look forward to having that justice come back upon itself."[15]

Obviously, Malcolm was very careful of how he presented his answer. For him to deny the facts regarding the enslavement of Africans by Muslim Arabs would have been deceptive and self-defeating to his religious mission. Yet for Malcolm X to dwell too heavily on the realities of slavery and racism in the Muslim world would have been an obvious inconvenience to his evangelistic claims, as well as to his personal Muslim loyalty. Perhaps Malcolm also feared that any attention paid to the past sins of the Muslim Arabs might also be used by Western apologists to divert the discussion and minimize the antiracist effort. Regardless, this approach was a far cry from his denial, while in the Nation, that Muslims took slaves at all.

Malcolm's account of the Hajj in *The Autobiography of Malcolm X*, then, was likewise intended to protect and promote Islam by idealizing Muslims and stylizing his own experience in Mecca. This is certainly clear in Malcolm's personal "reappraisal" of the white man. As his account would have the reader believe, it was after the Azzams intervened on his behalf that he "first began to perceive that 'white man,' as commonly used, means complexion only secondarily; primarily it described attitudes and actions. . . . But in the Muslim world, I had seen that men with white complexions were more genuinely brotherly than anyone else had ever been." Malcolm thus used his experience with the Azzams to demonstrate that both the religious and human societies of the Muslim world were "color-blind."[16]

Again, it seems clear to the critical reader that Malcolm had already begun to reappraise the white race long before his Hajj, just as he had already begun to reappraise the teachings of the Nation long before losing faith in Muhammad. Malcolm noted in his autobiography that in his declining days in the Nation, some white people "really got to me in a personal way." Their obvious concern and personal respect for him made Malcolm realize that "some of them were really honest and sincere." It was no major change, to be sure, but it was evidence that Malcolm X was reconsidering the difference between white complexions and white attitudes quite awhile before he went on the Hajj.

As a member of the Nation, Malcolm's belief had forced him to stand in total rejection of the white world. Consequently, his moral posture as a follower of Elijah Muhammad required the rejection of all the values of the dominant culture, while at the same time keeping him at arm's length from the Muslim "society" he had always admired. With Malcolm now religiously reintegrated into the world, Sunni Islam allowed him to maintain his moral posture without total acceptance or total rejection of the world of white people.

Malcolm's new place in Islam thus allowed him the more humane position of standing in-between whites, and judging them according to their personal values rather than standing entirely against them as a race. This was the religious experience Malcolm expressed in his autobiographical account. However, in order to advance his religious cause, Malcolm had to idealize his Hajj in the Muslim world—in effect using it as a model of desired human relations, and a kind of moral high ground from which to announce Allah's purpose for humanity in the matter of race.

Not long before he was to leave Saudi and continue his journey, Malcolm enjoyed an audience with Prince Faisal. Faisal told Malcolm that making him a guest of state was merely Muslim hospitality offered to the "unusual Muslim from America . . . with no other motives whatever." Faisal was obviously concerned if Malcolm now understood the orthodox Islamic religion, and Malcolm promptly assured him this was the reason for his Hajj. Faisal was apparently satisfied with Malcolm's sincerity, but advised him that good literature on Islam was abundant, and therefore sincere people had no excuse to be misled.

Malcolm made no further comment in the text about his meeting with Faisal, but the implicit meaning of the incident is clear. The Muslim ruler who had taken up the cause of the "unusual Muslim from America" and made him a guest of state was now giving Malcolm an exit interview. He had passed the test at the Hajj court and fulfilled all the rituals and requirements of the most sacred event in the Muslim world. Aware of Malcolm's imminent return to the United States and the attention he would undoubtedly draw, Faisal wanted to make sure that the former "Black Muslim" understood his responsibility to Islam.

Malcolm no longer had the excuse of lack of understanding; he had formerly misled people into believing what Faisal called "the wrong Islam." Now Malcolm was a true Muslim, and he was expected to bring orthodox Islam to the United States. The many sincere people seeking to know Islam should no longer be misled, the Prince concluded.[17] In the most gracious of Eastern terms, or so it would appear, the Hajji Malcolm had been given a mandate.

# 17

## The Final Year

*So I say that we must have a strong Africa.*

From the end of his Hajj in April 1964 until his assassination in February 1965, Malcolm X's story—already a challenging and detailed study—blossoms into a substantially more complex and fascinating account. This complexity is not due merely to the fact that he spent the last months of his life developing both a religious and a political organization. Nor is it due to the fact that he was simultaneously struggling against the Nation—a conflict which became quite heated by the summer of 1964.

Rather, Malcolm's last year was complex because he spent a good portion of his final months in the Dark World, and these extended travels accelerated his personal development—largely out of sight of the Western world. If Malcolm X has been an enigma, it is due to the failure of writers to do critical work on the international aspects of his life. Thus even a fine scholar might err in saying that Malcolm was not as "nationally or internationally known" as Martin Luther King, Jr. The Malcolm X of 1964–65 was indeed very much an international figure, which we are only beginning to appreciate now.

Malcolm X in this last year is a very different man from the Malcolm X of the Nation days in many ways. His scope is broadened, his tenor of speech seems more directed toward pedagogy, and his religious expressions are philosophical even when polemical. Yet he remained very much the revolutionist and "extremist" until his dying day. But now his thoughts on change— even change by means of physical force—were constructively explained and reasoned (when his interviewers gave him the opportunity) within a fundamentally humanitarian context.

Malcolm X tailored his presentations within the United States according to his perceptions of the political culture. Indeed, it has been said that Malcolm believed people in the United States were "politically parochial." He therefore communicated his ideas to his audiences in simplistic terms, often using metaphors. In contrast, in his "discourse outside of the American context . . . Malcolm spoke in grounded specifics and displayed a political astuteness and diplomatic sagacity" that frustrated even a prominent scholar: "I asked myself, Who is this man?"[1]

In his autobiography, Malcolm recalled in great detail his shorter tour of Africa, which immediately followed the Hajj—lasting from the end of April until May 21, 1964, when he returned to the United States. After leaving the "Holy World," Malcolm also visited Lebanon, Egypt, Nigeria, Ghana, Liberia, Senegal, Morocco, and Algeria. This first tour of 1964 occasioned a certain amount of celebrity for Malcolm. He provided Alex Haley with a variety of vignettes picturing some of the colorful moments of his tour. Most striking were his enthusiastically received speeches before African student organizations, fetes sponsored in his honor by various dignitaries, and his notable meeting with Ghana's leader, Kwame Nkrumah.

On the other hand, Malcolm devoted only a few lines to his extended return trip, which occurred from July through November 1964. He did note that he had met with a variety of African heads of state as well as religious leaders, and his communications and interactions on the African continent were very extensive.[2] Much of his time in the Muslim world and Europe was devoted to religious matters. In addition, Malcolm made two brief trips to Europe in December 1964 and February 1965 to show his interest in the African and African American expatriate communities there.

*The Autobiography of Malcolm X* is politically incomplete—not only because Malcolm's writing partner, Alex Haley, was not able to accompany him overseas on these tours, but because Haley apparently did not understand the sophistication of Malcolm's political evolution. To be sure, it was not the intent of Malcolm X to make his autobiography into a technical explanation of his political development; it was, instead, fundamentally the religious appeal of a devout revolutionist. In a somewhat wistful socialist interpretation, George Breitman's political observation of Malcolm's last year has correctly noted that Malcolm's evolution quickened in the last months of his life—especially during the last three months of December 1964 to February 1965.[3] Yet these final months could not have been documented in the autobiography because Malcolm and Haley were already in the final phases of manuscript preparation.

All these factors suggest that the Hajj marked an important turning point in Malcolm's career as an activist, and that attempts to analyze him politically must be carried out with a great deal of sensitivity. Students and scholars must consider the African, Asian, and European press, the limitations of documentation in the United States, and the inadequacies of *The Autobiography of Malcolm X* itself. Finally, one must bear in mind the biases of the socialists—who enjoy a publishing monopoly on Malcolm's speeches, especially those given in the final year of his life.

In this chapter I will present historical information that is needed to lay the groundwork for further discussion concerning the religious Malcolm X. What follows is a topical overview of Malcolm X's last year, presented along the lines of three important biographical themes: Malcolm and Africa, Malcolm and the Organization of Afro-American Unity, and Malcolm's tragic conflict with the Nation.

In 1964–65, Malcolm paid a great deal of attention to the political and social conditions in Africa. He spent about half of his last year in Africa, and the African political situation figured heavily in his stateside speeches, discussions, and organizational concerns as well. Malcolm noted with pride that, during his May 1964 visit to Ibadan University in Nigeria, a Muslim student organization awarded him a membership card as well as an African name. The students named Malcolm "Omowale," "the son has come home" in the Yoruba language. It was a fitting title for one whose Garveyite heritage remained at the heart of his attitude toward Africa.

In the summer of 1964, only a short time before he flew to Cairo to begin his second extended tour of the continent, Malcolm visited Omaha, Nebraska, his birthplace and one of the places where his parents worked on behalf of the Garvey movement. "America is the country of the past," Malcolm told reporters, "and Africa is the country of the future." It was an obvious slip on Malcolm's part to refer to an entire continent as a "country"; however, the statement reveals how deeply he identified with the entire

African homeland as *his* land. "I don't feel that I am a visitor in Ghana or in any part of Africa," Malcolm had already declared before an audience of Ghanaian students in May 1964. "I feel that I am at home."[4] Writing to a journalist in May 1964, Malcolm declared:

In the Arab world they loved me as soon as they learned I was an American Muslim, and here in Africa they opened their hearts and their arms to me when they learned that I was an African American, and I must confess that their joy and respect was greater still when they discovered I was "Malcolm X" of the Militant American Muslims. Africans in general and Muslims in particular, everywhere, love militancy."[5]

Malcolm, of course, loved militancy, too, and had no trouble fitting into the African revolutionary context. Julian Mayfield, the leader of the African American expatriate community in Ghana, recalled that Malcolm's months in Africa "were the happiest of his life. He won friends of high and low station everywhere he went."

John Lewis and Donald Harris, who were sent to Africa on a fact-finding tour by the Student Non-Violent Coordinating Committee (SNCC), arrived during Malcolm's second tour and wrote in their report: "Malcolm's impact on Africa was just fantastic. In every country he was known and served as the main criteria [sic] for categorizing other Afro-Americans and their political view." However, Malcolm's success in Africa was not based merely on political sentimentality or on his charismatic presence. He considered his personal and organizational relationship to Africa as a vital matter in the survival of both the African continent and Africans scattered throughout the Western Hemisphere.

During his tour in May 1964, Malcolm wrote to James Shabazz, his assistant in the Muslim Mosque: "Brother James, I have established a foundation which cannot be destroyed if I am killed tomorrow." Thus, Malcolm saw his work as foundational—the establishment of a basis upon which Africans and African Americans could unite and build a power bloc in the world. "His scope was broadening in ever-increasing concentric circles," Shabazz reflected of Malcolm's interest in Africa and in scattered Africans worldwide.

In this great partnership with Africa, Malcolm maintained it was necessary for African Americans to go back mentally, culturally, spiritually, philosophically, and psychologically to Africa.[6] He used the relationship of Jews in the United States to the Jews of the world as a model for the international Pan-Africanism he envisioned:

Just as the American Jew is in harmony (politically, economically and culturally) with World Jewry, it is time for all African Americans to become an integral part of the world's Pan-Africanists . . . we must "return" to Africa philosophically and culturally and develop a working unity in the framework of Pan-Africanism.[7]

Malcolm made a similar case in an article published in an African magazine: "We don't want to move over here physically. What we want is to have a cultural and psychological migration here, like the Jews have migrated to Israel philosophically and culturally." (Interestingly, after making a little-known visit to the Palestinian homeland on the Gaza strip in 1964, Malcolm stopped using Israel as an example, giving instead a Chinese analogy.)

Malcolm sought a two-way bridge between Africans and African Americans. He challenged Africans that they would never be respected until "the black man in America is also recognized and respected as a human being."[8] Likewise, Malcolm preached to his African American followers:

So I say that we must have a strong Africa, and one of my reasons for going to Africa was because I know this. You waste your time in this country, in any kind of strategy that you use, if you're not in direct contact with your brother on the African continent who has his independence.[9]

In February 1965, in the last speech Malcolm was to make, he told an assembly of Columbia University and Barnard College students that African Americans must "help Africa in its struggle to free itself from western domination. No matter where the black man is, he will never be respected until Africa is a world power."

Malcolm believed implicitly that the Western powers incited and maintained division within Africa. He told an audience of his followers that these powers made a constant effort, for instance, to incite divisions between East Africans and Asians, and between West Africans and Arabs. He also believed that indigenous Muslims and Christians were likewise provoked to fight in parts of Africa—all to secure the power of the West. "When you go over there and study this thing, you can see that it is not something that is indigenous to the African himself," he said.

Similarly, Malcolm believed unity among blacks in the Western Hemisphere was crucial, estimating that there were well over eighty million "Africans in the Americas." However, such unity was being hindered by the "well-designed plan" of the Western powers, whose sense of "frantic necessity" compelled them to keep blacks in the Americas from uniting further with Africans "in our swiftly emerging African fatherland."[10]

Malcolm returned from his first tour of the African continent in May 1964 with the intention of addressing the need for unity among people of African descent. However, he also felt that it was necessary to address the racial crisis confronting African Americans on the local level. He wanted to develop an organization, separate from the Muslim Mosque, that would promote the participation of a diverse group of African Americans without obligating its membership to participate in Muslim affairs. "We realized that many of our people aren't going to become Muslim; many of them aren't even interested in anything religious," Malcolm recalled. "So we set up the Organization of Afro-American Unity as a non-religious organization."

Malcolm first thought of calling this organization the Afro-American Freedom Fighters, a counterpart to the African revolutionary groups that had helped to liberate Algeria and Kenya. However, upon further consideration, he apparently found the Organization of African Unity (OAU) a better model, since it advanced the pan-African philosophy and was inclusive of all African independence movements. The OAU, founded in 1963, thus became the impetus for the founding and development of Malcolm's New York-based "Organization of Afro-American Unity" (OAAU), which maintained chapters in Africa and Europe and established an information bureau in Ghana. The philosophy of the OAAU was wholistic, focused on politics, economics, community improvement, self-defense and education. Its fundamental goal was "the acquisition of human rights" for African Americans, and the building of a black solidarity that would transcend "all organizational differences." [11]

When Malcolm made his second 1964 trip to Africa, his first stop was in Cairo. Here he attended the second OAU conference on July 17 to 21 as a representative and chairman of the OAAU and was granted observer status. He prepared a memorandum to the conference representatives, to whom he appealed that "our problems are your problems." Calling the U.S. government a tricky "neo-colonialist power," Malcolm urged the OAU to recognize the racial crisis in the United States as a human rights issue worthy of their attention and asking for their unified effort to bring it before the United Nations.

In response to Malcolm's appeal, the OAU passed a resolution that recognized that civil rights legislation of the United States government had failed to implement a solution to the racial crisis. In Africa, Malcolm took an unabashed position in exposing the U.S. government's hypocritical pursuit of friendship with African nations while racism remained a problem at home. "But how can she keep the Africans' respect," Malcolm declared in an

*Egyptian Gazette* interview, "when she allows such injustice to people of African descent in her own country?" [12]

At the time that Malcolm was undertaking such a task of international proportions, he was greatly frustrated in his attempts by his escalating clashes with the Nation. The Nation had not waited until Malcolm was out of the movement to declare war on him; as early as January 1964, the leadership of Mosque No. 7 in New York attempted to persuade some of its members to kill Malcolm. The plot failed, however, when the would-be assassin proved to be sympathetic to Malcolm.

The conflict between Malcolm and the Nation seems to have been significantly exacerbated by the Nation's attempt to evict him from his house in Queens. The Nation's attorney argued that because Malcolm was no longer a Nation minister, he should not reside in their parsonage. In answering the Nation, Malcolm countered that the house had been purchased for him by the movement during his tenure as their New York minister.

Malcolm was disturbed by the Nation's eviction attempt not only because it jeopardized the security of his family, but also because the movement would not allow him to argue his case in a private Nation hearing. "So they would rather go to the man whom they say is the devil to settle the differences rather than to settle it behind closed doors," Malcolm complained in an interview. "I have not wanted to do anything in public. And I've even kept my tongue, which is not my nature, you know." [13]

In June 1964, Malcolm no longer held his tongue. He fought back, using his knowledge of Muhammad's sexual abuses as the basis for what he apparently hoped would be a media blitz about the Nation. He appeared on talk shows in Boston, Philadelphia, and New York, provided information to newspapers, and used his own organizational platform to reveal details about Muhammad's illegitimate children. Most notable, however, was Malcolm's interview by Mike Wallace of CBS, in which he documented Muhammad's affairs and challenged the Nation's claim that the young women in question were Muhammad's wives. The former secretaries were not put in positions of respect or protection befitting their roles as "wives," Malcolm charged. "They have been debased." [14]

The immediate result was an upsurge of threats and attacks made against Malcolm X and his followers. One FBI source reported that, within Mosque No. 7, "war" had been openly declared on the Muslim Mosque, and members were encouraged to attack and drive Malcolm's followers out of town. When it became clear that violence was escalating, Malcolm wrote an "open letter" to Elijah Muhammad on June 23, 1964, suggesting his "calculated silence" would not spare him from being held responsible for the violent actions of Nation members. Malcolm further warned that "the writers of history" would declare him guilty, "not only of adultery and deceit, but also of MURDER." Appealing to Elijah Muhammad to "call off this unnecessary bloodshed," Malcolm suggested they should instead be working "in unity and harmony" to solve the problems of black people. "Historians," concluded Malcolm X, "would then credit us with intelligence and sincerity."[15]

Malcolm's letter brought only countercharges that he intended to kill Muhammad—to which Malcolm responded to the press: "We don't have to kill him. What he has done will bring him to his grave." In the meantime, Malcolm told an OAAU audience that he had no desire to fight the "Black Muslims, who are my brothers still"; however, it was apparently too late for Malcolm and the Nation to reach even a détente.

In July 1964, two of Muhammad's former secretaries brought paternity charges against him, which were answered by an official press release from Nation headquarters. In the statement, the Nation's top officials blamed Malcolm X, accusing him of maliciously attempting to disgrace Elijah Muhammad while at the same time they denied any guilt on Muhammad's part.[16]

*Muhammad Speaks* launched a series of attacks on Malcolm, the first of which was an open letter from one Nation minister who called him a hypocrite, a defector, and a notorious "Harlem hustler." In Chicago, a national official, John Ali, declared that Malcolm's "X" had been retracted and that he was now only Malcolm Little. However, Muhammad himself was apparently very careful not to address the issue of his sexual immorality, restricting his countercharges to comments about Malcolm's pride and departure from the Nation. Thus, he told one interviewer: "I suspended him, Malcolm took it for an insult to be set down for any length of time. He was too proud. A man seeking exaltation sometimes goes to extremes."

In September 1964, the civil court of Queens ruled in favor of the Nation, but stayed the execution of the eviction warrant until January 1965.[17] However, by the time of the decision, Malcolm had already been gone for two months, having left the United States to attend the OAU conference in July 1964. When he returned at the end of November, he publicly expressed his desire to avoid any further confrontations with the Nation. He told an OAAU audience that after having made an extensive tour of Africa and holding long discussions with many heads of state, his scope had broadened even further:

And I felt foolish coming back to this country and getting into a little two-bit argument with some bird-brained person who calls himself a Black Muslim. I felt I was wasting my time. I felt it would be a drag for me to come back here and allow myself to be in a whole lot of public arguments and physical fisticuffs . . . knowing that it would actually be more beneficial to our people if a constructive program were put in front of them immediately.[18]

Malcolm admitted that prior to his second tour abroad he had foolishly allowed the Nation to "jockey" him into participating in a war of words. He concluded that, consequently, when he returned to the United States the Nation refused to desist in their offensive. Indeed, in December 1964, the Nation sent a threatening telegram to Malcolm X and it was subsequently published: "Mr. Malcolm: We hereby officially warn you that the Nation shall no longer tolerate your scandalizing the name of our leader . . . regardless of where such scandalizing has been."

The "scandalizing" to which the message referred was apparently not an allusion to Malcolm's previous comments about Muhammad's sexual behavior, however, but to a letter that Malcolm wrote to *New York Times* journalist M. S. Handler in September 1964—while he was out of the United States. During his return trip to Mecca, Malcolm had written this letter, referring to Elijah Muhammad as a "religious faker" and declaring his intention to expose him as such. However, Malcolm's "Holy World" indignation toward Muhammad apparently abated after the remaining two months of his African tour, in October and November 1964. Consequently, when Malcolm returned to the United States at the end of November, the Nation was on the offensive. "He knew that he was not going to die an old man," Benjamin Karim remembered. Malcolm also knew that, for him, time "was fast running out."[19]

# 18

## Religious Revolutionist

*For the Muslims, I'm too worldly; for other groups,
I'm too religious.*

As it was conceived and created in March 1964, the Muslim
Mosque had no authentic religious standing in the Muslim world. Malcolm
X and two of his followers signed the prepared papers of incorporation on
March 9, 1964—the day after Malcolm's independence announcement.
The papers speak of the study and propagation of "the Islamic Faith and
Religion," but do not make any theological distinctions between the religion
of the Muslim Mosque and that of the Nation. However, one of the articles
did specify that the Muslim Mosque was established to impart the "Islamic
Religion in accordance with the accepted Islamic Religious principals."

About two months later, shortly after completing the Hajj, Malcolm wrote
to his Muslim Mosque constituency: "I hope that my Hajj to the Holy City
of Mecca will officially establish the religious affiliation of the Muslim
Mosque, Incorporated, with the 750,000,000 Muslims of the World of Islam
once and for all." It is necessary to underscore, then, that a fundamental
dimension of Malcolm's Hajj was, organizationally speaking, quite precon-
ceived. As such, Malcolm's pilgrimage was also a quest for religious authenticity in the Muslim world. This is important to note because it shows that
Malcolm's experience in Mecca was not a religious romance without root or

reason; it likewise shows that Malcolm's Hajj was not merely "a religious settling of accounts."[1]

Malcolm's religious mission was not simply a detail on his agenda, but the agenda itself. In December 1964 he told an interviewer that after he had formed the Muslim Mosque in March of that year, he immediately wanted to make the Hajj "to get a better understanding of Islam as it's practiced in the Muslim World and to establish ourselves with the orthodox Muslims." Once he had made official contact with the Muslim world, of course, Malcolm's new religious organization would be expected to conform to the orthodox standards and expectations of that world.

After completing the Hajj and his African tour, Malcolm met with the members of the Muslim Mosque in New York City on May 28, 1964. According to an FBI source, the meeting, which was held at Harlem's Hotel Theresa—also the site of Muslim Mosque headquarters—was attended by about two hundred people. Because the Nation had not yet begun its eviction efforts against Malcolm, he was not yet speaking negatively about Elijah Muhammad. However, during the question-and-answer period someone in the audience asked Malcolm if he had seen W. D. Fard while he was in Mecca. It was not only a reminder of whence he had come, but also how much work he now had to do as an exponent of traditional Islam. Malcolm told the questioner that members of the Muslim Mosque should disregard the old notions. From now on, Malcolm assured the audience, they would deal only with reality.

If the "ghost" of Fard haunted the Muslim Mosque, so did other vestiges of the Nation's cultic heritage. At a meeting at the Tusken Ballroom in New York on June 22, 1964, Malcolm announced that the Muslim Mosque, unlike the Nation, would be accountable for any monies collected from its membership. Sometime later, when the Muslim Mosque established a branch in Philadelphia, the new members were told they would not be asked for money unless necessary, and that the funds would remain at their own mosque. This policy signaled a departure from the kind of financial exploitation that typified the relationship of the Nation's headquarters with its branch mosques.[2]

Earlier during the month of June when Malcolm was between his two trips abroad, the membership of the Muslim Mosque in New York City was estimated at one hundred. He had additional supporters in Boston and Philadelphia, potential branch cities of the Muslim Mosque. After Malcolm left for his second, more extended tour from July through November, the Muslim Mosque began to suffer. According to FBI information, while Malcolm was away, only about fifteen people attended Muslim Mosque meetings regularly, and the interest on the part of the Muslims in Boston had waned almost entirely.

Worse, the Muslim Mosque began to have serious conflicts with Malcolm's other group, the OAAU. The conflict, which was apparently ignited by religious differences, seems also to have involved a power struggle between Muslim Mosque and OAAU officials. To counteract this problem, Malcolm directed that no one could serve as an officer in both organizations—a strategy he hoped would ensure the involvement of non-Muslims in the OAAU.

With Malcolm's return from the "Holy World" and Africa on November 28, 1964, both of his organizations were undoubtedly refreshed. FBI information described a very active Muslim Mosque in New York that offered not only religious instruction and prayer services for members several times a week, but also held judo classes and instruction in the Arabic language, with the latter two classes apparently open to the public.

Malcolm now no doubt had to make the members aware of the religious and philosophical changes necessitated by their new orthodox stance. Thus, at a Muslim Mosque meeting on December 23, 1964, Malcolm had to urge his followers not to condemn people on the basis of their color. He admitted that this was even hard for him to do, given all that he had said against white people in the past. It would probably have been even harder for Malcolm's followers to allow white brethren into the Muslim Mosque, which was an actual possibility—though it apparently never happened. One journalist later recalled that Malcolm liked to say the Muslim Mosque was open to people of all races. "The trouble is," Malcolm would add, "we haven't found any white people who want to be Muslims."

Though the Muslim Mosque's organizational papers had called for an official publication, there apparently never was one. Malcolm had spoken of starting a paper called *The Flaming Crescent*, but this was during the first weeks of the movement when the religious aspects of the Muslim Mosque were not yet sorted out. With the establishment of the OAAU and the release of its publication, the *Blacklash*, the idea of a regular Muslim Mosque publication seems to have been put aside.[3]

While no Muslim Mosque publication ever materialized, the organization did generate press releases that documented Malcolm's comments and activities while on tour. It also released informational fliers, such as one that presented a revealing explanation of the new Muslim Mosque—the organization as it had become with Malcolm's acceptance into the traditional Muslim world: "Created in fulfillment of the need to correct the distorted image of the religion of Islam that exists in the west. To offer to the American that religion that frees instead of enslaves, raises the morals, instead of lowering them, the religion that makes all men brothers."[4] The flier reiterated that the objective of the Muslim Mosque was not only to teach and propagate Islam, but to "correct" and "disseminate correct information on Islam." This theme of correction is significant because it was not part of the Muslim Mosque's founding papers.

These new emphases on correction of past religious errors and the wish to propagate a sound form of Islam are apparently the influence of Malcolm's extended time in the Muslim world as well as the increased influence of certain Muslim religious agencies on the Muslim Mosque. Most notable in this regard was the commissioning of Shaykh Ahmed Hassoun as a kind of missionary-teacher to the Muslim Mosque.

Hassoun, a Sudanese imam, was authorized and funded with a five hundred dollars a month stipend by the Saudi-based Muslim World League. His work, which was ultimately thwarted by Malcolm's assassination in February 1965, was essential to the advancement and success of the Muslim Mosque as a base for Islamic instruction. Hassoun, who adhered to the teachings of the prominent Wahabi sect of Saudi Arabia, not only served as an instructor in Islamic classes, but also taught Arabic. When Hassoun arrived in New York in December 1964, the Los Angeles *Herald-Dispatch* noted that he had come to help Malcolm X "correct the distorted image that the religion of Islam has been given by the hate groups in this country." An FBI source noted that additional instruction in Islam was provided to the Muslim Mosque through Dr. Shawarbi's New York–based Islamic offices.[5]

The Muslim world quite understandably sprang at the opportunity to advance Islam, which would not only give them an occasion to missionize in the African American community, but also to make a long-desired corrective strike at the Nation. Indeed, one of the fruits of the religious side of Malcolm's overseas sojourning was the endowment of "expense-free" scholarships to Islamic institutions made available to the Muslim Mosque. During Malcolm's second tour, he received twenty scholarships from the Cairo-based Supreme Council on Islamic Affairs (SCIA), which were designated for "young Afro-Americans" to study at Al-Azhar University. He likewise received fifteen scholarships for applicants wishing to study at the University of Medina in Saudi Arabia. The scholarships, which both the Muslim

Mosque and the OAAU advertised, were not only significant for academic reasons, but also as insurance against future distortions of Islam among African Americans.[6]

When Malcolm went on his second tour of 1964, he was criticized by some of his own followers in the OAAU, who griped that he was "going away when we need him most over here." Ethel Minor, who was a secretary in the OAAU, recalled that some of the membership even referred to Malcolm as "just another bourgeois nigger," because of his extensive tour of meetings with African heads of state. Others, while less mean-spirited, simply felt the second tour was superfluous.

Perhaps, in some sense, these troubling attitudes at home attest to David Graham Du Bois's broader assessment that "nobody understood, nobody had a clue what [Malcolm] was talking about." Thus, while Malcolm's organizational personnel bickered and criticized, he was in Egypt, delicately balancing revolution and religion in a manner elusive to most revolutionists and religionists alike. Du Bois, the stepson of the African American scholar-activist, W. E. B. Du Bois, had himself come to Cairo as an expatriate. He recalled that Malcolm X arrived in Cairo alone and without the fanfare he received during his first 1964 tour. In fact, Du Bois remembered, at first many of the religious officials at Al-Azhar University were not convinced of Malcolm's Muslim integrity.[7]

When news of criticism and dissension at home reached Malcolm, who was still in Cairo through September 1964, he wrote his followers a letter. He emphasized that his task in Africa was a "direct threat to the entire international system of racist exploitation." But by internationalizing the struggle of African Americans, Malcolm concluded, the foundation laid was firmly set, "and no one can hardly undo it." As to the reports of dissension, Malcolm expressed neither resentment nor surprise, noting that it was "normal" behavior in organizations—"history repeating itself."

Malcolm assured his followers of his commitment to human rights, organizational flexibility, and nonjudgmentalism. In tones reminiscent of a pastoral epistle, Malcolm continued by gently telling his dissenting followers that they were free to quit and even start their own organizations if they liked: "But wherever you go and whatever you do, remember that we are all still brothers and sisters and we still have the same problem. Let us not waste time condemning and fighting each other. We have already wasted too much time and energy doing this in the past."[8] Malcolm expressed his desire to avoid any further conflicts with Elijah Muhammad, and challenged both the Muslim Mosque and the OAAU to use the time of his absence wisely by working together. "I have so much faith in *Allah*, and in *right*, and in my people, that I believe I can come back and start from scratch if it is necessary and as long as I mean right *Allah* will bless me with success and our people will help me in this fight," Malcolm concluded. "I love all of you and pray *Allah* will bless all of you."

Malcolm's religious life could no longer be defined simply as one of disbelief in Elijah Muhammad. Likewise, Malcolm had now gone beyond the sincere appropriation and adoption of Sunni Islam that drove him to Mecca in the first place. Rather, Malcolm seems to have entered the last phase of religious development that may be referred to as "religiously" Muslim. This stage of development "reappropriates childhood's best attitudes, providing the needed context for being Jewish, Christian, Muslim or whatever. One no longer has a religion; one is religious in a particular way." The significance of Malcolm's first tour was that he truly *had* a religion; but the quiet triumph of his second tour abroad was that Malcolm now was developing his own particular way of being a Muslim.

Being "religiously" Muslim, in this case, involved two inner aspects, the first of which may be called "parable." "Parable," according to Gabriel Moran, is living with the awareness that problems may not have one single answer or that "logic" may not always be capable of providing solutions. "Living with a tension of opposites does not mean the paralysis that is non-action. Life demands activity, and the religious person is engaged in acting the best way he can discern," even though he lacks a "plan," and does not claim to know either God's justice or what is in God's mind.

This does not mean, however, that the religious person cannot recognize injustice. Quite to the contrary, he recognizes that "there are things wrong in the world, and someone must take the risk of stopping them." This outlook gives one a sense of belonging to a specific group and a particular history, allowing one to appeal to "my people" as an embodiment of "the people." "The beliefs of our people can now function not as blinders to a wider truth but as powerful stimuli to act on behalf of all."[9]

In many ways, this description of the "parable" aspect is well suited to Malcolm X in the summer and fall of 1964. It is interesting that Malcolm, who relived childhood memories of "Hector's Hill" while on the "Holy World Hilltop" of Arafat, had now been able to retrieve elements of his childhood religious experience—those that allowed him to form his own religious life and work according to his inner awareness of the divine, rather than the cultic divinity that had been mediated exclusively through Elijah Muhammad.

As a religious leader in his own right, Malcolm's words to his followers demonstrated that he no longer believed in herding souls with cultic discipline and diatribe; his appeal now was to his own discernment of Allah's will and purpose, and the kinship he felt for black people—which functioned as a powerful stimulus for action. Quite in contrast to the competing factions of his following, the issue for Malcolm was neither organizational preservation nor domination. He could surrender both the Muslim Mosque and the OAAU to the providence of Allah and start all over "from scratch" if necessary.

This was apparently the same sentiment Malcolm had expressed to Wallace Muhammad, the son of his former leader, in their December 6, 1964, meeting—a sentiment that so impressed Wallace that he apparently made note of it in a subsequent interview with the FBI, who stated that Wallace "advised that Malcolm X had convinced him that he (Malcolm X) was a true believer in the [o]rthodox Islamic religion. According to Muhammad, Malcolm X stated that he did not consider the OAAU or the [Muslim Mosque] as definite organizations and that *he could easily disband both of them.*"[10] This expression, like Malcolm's "start from scratch" comment in the letter to his followers, was neither a sign of bitterness toward his wavering disciples nor the symptom of growing disinterest.

Malcolm's willingness to "start from scratch" reflects the second inner aspect of his "religiously" Muslim stage. Moran calls this second aspect "detachment," but adds that parable is not thus abandoned but "deepened and enriched by the development of a contemplative center to life." Detachment is simply the willingness to wait, "the determination and the patience to stay at what one feels called to" because "the human vocation is to stay at one's post and do the best one can." However, in the growing contemplative center that characterizes detachment in the Eastern religious tradition, sometimes the struggle against injustice is undercut by extremes. In sharp distinction, Western religion favors a fundamental lack of detachment.

In Malcolm's case, detachment seems to have dominated his final months of life. Not only did he persevere in his work and ultimately return glory to Allah, but he sought to walk the steadfast and painful line that stretched between a contemplative life devoid of struggle against injustice, and a struggle against injustice that was altogether devoid of faith. "For the Muslims, I'm too worldly, for other groups, I'm too religious," Malcolm told some of his followers. "[F]or militants, I'm too moderate; and for moderates, I'm too militant. I feel like I'm on a tightrope."[11]

An interview in Cairo during his second tour of 1964 further reflects the depth and development of Malcolm's "religiously" Muslim stage. The interview, conducted by the African American activist Milton Henry, apparently took place after Malcolm's work at the OAU conference had concluded. During the interview, Henry stated that the Egyptians were a beautiful people and were also "beautiful people spiritually"—particularly in their apparent lack of color prejudice. Malcolm immediately seized on this comment, saying:

> But there's one thing though, brother, that you have to realize, and I think it's the underlying reason for the brotherhood that exists here in Cairo—this is a Muslim country, and the religion of Islam absolutely eliminates racism . . . it's the only spiritual force that has the sufficient strength to eliminate racism from the heart of the person. So that when a Muslim, *a true Muslim, who practices the religion of Islam* as it was taught by the prophet Muhammad, who was born and died in Arabia some fourteen centuries ago, *a true Muslim* never looks at a person and sees him just by the color of his skin. [12]

Malcolm's reference to a "true Muslim" is important, of course, because it continues to affirm the essential distinction he had already drawn between Sunni Muslims and Elijah Muhammad's Nation. However, this was not Malcolm's specific inference. Rather, it seems he was concentrating on the reality of the Muslim world in which he now dwelled, and on the fact that even in the "Holy World" an authentic Muslim is defined by prophetic praxis.

Malcolm's words show that he had now accepted the reality of a duality of principles in the Muslim world itself. Thus, Islam was a spiritual force that could absolutely eliminate racism and guarantee brotherhood, while Muslims in a Muslim world might nevertheless live beneath their calling. To Malcolm X, Islam was the solution, but not as a rational formula or an idealistic answer. Quite to the contrary, Islam became a question, a challenge, and a test that required the Muslim to work out brotherhood by the *practice* of faith, which undoubtedly included the struggle against injustice. Malcolm X had begun to develop his own way of being a Muslim—a way that distinguished the practicing Muslim from those who reduced Islam to a religion of ritual and tradition. However, in so doing, Malcolm began to question the status quo of the Muslim world itself.

Malcolm closed the interview with Milton Henry by advising him to make people in Detroit aware of orthodox mosques in their area. He emphasized again that Islam could produce "racial harmony and unity" even between blacks and whites in Detroit, if only they would seek its true form. "My next stop, if it be the will of Allah, will be Mecca," Malcolm told Henry. "I'm going back to Mecca, probably next week, and sharpen my spiritual eye." It appears, however, that Malcolm had already begun the process of Muslim spiritual refinement in a manner distinctly his own.

Marc Crawford has noted that when Malcolm became affiliated with the Muslim world, "he joined something far larger, far older, [and] far more substantial" than the Nation. "And it gave him a certain legitimacy that certainly he needed and had lacked," Crawford added. From the beginning, when Malcolm had announced the formation of the Muslim Mosque, he had openly admitted that despite his belief "in divine guidance, divine power, and in the fulfillment of divine prophecy," the only "credentials" he could claim was "sincerity."

Even after Malcolm made the Hajj, as Du Bois noted, as late as July 1964 a significant number of important Muslims were still skeptical about his sincerity. And while there seemed to be no overt opposition to Malcolm, his time in Egypt and Saudi during the second tour was apparently designated for achieving "ecclesiastical" recognition and acceptance—which went beyond the affirmation of his personal religious commitment by validating his role in the Muslim Mosque.

During Malcolm's extended stay in Cairo in July–September 1964, he befriended an Egyptian journalist and talked extensively with him about his life and goals. The journalist later recalled that Malcolm "was very proud of his Hajj document, which was attached to his passport and which he showed everybody."[13] He also remembered that Malcolm

spoke about the cause of the Negroes which he staunchly believed to be a just cause and also spoke about Islam which he embraced in true understanding and conviction. He spoke about how he strongly defended Islam against those who use Islam as a means of reaching their ends through Negroes.[14]

This reference to "those who use Islam as a means of reaching their ends" seems to suggest that Malcolm's indignation toward the Nation was continuing, and may even have heightened in the contemplation that distance afforded him. This account is particularly true to form because of the inseparable pairing of the black struggle with the promulgation of Islam that so typified Malcolm's religious thinking.

This pairing is obvious as well in a speech Malcolm made in Cairo on July 27, 1964, before the Shubaan Al-Muslimeen, a young men's Muslim organization similar to the YMCA. The speech reveals Malcolm's determination to fuse his role in the black struggle with that of the Muslim mission. In his presentation, Malcolm X appealed to his audience that "the case of the 22 million oppressed Afro-Americans is unique, much different from all other historic cases"—not only as a dark-skinned minority living among a white majority, but also because "we are over 6,000 miles from our Original Homeland." Malcolm declared further that if they, who were "in the majority here on this African Continent," had been oppressed by European colonizers, "how much more difficult is it for those of us who are a minority in America where we are still colonized by an enemy who outnumbers us?"

Being a Muslim he felt "duty-bound to fight for the spread of Islam until all the world bows before Allah." However, being also "one of the 22 million oppressed Afro-Americans," Malcolm declared, "I can never overlook the miserable plight of my people in America."

Therefore, my fight is two-fold, my burden is double, my responsibilities multiple . . . material as well as spiritual, political as well as religious, racial as well as non-racial. I will never hesitate to let the entire world know the hell my people suffer from America's deceit, and her hypocrisy, as well as her oppression.[15]

Malcolm charged that it was wrong for his listeners to condemn "the racist colonialism of South Africa," while keeping silent "about the racist neo-colonialism" of the United States. "In the Sight of Allah," Malcolm preached, "racism must be uncompromisingly condemned, both in South Africa and the United States." Obviously mindful that he was speaking to an international audience, Malcolm closed by challenging that the struggle of African Americans was not only a concern for Africans, but "must also be the concern and the moral responsibility of the entire Muslim World—if you hope to make the principles of the Quran a *Living Reality.*"[16]

In September 1964, Malcolm returned to Mecca, making an off-season visit, or Omra, which one United States Embassy official called "the little pilgrimage." The embassy at Jedda, in fact, prepared a somewhat detailed report about Malcolm's visit to Saudi that was based on an official interview and the press coverage provided by Jedda's *al-Bilad*. The embassy report emphasized that

Malcolm X stressed his pleasure at his visits to Saudi Arabia and their benefit to his personal spiritual development. He took pains during this conversation to deprecate his reputation as a political activist and dwelt mainly on his interest in bringing sounder appreciation of Islam to American Negroes.[17]

The report also said that Malcolm expressed happiness at being "far away from politics," which gave him a chance "to think about what was really essential."

On a whole, this report is fascinating in its description of Malcolm X for a number of reasons. First, it suggests that Malcolm made a visible attempt to emphasize his religious identity while deemphasizing his more well-known political role. Second, it shows that Malcolm, probably for reasons of expediency, sought to accommodate the embassy interviewer as much as possible. Thus the official described Malcolm as "assured but surprisingly unaggressive and undogmatic" and "rather disarming in describing his own activities." When asked about certain blunt statements he had made in Cairo, Malcolm minimized the whole issue by saying lightheartedly, "I shoot my mouth off a lot and don't always remember what I've said."

Finally, Malcolm seemed very much concerned to emphasize Islam and his desire to see it advanced in the United States. In fact, he not only spoke of the Muslim Mosque as his attempt to provide an Institute for Islamic studies, but made a point in his *al-Bilad* interview to express sharp criticism of the Nation and of Zionists in the United States who, Malcolm charged, were hindering the presentation of true Islam to the African American community in their distinctive ways.[18]

Malcolm's statements to the press in Jedda occurred around the same time that he wrote his zealous letter denouncing Elijah Muhammad as a "religious faker." The letter, which Malcolm wrote to a *New York Times* journalist on September 22, 1964, was undoubtedly his boldest religious denunciation of the Nation until that time. Though he had previously exposed Muhammad's moral depravation and had declared it as the reason for his own loss of faith, he had brought no such charges against the Nation as a whole.

Malcolm's letter was not without its personal elements, including his own *mea culpa* declaration, and the promise that he would never rest until he had "undone the harm" he had brought about by his previous "evangelistic zeal" in the service of the Nation.

For 12 long years I lived within the narrow-minded confines of the "strait-jacket world" created by my strong belief that Elijah Muhammad was a messenger direct from God Himself, and my faith in what I now see to be pseudo religious philosophy that he preaches. But as his then most faithful disciple, I represented and defended him at all levels . . . and in most instances, even beyond the level of intellect and reason.[19]

Along with this confession, Malcolm felt obligated to take the ignoble credit for turning "well-meaning, innocent Negroes" into blind fanatics whose faith in Muhammad now even exceeded his own. The "Islam" of Elijah Muhammad, Malcolm charged, was a "racist philosophy" deceptively labeled so as "to fool and misuse gullible people."

Having clarified his religious stance vis-à-vis the Nation and his former part in the movement, Malcolm then declared "emphatically" that he no longer wore anyone's "strait-jacket" and was now "a Muslim in the most orthodox sense"—a believer in Islam as it "is believed in and practiced by the Muslims here in the Holy City of Mecca." In Islam, Malcolm stated, all are brothers and equals before God and "as members in the Human Family of Mankind."

It seems likely that Malcolm's declaration was sincere and that it was not only fueled by genuine religious feeling but by the heightened experience of having returned to the "Holy World." Malcolm's zealous challenge to the Nation is even more understandable when one learns further details about his return to Saudi and the activities in which he took part. The same *New York Times* article that published Malcolm's letter revealed that Malcolm had spent an extended time studying with "ranking scholars of Islam" and "working with the Muslim World League."[20]

Malcolm was apparently undertaking a rigorous program of preparation and examination under the aegis of the leading religious figures of the Muslim world. His intensive preparation extended until October 1964, having been underwritten by the SCIA in Cairo which, according to Dr. Shawarbi, paid for the balance of Malcolm's travels in Saudi Arabia, Africa, and Europe. While in Saudi, Malcolm worked with the Mecca-based Muslim World League (MWL), a council of imams whose function it was to coordinate all the activities of Islamic organizations in the Muslim world.

In particular, Malcolm was supervised by the secretary general, Shaykh Muhammad Sarur Al-Sabban. Malcolm continued to correspond with the *New York Times* journalist, who reported that Malcolm "had worked all summer and into the fall . . . to prepare himself for his new role as an evangelist in the United States." Malcolm quite enthusiastically reported that the secretary general was a tall black man and an ex-slave who rose to power as minister of finance—perhaps an unwitting admission of the ironic blend of injustice and privilege that characterized the institution of slavery in the Muslim world.[21]

Sometime toward the end of Malcolm's ministerial preparation he faced what seems to have been a final examination before the rector of Cairo's Al-Azhar University. According to the certificate that was thereafter issued, "Malkulm X"—known also by his Muslim name, "Malik El-Shabazz"—appeared at the office of the supreme imam, Shaykh Hassan Maa'moun, who heard his affirmation of "the two Islamic Articles": "I confess that there is no God but Allah and that Mohammed is His Prophet, and Jesus is

His servant and Messenger. I ceased to believe in any other religion that contradicts Islam."

The certificate noted that Maa'moun's decision to approve Malcolm was based on the endorsements of the MWL and Malcolm's friend, Dr. Mahmoud Shawarbi. Maa'moun's certificate of recognition, then, was not concerned with vindicating Malcolm's personal faith, which he said was both "true and correct." Rather, it provided Malcolm with credentials as a religious teacher charged with "the duty to propagate Islam and offer every available assistance and facilities to those who wish conversion."

Back in New York, Dr. Shawarbi was undoubtedly basking in the pleasing sunlight of Malcolm's achievements in the Muslim world. In a telephone conversation monitored by the FBI, Shawarbi told Betty Shabazz that Malcolm would have a lot to do in assisting him upon his return to the United States. Shawarbi looked forward to "collaborating" with Malcolm, and he shared his dream of building an Islamic Center in the heart of New York City. Malcolm could even tour with him to raise funds, Shawarbi suggested.[22] However, it seems that Shawarbi, like the rest of the Muslim world, had an agenda that did not entirely overlap with that of Malcolm X. Malcolm had every intention of promulgating Islam, but he had no intention whatsoever of abandoning the struggle that was inseparably bound up with his religious identity.

While Malcolm's Muslim brethren seemed generally optimistic, or at least kept their criticism within private circles, one Muslim from the East increasingly sharpened his attack on Malcolm X in 1964–65. Abdul Basit Naeem, formerly Malcolm's close associate in the Nation, had continued to act as ally to Elijah Muhammad despite growing opposition to the "Black Muslims" by orthodox Muslims. In June 1964, when Malcolm X began aggressively to report Elijah Muhammad's sexual indiscretions to the media, the Nation held a rally in New York City's 142nd Street Armory in which Muhammad appeared. Shortly afterward, *Muhammad Speaks* featured an open letter of thanks from "the Messenger" to the Harlem community, as well as the apparent transcription of Naeem's speech. There was no doubt that Naeem's faithful support was once again being enlisted to add legitimacy to the Nation's Muslim claims; but it was also clear that Naeem (either voluntarily or by direction of Elijah Muhammad) engaged in some delicate oratorical surgery in order to close the wound left by Malcolm's break and the subsequent charges against Muhammad.

After praising Elijah Muhammad as a great teacher, reformer, therapist and individual of "sterling qualities," Naeem noted the current "crisis" facing the Nation. Declaring it his duty to attend the rally to speak out, Naeem noted his intention of discussing the removal "of an individual from the rolls of the Nation of Islam who once served as an important aide to The Honorable Elijah Muhammad." At no time was Malcolm mentioned by name, but the reference was clear as Naeem proceeded to advise his Harlem audience "not to fret over the winds blowing away a small splinter from the superb, super-structure of the Nation of Islam." This "splinter" was obviously "not properly attached or firmly connected with the main body," Naeem declared to his listeners, "and your fine House may well be better off without such loose pieces!" Naeem also warned the audience to refrain from "idle talk," which in the context of the "crisis" raised by Malcolm X was apparently an attempt to quell any further discussion of the several cases of Elijah Muhammad's illegitimate paternity. Naeem's final admonition was that Harlem's Muslims not be "carried away by the romance and apparent attraction of things 'Eastern.' " This was probably a sincere expression on his part. However, it was obviously also convenient to countering Malcolm's famous Hajj declarations in the "Holy World," and to preserving Elijah Muhammad's parochial vision.

That summer Naeem continued to speak out on behalf of Elijah Muhammad in *Muhammad Speaks*,[23] but in early 1965 it became impossible for Naeem to avoid addressing the Malcolm issue in an overt manner. Since Naeem had worked hard to appoint himself as a kind of liaison between the Nation and some leaders in the Muslim world (Naeem did not clarify who these leaders were), he was being queried from abroad regarding his continued support of the Nation in light of Malcolm's conversion to Sunni Islam—not to mention the opposition of Elijah's own son, Akbar Muhammad, to the Nation's teachings. However, Naeem probably grasped the occasion to again lend his support to Elijah Muhammad, who may have felt threatened when it became clear that Malcolm X had been authorized as an official Muslim representative by Al-Azhar University.

In two different issues of *Muhammad Speaks* in February 1965, Naeem addressed the issue of Malcolm X in vivid terms. "Speaking specifically of Malcolm X," Naeem announced, "I can safely state, having studied his motives, moods and moves as carefully and closely as circumstances permitted me during the past thirteen months, I find him positively undeserving of and unfit for the role of a Muslim leader in America, which he undeniably fancies for himself."[24] This was, among other things, an arrogant statement for Naeem to make, especially given that Malcolm's role as a Muslim leader was hardly fanciful after his studies and recognition at Al-Azhar. This statement may also reflect a certain disdain that he may have felt toward Arab Muslims, to which he had alluded before the audience at the 142nd Street Armory. In any case, the self-appointed Pakistani Muslim spokesman suggested that Malcolm's recent associations—perhaps with white social-ists—proved that he was a traitor even to his Arab and Muslim " 'well-wishers' abroad." Naeem further stated that if Malcolm could endure even nominally as a Muslim, it would not be due to personal strength but rather to his "previous training" under Elijah Muhammad. Finally, in a graceless display of mud slinging that was typical of the Nation's attacks on Malcolm at the time, Naeem concluded: "Those of us who know of the dubious and unimpressive moral background of Mr. Malcolm Little need not forget that if it were not for the Honorable Elijah Muhammad, our new champion of Afro-American Unity might—by his own admission—still be a pimp." Naeem also attacked Akbar Muhammad in the same article, but only by expressing great regret that Elijah Muhammad's own son lacked the wisdom to avoid, "even by implication," supporting Malcolm's "vicious campaign of belittling and slandering the Messenger."

In an article published only days before Malcolm's assassination, Naeem rounded out his previous attack by declaring his readiness to meet any challenger, whether Eastern or Western, who would dare to oppose Elijah Muhammad. Naeem recounted objectively that Malcolm had originally been removed from his pastoral position at Mosque No. 7, and that his request for reinstatement had been rejected. Seemingly blind to the Nation's hostile acts toward Malcolm, however, Naeem concluded that Malcolm's recent attacks on Elijah Muhammad's character were purely acts of "despera-tion and of deliberate and wilful vengeance." Finally, Naeem stated that Malcolm had done irreparable damage by sowing "seeds of dissension," and was therefore guilty of "immense disservice to the cause of our sacred faith (Islam)."[25]

Naeem's harsh treatment of Malcolm X demonstrates his own conception of the Muslim mission. First, it may be that, as a Pakistani, Naeem felt privately critical of the strong Arab orientation in the religious leadership of the Muslim world. If this was the case, it makes his treatment of Malcolm X all the more disappointing, since—as a Sunni Muslim—Malcolm was also apparently concerned that non-Arab (especially African) Muslims not be relegated to a secondary level of importance. Second, it seems that, whatever Naeem stood to gain financially from his association with the Nation, his personal loyalties were with the black community in the United States. This makes Naeem, again, a most unlikely critic of Malcolm X, who was proposing a program of genuine activism and progressive politics on behalf of the black community. Instead of supporting Malcolm's Muslim Mosque and OAAU organizations (as he had supported Nasser's movement in Egypt), Naeem remained loyal to the decidedly nonpolitical, cultic, and conservative program of Elijah Muhammad. For whatever reasons—personal, religious, or economic—Naeem clung to Elijah Muhammad and condemned Malcolm X. However, though Naeem had departed from the Muslim norm in rejecting Malcolm, he did share with the orthodox a lack of appreciation for Malcolm's continued commitment to the politics of black liberation.

For his part, Malcolm had hardly misled the Muslim world into thinking that he would conform to their conception of a missionary. From the first exuberant declarations of his Hajj, to his studies in Saudi in the late summer of 1964, Malcolm had never stopped talking about the struggle of his people, and he had certainly never suggested that his role as a true Muslim would minimize that struggle. Malcolm had turned the occasion of his Cairo address before the Shubaan Al-Muslimeen into a theo-political declaration, calling for both the triumph of Islam and the global struggle of the Muslim world against the oppression of African Americans.

Malcolm's letter from Mecca in September 1964 also spoke of forgetting "politics and propaganda," and approaching the racial problem "as a Human Problem which all of us as human beings are obligated to correct." Even in speaking to the official at the United States Embassy in Jedda, Malcolm had repeatedly used the word "humanism" to describe his philosophy of race and racial relations. He was clearly evidencing a new theology of racial reconciliation—one that took as a given a single human race rather than a black-white racial dichotomy. However, Malcolm was not implying by this an abandonment of the struggle, nor a willingness to minimize the realities of his people's racial oppression. In short, his religious "change did not imply that Malcolm's political understanding had become less radical." [26]

# 19

## Fighting in the Way of God

*I'm speaking now from what I think.*

One writer who observed Malcolm X very closely outside of the United States recalled that he "was a very explicit man, and his analysis of the spiritual and material condition of his people was nothing if not searing in its objectivity and explicitness." However, the searing analysis of Malcolm's political thought, all too often excised and appropriated by revolutionists, must be reset into the framework of Malcolm's religion and spirituality if it is to be fully understood.

Malcolm fundamentally perceived religion as a wholistic experience that "included every aspect of one's life—economic, political and social." That he grew frustrated by the "narrow confines" of the Nation is no surprise. After the Hajj, Malcolm declared that Elijah Muhammad not only taught "hate," but he offered "something that is unobtainable." Malcolm said further, "I believe the black man needs something more. I try to show my followers how they can get something more."[1]

Getting "more" for black people meant real political, social, and economic strategies, which excluded the "pie-in-the-sky" nonpolitical stance of Christians and the imaginary exodus promised by Elijah Muhammad. Even in the first weeks of his independence, Malcolm told a Muslim Mosque audience: "A preaching or a gospel is no better than its ability to be carried out in a manner that will make it beneficial to the people who accept it." He decried any kind of gospel that did not "do something for you and me right here, right now." "In the past," Malcolm concluded, "most of the religious gospels that you and I have heard have benefitted only those who preach it."

Malcolm believed implicitly that Islam was the kind of gospel that could provide for the concerns of the here-and-now. Indeed, even with the acceptance of orthodoxy, Malcolm never seems to have reproached Elijah Muhammad for having negated the "hereafter" in his teachings. However, he did insert a comment in his autobiography regarding the Nation's nihilistic view of death: "I was to learn later that Mr. Muhammad's teaching about death and the Muslim funeral service was in drastic contradiction to what Islam taught in the East."[2] Although he later accepted the Qur'an's teachings on life after death, it was characteristic of Malcolm X to weigh a religion's integrity according to its present value, not its future rewards. Thus, Malcolm told one interviewer:

The religion of Islam actually restores one's human feelings—human rights, human incentives—his talent. It brings out of the individual all of his dormant potential. It gives him the incentive to develop to be identified collectively in the brotherhood of Islam with the brothers in Islam. [3]

Besides the obvious autobiographical connotations of this description of Islam, it is clear that Malcolm believed it was a wholistic religion that presented collective as well as individual opportunities to "restore" humanity. This was significant for two reasons: Islam could be collectively applied to the condition of the African American community, and consequently the struggle of African Americans would become a relevant issue to the "brotherhood of Islam."

In this light, it is clear that Malcolm's challenge to a Muslim audience in Cairo, to make the principles of the Qur'an a "living reality," was not simple rhetoric. He believed that in order for Islam to be realized as it is presented in the Qur'an, it had to be fleshed out in social and political action that harmonized with the spiritual claims made by Muslims. "The Muslim World is forced to concern itself from the moral point of view in its own religious concepts," Malcolm wrote after the Hajj, "with the fact that our plight clearly involves the violation of our *human rights*." He continued:

The [Qur'an] compels the Muslim World to take a stand on the side of those whose human rights are being violated, no matter what the religious persuasion of the victims are. Islam is a religion which concerns itself with the human rights of all mankind, despite race, color, or creed. It recognizes all (everyone) as part of one Human Family.[4]

Malcolm's intention, apparently, was to suggest that even though much of the African American community was considered to be Christian, the Muslim world was nevertheless obligated to "take a stand" for their human rights. Thus, in Malcolm's thought, it was insufficient for Islamic advocates to claim their religion was a transracial faith if they were not also prepared to intercede for human rights across all boundaries of race *and* religion.

In a presentation on racism made late in January 1965 at Dartmouth College, Malcolm declared: "We must approach the problem as humans first, and whatever else we are second. . . . It is a situation which involves humans not nationalities. It is in this frame of reference that we must work." This was again reflective of the "humanism" and "human problem" themes he had introduced while in Saudi. Malcolm's appeal here was not to humanism in the sense of secular philosophy, but rather to a theistic humanism mandated by the Qur'an. Malcolm believed, therefore, that the Qur'anic paradigm for dealing with issues like racism and injustice was a theistic philosophy of human rights.

Quite contrary to the theistic themes of the civil rights struggle, however, Malcolm steadfastly maintained that the Qur'an's humanism did not rule out the use of just force against injustice. In an interview at Dartmouth's radio station, Malcolm was asked if the use of force against injustice could be avoided and perhaps replaced by a "more peaceful weapon." Malcolm undoubtedly recognized that the student interviewer's sincere inquiry reflected the popular nonviolent philosophy of the day. He calmly reasoned in response: "If a peaceful weapon could be used to correct the situation I'd be as much for it as anybody else. But I'm a realist, and I've watched this 'peaceful' approach."[5]

Malcolm pointed out to the student that the United States government never used a "peaceful" approach in dealing with its enemies, "not when her interests are at stake." He emphasized that blacks, therefore, will also react as all humans do when their interests are at stake. When the student interviewer asked Malcolm if this teaching was consistent with Islam, he responded:

The Qur'an says, "Fight against those that fight against you." This is what I love about the—this is one of the things that I love about the Muslim religion. It's a religion of peace, but at the same time you see the intelligence of it, because it says,

"Fight against those who fight against you"—don't initiate acts of aggression; don't attack people indiscriminately. But at the same time the religion of Islam gives one the right to fight when he's fought against.[6]

Interestingly, Malcolm's first inclination was to admit that what he loved most about Islam was its tolerance of self-defense. He seems to have checked himself in order not to give the impression that self-defense was the only appeal Islam had for him. Given his religious training in childhood, and his mother's reverence for Jesus as a prophet (but not as a divine figure), it would seem that Islam had other religious attractions for him. However, that the Qur'an sanctioned physical struggle as "fighting (or striving) in the way of God" was a central factor in Malcolm's belief that Islam was able to "restore" human dignity.

It appears that Malcolm's appreciation for this Qur'anic precept—and his desire to contextualize it in the case of the black struggle—was a tender issue, nevertheless. In particular, it seems that certain Muslim officials were put off by Malcolm's image as a "violent" revolutionist, and that some who should have known better were troubled by Malcolm's media image and his continued commitment to the black struggle in the United States. As early as the Hajj, Malcolm's friend, Dr. Mahmoud Shawarbi, expressed sentiments that perhaps assumed a bit too much of Malcolm's conversion. An interviewer for the *Washington Post* noted: "Dr. Shawarbi appeared confident that Malcolm would abandon his call for Negroes to arm themselves and form rifle clubs. He also predicted Malcolm's political organization will grow because whites may join."

Shawarbi not only expressed his belief that all people should be able to join the Muslim Mosque (which was characterized as a political movement), but that Malcolm should go about things "quietly and Islamically" so that his movement would grow. Shawarbi concluded of Malcolm: "In this way he will be serving his whole country, his own group and his new religion and setting a good example of a true Muslim for the American people."[7] However, Shawarbi could not have created a more misleading impression about the "new" Malcolm X. Indeed, it is possible that this and other "optimistic" statements by religious and political well-wishers contributed to the troublesome notion that Malcolm had undergone some sort of transmutation while in Mecca. Probably for this reason, in the initial weeks of his return from the Hajj and Africa, Malcolm X repeatedly corrected this assumption in interviews.

When one journalist asked Malcolm to compare the outlook of his "former self" with his new approach, he responded directly to the question's implications:

There has been no metamorphosis. Travel broadens your scope. My conclusion after getting outside the country and looking back was that most Negro leaders and Negro organizations are too selfish, organization-wise, and can't see the problem outside the context of their organizations. . . . I think that my scope was broadened sufficiently to enable me to work with anybody for a solution to the problem.[8]

Malcolm was apparently trying to make his interviewer cognizant of the difference between a broadening of his understanding and any notion of "metamorphosis." His breadth of understanding allowed Malcolm to maintain his "Muslim continuity" and the black struggle. A "metamorphosis" explanation, however, represented the earliest attempt to reinterpret Malcolm X—an approach that has become standard in the popular explanation of his conversion to Sunni Islam.

Shortly afterward, Malcolm made the same correction, using the same terminology, in another interview. As a result, the journalist noted that Malcolm's "conversation . . . indicated that he still regards the white man as the Negroes' No. 1 enemy and that his future course will be to fight that enemy." Indeed, he added: "No 'metamorphosis' resulted from his pilgrimage to Mecca, Malcolm said. He remains inflamed over the American Negro's condition and thinks only a revolution will correct it."[9] Even though violence was the "last thing" the black man wanted, Malcolm stated, "he must protect himself." He explained further that, even though he had abandoned the Nation's racial anthropology, he was not relinquishing his belief in the diabolical nature of racism in the United States:

Anyone . . . mind you, I am saying anyone . . . who overtly, intentionally, and knowingly deprives another of his human right[s] is a devil. I said anyone who does this is a devil. And, if he consciously, knowingly and intentionally deprives the man of knowledge that will enable him to correct his condition, he is a double devil. And this devil has to go.[10]

Similarly, in Malcolm's more publicized television interview with Mike Wallace on June 8, 1964, he further emphasized, "I've broadened my scope—travel broadens your scope, it gives you a wider understanding." He added that his experiences among college students, "even as a Black Muslim . . . showed me that they were genuinely concerned—some weren't genuinely concerned—but many of them were. And this element is increasing."

When Wallace pointed out that this represented "a considerable change of opinion," Malcolm responded that it was not so much a change of opinion as it was his new freedom to articulate his own thoughts. "Formerly I spoke for Elijah Muhammad. And everything I said was, 'Elijah Muhammad teaches us thus and so.' I'm speaking now from what I think, from what I have seen, from what I have analyzed, and the conclusions that I have reached."

It seems that Malcolm endeavored to demonstrate that while his break with Muhammad was genuine, and his thinking was no longer hindered by his former commitment to the Nation, he still had a legitimate case against whites in the United States. Malcolm likewise remonstrated that his experience in Mecca was only a broadening of his scope—that it entailed a widening of his vision and a clarification of his focus as it already had been. He had not evolved or metamorphosed into a new creature—Malcolm had always considered himself both a Muslim and an activist in the cause of black people. "Progressive programs and ideas were in Malcolm's natural makeup," his sister Ella Collins recalled. "He inherited it."

Malcolm was subjected to further scrutiny and criticism on the part of Muslim leaders, particularly when an abridged version of his autobiography was published in the *Saturday Evening Post*. The article, "I'm Talking to You, White Man," raised a good many orthodox eyebrows in the Muslim world and greatly disturbed Malcolm X himself. The article even irritated Dr. Shawarbi, who called Betty Shabazz to ask why Malcolm—who was in Egypt—had revealed so many stories from his earlier life. He complained that certain "ambassadors" from the East had queried him about Malcolm's character, which forced Shawarbi to explain that Malcolm "had no one to guide him when he was young." In defense of her husband, Betty pointed out that Malcolm's autobiographical work originated while he was still within the Nation, and therefore merited some changes. She also reasoned that when Malcolm "was a Black Muslim *he told bad things about himself to make Elijah Muhammad look good and give himself no credit for anything.*"

It seems that Betty Shabazz realized what many readers of Malcolm's story have not since understood: *The Autobiography of Malcolm X* was fundamentally shaped as a vehicle for religiously enhancing both the Nation and Elijah Muhammad himself. The fact that Betty felt her husband went so far as to deprecate his own role in the Nation underscores the fundamental honesty of Malcolm's autobiography and his testimony of having had the utmost faith in Elijah Muhammad. Fortunately, Shawarbi was most understanding, and assured Betty that the Qur'an taught that "sometimes the bad things are good." Perhaps, Shawarbi added, Malcolm's break with Elijah Muhammad had "all turned out to be a blessing for Malcolm." It undoubtedly had been a blessing to Malcolm. However, it was equally a blessing to Shawarbi's missionary goals, and he probably continued to anticipate that Malcolm would come his way, "quietly and Islamically."[11]

In Cairo, Malcolm was disturbed by the copies of the *Post* article sent to him by his wife, but his reasons were different from those of his Muslim friends and critics. On September 16, 1964, Malcolm wrote to Alex Haley, gently reproving him for not updating the article "to fit my present thinking." Malcolm was disturbed by a number of details that misrepresented his actions toward family and toward black people in general, and he felt that this only gave " 'take-off' material" to the editors of the *Post*, who had inserted a very biased editorial about him in the same edition.

Malcolm was particularly concerned, however, that Haley properly present the maturation and broadening of his thinking, and that he not present him in the post-Hajj period as thinking of whites in the terms of the Nation:

The only time [the book] should have me referring to them as devils is when it is in the context (and period) dealing with the time when that is what I was teaching. But it should remain only in *that* context. The end of the book should not have me (speaking in the 1st person and in the present tense) still referring to them as devils.[12]

Malcolm emphasized that "*time tenses*" had to be used in his story in order to keep his words and thoughts properly contextualized. "This is very important," he underscored. "And this is the only thing about the book that I absolutely insist upon."

Beyond the issues raised in the publication of his autobiography, Malcolm's more serious concern was reserved for what seems to have been an emerging conflict of interest between his political program and that of his missionary-minded Muslim associates. Throughout his last months, Malcolm had not only developed the revolutionary program of the OAAU, but he had refused to back away from his politically active Muslim stance. In December 1964, Malcolm showed anything but "quiet" inclinations in his approach to Islam.

On December 3, 1964, in fact, Malcolm was invited to participate in a debate at the Student Union of Britain's Oxford University. The theme was clearly political and controversial and was based on the proposition, "Extremism in defense of liberty is no vice, moderation in the pursuit of justice is no virtue"—a statement that had been made previously by former U.S. presidential candidate, Barry Goldwater. Malcolm took one of the positions in defense of the statement, skillfully putting it in the context of the African American struggle.

In his presentation, Malcolm emphasized his belief in Islam and his fulfillment of all the requirements of the religion, including the Hajj. He then demanded that since the system of the United States was based "upon the castration of the black man," none of the current legislative or civil rights programs could work to bring meaningful change. Malcolm charged that the U.S. government showed either its inability or unwillingness "to do whatever is necessary to protect life and property where the black American is concerned." Therefore, Malcolm concluded, because African Americans realize this,

we are not human beings unless we ourselves band together and do whatever, however, whenever is necessary [sic] to see that our lives and our property is protected. And I doubt that any person in here would refuse to do the same thing were he in the same position—or I should say were he in the same condition. [13]

Malcolm made other stops and speeches while in England, one of which was before three hundred Muslim students in London's Malaysia Hall on December 5, 1964. During his address Malcolm had occasion to refer to Martin Luther King, Jr., whose visit to England happened to have overlapped with his own. A reporter for the *Manchester Guardian* noted that Malcolm was "barbedly generous" to the nonviolent Christian leader. "I'll say nothing against him," Malcolm declared. "At one time the whites in the United States called him racialist, an extremist, and a Communist. Then the Black Muslims came along and the whites thanked the Lord for Martin Luther King." The journalist concluded that Malcolm seemed "relaxed, mellifluous and reasonable"—hardly the stereotype of Malcolm X that prevailed in the media. His backhanded compliment continued with the statement that Malcolm "has the assurance of Dr. Billy Graham and details are swamped by the powerful generalities of his message. And no one should doubt the power."

To be sure, the "power" of Malcolm's presentation was not revolutionary rhetoric, nor were his activist Muslim sentiments without action. While Malcolm was in Africa on his second tour of 1964, he actually made an offer to an OAU delegate to raise an army of African Americans to assist in driving out white mercenaries from the Congo. His plan for an "Afro-American Freedom Brigade" went as far as the recruitment of one hundred blacks by the OAAU to fight in what Malcolm anticipated would be an "African revolution." Back in New York City, in December 1964, Malcolm arranged for Muslim Mosque members to join OAAU members in a protest demonstration at the United Nations. According to an FBI source, the theme of the demonstration was to urge the United Nations to "take action against the United States for crimes committed against the American Negro all over the United States."

Malcolm X was no doubt aware that his revolutionary activities and reputation did not appeal to the conservative elements of the Muslim world. Certainly, he understood that religious affiliations tended to bridle the movements of the free-spirit—a lesson he had learned early from his mother, Louise. In May 1964 Malcolm told a television audience that "usually when you're working with a religious group or within a religious framework, you're already in a position to be in constant opposition to other people whose religious persuasion happens to be different." The kinds of tensions Malcolm had known while in the Nation were intense and inhibitive. But his new place in the Muslim world was, apparently, not without some opposition from certain Muslims with a different "religious persuasion."[14]

This is most clearly evidenced in Malcolm's correspondence with Said Ramadan, the director-general of the Islamic Centre in Geneva, Switzerland. In a letter of January 11, 1965, Malcolm responded to Ramadan's invitation to come and speak at the Centre, stating that it "is always a blessing to be able to tell the world what ALLAH and ISLAM has [sic] done for me and for our people here who have accepted it in America." Malcolm mentioned his attempts to "reorganize" the Muslims "into True Islam" since returning from his second trip, as well as the opposition he was facing from the Nation.

Malcolm noted that Elijah Muhammad would even use murder to oppose this effort, and that the Nation's animosity was aimed especially at him, which meant he was not only busy in his Muslim endeavors but "quite busy just trying to stay *alive*." Apart from these issues, Malcolm noted that the Saudi vice-minister of foreign affairs, H. K. Sayyid Omar El-Saghaf, had failed to follow through with a promise to provide the Muslim Mosque with finances for renting a "suitable" place of worship. "If we had stronger support from the Muslim world," Malcolm complained, "it would be very easy for us to spread True Islam here in the country."[15]

It is possible that the inadequacy of "support from the Muslim world" that Malcolm lamented was, in part, due to his continued revolutionary stance, his activities and statements in Africa, and his obvious intention of making his own way—in contrast to the more conservative expectations of certain

Muslim colleagues and benefactors. It is also likely that the paucity of financial assistance offered to Malcolm and the Muslim Mosque resulted from political expediency on the part of Saudis and others who feared offending the U.S. government. In any case, it seems that certain leaders in the Muslim world simply did not understand or sympathize with Malcolm's militant black struggle.

Just prior to his assassination, in fact, Malcolm X was preparing a lengthy correspondence to Ramadan. In it he answered a number of questions Ramadan had asked with regard to the work of the Muslim Mosque. Malcolm's letter assured the director-general that the "sole interest" of his organization was to "help undo the distorted image we have helped spread about Islam." In the same answer, Malcolm apparently felt constrained to defend his political agenda to Ramadan, pointing out that his other organization, the OAAU, was established "in a white racist society" to unite blacks "regardless of religious affiliation."[16]

The seventh question that Malcolm was to answer, however, was clearly critical of his political stance. "How could a man of your spirit, intellect and worldwide outlook," asked Ramadan, "fail to see in Islam its main characteristic, from its earliest days, as a message that confirms beyond doubt the ethnological oneness and quality of all races, thus striking at the very root of the monstrosity of racial discrimination[?]"

Assuming that this unwarranted rebuke was probably hurtful to Malcolm, his response was nevertheless patient and self-assured in tone. He responded that being an African American, he felt his "first responsibility" was to "my 22 million fellow Black Americans who suffer the same indignities because of their colour as I do." Further, Malcolm stated that he did not believe his "personal problem" with racism could be solved until it was solved for all African Americans. He then returned the stroke to Ramadan, albeit gently: "Much to my dismay, until now the Muslim World has seemed to ignore the problem of the Black American, and most Muslims who come here from the Muslim World have concentrated more effort in trying to convert white Americans than Black Americans."[17]

At this point, however, Malcolm's words to Ramadan assumed the style of a lecture about the failure of the Muslim world to proselytize in the African American community. Switching to an agricultural metaphor, Malcolm told the director-general of the Muslim Centre that "farming efforts" should be concentrated on "the most fertile soil"—and since whites had largely proven unresponsive to Islam, Malcolm scolded,

I should think the Muslim World would realize that the most fertile area for Islam in the West is the Black American. This in no way implies discrimination or racialism, but rather shows that we are intelligent enough to plant the Good Seed of Islam where it will grow best . . . later we can "doctor up" or fertilize the less fertile areas, but only after our Crop is already well-planted in the heart and mind of these Black Americans. [18]

Unrelenting, Malcolm broadened the discussion to Muslim attitudes toward Africa, and toward education in general. He blamed the failure of Muslim educators to allow non-Muslim Africans to become advanced beyond their Muslim peers, and he noted that "Muslim religious leaders of today need a more well-rounded type of education." He also wrote that unlearned Muslim leaders kept their people equally unlearned so as to dominate them. "They keep the people narrow-minded because they themselves are narrow-minded." These disturbing limitations, Malcolm noted, were particularly imposed on women—an unfortunate fact, since he also found that the positions of women in African and Middle Eastern nations tended to typify the general conditions in those countries.

Malcolm also advised Ramadan that Muslim educators had to reevaluate and clearly spell out the Muslim position on education, especially for women, and follow this up with a vast program. Malcolm's Garveyite nature was clear in his insistence that Africa was his "Fatherland," and that he was primarily interested in seeing the continent "free of outside political and economic influence that has dominated and exploited it."

Finally, Malcolm underscored that given the "almost inseparable" relationship of the Arab image with the "Image of Islam," the Arab world had "a multiple responsibility that it must live up to. Since Islam is a religion of Brotherhood and Unity those who take the lead in expounding this religion are duty-bound to set the highest example of Brotherhood and Unity." To assure this, Malcolm told Ramadan that the SCIA in Cairo and the MWL in Mecca ought to hold a religious "summit" to promote solutions to "the present plight of the Muslim World." He closed with a prophetic-styled threat, warning Ramadan that if the leadership of the Muslim world did not assert itself in this matter, "other forces" would rise to remove their "Power Centres," placing them elsewhere. "ALLAH CAN EASILY DO THIS." [19]

Malcolm's answers and comments to Said Ramadan highlight two important points. First, they reaffirm that in some quarters of the Muslim world, Malcolm X was completely misunderstood, if not disliked, because he insisted on pressing the issue of white racism and the struggle of African Americans. Malcolm's criticism of the Muslims' partiality toward whites was not a new observation on his part: he had already leveled that charge against his orthodox Muslim critics while he was in the Nation.

It is interesting that Dr. Shawarbi had admitted to Betty Shabazz that a Muslim colleague in New York City was not only critical of Malcolm, but was not happy about letting "anyone of every race become Muslims"—a private admission that not all of the Muslim brotherhood was as "colorblind" as Malcolm had declared them to be. It seems, then, that the Muslim world's outreach in the West had generally fallen into the same racial rut that European Christians had so deeply engraved into the religious landscape of the United States.

Second, these comments to Said Ramadan cast greater light on Malcolm's gentle innuendo in *The Autobiography of Malcolm X* that "the Arabs are poor at understanding the psychology of non-Arabs and the importance of public relations." Not only were they too passive in their missionary hopes, said Malcolm, but they didn't understand "the outside world."[20] However, in Malcolm's more explicit comments to Ramadan, he shows that this "outside world" so misunderstood by the Arabs also included Africa and other non-Arab countries, even those that had Muslim populations.

The failure to reach out to their non-Arab brethren, especially in terms of educational programs, kept these peoples limited in their development. Malcolm did not say so specifically, but there is a sense that he recognized a kind of Arab hegemony—the status quo of Arab domination that confined non-Arab Muslims to second-class citizenship in the Muslim world. Certainly this was the case with "the outside world" of women, which the patriarchal Muslims failed to perceive as being key to progress, even in their own Muslim societies. All in all, it appears that Malcolm's private comments to Said Ramadan serve as an important complement, and even a corrective, to his more publicized missionary-oriented declarations about the "Holy World."

At the individual level of his religious experience, it seems that Malcolm likewise approached Islam in a manner distinctly his own. As such, it is possible to see that in terms of the last stage of the "religiously" Muslim, Malcolm X had indeed recovered "childhood's best attitudes." Perhaps this is illustrated in his letter written from Saudi to a *New York Times* journalist in September 1964, when Malcolm openly proclaimed his friendship with people from many different religions, including atheists and agnostics. In that warmly humanist moment, Malcolm wrote: "It takes all these religions" among other human differences "to make the Human Family and the Human Society complete."

This statement might seem awkward—and even contradictory—when set against Malcolm's theo-political presentation before the Shubaan Al-Muslimeen. There, Malcolm had declared before an audience of Muslims that he felt "duty-bound" to fight for the advance of Islam, "until all the world bows before Allah." The question, then, is how it could be—in Malcolm's understanding—that all the world's religions together made humanity "complete," while at the same time Islam had to overtake all other religions.

Perhaps the best way to approach this question would be first to note examples of Malcolm's personal approach to advancing Islam. Michael Abdul Malik, a Caribbean-born black activist, met Malcolm when he visited England in 1965. Malik, who was not yet a Muslim, recalled that Malcolm spoke of the Qur'an as the "wonderful book" in which were answers to any problem. Another man who was profoundly touched by Malcolm's personal faith was Hakim Jamal, an ex-Nation member who recalled a dangerous trip to Los Angeles that Malcolm made in an attempt to help two of Muhammad's former secretaries. During that visit, Malcolm urged Jamal not to turn from Islam altogether, but only to turn from Elijah Muhammad. "It can help you, brother—believe me, I know this to be true."

Finally, David Graham Du Bois was likewise deeply impressed with Malcolm's religious sincerity. Du Bois recalled that Malcolm spoke of religion in general as a way of putting moral "blinders" on people to keep them from going astray. Subsequently, Du Bois incorporated his meetings with Malcolm into a historical novel about African American expatriates in Cairo—a story that leans quite obviously toward autobiography, and which presents almost photographic vignettes of the private Malcolm X.

Du Bois recounts Malcolm's discussions with him in Cairo, where Malcolm is to have told him that he would provide Islamic instruction to his followers if they desired it: "But no one will be forced to adopt Islam or to follow the Moslem teachings. Ideally, those who do follow Islam will provide an example of high moral behavior as well as dedication to our people that will win others to Islam." Du Bois's Malcolm displayed a serenity "that dominated every aspect of his person in all the great and small situations." Determined to correct the errors he had committed as Muhammad's spokesman, Malcolm assured Du Bois that he believed Allah would help him "travel the right road."

Du Bois's recollection is strengthened by an Egyptian interview with Malcolm, which took place in Cairo during the same time. Here, Malcolm said his name, Shabazz, signified his religious determination, implying he would not be misled "from the right path of Islam."[21] In discussing his personal religious life, Du Bois' Malcolm also says: "For me religion . . . Islam . . . has been like a harness, a guide to how I should behave. You know the life I led before I found the Nation. Everybody knows. I needed to be reined in. I needed guidelines . . . limits beyond which not to go. Islam provides these for me."[22] The Malcolm X who emerges from these various recollections is hardly the intense proselytizer that the Muslim world may have preferred. Still, he was a devout believer, and one who did not hesitate to share his religious experience with others. Malcolm obviously perceived his religion as a strong moral safeguard, and a system of controls that could both maintain and repair the human condition. For Malcolm, Islam was "a *Way of Living* . . . a guidance, [and] an uplifting Direction."

The fact that Malcolm could speak of all the world's religions as being necessary to "make the Human Family and the Human Society complete," does not negate his personal commitment to the advancement of Islam. Indeed, in autobiographical reflection, Malcolm shared his belief that one day Arabic would be "the most powerful spiritual language of the future"— words that could hardly be mistaken for religious compromise. He was, after all, a believing Muslim. His witness in this regard was constant in his public presentations and interviews, such as his speech at the Harvard Law School Forum in December 1964: "I'm a Muslim, which means that I believe in Allah, the same God that many of you would probably believe in if you knew more about Him. I believe in all of the prophets: Abraham, Moses, Jesus, Muhammad."

Yet if one characteristic distinguishes Malcolm's approach to Islam, it is that he appears to have been very comfortable with religious variety. Specifically, he seems to have perceived all the world's religions as enjoying a certain legitimacy, based not in the correctness of their theologies, but in their interrelatedness with the peoples and cultures to which they belonged. Malcolm's Islam thus evidenced both the basic religious eclecticism and the strong racial identification of his parents. Being a Garveyite son, it was natural for Malcolm X to view religion primarily through the lens of race-consciousness; as the son of Louise Little, it was equally natural for Malcolm to base his understanding of the Islamic mission on eclectic, receptive religious terms, instead of the narrower ground of religious fundamentalism.

In a speech Malcolm made in between his two 1964 trips abroad, he told a Muslim Mosque rally audience: "As a Muslim, I tell you try and get closer to God, believe in God, get a strong faith in *some* kind of [g]od and you'll find that it'll enable you to display a higher moral character." Drawing on his religiously eclectic roots, Malcolm seems to have been expressing his belief that theism, even non-Abramic theism ("*some* kind" of god), had specific moral value. Nevertheless, getting "closer to," and believing in *God*, in Malcolm's thinking, would probably still mean believing in Allah, the God of all the prophets.[23]

Thus, even within the context of the Abramic religions, Malcolm appeared to believe that Islam was the most advanced in its knowledge of God, a point he did not hesitate to emphasize further in the Harvard address: "Most of you are Jewish, and you believe in Moses; you might not pick Jesus. If you're Christians, you believe in Moses and Jesus. Well, I'm Muslim, and I believe in Moses, Jesus, and Muhammad. I believe in all of them. So I think I'm 'way up on you.' "[24] Malcolm's reasoning before his Harvard audience was that, as Jews and Christians, they would embrace the God of Islam if they only "knew more about Him." In order to do so, however, Jews and Christians would have to accept the Islamic understanding of Moses, Jesus, and Muhammad. Malcolm's expression seems to suggest his belief that Islam was the most progressive stage of Abramic monotheism—an integral claim of the Muslim mission.[25]

Nevertheless, Malcolm's "map" of world religions was primarily drawn along lines of race. Malcolm told another interviewer:

I can hardly separate the racial ingredient from any religion. When you really study them very closely, all of them have their racial characteristics. The Christian religion predominates in what we know as white European countries. . . . And even your Buddhist religion, your Hindu religion—they follow along a pretty set racial pattern.[26]

To Malcolm, religions expressed the various distinctive voices of humanity, and it was in this religious "racial pattern" that he recognized the totality of humanity. "The Africans are returning to Islam and other indigenous religions," Malcolm happily declared in 1965. "The Asians are returning to being Hindus, Buddhists and Muslims."

Still, Malcolm felt that of all the world's religions, Islam was the most flexible and was therefore able to "jump over" more racial boundaries— spanning the continents beyond the reach of Buddhism, another prominent Dark World religion. Indeed, Malcolm added, "Islam has made its inroads into countries that it has never conquered. *It just enters spiritually and conquers.*" Certainly, Malcolm told another interviewer, compared to Christianity, Islam in Africa was "a very powerful force" that had "won more acceptance."

It was the idea of "spiritual conquest," however, that appealed to Malcolm the most, and it seems likely this was what he had in mind when he told his Muslim audience in Cairo that he felt "duty-bound to fight for the spread of Islam." Since, for Malcolm, an individual's choice of religion was "personal business," religious conquest could only take place on a spiritual level: "Mankind's history has proved from one era to another that the true criterion of leadership is spiritual. Men are attracted by spirit. By power, men are *forced*. Love is engendered by spirit. By power, anxieties are created."[27] Clearly, toleration undergirded Malcolm's entire understanding of religious mission.

While his "spirit vs. power" theme has often been quoted in social or political contexts, it is important to emphasize that Malcolm was speaking here primarily in a religious context. Islam, as Malcolm X understood it, could not be forced upon people, especially those dwelling in different lands and cultures. The true Muslim could only advance his religion by spiritual conquest, and this meant that the Islamic mission could only succeed by setting an example of leadership that was attuned to the spiritual values of love and justice.

# 20

## Closing the Book

*I was faithful to that organization, and to that man.*

During the interview in Cairo by Milton Henry, Malcolm noted that "very narrow, backward, almost childish" attitudes seemed to prevent the unity of African Americans. In this regard, Malcolm emphasized what he considered to be the selfishness of religious groups: "Any group, any group that can't work with all other groups, if they are genuinely interested in solving the problems of the Negro collectively—why, I don't think that that group is really sincerely motivated toward reaching a solution."

Malcolm was clearly making a broad criticism that included all major black denominations, sects, and cults. However, it is likely that he spoke these words with the Nation in mind. Throughout the last year of his life, it was impossible for Malcolm to escape the Nation; when its intrusive presence did not threaten him physically, he was still haunted by the religious past he shared with Muhammad's Muslims.

As to Malcolm's transition from cult to orthodoxy, it had been completed when he identified himself with a new group of highly committed members. Those who abandon cults and enter orthodoxy invariably "close the book" on the past, viewing their former religious experiences as temporary episodes.

Invariably, the old view is finally and thoroughly repudiated and "disarmed of its interpretative validity by the individual's new faith."

In making thc Hajj, Malcolm was able to cut himself free from his former religious faith in Elijah Muhammad. However, throughout the last year of his life, he spent a great deal of time talking about the Nation. To be sure, the hostility and attacks launched against Malcolm and his followers— beginning with the eviction suit and ending with the firebombing of his house—may have inflamed him, prompting some harshness in his statements. Nevertheless, his overall assessment of the Nation, particularly from the standpoint of his religious thinking, seems fairly consistent in both earlier and later comments, and in statements made abroad and in the United States.

Malcolm ultimately concluded that "what Elijah Muhammad is teaching is an insult to the entire Muslim world, because Islam . . . has nothing to do with color." However, unlike others who were prepared to dismiss the Nation as a pseudo-religion, he emphasized that it possessed a true religious nature. In late January 1965, Malcolm appeared on a television program in Chicago and declared: "No one can say that what [Muhammad] teaches is not a religion, but it is not the religion of Islam. The religion of Islam is based upon brotherhood." Malcolm further suggested that, given the lack of understanding about Islam in the United States, "it is easy for any phony or faker to come along with a concocted, distorted product of his own making, and say this is Islam."[1]

As for the nature of the "concocted" religion of the Nation was concerned, Malcolm stated that since Elijah Muhammad had failed to steer his followers toward traditional Islam, the Muslim world had rejected him entirely. As a result, "It created a situation where we were in what we called a religious movement," which was really "a religious vacuum." Unwanted by the true Muslim world, and outside of the Christian world as well, the Nation had become a religious "hybrid." Indeed, the Nation was a "religious-political hybrid," alienated from the very struggle they claimed, and ever confined to the sidelines of that struggle.

The supposed militancy of the Nation as a movement, Malcolm told an interviewer, was really not true of the entire organization. It was only the New York branch (and thus Malcolm) that was militant. Only because of the high-profile attention Malcolm X had received from the press had "extreme militancy" been projected onto the entire Nation—despite Elijah Muhammad's basic nonpolitical stance. Even their "anti-white" reputation was not so much a political fact as it was a theological doctrine, Malcolm concluded.

In contrast to the pseudo-characteristics of the Nation, Malcolm testified from personal experience that the movement was highly restrictive. In an interview published in the Jamaican *Sunday Gleaner,* Malcolm revealed that though he had always wished to visit the Caribbean, he was not permitted to do so. "As a Black Muslim, in the Black Muslim Movement, I couldn't go because Mr. Muhammad never encouraged his followers, as such, to go anywhere. They were confined right here to the shores of America." [2]

Elijah Muhammad's insecure parochialism continued even after the supposed ground-breaking Middle Eastern and African tours that he and Malcolm had taken in 1959–60:

I went as an emissary for Mr. Muhammad. In fact, I was the one who set up the entire trip that Mr. Muhammad himself took. I will say this that the only reason I never went back was because Mr. Muhammad wouldn't let me go back. He has never encouraged any of his followers to visit Mecca, or to visit Africa. [3]

Apparently, Muhammad's restrictions served to prevent his followers from broadening their horizons—which would have inevitably meant the discovery of his faulty teachings. The teachings themselves were narrow and restricting, and Malcolm told another interviewer that eventually "the young, thinking Muslims" began to see that Muhammad's talk of a separate state for the Nation was no different from the black Christian teachings they had criticized as "pie in the sky." Malcolm and the other "thinking Muslims" apparently began to see that no effort was being made to make a separate state materialize.

In fact, according to Malcolm's later reflections, Elijah Muhammad had never *actually* espoused a separate black state, and thus his ideology was as void of content as his "Islam" was void of authenticity. "But at no time did he ever enter into any kind of activity or action that was designed to bring any of this into existence," Malcolm concluded. "And it was this lack of action that led many of the activists within the movement to become disillusioned and dissatisfied and eventually leave it."

Probably, in terms of the Nation's restrictions, this "lack of action" had wounded Malcolm the most—especially after the 1962 police attack on the Los Angeles mosque. "Some of our brothers got hurt and nothing was done about it. Those of us who wanted to do something about it were kept from doing something about it. So we split." [4] Malcolm was obviously offering here a simplified version of his break with Muhammad, but it underscores the great frustration he had felt about the Nation's stifling, nonactivist leadership.

Malcolm told an *Ebony* journalist that Elijah Muhammad had "agreed to let me present him as the prophet and messenger of Allah." In so doing, Malcolm recalled in another interview, his work had virtually become synonymous with the Nation: "I represented him probably more diligently than all of the rest of his representatives combined." Indeed, he added: "I represented an organization and organizational thinking. Many of my own views that I had from personal experience I kept to myself. I was faithful to that organization and to that man."[5]

Speaking in a radio interview several days before his death, Malcolm confessed that the reason for his former zealous labors on behalf of the Nation was his absolute faith in Elijah Muhammad:

There's not one person who is a Muslim who believes in Elijah Muhammad today who believes in him more strongly than I did. When I was with him I believed in him 100 percent. And it was my strong belief that made me go along with everything he taught. And I think if you check back on my representation of him while I was with him, I represented him 100 percent.[6]

Malcolm characterized his belief as "blind faith" and admitted to the readers of the *Egyptian Gazette* that he had permitted himself "to be used by Elijah Muhammad" to "make sweeping indictments of all white people." Malcolm told his own followers that because of his absolute trust in Elijah Muhammad, "I didn't try to see him as he actually was." Consequently, as Malcolm wrote to Alex Haley, he gave himself to years of "defending Elijah Muhammad's DEFENSELESS position."[7]

The postinvolvement phase in the life of the cult defector is one of sifting events and experiences, separating good from bad. As a result, voluntary defectors often defend certain aspects of their former organization while criticizing others. This kind of selectivity and separation of the more highly valued facets of one's membership gives an indication of careful reflection on the part of the individual.[8]

The process by which Malcolm selectively reflected on his involvement in the Nation can be observed in the commentary he constructed concerning both his break with the Nation and its tragic organizational decline. For Malcolm, the key to understanding the unfortunate deterioration of the movement required an understanding of Elijah Muhammad's contributions as a moral and spiritual leader, and his subsequent downfall. Thus, by imputing a kind of spiritual "golden age" to the Nation's history, Malcolm was able to selectively salvage aspects of his own experience within the movement.

Speaking about the Nation before the OAAU on February 15, 1965, Malcolm declared that it "was not a criminal organization at the outset."

It was an organization that had the power, the spiritual power, to reform the criminal. And this is what you have to understand. As long as that strong spiritual power was in the movement, it gave the moral strength to the believer that would enable him to rise above all his negative tendencies.[9]

Malcolm emphasized that he knew this from his own personal experience, and from observing "thousands of brothers and sisters" who were reformed "overnight, just through faith and faith alone." This spiritual force, then, gave the Nation the "moral discipline" it needed to become a feared and respected organization. In the same radio interview just prior to his death, Malcolm made a similar case for the Nation. Whatever else one might say of the Nation, Malcolm reasoned that at one time the organization was morally disciplined. "And there was that force within it, which was a spiritual force, that made the rank-in-file one who believed in it capable of abstaining from many of the moral weaknesses."

Malcolm had apparently begun this sorting process much earlier, as can be seen in his June 1964 interview with Mike Wallace, where in the face of the Nation's mean-spirited campaign to evict him, Malcolm pointed out that the Nation had formerly possessed the ability "to reform the morals of the so-called Negro community," eliminating drug and alcohol abuse and sexual promiscuity. Obviously, Malcolm continued this reflective selectivity until the time of his death. He did so, in fact, not just in public statements where religion was not the main issue, but in the more demanding report to the director-general of the Islamic Centre. In answering Said Ramadan's questions—the last official document he would compose—Malcolm likewise maintained that the Nation had enjoyed an "iron discipline," as long as belief in Elijah Muhammad's "infallibility and high moral character" was maintained. In a speech he made in Detroit on February 14, 1965, Malcolm's reflective selectivity went so far as to point out that his own consistent shirt-and-tie look was "a holdover from the Black Muslim movement," which taught its membership "to be very careful and conscious" of appearance—"a positive contribution" amid the Nation's many "liabilities."

More interesting was Malcolm's determination to point out to Said Ramadan what he apparently felt was another positive contribution—that even with the Nation's decline, those who were leaving the movement in disillusionment "never return to the church, they never return to Christianity." [10] Thus, by presenting the Nation as having had a genuine spiritual force and power and the ability to make enduring contributions that complemented Islam, Malcolm was able to select the aspects of the Nation that had meant the most to him—thus recovering a vestige of integrity from the wreckage of religious "deviation," and likewise salvaging his own religious sincerity in the process.

Malcolm told a television interviewer that he had believed in the Nation's divinity more than Elijah Muhammad himself did, but had not realized it until Muhammad "was confronted with a crisis in his own personal moral life and he did not stand up as a man." Malcolm likewise told a reporter: "When I lost my confidence in Muhammad as a person, I began to reexamine his philosophy, perhaps objectively for the first time, and his doctrine— his entire organization and behavior pattern." "When I ceased to respect him as a man," Malcolm told a Canadian interviewer, "I could see that he also was not divine. There was no God with him at all." Malcolm wrote to Said Ramadan that when Wallace Muhammad exposed his father "as a very immoral man who had deceived and seduced seven of his young secretaries . . . the moral discipline of the entire movement decayed and fell apart." [11] With this decay came the decline of the Nation:

But after the real faith, the religious side, or the real spiritual power began to fade from the Black Muslim movement, the power that used to enable the brothers and sisters to let their higher tendencies dominate, rather than their lower tendencies, it was switched around. . . . So now you have an organized group of people who do not have the moral strength to rise above or contain themselves from falling victim to their own low desires. [12]

It is interesting that Malcolm pinpointed the decline of faith within the movement at the time when he personally learned of Elijah's sexual sins in 1963. However, it seems that Malcolm was here applying his own experience of religious disappointment to the entire organization. Elsewhere he had noted that the spiritual decline of the Nation had begun as early as 1960, when Elijah Muhammad returned from his off-season pilgrimage to Mecca. When Muhammad had returned to the United States, "the whole trend or direction that he formerly had taken began to change. And in that change there's a whole lot of other things that had come into the picture," Malcolm revealed. At this point, Elijah Muhammad "began to be more mercenary. More interested in money. More interested in wealth. And, yes, more interested in girls."

The reference to "a whole lot of other things" quite probably signified the placement of Elijah's family members into positions of power, which Malcolm also cited as a major cause of deterioration. These assessments by Malcolm show something of his own reflections and his ability to look back and see that the movement had actually begun to decline before his "blind faith" had allowed him to see it. He knew that "the real rot" had set in before Muhammad was exposed; but because Malcolm could not conceive of the Nation religiously without Muhammad, he tended to center its actual decline at the point when he came to terms with Elijah Muhammad's imperfection.[13]

On February 15, 1965, speaking about the Nation before an OAAU audience, Malcolm announced: "I, for one, disassociate myself from the movement completely. And I dedicate myself to the organizing of Black people into a group that are interested in doing things constructive, not for just one religious segment of the community, but for the entire Black community."[14] This was Malcolm's way of emphasizing the OAAU's new "action program," but it was also a sober assessment of the Nation as he now perceived it. Malcolm realized that the Nation had become "a machine" that killed, maimed, and crippled, "a criminal organization" dominated by nepotism, greed, and self-interest. "Muhammad is the man," Malcolm told a reporter for *The Village Voice*, "with his house in Phoenix, his [expensive] suits, and his harem. He didn't believe in the black state or getting anything for the people."[15]

Just as Malcolm did not approach this analysis painlessly, he likewise had not done so without holding himself responsible while also attempting to redeem the Nation. In the summer of 1964, Malcolm told a journalist in Cairo that he was "launching a campaign against the falacies [sic] that dominate the Muslim community in America." That campaign, according to Malcolm, entailed convincing members of the Nation "that Islam is not a religion of taxes, and that they have not got to pay for saying their prayers in the mosque, as somebody has misled them."

David Graham Du Bois recalls Malcolm X in Cairo, lamenting that he once believed in Elijah Muhammad; "but my eyes are open now. I've got a lot to make up for." He told Du Bois that many Muslims had believed in him once, and he had led them wrong. "I'm now in the hands of Allah." Malcolm told an *Egyptian Gazette* reporter that he believed "the only salvation" for the Nation was Sunni Islam—a hope that he apparently clung to in his preparations for the Hajj. Still, the memory of his painful departure from the Nation was vivid in his mind: "I can't tell you what it was like to me to lose faith in him."

Now that he had corrected and clarified his faith in Islam, Malcolm announced he was "striving to live the life of a true Muslim," being careful "not to sentence anyone who has not first been proven guilty." As for the Nation, Malcolm recognized that the movement had "lost that indefinable energy and zeal that brought it to preeminence. Elijah through his personal indiscretion has revealed himself as a religious fake. It is inevitable that his followers will fall away." That "indefinable energy," as Malcolm called it, was not true Islam, and yet it was a religious force. It was the concoction of a faker, a new religion that Malcolm X now realized had used biblically laced explanations in a manner typical of a "religious cult."

As to his own work, Malcolm X's mission was no less religious in character. But instead of depending on a cultic, end-of-the-world solution, he emphasized activism. "We must begin to fight back," Malcolm explained to students at Dartmouth College. "Things have gone beyond the point that we can answer them with religious action." [16] "Elijah believes that God is going to come and straighten things out," Malcolm told students at Tuskegee Institute on February 3, 1965.

But whereas Elijah is willing to sit and wait, I'm not willing to sit and wait on God to come. If he doesn't come soon, it will be too late. I believe in religion, but a religion that includes political, economic, and social action designed to eliminate some of these things, and make a paradise here on earth while we're waiting for the other. [17]

Malcolm X had now truly closed the book on his Nation years. The man he had once adored as the "Messenger of Allah," the "Holy Apostle," and the "Honorable Elijah Muhammad" was now simply "Elijah." The "religious action" of Muhammad's program became inadequate. The vision of Fard's coming kingdom was irrelevant.

Several weeks before his death, Malcolm appeared on a Chicago television program, answering questions about his former involvement in the Nation and his subsequent conversion to Sunni Islam. Conversation led to comparisons between the Nation and the KKK, and the program's host asserted that the two organizations were fundamentally equal insofar as "racial hatred" was concerned. Malcolm differed, insisting that the Klan was inseparable from white society, which had "absolutely failed to fulfill its promise for twenty-two million black Americans." The Nation, Malcolm concluded, was only "the result of the failure of a society, of the hate that exists in the American society."

Malcolm X could not escape the themes of racism and racial violence that had surrounded him since infancy. As Marcus Garvey had once insisted that the Klan was inseparable from white society, so Malcolm X likewise reminded whites that *they* were responsible for both the KKK and black separatist groups. Malcolm emphasized that, as a Muslim, he did not judge people by skin color, but still had to face the fact that brotherhood was not a reality in the United States. "I have to take a stand that is uncompromising," Malcolm X concluded, "on the side of my people, against any person that stands in the way of our being recognized and accepted as human beings in the same context with all of humanity."

Now Malcolm X had his own religious philosophy, perhaps inevitably similar to that of Marcus Garvey, whose religion "was concerned primarily with essentials."[18] For Malcolm, religious issues were above all those that pertained to the lives and struggles of *his* people living on this side of paradise. It is no wonder, then, that in the final chapter of his autobiography, Malcolm compared his childhood meditations on "Hector's Hill" with his revelations in Mecca. For Malcolm X, the religion of the prophets and the religion of his parents were very much the same.

# Now He's Gone

*Once you are dead your troubles are over. It's those living that are in trouble.*

In 1965, the Audubon Ballroom stood between two distinct neighborhoods. South of the ballroom was a black and Puerto Rican area where people lived in jammed apartment houses, left unoccupied after whites fled from the upper Manhattan area to the Riverdale section of the Bronx and beyond. North of the ballroom were the "old-time tenants," including many ethnic and religious groups. The Audubon was situated on 166th Street, bordered on the west by Broadway and on the east by St. Nicholas Avenue. Running north and south, these avenues meet just north of the ballroom and then diverge again—framing the Audubon in an unusually short block. Named after a thoroughfare in Manhattan, the ballroom was only an indirect namesake of John J. Audubon, the famous ornithologist. By the time Malcolm X used it for his organizational rallies, the Audubon was already old; it had seen better days. Still, those who attended dances there had learned to ignore the sickly green color of the walls and its naked light fixtures. The surrounding neighborhood likewise learned to tolerate the Audubon; nobody seemed to mind the uproar created whenever dances were over and people spilled noisily onto the streets.

The structure was comprised of two second-floor ballrooms, the smallest of which was the Rose Room, with a capacity for 575 people. In contrast, the Audubon Grand Ballroom, with room for 1,500 people, boasted the largest dance floor in New York City. Upon entering the main entrance into the small, first-floor vestibule, people could either walk up one flight of steps or take an elevator to the main lobby. From the lobby, they could enter either one of the two ballrooms, passing first through a lounge area. The Grand Ballroom was lined with booths on either side of the room, and its small stage was of sufficient depth to accommodate theatrical performances. The ample floor space of the Grand Ballroom allowed for many seats during conferences; wooden chairs were set up beforehand according to the preferences of the hosting organization.

On Sunday, February 21, 1965, two events were scheduled for the Audubon Grand Ballroom: a George Washington's Birthday dance (sponsored by a local church) was booked for that evening, preceded in the afternoon by a rally of Malcolm's OAAU. The two events couldn't have been more different, thematically speaking. One celebrated the birth of the founding president of a nation steeped in white supremacy, the other solemnized the awakening black consciousness of that nation's foremost victims. Though Malcolm's blood was spilled on the stage of the Audubon that afternoon, the George Washington's Birthday dance apparently went on as scheduled. By Sunday night, one journalist noted, every "sign of violence had been removed."[1] Of course, he was incorrect: the back wall of the stage was pocked by bullets, leaving marks that scarred the Audubon as long as it remained—the engravings of violent men that too many have since exploited in order to buttress their warped accounts of the man called Malcolm X.

Though politically and religiously motivated murders are as old as the human race, the original "assassins," according to history, were Muslim zealots who expressed their dissent through violence. Born out of the religious and social upheavals of the eleventh-century East, the assassins used daggers along with doctrine to oppose the dominant beliefs of the Muslim world. Apparently they also attacked the military presence of Christendom, which relayed news of these terrible assailants to Europe, calling them assassins—a term apparently based on the Arabic word for "hashish users." Whether or not the original assassins used narcotics to prepare themselves for their terrible work, it is clear that they were driven largely by religious unrest and by the desire to eradicate those who represented the evolving orthodoxy of the Muslim world.[2] In one sense, then, Malcolm X was truly assassinated—murdered by religious dissenters, brutally and publicly assaulted by representatives of a "Muslim" organization that refused to submit to the consensus of the Muslim world.

Of course, this is only one way of looking at Malcolm's assassination. Malcolm X was also killed for personal reasons—jealousy, resentment, and sheer hatred that reverberated down the chain of command from the highest echelons of the Nation. Likewise, from the first moments following the assassination, there has always been good reason to believe Malcolm X was targeted by forces outside of the African American community, particularly the government. Now, nearly three decades after his death, scholars and other assassination theorists are building a substantial case that Malcolm's death was—at the very least—encouraged, monitored, and unofficially sanctioned by the surveillance community. However, even this conservative evaluation does not answer all the questions that have been raised, particularly those that suggest an international plot since Malcolm X ultimately represented two forces feared by the West: worldwide black solidarity and the advancement of Islam.[3]

What *is* absolutely clear is that Malcolm X died in a manner totally foreign to the intellectual and religious life he had led both within the Nation and independently. Despite his former "Black Muslim" invocation of Allah's wrath upon the white man and his later independent calls for organized black self-defense against racist attacks, Malcolm X lived an essentially nonviolent life without committing himself to philosophical pacifism. Contrary to all the distorted, sensational characterizations by the press, Malcolm was consistently committed to dialogue, education, debate, and religious critique—all constructive, civilized, and acceptable forms of dissent according to the ideals of Western culture.

When Malcolm X did advocate the use of physical force, he maintained that such a response should be reserved only for those who spoke exclusively the language of brute violence and militarized racial domination. Had Malcolm X been an advocate of sheer racial "violence" as the media so vehemently portrayed him, he would have been personally antagonistic toward all whites—which he clearly was not, even within the Nation. Further, in those last, tragic days he demonstrated his willingness to defend himself, even from black attackers. Thus, if Malcolm X was guilty of anything, he was guilty of not being a pacifist, and of believing in the fundamental human right of self-defense. In this light he was no less guilty than most patriotic citizens in the United States. But unlike many of his critics, Malcolm X had a higher regard for free speech and human rights.

Malcolm X's last moments were recorded on tape—not a surprising event, since he died in the process of giving a speech. What follows is a detailed transcript of that fateful moment, as Malcolm's assistant, Benjamin (Goodman) 2X (now Karim), concluded his introductory remarks:

*Benjamin:* And without any further ado, I bring before you Brother Minister Malcolm, and I pray that you and I will listen—listen, hear, and understand. Thank you.
  *(Malcolm approaches the lectern, with approximately 7 seconds of applause.)*
*Malcolm:* Salaam Alaikum.
  *(Voices from the audience respond: "Walaikum Salaam." From a different part of the ballroom is the shouting of a man, angrily rebuking: "Get your hand out of my pocket!" The sound of chairs overturning. . . .)*
*Malcolm:* [In a tense voice] Hold it, hold it, hold it, hold it, hold it [pause]. Hold it, hold it, hold it, hold it [pause]. Hold it—
  *(Shotgun blast)*

"Then time stopped," recalled Robert Allen, who sat with a friend in the audience. "An ear-splitting blast, a flash glimpsed from the corner of my eye." Another member of the audience, Patricia Russell, saw men at the front of the ballroom stand up and fire, and then Malcolm clutched his chest and fell backward. Malcolm's wife, Betty, saw it too. Russell recalls that Betty cried out, "They are killing my husband!" Even as Malcolm lay dead or dying, the three assassins kept firing, two with handguns, the third emptying the second shell from his sawed-off shotgun. Malcolm probably saw his assassins stand, but had little time to react. He did not hear the rest of the gunfire, the cries and shouting, the crashing of chairs, the scuffling of fleeing assassins, or the screams of his wife.[4]

Below the Audubon, on the first floor, was a storefront synagogue, where a few elderly men had congregated in preparation for prayers. They heard the shots. Next door, on Broadway, the manager of the San Juan Theater also heard the shots. He ignored them, perhaps thinking the sounds had come from inside the theater, where a movie, *El Padre Pistolas* was being shown. But shortly, New York City and the rest of the world became aware of what had transpired in the Audubon that Sunday afternoon.

In Detroit, service was being conducted as usual in the Nation's Mosque No. 1. During his sermon, Minister Wilfred X, Malcolm's brother, was apparently interrupted with word of the assassination. An FBI source in the audience reported that Wilfred was visibly shaken by the news, but proceeded with his message. At the conclusion he announced what had happened to Malcolm and—hiding his own pain—sought to comfort the audience. After all, Mosque No. 1—when it was still "Temple No. 1"—was Malcolm's home congregation. This was where he had started out as a young parolee in 1952. Many there had come into the Nation because of Malcolm's preaching. "No sense in getting emotional about this," Wilfred encouraged, "for this is the kind of times we are living in. Once you are dead your troubles are over. It's those living that are in trouble."

Wilfred's controlled behavior was wise. However hurt or even resentful he might have felt toward the Nation's leadership in the matter of his brother's death, Wilfred surmised that for the safety of his family and himself he could not afford to express even the slightest criticism. Malcolm's brother Philbert X had already taken the easiest way out—he had willingly cooperated with Mr. Muhammad's family in publicly denouncing Malcolm as a traitor almost a year before. Wilfred, the eldest, had perhaps always carried the brunt of his siblings' grief since the loss of their father. He had apparently remained painfully quiet throughout the period of Malcolm's silencing and during the eleven months of his independence, perhaps hoping that the worst could be avoided. It could not. Now that Malcolm was gone, Wilfred realized that it was the living who had the real troubles; one wrong word or action could have easily brought the wrath of the Nation's zealots upon him and his family. Wilfred recognized, as he said later, that he had his "hand in the lion's mouth."[5]

Mosque No. 1 not only had its FBI informants, but undoubtedly it was also infiltrated by those who would readily report back to Elijah Muhammad the slightest dissent expressed by Wilfred. Yet Wilfred's greatest crisis was yet to come. A week after the assassination, the Nation gathered in its annual convention in Chicago, and Wilfred was expected to attend as usual. Called "Savior's Day," the convention was the Nation's theological counterpart to Christmas, since it was held in celebration of the birth of W. D. Fard, the master and savior proclaimed in Elijah Muhammad's gospel.

Elijah Muhammad had already pleaded the innocence of the Nation in the matter of Malcolm's death. In a press conference the day after the assassination, Muhammad declared: "We have never resorted to no such thing as violence"—a statement that was either a bold-faced lie or, less likely, a demonstration of the elder's imperfect knowledge of the Nation's affairs. The current issue of *The Saturday Evening Post*, in fact, carried a detailed story by an ex-Muslim from Boston who not only exposed the Nation as a fraud, but who had been brutally beaten by enforcers from the

Boston mosque. Stories of other beatings and killings were beginning to grow, confirming Malcolm's recent charge that the Nation had become a "criminal organization." Further, in the week between Malcolm's death and the Savior's Day convention, Elijah Muhammad told *Chicago's American* that Malcolm X was "the most open and strongest hypocrite that I have ever had among my followers for the last 33 years . . . he wanted to be the boss rather than a follower."[6]

Elijah Muhammad's statements are very revealing. Referring to Malcolm X as a "hypocrite," according to the Nation's vocabulary, was a serious charge. The "hypocrite" was not a phony nor, in the classical sense, an actor. Rather, the Nation perceived "hypocrites" as schismatic opponents, especially those who had left in order to open their own sectarian mosques. This notion of the hypocrite as schismatic opponent undoubtedly dated back to the days when Elijah Muhammad and his beloved leader, W. D. Fard, fought quite literally against dangerous competitors in Detroit and Chicago. "Hypocrites" had later forced Elijah Muhammad into a period of wandering and preaching in the early days, and now he was accusing Malcolm of having been the worst hypocrite he had faced in his ministerial career. It seems to have been an inadvertent admission of—and perhaps even a rationale for—the Nation's murderous assault on Malcolm X.

The fact that Muhammad excoriated the dead Malcolm for wanting to be "boss" rather than "follower" also suggests that the elder had come to see Malcolm increasingly in the light of the schismatic factionalism and warlike competition that typified the early years of the Nation. The history of cultic black Islam has not been an unbroken chronology of apostolic succession but a series of factional competitions in which only one leader could ultimately become "boss." It was a system that, in some ways, resembled the struggle of Mafia dons competing for the position of *capo di tutti cappi*—boss of all the bosses. Malcolm X would not be the last "hypocrite" to challenge Mr. Muhammad and pay dearly for it.

Wilfred X attended the convention in Chicago, and found that he was expected to speak publicly against Malcolm before the entire assembly, and to do so in terms previously spelled out by Elijah Muhammad. As Wilfred recalled later, he carefully managed to do otherwise, succeeding only by refocusing the attention of the assembled black nation upon the glory of Elijah Muhammad and the infamy of whites. As far as Malcolm X was concerned, Wilfred said essentially what he had told his own congregation: "My brother is dead, and there is nothing we can do to bring him back." Only later did Muhammad realize that Wilfred had actually managed to evade his directives. For years to come, Wilfred and his family survived by such discretion. "It was like walking into a snake pit," he remembered of his later encounters with Elijah Muhammad and the Nation's leadership. Gradually, Wilfred was able to edge his way out of the movement, and after many years left the Nation's ministry to pursue another livelihood.[7]

Of course, the week after Malcolm's death, Elijah Muhammad had concerns of his own. Not only was Mosque No. 7 in Harlem firebombed and destroyed (it was supposedly done by Malcolm's followers, but no arrests were made, and Malcolm's followers deny having retaliated), but rumors were flying that Malcolmites were planning to kill Elijah Muhammad in retaliation. The focal point of concern was the Savior's Day convention, since Muhammad would be vulnerable before such a large audience in Chicago's Coliseum. *Chicago's American* reflected this concern in a cartoon entitled "Conventioneer?" that pictured Death (a skeleton in black robe with a scythe) milling into the Coliseum with the rest of the attendees. The concern over possible retaliation was not just in the minds of the press; according to one journalist, the entire Chicago Coliseum had been checked for bombs by the police department and would be infiltrated by plainclothes detectives during the meeting—supplying the same kind of security that is provided for the president of the United States.

This, apparently, did not entirely soothe Mr. Muhammad's apprehensions. On the second day of the convention, Muhammad shrieked out a warning before an audience of 2,500 followers: "If you want to snuff out the life of Elijah, you're inviting your own death." However, Muhammad's worst fears never materialized. He never faced any retaliation, and during the convention he even enjoyed the validation of his son Wallace. The younger Muhammad returned to the Nation after his own orthodox Muslim organization had apparently fizzled. Wallace had not only left the Nation in favor of orthodoxy, but had been associated with Malcolm, and was known to have been both a source of information and counsel to him. In the hope of reinstatement into the Nation, Wallace publicly vowed he would now "take orders" from Elijah Muhammad.[8]

In general, the mainstream press was much more concerned with covering the aftermath of Malcolm's assassination than with the Nation's Chicago convention. Certainly, there was a multitude of editorials and articles that appeared to gloat over the assassination, harping on the supposed inevitability of a violent end to such a "violent" life. The morning after the assassination, the *New York Times* editorialized: "He was a case history, as well as an extraordinary and twisted man, turning many true gifts to evil purpose." Still others, like the editor of Cleveland's *Plain Dealer,* tended to be slightly more sympathetic toward Malcolm, "an apostle of violence." Misguided and bitter as he was, the editor stated, Malcolm's troubled youth had flowered in racial hatred. Malcolm X had ultimately been "removed by the very tactics he so long espoused," but his killers would have to be punished "as a deterrent to a continued use of force." Some accounts of Malcolm's death, such as that in *Newsweek,* were both sarcastic and contemptuous. Calling Malcolm X a "desperado," the article noted his conversion to Islam in 1964. "But his own overwhelming talent was still talk; he always followed his agile tongue instead of his wasted mind."

Some black newspaper editors perhaps felt constrained to lean in the direction of the "apostle of violence" image, though more out of prudence than spite. Omaha's *Black Dispatch* featured an editorial that spoke of Malcolm as a preacher of violence and as an embittered black nationalist. "We do not want another Malcolm X," the editorial stated, "for he failed to see any good in any white man." Then in a somewhat peculiar if not untenable twist of interpretation, the editorial sympathetically closed by recalling Malcolm's "chickens coming home to roost" comment after the assassination of President Kennedy in 1963. "We take him to mean that after a hard day scratching for the things to survive, he had come home to [rest] from the toils. Malcolm X now has done just that." This little editorial, while awkwardly expressed, serves to illustrate the feelings of many African Americans toward Malcolm X. Though apparently quite concerned not to offend whites, the editor admired and respected Malcolm X and refused to allow Malcolm's own words to be turned against him to the satisfaction of the whites.

Closer to home, at the office of Harlem's *New York Amsterdam News,* editor James Hicks could have cared less what white people wanted to hear about the fallen Malcolm. "If you're looking for some reading material which will help you rejoice about the death of Malcolm X, you'd better turn the page—or better still look for another newspaper," Hicks wrote during the week of the assassination. Hicks shared his deep grief at the loss of his friend Malcolm X, and shared with readers a little about their friendship and Malcolm's work as a columnist for the *Amsterdam News.* Hicks concluded that while he did not agree with the Nation's call for a separate black state, Malcolm had done an amazing job of rehabilitating many ex-cons and drug addicts in his service to the Nation. Interestingly, though, Hicks made no comment about the independent Malcolm X and his political platform; he closed by saying he hoped that the "secret" of rehabilitating wayward people "did not die with Malcolm X."

Even more so, the civil rights leaders, whatever their personal feelings were toward Malcolm X, wasted no time in employing his death to underscore their own concerns. In life, Malcolm X had provided the civil rights leadership a frightening racial scapegoat to hold up before the public—knowing that the "Black Muslims" made the civil rights programs seem much more palatable to whites. Now, in death, the "apostle of violence" lent himself one last time to the civil rights leadership. Dr. Martin Luther King, Jr., stated that he was "deeply saddened and appalled" at Malcolm's death, and observed that this society was "still sick enough to express dissent with murder." "This vicious assassination," King concluded, "should cause our whole society to see violence and hatred are evil forces that must be cast into unending limbo."

Whitney Young, the director of the Urban League who had taken the heat of Malcolm's Nation criticisms, declared that Malcolm X "is survived by his Harlem, the ghetto which created him and shaped him." However, unlike King, Young seems to have gotten in a last hit at Malcolm, albeit mildly. "I have never been concerned about Malcolm X in particular as much as the frustration, hopelessness, bitterness and despair which exist." Malcolm X, Young concluded, "belonged to the past. His dream was for a separate black state, for two nations within one"—an answer coming a century too late for "America's Negro citizens." However inaccurate his assessment, Young was quite capable of using the dead Muslim leader to enhance his own program: "Malcolm X is our victim. . . . It will not do to condemn the violence which killed him, or the violence he espoused, until we have wiped out the misery and ignorance which produces violence."[9]

A somewhat unusual notation regarding Malcolm's death appeared in *Christianity Today*, the leading conservative white Evangelical publication—unusual because the magazine probably had never made any extensive religious observations about the Nation or Malcolm X, despite the impact they potentially had upon the black Christian community. *CT*'s writer could not resist pointing out the "ultimate irony" that Malcolm's funeral would be conducted inside a Harlem Christian church even though he was an "Islamic Negro nationalist." Of course, given Malcolm's status in the Harlem community and his large but silent following of black Christian supporters nationwide, there was nothing ironic in the use of a Christian church. Had it not been for a number of telephoned bomb threats, other Harlem churches would likely have been willing to host the solemn occasion. If anything, *CT*'s arid, encyclopedic account reflected the indifference of white Evangelicals toward blacks in general, as well as the failure of the premier Evangelical Christian magazine to educate its readership about black issues. Bringing up the rear in matters of race and racial justice, *CT* typified the white Evangelical movement itself; only after Malcolm X had been literally blasted into eternity did they show even slight interest in the "Black Muslim" phenomenon, a religious reality that was already quite familiar to their ecclesiastically segregated black Christian brethren.[10]

That Malcolm was admired and appreciated in the black, traditionally Christian community is no exaggeration. This is perhaps best typified by the observations of one journalist, who went to Selma, Alabama, shortly after Malcolm's assassination. Malcolm had, in fact, spoken in Selma only three weeks before. The journalist noted that when he arrived at the joint office of the Student Nonviolent Coordinating Committee (SNCC) and the Southern Christian Leadership Conference (SCLC), he found a sign on the door that read: "This office is in mourning for Malcolm X." One of Selma's leaders made the point even more clear:

[Malcolm] was very well received. . . . The problem is that many more people agreed with him than will admit it. . . . It wasn't fashionable due to the image people had of Malcolm as a bad thing, a fiery renegade, a fanatic. The press was responsible for this false image. . . . It is tragic that most people didn't understand the effect he was having on international relations, the unifying effect he was having on black people all over the world.[11]

If one reaction to the assassination epitomized this distorted image of Malcolm as an evil renegade, it was that of the preeminent gossip-monger, Walter Winchell. A week after the assassination, Winchell published perhaps the most profoundly bigoted and slanted analysis in his column: "Malcolm X was a victim of his own exaggeration. He never reconciled the truth with his private delusions. He was a petty punk who pictured himself as an heroic figure." Winchell slammed Malcolm as a convicted thief, dope addict, and pimp who preached hatred and terrorism. He wrongly commented that Malcolm's conflict with the Nation was actually about the movement's vast real estate holdings, not about ideology. Finally, Winchell made the gratuitous complaint that Malcolm's death had "received more newspaper space than the passing of Nat King Cole, the gentleman. . . . The Devil attracts the biggest headlines."

Quite unintentionally, or so it would appear, Jim Powell of Chicago's

*New Crusader*, writing during the week of the assassination, put Winchell in check. Rather than contrast Malcolm with Nat King Cole, he paid tribute to both. Powell was apparently in attendance at a Chicago Christian church at the time the announcement was made that Malcolm had been killed. Ironically, it interrupted a memorial service for Nat King Cole, who had died earlier that same month. Writing warmly of both black men, Powell eulogized: "Malcolm X, a Black Nationalist, they call him, but a man fighting for a place in the [s]un is what I call him." Had Malcolm X lived, Powell continued, he would likely have grown in popularity and power. "And do not think one minute that he was not needed. As long as America produces Ku Klux Klans, John Birchers, Nazis and other bigoted sects, the likes of Malcolm X to meet them on their own terms is needed."[12]

While Powell's thoughtful tribute to Malcolm and Cole served as a spontaneous rebuttal to Winchell's imprudent remarks, in another journalistic event, a columnist from the *New York Amsterdam News* quite deliberately went about countering the disdainful commentary of another Malcolm X critic. After Malcolm's assassination, Carl T. Rowan, the director of the United States Information Agency (USIA), was apparently disturbed by an outpouring of praise and eulogy for Malcolm from foreign countries, especially African ones. In a speech made before the Foreign Service Association shortly after the assassination, Rowan, an African American, complained that African reactions had been based on "misinformation and misrepresentation." Specifically, Rowan noted that one of the tributes had portrayed Malcolm as a hero to the integration movement, and another as a martyr. Insofar as the movement for integration was concerned, Rowan was correct to object; but his efforts went beyond repairing misconceptions of that sort.

Rowan outrightly admitted that he asked his colleagues in the USIA "to do an extra-zealous job of getting out the facts, of informing the world in order that we might minimize damaging reactions based on emotion, prejudice and misinformation." In order to do so, Rowan openly referred to Malcolm as a "Negro who preached segregation and race hatred." Further, Rowan was widely quoted as saying he could not understand why so much had been made about the death of an ex-convict and ex-dope-peddler who had become a racial fanatic.

Interestingly, one of the most poignant rejoinders to Rowan came from a white columnist, Gertrude Wilson, whose "White-On-White" feature was regularly published in Harlem's *New York Amsterdam News*. Over the years, Wilson had developed an admiring friendship with both Malcolm and Betty, though largely through telephone conversations. In her column, Wilson recounted Rowan's speech before the Foreign Service Association and his espoused intention of "correcting" supposedly mistaken assumptions about Malcolm X on the part of Africans.

Wilson took particular aim at Rowan's reference to Malcolm's youthful days as criminal and drug dealer. "Perhaps the most amazing thing about Malcolm X is that he was all of the things which Mr. Rowan says—and he rose above them." Rowan, Wilson contended, had entirely missed what Malcolm X represented to African Americans. Malcolm's new organization may not have accumulated a large number of followers at the time of his death, Wilson said, "but the spirit of independent manhood which he epitomized for hundreds of thousands of Negroes was something which reached out—yes, even to Africa." Wilson added that Malcolm X had many admirers nationwide, openly and secretly, and at all levels of society. Malcolm's friend then closed with a final jab, effectively underscoring Rowan's flawed assessment: "If Mr. Rowan does not like what he sees written in admiration of Malcolm X in the African and Asian press, it would be well for Mr. Rowan to look homeward for an answer." [13]

Not all of Malcolm's critics in life remained so hard on him once he was dead. Most notable was the white liberal journalist, James Wechsler, who had been particularly sharp in opposing Malcolm X in his last, independent year. Wechsler claimed that his trouble with Malcolm originated during his speech before the Militant Labor Forum in New York City on April 8, 1964. (At this point, the newly independent Malcolm had founded the Muslim Mosque, but he had not yet made the Hajj.) His presentation, entitled "The Black Revolution," was made before a largely white audience, whose response to Malcolm was very mixed.

In style, the intensely political presentation was a far cry from Malcolm's former Nation sermons, which were always filled with biblical illustrations and allusions. However, Malcolm was only amplifying the black nationalism he had espoused in the Nation; he likewise reiterated his same criticism of white liberals as phonies who practiced "lip-profession."

What particularly turned Wechsler against Malcolm, however, was what occurred after the speech, in the question-and-answer period. According to Wechsler, a "gentle, gray-haired" white man named Will Lipson "rose in the rear of the hall and tried to touch Malcolm's conscience." The elderly questioner began by asking whether he might call Malcolm "brother in the name of humanity." Malcolm apparently agreed—an interesting point considering Malcolm had not yet made his famous pilgrimage to Mecca nor proclaimed his "universal brotherhood" stance.

The elderly Lipson then suggested that, under Malcolm's direction, the entire audience should rise for one moment in honor of a white minister who had recently died in an accident during a civil rights protest in Cleveland, Ohio. According to Wechsler, who was in attendance, Malcolm refused in an "icy tirade." Wechsler reported the incident in the *New York Post*, quoting Malcolm as saying he would not use his energy "applauding the sacrifice of an individual white man." Wechsler, who first met Malcolm when he was still in the Nation, concluded that he had previously tried to understand the Muslim activist and sought to avoid burlesquing him as a "cosmic joke." However, after the Lipson incident, Wechsler concluded, "Malcolm finally and totally lost me."[14]

Unfortunately, Wechsler was being overly sensitive and had taken Malcolm's rebuttal personally—so personally, in fact, that his own conscience had missed Malcolm's point. Actually, Malcolm's reaction to Lipson's request was not met with an "icy tirade" but what appears to have been a passionate reminder that white liberals ought not to allow their individual sacrifices to distract them from the overwhelming suffering of black people worldwide. Wechsler did not report that Malcolm had responded by challenging the audience to rise also in honor of two slain black leaders, Patrice Lumumba and Medgar Evers. What the white civil rights worker had done was "good," Malcolm concluded. "But the day is out when you'll find black people who are going to stand up and applaud the contribution of whites at this late date."

Malcolm also reminded Lipson and the rest of his audience that millions of Africans had been uprooted and destroyed in the slave trade, and that the bones of black people "fertilized the soil of this country." Actually, Wechsler's belief that Malcolm's "conscience" needed to be "touched" suggests a good deal more about his own white liberal narcissism than it did about Malcolm's humanitarian sensitivity.[15]

Unfortunately, Wechsler was not satisfied with his retort to Malcolm in the *Post*. He prepared a more extensive criticism of Malcolm for *The Progressive*, which appeared in June 1964. Of course, as fast as things were occurring in Malcolm's life, by the time Wechsler's article appeared, its criticisms were not only questionable, but dated as well. In the article, Wechsler recalled his first encounter with Malcolm X, sometime in 1963, as a fellow guest on the Barry Gray radio program in New York. Wechsler recalled his horror at Malcolm's harsh denunciations of the "established Negro leadership," especially the pioneer activist, A. Philip Randolph. According to Wechsler, Malcolm's reason for opposing Randolph was stated outright:

"Randolph fought Marcus Garvey." Wechsler apparently had no appreciation for (or lacked awareness of) Malcolm's family roots in the Garvey movement. Instead, he called Malcolm a "self-righteous, self-possessed, self-proclaimed young savior."

In the same *Progressive* article, Wechsler again recounted the April 1964 episode at the Militant Labor Forum, and pointed out that, by then, Malcolm was out of the Nation, but "was now more than ever committed to a hell-raising role in the civil rights battle." Interestingly, he revealed what he had not mentioned in his *Post* column: Wechsler *himself* had first raised the issue of the dead civil rights worker to Malcolm, prior to the request by Lipson that the audience stand in tribute. In contrast to Lipson's gentle approach, which Malcolm honored, Wechsler had apparently antagonized him by interrupting with comments that put Malcolm on the defensive. Malcolm, who was not easily intimidated, responded in kind to Wechsler:

We're not going to stand up and applaud any contribution made by some individual white person when 22 million black people are dying every day. What [the dead civil rights worker] did—good. Hooray, hooray, hooray. Now Lumumba was murdered, Medgar Evers was murdered, my own father was murdered. You tell that stuff to someone else. It's time that some white people started dying in this thing.[16]

It was an admittedly harsh response, but nonetheless valid—especially considering the fact that even Wechsler later admitted he had not been "aloof" in his verbal approach toward Malcolm. Wechsler's personal prejudice against Malcolm had obviously emerged during that meeting, and Malcolm had merely reacted to it, albeit strongly. When, afterwards, the elderly Lipson expressed a willingness to call him "brother," Malcolm nevertheless accepted the kindness and acknowledged that the dead civil rights worker had done "good." However, it was apparently not enough to satisfy Wechsler's wounded pride. He concluded his *Progressive* article by stating that his real gripe with Malcolm was "his alienation from reality and his attempt to lead people down a dead-end road."

With Malcolm dead, Wechsler spoke of him with far less acrimony. In the *Post*, he inevitably recounted his memorably contentious meetings with Malcolm X, but added, "All that was many long months ago." In tempered reflection, Wechsler augured that "rival historians" would someday recall Malcolm X in many different ways, from his "squandered genius" and "messianic inspiration" to his "private gentleness" and "tortured soul." Wechsler stated his belief that "there is enough in the record of his last months on earth to suggest" that Malcolm hoped to leave behind more than "wild cries for revenge" as his legacy. "As for myself," the journalist admitted, "I might be a wiser man if I had known him better."

While Wechsler's analysis of the fallen Malcolm was both halcyon and personal, James Baldwin's most notable response to Malcolm's death was issued, not from the pen, but in a public declaration—and in much broader terms. Baldwin had apparently been informed of the assassination upon arriving in London, where he had gone to promote the new European edition of his novel, *Another Country*. When reporters besieged the writer for a reaction to the death of Malcolm X, he screamed at them: "You did it! It is because of you—the men who created this white supremacy—that this man is dead. You are not guilty, but you did it. . . . Your mills, your cities, your rape of a continent started all this." [17]

Meanwhile, the story of Malcolm X, which had begun in the history of black resistance, was now slowly and painfully drawing to a close in New York. Ted Poston, another *Post* journalist, recalled sitting with Betty in the home where she was staying with the children. It was shortly after the assassination, and Malcolm's widow sat watching the television reports. When Elijah Muhammad appeared on the screen, denying that the Nation used violence, she scoffed, "So Elijah Muhammad no longer believes in violence."

Turning her attention from the television, Betty recalled that Malcolm "had a very warm relationship with his family." She noted that even though he had made two long trips overseas in 1964, Malcolm wrote almost every day. "And I could always expect a telephone call." Then she added sorrowfully: "The greatest emptiness is that I'll never get a letter again; no letter, no phone call. The children always ask for him when he's away. How will I tell them he won't come home again?" Gertrude Wilson, the white journalist from the *Amsterdam News*, was also there. She recalled that Betty turned to speak, her eyes wide with shock and grief: "They've taken him away from me, Mrs. Wilson." Her voice, the journalist later wrote, "was the sound of heartbreak."

Later, Betty, accompanied by her attorney Percy Sutton, held a press conference at George's Supper Club in Queens. "The magnitude of his work will be felt around the world," she told reporters. "I think he accomplished more than can be realized at this moment." Wearing her green cloth coat throughout the interview, Betty's words turned again to personal memories of Malcolm: "He loved me and he loved the children dearly. . . . That's why I never traveled with him, because he never trusted anybody but me with the children." [18]

In the meantime, Malcolm's remains were being prepared for viewing, not in Queens, but in his beloved Harlem. After the autopsy, Malcolm's death certificate was recorded, noting cause of death as multiple shotgun slug and bullet wounds to the chest, heart, and aorta. The death certificate bore only the name of his mother, Louise Helen Little, and noted that Malcolm had resided in New York City for thirteen years (it was actually eleven years). Under the section, "business or industry," Malcolm's profession was simply listed as "Islam."

In Harlem, Malcolm's body came into the care of Joseph Hall, the owner and director of the Unity Funeral Home at 8th Avenue and 126th Street. During Malcolm's tenure as the minister of Mosque No. 7, Hall had provided funeral service for members of the Nation. As Malcolm X recalled in his autobiography, the Nation's "Muslim" funeral services were as unorthodox as the rest of their theology. No flowers, songs, or tears were permitted; as far as the Nation was concerned, there was no afterlife. Instead, all honors and gifts were to be translated into monies for the bereaved family. Then, thin rounds of candy were distributed and taken in unison. "We won't cry," Minister Malcolm would tell his grieving parishioners, "just as we don't cry over candy. Just as sweet candy will dissolve, so will our brother's sweetness that we have enjoyed when he lived now dissolve into a sweetness in our memories."

Now Malcolm was dead, but the Nation would not bid him such a sweet farewell. Instead, Malcolm's 6-foot, 9-inch bronze coffin required the installation of a special glass covering for the viewing—in case members of the Nation slipped by the police guard to desecrate the body. Ironically, there was a bit of unorthodoxy practiced in regard to Malcolm's funeral. Muslim tradition required burial before the sun had twice risen and set over the deceased believer. Betty chose to break with the practice, extending the viewing dates in order to allow African dignitaries enough time to attend. Malcolm's body was thus prepared and dressed in suit and tie for viewing from Tuesday, February 23, until Friday afternoon, February 26. Though the entire viewing period apparently went without problems, one quirky error in the funeral preparations managed to slip into the pages of history. When a small, oblong brass plate for the coffin was inscribed with Malcolm's Muslim name, the engraver confused Malcolm's title, making it read: "*La* Hajj Malik Shabazz," instead of "El Hajj Malik Shabazz." (When Alex Haley mentioned the coffin plate in the epilogue to *The Autobiography*, however, he made no mention of the error—apparently correcting it for the sake of his readers.)

During that four-day viewing at the Unity Funeral Home, as many as 30,000 people filed in to pay their last respects. Among those who came, one Harlem woman perhaps best summed up the feelings of the community. "I saw that boy speak when he was alive," the elderly woman declared. "Now he's dead and I don't know what I feel except mad." By the end of the week, in the closing hours of viewing on Friday afternoon, people were still gathered outside to catch a last glimpse of Malcolm X. Those who came after the funeral home had closed lingered in the subfreezing temperature outside. "I guess I'm too late," one man from the Bronx told a reporter. "I wanted to see him, just once. It is part of history." A woman pleaded with the police who had been stationed at the funeral home all week. "I just wanted to put this rose near him," she implored to no avail.

One bearded youth adopted a different approach—a bitter reminder that Malcolm X also had enemies in Harlem. The young man, who looked to be about twenty years old, went "half-skipping and half-dancing past" Malcolm's lingering admirers and hooted, "He messed with the wrong man. . . . Don't mess with the Messenger." Still, it was clear that most of those waiting in the cold were admirers. One college student stood listening to the music being piped onto the streets from a record store: "I couldn't go to look at him now. I want to remember him standing on his own feet telling off the man." As darkness fell on Harlem that Friday evening, secret preparations were made to move Malcolm's coffin to a church with a heavy police escort that same night.[19]

There was a kind of biographical resonance in the particular church setting of Malcolm's funeral service. Despite his forceful anti-Christian rhetoric during his Nation years and his later conversion to orthodox Islam, Malcolm's personal rapport with Christian clergyman was always respectful, if not warm. One young Christian minister who had met with Malcolm over lunch at Harlem's Theresa Hotel later eulogized him as bearing a likeness to Christ.[20] Certainly, even if other clergy did not share that lofty assessment, the fact that Malcolm's body found rest in a church was neither an irony nor a miracle.

The resonant theme was sounded in the fact that, of all the Protestant denominations, Malcolm X's funeral would be held in a Pentecostal church. As a child, Malcolm liked Pentecostal ("Holy-Roller") churches the least. In his autobiography he characterized it as "spooky." However, when many of Harlem's churches closed their doors to Malcolm's funeral for fear of bomb threats, Bishop Alvin Childs, pastor of the Faith Temple Church of God in Christ, took in the remains of the Muslim leader as a "humanitarian gesture." Of course, like all the older black Christian denominations, the Church of God in Christ (COGIC) could trace its origins to white racial rejection. The resonance itself, however, was that black Pentecostalism, like Malcolm X, was a phenomenon born in the twentieth century—both having known the rejection of modern white Christians.

On Saturday February 27, the day of the funeral, the church "was like an armed camp—cops everywhere," a writer later recalled. "They patrolled the streets and roof tops; the tactical squad was out in force. Inside the church both uniformed and plainclothes police were in evidence, and a 'choir' of newsmen and photographers." All the attention given to the dead Malcolm X was not intended as an honor; it was, in fact, a bitter reminder of the failure of both the police and the media to heed Malcolm's claims that his life was in danger. Shortly after the assassination, Betty had complained to Ted Poston of the *New York Post*, "The newspapers and the radio and television people too, they didn't want to take [Malcolm] seriously. . . . They even tried to make people think that he bombed our house—and with our children in it."

The bombing of the house had preceded the assassination by one week, and Malcolm's critics in the media (probably with the encouragement of the FBI) had accused him of orchestrating the calamity for political reasons. Malcolm flatly denied the charge and sent Betty and the children to stay with friends. They had been shopping for a new house on the day before the assassination. Now, with Malcolm gone, reporters were still asking Betty about the bombing the week before, still intimating his possible involvement. Her response was appropriately sharp: "Now, the press will probably say that he shot himself."

The peculiar absence of the police at the Audubon on the day of the assassination and their almost apathetic attitude when finally appearing on the murder scene are well-documented situations. In fact, Betty Shabazz denied the police department's contention that they had made numerous attempts to offer Malcolm police protection: "It's a lie," she told a journalist. Certainly, the police—at the very least—were guilty of what one writer calls "cool disinterest" about providing protection while Malcolm X was alive. Now that he was dead, they were conspicuously placed inside and outside of Faith Temple, including eight uniformed officers who stood around the coffin during the funeral service. Had Malcolm X received such unsolicited protection in life, perhaps his murder might have been averted. Unfortunately, it appears that both local and federal constabularies were more than willing to stand by and observe—perhaps with a bit of relish—while Malcolm's last days came painfully to a close.[21]

When Malcolm's body was displayed in the sanctuary of Faith Temple, he was no longer dressed in a suit. Shaykh Ahmed Hassoun, the Sudanese missionary-teacher sent by the Muslim World League to assist the Muslim Mosque, performed his last service to Malcolm by washing the body in a special oil and dressing it in a *Kafan*, the traditional Muslim burial shroud. The last time Hassoun had seen Malcolm alive was in the Audubon Ballroom's small dressing room. Malcolm was obviously under a great deal of stress and had snapped at a staff member. The elderly teacher sought to calm him, earning a gruff response. Pressure was building, and the expectation of attack, along with the burden of his work and family, was weighing heavily on him. "I'm just about at my wit's end," Malcolm explained apologetically to the staff worker. She said she understood, but as he walked out of the room to face his assassins, Malcolm X questioned aloud whether anyone really understood.

After the assassination, the elderly Shaykh could only dress Malcolm for the grave. The FBI observed that soon afterward, Shaykh Hassoun's relationship with the Muslim Mosque began to deteriorate. For reasons that are unclear, the Shaykh stopped teaching classes in Arabic at the Muslim Mosque headquarters after Malcolm's death. He developed health problems and was hospitalized; upon release from the hospital, the Shaykh apparently severed his involvement with the Muslim Mosque and returned to his native Sudan. One FBI source suggested a significant reason for the break was that after Malcolm was gone, Muslim Mosque members began to mistreat the elderly man. Hassoun even suspected the Muslim Mosque's executive secretary, who shared his apartment, of stealing his money. This did not spell the end of the Islamic mission among African Americans, though it apparently signaled the demise of the Muslim Mosque. Ironically, Elijah Muhammad's son, Wallace (now Warith Deen Muhammad), would regain acceptance in the Nation and, upon his father's death in 1975, spearheaded the most significant orthodox Islamic movement among Muslims indigenous to the United States.

The hour-long funeral service was presided over by Ruby Dee, the actress whose husband, Ossie Davis, eulogized Malcolm in the often quoted phrase, "A Prince! Our own black shining prince!" While still in the Nation, Malcolm had obtained *ex cathedra* permission to attend his friend Ossie's 1961 Broadway comedy hit, *Purlie Victorious*. Dee (who had also joined with other black entertainers in starting a fund for Malcolm's children) and Davis read national and international messages of condolence. One came from Whitney Young, whom Malcolm had once lampooned as "Uncle Whitney"; another came from Kwame Nkrumah, prime minister of Ghana, who had granted Malcolm an audience during his first visit to Africa in 1964.

Betty sat in the second row, with police escort, in widow's black. One member of the press, ever faithful to his duty of elevating the white archetype, referred to her as a "black Jacqueline Kennedy." It was supposed to be a compliment and Haley recorded it as such in his epilogue. However, Malcolm X was always critical of whites for their insistence upon measuring blacks according to a white "yardstick"; even his widow could not escape it— as if the wives of white martyrs had a monopoly on dignity and beauty in crisis.

In the audience of approximately one thousand people was a host of civil rights dignitaries: Andrew Young, assistant to Martin Luther King, Jr., Bayard Rustin, James Farmer, strike leader Jesse Gray, and labor leader L. Joseph Overton. Also seated were Malcolm's friends from the entertainment world Dick Gregory and Michael Olatunji, the African drummer.

Gregory, a comedian, was also a civil rights activist and had come to know Malcolm while he was still in the Nation. Gregory had early tested Malcolm's loyalty to Mr. Muhammad. Apparently he had conferred with Malcolm about the possibility of getting Elijah Muhammad to authorize his followers to purchase his comedy recording *en masse*. The deal was as good as done when Gregory slipped in a comment to the effect that he and Malcolm should think up another way of getting one over on Mr. Muhammad. Malcolm immediately rescinded the agreement. Later, when Malcolm's faith in Mr. Muhammad was collapsing and word of the latter's sexual indiscretions had begun to leak out, Gregory met Malcolm backstage at the Apollo Theater and openly insulted Muhammad. Malcolm recalled the incident, how his first "instinct" was to "attack" Gregory. Instead, Malcolm wrote, "I felt weak and hollow." Gregory seems to have recognized that weakness, and he backed off.

After Malcolm was gone, Gregory remembered him as "a living denial of that old cliché, 'clothes make the man.' No matter what Malcolm X was wearing, his manhood and his very special human dignity shone through." Gregory concluded: "Kings wear their crowns on top of their heads. Malcolm's crown was on the inside. Malcolm X showed me the difference between a crown and a halo." While he was alive, Malcolm had paid Gregory an equally high compliment. At one OAAU meeting in December

1964, Malcolm invited Gregory to speak and made an informal announcement of Gregory's new book, *Nigger*. After some fraternal jesting regarding the title of the book, Malcolm introduced Gregory as a real "dyed-in-the-wool" African revolutionist. "He doesn't want to be, but he is," Malcolm concluded happily.[22]

Before Davis's "black shining prince" eulogy, the young Muslim, Omar Osman, paid tribute to Malcolm. Speaking on behalf of the Islamic Centre in Geneva, Switzerland, Osman acknowledged that the Muslim world recognized Malcolm as a "blood brother" and a hero who had died on the battlefield of faith in Islam. Osman's comments drew great applause, just as his reference to Carl Rowan's USIA remarks drew hisses.

This was no mere duty of religious statesmanship for Osman; he knew Malcolm well. While Malcolm was still in the Nation, it was he who had confronted him from the audience of Mosque No. 7, challenging the Nation's version of "Islam." He had also corresponded with Malcolm and found him to be quite sincere in his interest in orthodox Islam. When Malcolm made the Hajj, he wrote to Osman, "For the past week I have been utterly speechless and spellbound by the graciousness I see displayed all around me by people of *all colors*."

Finally, in January 1965, Osman had arranged to have Malcolm come to speak to the students of Dartmouth College, where he was a student. After the funeral, Osman wrote a tribute to Malcolm in the campus newspaper, *The Dartmouth*: "They accused him of violence and he was never involved in any violence, private or public, overt or covert. They accused him of preaching segregation and being a racist and he never advocated any of this since his return from the pilgrimage to Mecca." The young Muslim student closed his tribute with a verse of poetry: "Yes, of what race, colour, land he was I care not. But this much I care he was my Brother."

Outside of Faith Temple, which was filled to capacity, speakers had been set up so that the crowds on the streets could hear the eulogies. Besides those standing right outside, hundreds in the church's vicinity watched and listened from windows. Inside, after Davis's masterful eulogy, a prayer was recited by another religious dignitary, his Muslim appeal echoing through the Pentecostal church. Malcolm's coffin sat upon a platform draped in dark red velvet, every sign of Christian worship covered lest the funeral be nullified and Malcolm be declared an unbeliever.

Lamps stood at either end of the coffin, and a beautiful blanket of flowers banked beside the body—a last, loving tribute from Betty. The blanket's mass of red carnations, measuring 17 by 25 inches, required three specially designed easels for support. In the center of the field of red was a three-dimensional star and crescent, the sign of Islam, modeled in white carnations.

The prayer completed, the time had come for the coffin to be closed. Betty approached, peering down in final farewell. As she did, the church was filled with the sounds of moans and shrieks, as if all were sisters, mothers, and daughters with her in that rueful moment.

The funeral completed, Malcolm's coffin was carried outside. The neighborhood seemed to be blossoming with black humanity—the streets, the windows of nearby buildings, and even the fire escapes were filled with Harlemites waiting to catch a last glimpse of Malcolm X. "It was an impressive display of the warm feeling they had for Malcolm and his ideas," one observer later noted. However, for Harlem, it was all over in an instant. A funeral procession of over fifty cars sped Malcolm's remains toward his final resting place. The same observer, who also drove in the motorcade, felt that the whole affair had been rushed out of the city by the police—"the feelings of Harlemites didn't matter at all." The police escorted Malcolm's motorcade as far as the city limits, where they passed responsibility to the hands of the Westchester County police, who in turn escorted the somber procession to the place of Malcolm's final rest. And there, miles from his beloved Harlem, "Night fell over the earthly remains of El-Hajj Malik El-Shabazz, who had been called Malcolm X."[23]

Not long after Malcolm's burial, when stories of the "apostle of violence" were still abundant in the press, a Christian minister named W. E. Sanders wrote a tribute to him that appeared in Cleveland's *Call & Post*. It was an unusual eulogy, not merely in its great warmth toward Malcolm X, but in its lofty, almost Garveyite black nationalist tones. "The eternal star of Malcolm X now illumines the heavens. A tall oak in the forest of Black Nationalism has fallen. A militant advocate of African universality lies dead," Sanders wrote.

Malcolm the man was to be measured "by the depths from whence he climbed" and the love he showed for his black countrymen. Sanders continued by comparing Malcolm to Booker T. Washington, Marcus Garvey, and Patrice Lumumba, and called on his readers to renew "the cry of 'Europe for the Europeans,' 'Asia for the Asians,' 'Africa for the Africans,' and 'the Americas for us all.' " Only the "black facts of truth" would be acceptable, Sanders concluded as he rhetorically consigned Malcolm to the sod. "For we know that Malcolm X has a rendezvous with God."

Malcolm's widow Betty also had a rendezvous with God. Before leaving

New York, Betty had remembered her husband as a man whose family life and mission were inseparable. "He was obsessed with the idea that his children and upcoming generations should not have to face the kind of conditions that his generation faced," she told the *Amsterdam News*. As for the outpouring of support shown her on behalf of Malcolm, Betty expressed her gratitude and her certainty that Malcolm "was worthy of their tribute."

Now she was on her way to Mecca, like Malcolm, a Hajji crying, "Labbayka! Here I come, O Lord!" It had been a year since Malcolm had made the pilgrimage, and now another Hajj season had already come. And while Harlem's citizens flowed busily along Malcolm's streets, Betty was tracing his tracks in the ancient paths of Mecca—finally sharing his happy pilgrimage, just as she had shared his burden. "The brotherhood that I have heard preached about all my life is here," Betty wrote back to the people of Harlem. "This ancient city with its beauty and sereneness is indeed something for all men to behold."

Back in Harlem, Malcolm was still missed, especially by those who had looked to him for guidance. On May 19, 1965, when Malcolm would have turned forty years old, followers and admirers staged a commemorative affair at Harlem's Rockland Palace. Along with the oratory, a lone portrait of Malcolm X was mounted on the stage. At the door, Malcolm's transcribed speeches were sold, foreshadowing a Malcolm X print legacy that has since blossomed into a significant market.

Meanwhile, down on 125th Street, a banner was suspended on the Theresa Hotel proclaiming May 19 as "Malcolm X Day." A journalist from the *New York Post*, observing the day's celebration, found himself standing with one of Malcolm's grieving followers at the corner of 125th Street and 7th Avenue. The despondent disciple, whom he called only "William X," was obviously a former "Black Muslim" who had followed Malcolm out of the Nation.[24] William X just stared up at the Theresa and its Malcolm X Day banner. He undoubtedly appreciated the celebration of Malcolm's birthday, the special meeting farther uptown, and the many words that had been spoken. But the wound was too fresh, and the loss too great. "He was special," William X told the journalist. "Now he's gone and all the memorials in the world will not bring him back."

# Author's Note

Any intellectual work is influenced, whether minimally or definingly, by the context of its origin. In this light, it is important to acknowledge that this book is by an Evangelical Christian. Some might argue that being a Christian could constitute an advantage in studying Malcolm's religious life; a Muslim might, for instance, feel less comfortable emphasizing the essential theme of religious propaganda that is central to the study of Malcolm's autobiography. But I think it important to observe that I, too, have invariably been tempted in my own way as a religious writer.

Though I have never been personally bothered by the Nation of Islam's "white devil" anthropology, my own religious feathers were on occasion ruffled in studying a movement that made a blanket condemnation of Christianity while at the same time making use of both its scriptures and theological constructs. However, I have deliberately refrained from engaging in any religious debates with the Nation and the legacy of its founders and activists. I believe it is crucial to acknowledge this interplay between subject and author, not as a form of apologia, but as recognition that this book, like any other, emerges out of a specific historical, religious, and cultural context.

Thus, while this is a Christian's book, it is *not* a *Christian* book on Malcolm X.

# A Note on Biographies

In preparing this book, I intensively studied *The Autobiography of Malcolm X*, as well as all of Malcolm's available published speeches that he delivered both as a minister in the Nation of Islam and as an independent leader. I also found Peter Goldman's *The Death and Life of Malcolm X* (Chicago: University of Illinois Press, 1979) to be extremely helpful and eloquently written. Goldman's honest, sympathetic view of Malcolm X is that of a white liberal, but he offers little regarding Malcolm's youth, and the book presents a very conservative theory of the assassination that has been criticized by others. Nevertheless, Goldman's book remains foundational to any biographical study of Malcolm X, drawing as it does on interviews, publications, and the author's own journalistic relationship with Malcolm X.

Another important book is James Cone's more recent *Martin & Malcolm & America* (Maryknoll, N.Y.: Orbis Books, 1991). This work is the first critical religious analysis of Malcolm X and is both scholarly and highly readable. Perhaps the only limitation of this book is its broad scope as a double biography of Martin Luther King, Jr., as well as Malcolm X. Cone presents Malcolm's religious life and development through the lens of his own black theology presuppositions, and his study offers a rich analysis and a fine resource for students of Malcolm's life. As a double biography it is superb—far surpassing the less scholarly, more sensational book by Louis Lomax, *To Kill a Black Man* (Los Angeles: Holloway House, 1987), which also recounts the lives of King and Malcolm X. Eugene Victor Wolfenstein's *Victims of Democracy: Malcolm X and the Black Revolution* (London: Free Association Books, 1989) is a significant work of scholarship. However, since Wolfenstein is a political psychohistorian, his biography is centered around a Marxist-Freudian analysis that skews the religious perspective.

The publication of Bruce Perry's *Malcolm: The Life of a Man Who Changed Black America* (Barrytown, N.Y.: Station Hill Press, 1991) merits a critical analysis in and of itself. Perry must be credited for being the first Malcolm X biographer to break significantly with the assumption that Malcolm's autobiography could be accepted uncritically. He was apparently the first to initiate extensive research into primary sources (such as Malcolm's prison file, correspondence, school records, etc.). Perry also claims to have conducted many interviews with Malcolm's associates from boyhood to manhood. These basics make Bruce Perry's work the most extensive biography to date. Besides introducing readers to important primary and secondary resources, Perry's greatest contribution is to provide a biographical chronology of Malcolm's life, one that both complements and corrects Malcolm's autobiographical recollection. Thus, in its general historical framework, Perry's biography is highly valuable for students.

But Perry's book is marred by his determination to present Malcolm as a psychohistorical basket case. Whereas the traditional anti-Malcolm bias depicts him as a "violent" man, Perry proposes to attack, not Malcolm's ideology, but his psychology. To do so, he builds his interpretation on a dubious portrayal of Malcolm's parents as abusive, immoral, and psychologically troubled people. Perry's Malcolm is ultimately a lost child in a man's body whose rebellion against white society is really rebellion against adults, largely premised on fear and even sexual confusion. Perry's work hardly does justice to the resources and research opportunities he had been afforded. A careful reading of the book and its endnotes will reveal a number of serious problems. First, Perry presents many interviews, but it is clear that he weighed neither the integrity nor reliability of his interviewees and apparently used even the most controversial recollections without informing the readers of possible bias.

Second, Perry at times "twists" primary and secondary sources into making them say what they do not even infer. In reading the Michigan State Police report on the burning of Malcolm's childhood home, the purported evidence hardly suggests that Earl Little was an arsonist. Yet Perry has Malcolm's father running in the dark of night, knocking on his neighbors' doors as part of a ploy, even though the police record shows that a neighbor had done the knocking in order to find a phone to call the police. In an entirely different case, I noted the same disingenuous use of a newspaper quotation from a 1963 speech to strongly intimate something of a homosexual confession, even though the context of Malcolm's words is neither personal nor related to homosexuality. Unfortunately, this tendency to read psychosexual confessions into Malcolm's public words is repeated a number of times throughout Perry's text and notes and only serves to lessen the reader's faith in his work.

While Perry's work is not the only biography indifferent to Malcolm's religious life, his seems to be singularly antagonistic toward the idea of conversion and belief in Malcolm's story. The irony of *Malcolm: The Life of a Man* is that its best contributions are probably inadvertent. Bruce Perry has unquestionably made a niche in the terrain of Malcolm X biography, so students should not ignore his work but also not take it seriously.

A good many personal remembrances of Malcolm have been recorded in various books. Perhaps among the best of these are the following: Hakim A. Jamal, *From the Dead Level: Malcolm X and Me* (New York: Random House, 1971); Benjamin Karim, with P. Skutches, *Remembering Malcolm* (New York: Carroll and Graf, 1992); David Graham Du Bois, . . . *And Bid Him Sing* (Palo Alto, Calif.: Ramparts Press, 1975); and Michael Abdul Malik, *From Michael de Freitas to Michael X* (Great Britain: Andre Deutsch, 1968). Of these four, the first two are recollections by authors who were admiring followers of Malcolm X both within the Nation and later (and Jamal also recalls Malcolm the hustler). The latter two books are remembrances of Malcolm in 1964–65 and grant rare glimpses of Malcolm X abroad. While Du Bois's is rightly classified as historical fiction, there is little doubt that his main character, an African American expatriate in Egypt, is largely autobiographical. Du Bois met Malcolm in Egypt and his portrayal of Malcolm is quite trustworthy.

Other sketches of Malcolm may be found in the following writings (alphabetically listed by author): Maya Angelou, *All God's Children Need Traveling Shoes* (New York: Random House, 1986); Harry S. Ashmore, *Hearts and Minds: The Anatomy of Racism from Roosevelt to Reagan* (New York: McGraw-Hill, 1982); James Farmer, *Lay Bare the Heart: An Autobiography of the Civil Rights Movement* (New York: Plume/New American Library, 1985); Dick Gregory, *Up from Nigger* (New York: Stein & Day, 1976); *My*

*Life of Absurdity: The Later Years; The Autobiography of Chester Himes* (New York: Paragon House, 1976); Haynes Johnson, *Dusk at the Mountain: The Negro, the Nation, and the Capital—A Report on Problems and Progress* (Garden City, N.Y.: Doubleday, 1963); Leslie Alexander Lacy, "African Responses to Malcolm X," in *Black Fire: An Anthology of Afro-American Writing*, ed. LeRoi Jones and Larry Neal (New York: Morrow, 1968); C. Eric Lincoln, *My Face Is Black* (Boston: Beacon Press, 1964); Gordon Parks, *Voices in the Mirror: An Autobiography* (New York: Doubleday, 1990); Art Sears, Jr., "Malcolm X and the Press," and Lebert Bethune, "Malcolm X in Europe," both in *Malcolm X: The Man and His Times* (New York: Collier Books, 1969), 106–13 and 226–34; and David Gallen, *Malcolm X: As They Knew Him* (New York: Carroll & Graf, 1992). Some of these recollections, however, may not be entirely reliable about details and should be studied carefully.

Finally, Malcolm X is featured highly in books written about the Nation of Islam in the early 1960s. Louis Lomax, *When the Word is Given . . .* (Cleveland: World Publishing, 1963), features Malcolm somewhat sensationally—an approach quite characteristic of Lomax's work on the Nation. On a more scholarly level, C. Eric Lincoln's classic, *The Black Muslims in America* (Boston: Beacon Press, 1960), in its original and revised editions, documents Malcolm's role in the Nation at its zenith. My personal favorite is E. U. Essien-Udom, *Black Nationalism: The Search for an Identity in America* (Chicago: University of Chicago Press, 1963), from which the student may glean some particularly rich statements and vignettes of Malcolm X in the Nation.

# Notes

Terms pertaining to FBI documents are taken from Ann Mari Buitrago and Leon Andrew Immerman, *Are You Now or Have You Ever Been in the FBI Files* (New York: Grove Press, 1981), glossary section, 159–214. A single asterisk (*) denotes an adaptation from the Buitrago glossary, and a double asterisk (**) denotes an original definition, both from *BEST*.

The first two sets of digits in a file citation form are unique to that file. For example, Elijah Muhammad's FBI Headquarters file is 105-24822; his FBI Chicago field office file, however, would not have the same number. The third set of numbers that appear in an FBI file citation is the number of a particular document. Thus, 105-24822-100 is "*EM/HQ*-100," the final number pertaining to document "No. 100" in Elijah Muhammad's FBI Headquarters file. Since the FBI kept a number of files on Elijah Muhammad, Malcolm X, and their organizations, any single document cannot be properly cited without its file number designation and its unique document number. The reader should note that even newspaper clippings kept on file were individually serialized by the FBI and are noted accordingly in this study, along with their footnote citations.

The following abbreviations are used in the notes.

ACLU   American Civil Liberties Union Papers, Seeley G. Mudd Manuscript Library, Princeton University, Princeton, New Jersey.

| | |
|---|---|
| Airtel* | An internal FBI communication, urgent enough that it must be typed on the day it is dictated, but routine enough to be sent by air mail rather than teletype. Often serves as a cover letter for an LHM. |
| AMP | Allan Morrison Papers, Schomburg Center for Research in Black Culture, New York Public Library. |
| AMX | *The Autobiography of Malcolm X.* |
| BEST | Best Efforts, Inc., Archives, Highland Park, Michigan. |
| BOSS | Bureau of Special Services and Investigations, New York City Police Department. |
| Caption | The titles and subtitles of FBI documents (e.g., "Malcolm K. Little; IS-NOI"). |
| CORE | Congress On Racial Equality. |
| DS/MX | United States Department of State files on Malcolm X. |
| ELSUR* | Electronic surveillance; includes TESUR. |
| EM/HQ** | FBI Headquarters (or "Bureau") file on Elijah Muhammad (105-24822). |
| FBI | Federal Bureau of Investigation. |
| IS* | Internal Security; subcaption (see below) of an FBI document, followed by a hyphen, denoting a "subversive" investigation of an organization (e.g., "IS-NOI"). |
| LHM* | Letterhead Memorandum; FBI summary report intended for dissemination to other agencies; conceals confidential sources; often enclosed in an airtel. |
| MCI** | Muslim Cult of Islam. Early (pre-1957) FBI name for NOI. |
| MKL | Malcolm K. Little. FBI abbreviation. |
| MMI | Muslim Mosque, Inc. |
| MMI/HQ** | FBI Headquarters (or "Bureau") file on the Muslim Mosque, Inc. (100-441765). |
| MMI/NY** | FBI New York Office file on the Muslim Mosque, Inc. (100-152759). |
| MSP | Massachusetts State Prison. |
| MSTA | Moorish Science Temple of America Collection, Schomburg Center for Research in Black Culture, New York Public Library. |
| MX/ELSUR** | FBI New York Office ELSUR subfile on Malcolm K. Little (105-8999-Sub 1); specifically, the logs of the TESUR on Malcolm X's home telephone. Extracts in Clayborne Carson, ed., etc. |
| MX/HQ** | FBI Headquarters (or "Bureau") file on Malcolm K. Little (100-399321), as processed in 1982–83. See also SR. |
| MX/NY** | FBI Headquarters (or "Bureau") file on Malcolm K. Little (105-8999). |
| MXS | Malcolm X Scrapbooks, Volumes I–III, in the Schomburg Center for Research in Black Culture, New York, N.Y. |

NAACP   National Association for the Advancement of Colored People.

NOI   The Nation of Islam. FBI reference.

N.R.**   Not recorded; denotes an FBI document, or serial (see below), that was not numbered or "serialized" when filed. When followed by "after [serial number]," indicates that the document was filed after (but not immediately behind) the cited serial; when followed by "behind [serial number]," the document was filed immediately behind (or "under") the cited serial; when followed by "before [serial number]," the document was filed immediately before (or atop) the cited serial.

NYU   Institute of Afro-American Affairs, New York University.

OAAU   Organization of Afro-American Unity.

OAAU/HQ**   FBI Headquarters (or "Bureau") file on the Organization of Afro-American Unity (100-442235).

OO**   Office of Origin; subcaption (see below) of an FBI document, followed by a colon, denoting the FBI field office that had primary responsibility for an investigation (e.g., "OO: New York").

PF   Prison File of Malcolm Little, Department of Correction, Commonwealth of Massachusetts, Boston.

PRF*   Parole File of Malcolm Little, the Department of Correction, Commonwealth of Massachusetts, Boston.

Redaction   Deletion.

Report**   FBI communication, often quite long, from a field office to Headquarters, with copies to other interested field offices; intended for dissemination to other government agencies.

SA   Special Agent, the title of any FBI agent.

SAC*   Special Agent in Charge, the head of an FBI field office (except Los Angeles and New York, which were headed by Assistant Directors).

SE   Special employee of FBI; not an agent or clerk.

Serial**   An individual document within an FBI file. Each serial in a file has a different number.

SM*   Security Matter; subcaption (see below) of an FBI document, followed by a hyphen, denoting a "subversive" investigation of an individual; the letter following it indicates the nature of the investigation, as in "SM-C."

SM-C   Security Matter-Communist. See SM.

Source   Designation for any supplier of information to FBI, human or otherwise. Human sources tend not to be paid and given their positions are likely to have access to information (e.g., landlord or employers).

SR**   Scholarly Resources, Inc., microfilm of MX/HQ, published as *Malcolm X: FBI Surveillance File*, 2 reels (Wilmington, DE,

1978). MX/HQ was processed and released twice by the FBI— first in the mid-1970s (the SR version), then again in 1982–83 (available through the Freedom of Information–Privacy Acts Section, Information Management Division, FBI, which can be viewed in the FBI Reading Room, FBI Headquarters, Washington, D.C.). The SR version is generally more heavily redacted, omitting file numbers, serial numbers and subcaptions.

Subcaption    The subtitle in the caption (see above) of an FBI document following an initial semicolon (e.g., "Malcolm K. Little; IS-NOI").
SR-MSP      Special Report, Michigan State Police.
TESUR      Technical (i.e., telephone) surveillance by FBI.
UNIA       Universal Negro Improvement Association.

## Notes to the Introduction

1. *The Autobiography of Malcolm X*, with Alex Haley (New York: Grove Press, 1965), 235; henceforth, *AMX*. Orrin Evans, "Malcolm X Comes to Phila[delphia] to 'Reorganize Muslims,' " *Evening Bulletin* (Philadelphia), 30 December 1964, 3, *BEST*; Mary Seibert McCauley, "Alex Haley, A Southern Griot: A Literary Biography," Ph.D. diss. (George Peabody College for Teachers of Vanderbilt University, 1983), 88.

2. All the original chapter titles of *The Autobiography of Malcolm X* were set forth in an approval letter, Malcolm X (Malik Shabazz), East Elmhurst, N.Y., to Paul R. Reynolds, Paul R. Reynolds & Sons, New York, 21 March 1964, in the Rare Book and Manuscript Library, Columbia University, New York. The original agreement between Malcolm, Haley, and the publisher even allowed Haley to include his own "Afterword" in the book. See also Brenda J. Gilchrist, "The Final Chapters; Rest of Haley Book about Malcolm X to Be Released Soon," *Detroit Free Press*, 18 March 1993, 1B.

3. John Paul Eakin, "Malcolm X and the Limits of Autobiography," *Criticism* (Summer 1976): 241–42.

## Notes to Chapter 1

1. Albert Murray, *The Omni-Americans: Some Alternatives to the Folklore of White Supremacy* (New York: Vintage Books, 1983), 62; August Meier and Elliott Rudwick, *From Plantation to Ghetto* (New York: Hill and Wang, 1976), 234 and 236; C. Eric Lincoln, *The Black Muslims in America* (Boston: Beacon Press, 1973), xxiv; James Weldon Johnson, *Black Manhattan* (copyright 1930 by James Weldon Johnson; rpt., n.p.; New York: Atheneum, 1977), 256.

2. "Garvey Denounced at Negro Meeting," *New York Times*, 7 August 1922, 7; "2,000 Negroes Hear Garvey Denounced," *New York Times*, 21 August 1922, 11; Tony Martin, *Race First: The Ideological and Organizational Struggles of Marcus*

*Garvey and the Universal Negro Improvement Association* (New York: Dover Press, The Majority Press, 1976), 6, 23; idem, "Garvey and Scattered Africa," in *Global Dimensions of the African Diaspora*, ed. Joseph E. Harris (Washington, D.C.: Howard University Press, 1982), 244.

3. Theodore Draper, *The Rediscovery of Black Nationalism* (New York: Viking Press, 1969), 46; contrary to the suggestion that Garvey's UNIA motto was a "paraphrasing" of a line by Alfred Lord Tennyson, it seems more likely that this motto was inspired by St. Paul's declaration, "One Lord, one faith, one baptism" (Ephesians 4:5). Cf. Marcus Garvey, *Marcus Garvey: Life and Lessons*, ed. Robert A. Hill and Barbara Bair (Berkeley: University of California Press, 1987), xxxi; Leonard E. Barrett, *Soul Force* (Garden City, N.Y.: Anchor/Doubleday, 1974), 134–35; Marcus Garvey, "The Philosophy of Marcus Garvey," in *Black Protest: History, Documents, and Analyses: 1619 to the Present*, ed. Joanne Grant (Greenwich, Conn.: Fawcett Publications, 1968), 203; E. U. Essien-Udom, *Black Nationalism: A Search for an Identity in America* (Chicago: University of Chicago Press, 1962), 37 and 38, n. 43.

4. Essien-Udom, *Black Nationalism*, 37, 39; Adolph Edwards, *Marcus Garvey: 1887–1940* (London: New Beacon Books, 1972), 13–14; Martin, *Race First*, 92–93, 70–72; "Garvey Preaches Faith in Black God," *New York Times*, 4 August 1924, 7; "Negroes Acclaim a Black Christ," *New York Times*, 6 August 1924, 3; Barrett, *Soul Force*, 135.

5. Barrett, *Soul Force*, 144.

6. Edward Wilmot Blyden (1832–1912) was a brilliant Liberian statesman and scholar who was born in St. Thomas, Virgin Islands. As an educator, ordained Presbyterian minister, and a pan-Africanist, Blyden was deeply impressed with Islam's progressive influence on the African people. While Blyden never renounced the essence of Christianity, he argued that Islam was a better religion for the black man than traditional Christianity. Blyden argued this case in his scholarly masterpiece, *Christianity, Islam and the Negro Race* (London: W. B. Whittingham and Co., 1887; rpt. Edinburgh: Edinburgh University Press, 1967).

7. Martin, *Race First*, 74–77, 151–67, 174–92; Edwards, *Marcus Garvey, 1887–1940*, 12, 16; Essien-Udom, *Black Nationalism*, 39.

8. Edwards, *Marcus Garvey: 1887–1940*, 20, 23–24; Martin, *Race First*, 193–95; Essien-Udom, *Black Nationalism*, 40; Roi Ottley, *New World A-Coming* (New York: Arno Press and New York Times, 1968), 72–73; Draper, *The Rediscovery of Black Nationalism*, 72. It should be noted that Islam had been introduced to the shores of the United States during the slave trade. There are significant accounts of African American slaves who either practiced or remembered the practice of Muslim religion. However, these Muslim pioneers in the West apparently had no enduring influence, and no apparent connection with twentieth-century Islamic-styled movements of the black urban north. See Albert J. Raboteau, *Slave Religion: The "Invisible Institution" in the Antebellum South* (New York: Oxford University Press, 1980), 46–47; and Morroe Berger, "The Black Muslims," *Horizon* (Winter 1964): 53–55.

9. Essien-Udom, *Black Nationalism*, 33; Arthur Huff Fauset, *Black Gods of the Metropolis; Negro Religious Cults of the Urban North* (New York: Octagon Books, 1970), 41; Noble Drew Ali, *Koran Questions for Moorish Americans* (Chicago: Moorish Science Temple of America, 1928?), questions no. 89–91, in Moorish Science Temple of America collection, Schomburg Center for Research in Black Culture, New York; henceforth, *MSTA*. Certificate of registration for Cook County, Illinois, 29 November 1926, *MSTA*.

10. Fauset, *Black Gods*, 42–43; Noble Drew Ali (reincarnated Mohammed, 3rd), *Moorish Literature* (N.p.: Noble Drew Ali, 1928), 18, 10–12, *MSTA*; Essien-Udom, *Black Nationalism*, 35; Edwin E. Calverly, "Negro Muslims in Hartford," *The Muslim World* (October 1965): 343; Drew Ali, *Koran Questions for Moorish Americans*, question no. 64, *MSTA*.

## Notes to Chapter 2

1. For an overview of the Nation, see Lawrence H. Mamiya, "From Black Muslim to Bilalian: The Evolution of a Movement," *Journal for the Scientific Study of Religion* (June 1982): 138–52; Clifton E. Marsh, *From Black Muslims to Muslims: The Transition from Separatism to Islam, 1930–1980* (Metuchen, N.J.: Scarecrow Press, 1984); Steven Barboza, "A Divided Legacy," *Emerge* (April 1992): 26–32.

2. Hatim Sahib, "The Nation of Islam," thesis, University of Chicago, 1951, 87–93; Bob Lucas, "First Magazine Interview with Elijah Muhammad Black Muslim Leader," *Cavalier* (January 1964): 11–12, 89–93; *AMX*, 207–8.

3. Erdmann Doane Beynon, "The Voodoo Cult among Negro Migrants in Detroit," *American Journal of Sociology* (May 1938): 894–907; Sahib, "The Nation of Islam," 73–74; Arna Bontemps and Jack Conroy, *Any Place but Here* (New York: Hill and Wang, 1966), 216–23; Lincoln, *The Black Muslims*, 14; Essien-Udom, *Black Nationalism*, 45; Benjamin Karim, with P. Skutches and D. Gallen, *Remembering Malcolm* (New York: Carroll and Graf, 1992), 134; Wallace Deen Muhammad, *As the Light Shineth from the East* (Chicago: WDM Publishing, 1980), 27. *BEST* has first noted the striking resemblance of a Garveyite organizer named "Farr" to W. D. Fard. Cf. Robert A. Hill, ed., *The Marcus Garvey and Universal Negro Improvement Association Papers*, vol. 4 (Berkeley: University of California Press, 1985), 233–34, 236–37, 311–12. A police photograph of W. D. Fard is found in Malu Halasa, *Elijah Muhammad: Religious Leader* (New York: Chelsea House, 1990), 51.

4. Beynon, "The Voodoo Cult," 898. Cf. Elijah Muhammad, *Message to the Blackman in America* (Newport News, Va.: United Brothers Communications Systems, n.d.), 1–2, 4–5.

5. Sahib, "The Nation of Islam," 85, 72, 183; Beynon, "The Voodoo Cult," 901; Bontemps and Conroy, *Anyplace but Here*, 219.

6. Sahib, "The Nation of Islam," 71, 74, 90–94, 96; Beynon, "The Voodoo Cult," 903; Elijah Muhammad, *The Supreme Wisdom: Solution to the So-called Negroes' Problem* (n.p., 26 February 1957; rpt., Newport News, Va.: National Newport News and Commentator, n.d.), 15; Essien-Udom, *Black Nationalism*, 44; Lincoln, *The Black Muslims*, 199.

7. Sahib, "The Nation of Islam," 77–81, 86–87; Essien-Udom, *Black Nationalism*, 63–67; Beynon, "The Voodoo Cult," 906–7; "Moslem Put under $5,000 Bond for Failing to Sign for Draft," *Evening Star* (Washington, D.C.), 10 May 1942, *BEST*; "$5,000 in Cash Donated to Free 'Mohammed'," *Evening Star* (Washington, D.C.), 24 July 1942, *BEST*; " 'Speaks Only to God': Jury May Reverse 'Allah' in Draft Case Today," *Washington Daily News*, 23 November 1942, *BEST*.

8. Sahib, "The Nation of Islam," 82–84, 19, 237–39; Marsh, *From Black Muslims to Muslims*, 117; Muhammad, *As the Light Shineth from the East*, 17, 19–20.

9. Marsh, *From Black Muslims to Muslims*, 55; Muhammad, *Message to the Blackman*, 38, 157–59, 266–69; Essien-Udom, *Black Nationalism*, 205–6, 218–21, 136–38, 228–29; Lincoln, *The Black Muslims*, 84; *Muslim Daily Prayers* (Chicago: University of Islam, 1957), *BEST*; Sahib, "The Nation of Islam," 94–95, 171–72; Muhammad, *The Supreme Wisdom*, 25–27, 40.

## Notes to the Prologue to Part Two

1. AMX, 164. Three separate accounts of Paul's conversion are found in the biblical (New Testament) book of Acts 9:1–22, 22:3–16, and 26:9–18.

2. Letter of Malcolm X to Elijah Muhammad, 19 July 1960, 1, *BEST*.

3. AMX, 164–65.

4. AMX, 188.

5. AMX, 188 and 190; Eugene Victor Wolfenstein, *The Victims of Democracy: Malcolm X and the Black Revolution* (London: Free Association Books, 1989), 221–22; Perry, *Malcolm: The Life of a Man Who Changed Black America* (Barrytown, N.Y.: Station Hill Press, 1991), 128.

## Notes to Chapter 3

1. AMX, 1–2. Bruce Perry has shown that Malcolm's mother's name was actually Louisa, but that she was known as Louise after she came to North America. Since she apparently accepted the latter, and since this is likewise the name recalled by Malcolm, in this study Malcolm's mother will be referred to as Louise Little. Perry, *Malcolm: The Life of a Man*, 5; Ted Vincent, "The Garveyite Parents of Malcolm X," *The Black Scholar* (April 1989): 10–13; Wilfred Little Shabazz, interview by author, 14 August 1992, Detroit, Michigan; henceforth, Wilfred Little Shabazz Interview, 14 August 1992.

2. AMX, 6, 395; Malcolm X, *By Any Means Necessary: Speeches, Interviews and a Letter by Malcolm X*, ed. George Breitman (New York: Pathfinder Press, 1985), 25.

3. AMX, 6 , 3; Vincent, "The Garveyite Parents of Malcolm X," 10–12; Edwards, *Marcus Garvey: 1887–1940*, 13–14; Wilfred Little Shabazz, in *Malcolm X: Make It Plain* (New York: Viking, 1994), 23.

4. AMX, 2–3. Malcolm's brother Wilfred described his father as being a very muscular man, "very strong, not only physically, in other ways too. He had come out of Georgia, where he'd grown up on a farm." Wilfred Little Shabazz, in *Malcolm X: Make It Plain*, 15; Perry, *Malcolm: The Life of a Man*, 3 and 385.

5. Robert Millette and Mahin Gosine, *The Grenada Revolution: Why It Failed* (New York: Africana Research Publications, 1985), 14–16; AMX, 2. Bruce Perry says Malcolm's maternal grandfather was a Scotsman; see Perry, *Malcolm: The Life of a Man*, 2–3. According to Robert Little, in her advanced years Louise Little surprised her family by demonstrating exceptional familiarity with the French language. Robert Little, interview by author, 2 April 1992, New York. Note also the recollection of Malcolm's brother Abdul Aziz Omar (nee Philbert Little) that part of their home training as children included lessons in French; *Malcolm X: Make It Plain*, 16.

6. Earl Little's voice described by Wilfred Little Shabazz, interview by author, 15 August 1992, Detroit; henceforth, Wilfred Little Shabazz Interview, 15 August 1992. Vincent, "The Garveyite Parents of Malcolm X," 11; Abdul Aziz Omar, in *Malcolm X: Make It Plain*, 16, 24; AMX, 2, 7–9, 11, 28.

7. Wilfred Little Shabazz Interview, 15 August 1992.

8. Malcolm X, *Malcolm X Speaks: Selected Speeches and Statements*, ed. George Breitman (New York: Grove Press, 1982), 36. Wilfred Little Shabazz, telephone interview by author, 27 November 1992. Wilfred Little Shabazz expressed great concern over Bruce Perry's biographical treatment and concluded that Perry must be "sick" to deny the Klan attack on his parents' home.

9. Joel Williamson, *The Crucible of Race: Black-White Relations in the American South since Emancipation* (New York: Oxford University Press, 1984), 472; Wolfenstein, *The Victims of Democracy*, 46; " 'K.K.K.' Sends Human Hand; Negro Editor Gets Warning with Mail Enclosure," *New York Times*, 6 September 1922, 19; "Garvey Assails Ku Klux," *New York Times*, 10 July 1922, 17; "2,000 Negroes Hear Garvey Denounced; Speaker Declares Ex-President General Is Ally of the Ku Klux Klan," 11. See Tony Martin's insightful analysis of the "symbiotic" relationship that existed between Garvey and white racist organization leaders, in Martin, *Race First*, 344–55.

10. Special Report by G. W. Waterman, B.C.I. [Bureau of Criminal Investigation/s?], Michigan State Police, Case #2155, n.d. [late February/early March 1930], 1, *BEST*; henceforth, *SR-MSP*; AMX, 3 and 2. See comments by Abdul Aziz Omar and Wilfred Little Shabazz, in *Malcolm X: Make It Plain*, 21; Perry, *Malcolm: The Life of a Man*, 9.

11. Perry, *Malcolm: The Life of a Man*, 9–10; *SR-MSP*, 1–2; analysis and reference to article in *Lansing Capital News*, 11 November 1929, 10, in letter from *BEST* to author, 6 November 1993, 1; *AMX*, 4; sworn statement by Earl Little, 11 November 1929, in *SR-MSP*, 1–2; Wolfenstein, *The Victims of Democracy*, 48.

12. Wolfenstein, *The Victims of Democracy*, 144; Vincent, "The Garveyite Parents of Malcolm X," 12–13; observations regarding Michigan State Police file on the Black Legion, letter from *BEST* to author, 6 November 1993, 2; *AMX*, 7, 10; Wilfred Little Shabazz interview, 15 August 1992; James Cone, *Martin & Malcolm & America* (Maryknoll, N.Y.: Orbis, 1991), 43; Report of Trooper [Laurence J.] Baril, 28 September 1931, in *SR-MSP*.

13. Karim, *Remembering Malcolm*, 172; Cone, *Martin & Malcolm & America*, 43. Reference to Malcolm's 1963 statement to Elijah Muhammad in letter from *BEST* to author, 8 April 1993, 2.

14. *The Negro Protest: James Baldwin, Malcolm X, Martin Luther King Talk with Kenneth B. Clark,* ed. Kenneth B. Clark (Boston: Beacon Press, 1963), 18–19.

15. Hans J. Massaquoi, "Mystery of Malcolm X," *Ebony* (September 1964), 45; Wolfenstein, *The Victims of Democracy*, 45–46, which notes that by the end of 1924 there were probably one and a half million Klansmen nationwide, and the KKK was particularly entrenched in lower-middle and working-class in large cities and small towns in the South and Midwest; cf. Perry, *Malcolm: The Life of a Man*, 12 and 390, and Wolfenstein, *The Victims of Democracy*, 43; *AMX*, 10; observation about police report's silence in letter from *BEST* to author, 6 November 1993, 2.

## Notes to Chapter 4

1. *Malcolm X Speaks*, 135.

2. AMX, 371.

3. AMX, 2, 8, and 371; Gabriel Moran, *Religious Education Development: Images for the Future* (Minneapolis: Winston Press, 1983), 136, 147, 130; Hexham and Poewe, *Understanding Cults*, 60. The psychobiographical interpretations are found in Perry, *Malcolm: The Life of a Man*, 2 and 384; Wolfenstein, *The Victims of Democracy*, 97.

4. Hexham and Poewe, *Understanding Cults*, 61–62; AMX, 1; *The Negro Protest*, 18; "Mystery of Malcolm X," 44; and Malcolm X, "I'm Talking to You, White Man," *Saturday Evening Post*, 12 September 1964, 31; Wilfred Little Shabazz Interview, 14 August 1992.

5. Wilfred Little Shabazz Interview, 14 August 1992.

6. *AMX*, 7, 17.

7. Wilfred Little Shabazz Interview, 14 August 1992.

8. Hexham and Poewe, *Understanding Cults*, 6; Robert Little Interview, 2 April 1992; Wilfred Little Shabazz Interview, 14 August 1992; *AMX*, 5 and 39. Malcolm wrote that one of his brothers, Philbert (Abdul Aziz Omar), "loved the church" and was temporarily active in the black Pentecostal "holiness" movement—an orthodox Christian movement; cf. 5 and 153. However, Philbert eventually left behind orthodox Christianity to join the Nation—which may suggest he was no less a religious eclectic than the rest of the family.

9. *AMX*, 11–13; Yvonne Little Woodward and Wilfred Little, in *Malcolm X: Make It Plain*, 26 and 28.

10. *AMX*, 14, 17–20, and 35; Yvonne Woodward, in *Malcolm X: Make It Plain*, 29; Robert Little. Interview by Clara Hemphill, " 'Keep Children Connected to Family,' " *New York Newsday*, 13 May 1991, 69.

11. *AMX*, 25–39 and 43; Bill Cunningham and Daniel Golden, "Malcolm: The Boston Years," *Boston Globe Magazine*, 16 February 1992, 26; Massaquoi, "Mystery of Malcolm X," 45. "Subject wrote to his half sister, Mrs. Ella Collins requesting permission to come to live with her. She in turn sent for him and he arrived here in Boston at the age of 13 years. Subject refused to go to school"; C. Peterson, "Family & Personal [H]istory, Malcolm Little M.S.P. 22843, Interview with Mrs. Ella Collins, half-sister," 17 May 1946, Prison File of Malcolm Little, the Department of Correction, the Commonwealth of Massachusetts. Henceforth, *PF*.

12. *AMX*, 44 and 55–56; Murray, *The Omni-Americans*, 50–52. Emphasis in the text. Malcolm pointed out the actor Sidney Poitier as an admirable example, among others, of a black man who kept his natural hair style all along. Poitier, in fact, very much fits Murray's description. In the civil rights era, Sidney Poitier was on the vanguard of the integrationist movement, and his strong stance in this regard was reflected even in his films.

13. Cunningham and Golden, "Malcolm: The Boston Years," 27; *AMX*, 5; Herbert Krosney, "America's Black Supremacists," *The Nation*, 6 May 1961, 391.

14. *AMX*, 15 and 391; Cunningham and Golden, "Malcolm: The Boston Years," 26; "Says His Movement Will Live," *Boston Herald*, 23 February 1965, 13, *PF*.

15. Perry, *Malcolm: The Life of a Man*, 92–93; Cunningham and Golden, "Malcolm: The Boston Years," 27. Both accounts appear to be based on interviews with Malcolm Jarvis, though only Perry's account actually cites Jarvis. There is a discrepancy between the two accounts as to where the incident actually took place. In Perry's account, the scene occurred at a club called The Little Dixie; in the shorter account by Cunningham and Golden, the scene was Wally's Paradise.

16. Yael Lotan, " 'No Peaceful Solution to Racialism': An Exclusive Interview with Malcolm X," *Sunday Gleaner Magazine*, 12 July 1964, 5.

*Notes to Chapter 5*

1. Nat Hentoff, "Elijah in the Wilderness," *The Reporter*, 4 August 1960, 39; Peter Goldman, *The Death and Life of Malcolm* X (Chicago: University of Illinois Press, 1979), 30–31.

2. Louis Lomax, *To Kill a Black Man* (Los Angeles: Holloway House, 1987), 27–28; Goldman, *The Death and Life*, 29.

3. AMX, 71; Johnson, *Black Manhattan*, 145–56; James Egert Allen, *The Negro in New York* (New York: Exposition Press, 1964), 33–35.

4. "Police and Court Data," Malcolm Little #22843, 23 July 1946, 2, *PF*. Malcolm worked for the New Haven Railroad from June to September 1941, January to October 1942, and again for several weeks in March 1943. William Worthy, "The Nation of Islam: Impact and Prospects," *Midstream* (Spring 1962): 35; AMX, 76–79.

5. AMX, 31, 119, and 171; Goldman, *The Death and Life*, 30. The elderly racketeer who Goldman says remembered Malcolm in Harlem, said Malcolm was a "john-walker"; Perry, *Malcolm: The Life of a Man*, 377 and 76 (n., 399); author's transcription of Malcolm X on *City Desk* (Chicago: WMBQ-TV, 17 March 1963), videotape in the Schomburg Center for Research in Black Culture, Harlem, New York. Malcolm X, interview by Douglas Geoffrey Bridson, 2 December 1964 (London: BBC Broadcasting House), edited and transcribed by Paul Lee of *BEST*; henceforth, Malcolm X, Bridson Interview.

6. Clarence Atkins, interview by author, 17 July 1992, New York; henceforth, Clarence Atkins Interview. AMX, 68, 76, and 94. Malcolm said of Sophia that "she just seemed to love all Negroes. . . . She swore that a white man couldn't interest her"; Cunningham and Golden, "Malcolm: The Boston Years," 28. Bea is identified by her married name, Bazarian. See also Perry, *Malcolm: The Life of a Man*, 56 and 75.

7. AMX, 96–97.

8. Clarence Atkins Interview; AMX, 89, 92, 97, 120, and 31; Perry, *Malcolm: The Life of a Man*, 77–78 and 83.

9. Clarence Atkins Interview; Bruce Perry and Malcolm's brother, Abdul Aziz Omar, on *Talk from the Heart*, with Al Kresta (Detroit: WMUZ-FM, 2 February 1993). In this radio interview, Omar called in to take issue with Perry, expressing great disturbance over his unwarranted, negative portrayal of Earl and Louise Little, and his questionable suggestion of Malcolm's homosexuality; "Why Malcolm X Quit the Black Muslims," *Sepia* (May 1964), 60; Lotan, " 'No Peaceful Solution to Racialism'," 5.

10. AMX, 155, 86, 135, and 97; Saint Augustine, *Confessions*, trans. R. S. Pine-Coffin (Baltimore: Penguin Books, 1961), 43.

11. AMX, 97; Louie Robinson, "Redd Foxx—Prince of Clowns," *Ebony* (April 1967), 91; Clarence Atkins Interview. Author's emphasis. Indeed, Atkins credits

Malcolm X for his own study and expertise on Garvey and the UNIA; Hentoff, "Elijah in the Wilderness," 39.

12. Clarence Atkins Interview; Wilfred Little Shabazz Interview, 14 August 1992; Malcolm Jarvis, in *Malcolm X: Make It Plain*, 54; AMX, 81, 97, and 113; "Police and Court Data," Malcolm Little, #22843, 23 July 1946, 2, *PF*. In the autobiography, Malcolm said he worked at Small's from after his birthday in 1942 until early 1943, which would have been the better part of a year. However, Clarence Atkins did not think Malcolm worked at Small's very long, and Malcolm's prison record notes that Malcolm was working at Jimmy's Chicken Shack from 1942 to 1944.

13. "Police and Court Data," Malcolm Little, #22843, 23 July 1946, 2, *PF*. Malcolm worked at Mr. Goldstein's Lobster Pond on 42nd Street in Manhattan from July through September 1944; AMX, 89, 99, 103–104, 110, and 115; Clarence Atkins Interview; Malcolm X, "I'm Talking to You, White Man," 40.

14. AMX, 106 and 72. Apparently Malcolm also made extended visits back to Boston and Lansing, where he worked temporarily at legitimate jobs and also engaged in a variety of criminal activities, and even got in trouble with the law. Perry, *Malcolm: The Life of a Man*, 82–86. The location of the draft board noted in Boston Office Report, "Malcolm K. Little; Security Matter-C; Security Matter-MCI," 4 May 1953, 2, Reel 1, *SR*.

15. AMX, 106–8.

16. AMX, 134; SAC, New York to FBI Director, "Malcolm K. Little; Security Matter-MCI," 28 January 1955, 1, Reel 1, *SR*; Perry, *Malcolm: The Life of a Man*, 89. Given his peculiar biographical motivation, Perry is particularly concerned to emphasize that Malcolm was "run out of Harlem," and that he had never been the "tough guy," standing up to West Indian Archie, as he claimed. He also notes that Jarvis claims to have initiated the call to Sammy in Harlem, and not the other way around, as Malcolm claimed.

17. Clarence Atkins Interview.

## Notes to Chapter 6

1. AMX, 139–44, 149–51; "Malcolm Little MSP #22843, Middlesex Superior Court Charges," 2, *PF*; "Preliminary Record, Malcolm Little MSP #22843," 2–3, *PF*; Perry, *Malcolm: The Life of a Man*, 100–101 and 420–21; case report on Malcolm Little #22843 by John F. Rockett, 7 May 1946, 1, *PF*; "Institution History of Malcolm Little," May 1951, *PF*; Helen Dudar, "The Muslims and Black Nationalism; Part V: What Does Malcolm Want?" *New York Post*, 10 April 1964, 49.

2. Cunningham and Golden, "Malcolm: The Boston Years," map insert, "Crime and Punishment," 18; "Institution History of Malcolm Little," *PF*; AMX, 143 and 153–54; Perry, *Malcolm: The Life of a Man*, 104 and 106, 422–23; "Transfer Summary," 10 January 1947, *PF*; "Massachusetts State Prison Psychometric Report,"

1 May 1946, *PF*; "Preliminary Record," 1, *PF*. In an interview with a case worker two months later, Malcolm again claimed his mother was white; see "Department of Corrections Case Worker's Report," 13 May 1946, *PF*.

3. "Preliminary Record," 3, *PF*, AMX, 154–55.

4. Malcolm X, Bridson Interview.

5. Malcolm X, Bridson Interview; AMX, 153; "Mr. Muhammad and His Fanatic Moslems?" *Sepia* (November 1959): 26; "Malcolm X," interview by Alex Haley, in *The Playboy Interview*, ed. G. Barry Golson (N.p.: Wideview Books, 1981), 49. This Malcolm X interview originally appeared in the May 1963 issue of *Playboy*.

6. AMX, 155, 172, and 29; Perry, *Malcolm: The Life of a Man*, 108; "Massachusetts State Prison Psychometric Report," 1 May 1946, *PF*.

7. Malcolm X, Bridson Interview; "Transfer Summary," 10 January 1947, PF; AMX, 155–56; "Massachusetts State Prison, Commitment and Booking Data," n.d., *PF*. This report is apparently based on the "Preliminary Report" for Malcolm Little, #22843, 8 March 1946, 3, *PF*.

8. "Institution History of Malcolm Little," May 1951, *PF*; Concord Reformatory was located approximately fifteen miles northeast of Boston. See Cunningham and Golden, "Malcolm: The Boston Years," map insert, "Crime and Punishment," 18; letter of Malcolm Little to Mr. Dwyer, Norfolk Prison Colony Transportation Board, 28 July 1947, *PF*; AMX, 156; Wilfred Little Shabazz Interview, 14 August 1992.

9. Letter from Malcolm Little to Mr. Dwyer, Norfolk Prison Colony Transportation Board, 28 July 1947, *PF*.

10. Malcolm Little to Dwyer, 28 July 1947.

11. AMX, 158–59; Cunningham and Golden, "Malcolm: The Boston Years," 30 and 35, and map insert, "Crime and Punishment," 15; "Institution History of Malcolm Little," May 1951, *PF*; Wilfred Little Shabazz Interview, 14 August 1992. Norfolk Prison Colony was located about twenty miles southwest of Charlestown Prison, where Malcolm was first incarcerated.

12. AMX, 159–69, 171, 156; Perry, *Malcolm: The Life of a Man*, 114 and 116; Wilfred Little noted, "He studied Buddhism while he was in there [prison]." Wilfred Little Shabazz Interview, 14 August 1992; "Transfer Summary for Malcolm Little," Massachusetts Department of Corrections, 23 March 1950, PF; Hexham and Poewe, *Understanding Cults*, 95 and 103; Stuart A. Wright, *Leaving Cults: The Dynamics of Defection* (West Lafayette, Ind.: Society for the Scientific Study of Religion, Purdue University, 1987), 6 and 8. Neither Wright nor Hexham and Poewe refer to Malcolm X in their studies. References to their work throughout this book represent only my application.

13. Hexham and Poewe, *Understanding Cults*, 12–13; AMX, 171–81; Perry, *Malcolm: The Life of a Man*, 119–20.

14. Robert James Branham, " 'I Was Gone on Debating': The Prison Debates and Public Encounters of Malcolm X," MS (Lewiston, Maine: Bates College, n.d.),

8–10, *BEST*; "Abolishment of Capital Punishment: The Death Penalty Is Ineffective as a Deterrent; 2nd Speaker, Malcom [*sic*] Little," *The Colony* 21 (1 January 1950): 9, *BEST*; AMX, 185.

15. AMX, 187–90. Jeremiah Shabazz, interview by author, 17 May 1993, Philadelphia. Henceforth, Jeremiah Shabazz Interview; Hexham and Poewe, *Understanding Cults*, 60–61; Wright, *Leaving Cults*, 9.

## Notes to Chapter 7

1. Perry, *Malcolm: The Life of a Man*, 132 and 429. Perry states that Malcolm told the prison authorities at Norfolk that he would not take the inoculation because of the Nation's teachings, and that he knew the consequences would involve transfer. He also says that inoculation was mandatory at Norfolk because the facility's well water was chemically untreated.

2. AMX, 186, 190–91; "Transfer Summary for Malcolm Little," Massachusetts Department of Correction, 23 March 1950, PF; Perry, *Malcolm: The Life of a Man*, 133. Perry says that while Malcolm was in Norfolk he had studied library books on constitutional law and that those books eventually vanished; also, reading material sent by his sister Ella also disappeared. "Institution History of Malcolm Little," May 1951, PF; Massachusetts State Prison Report of Psychiatrist, 4 May 1951, PF.

3. AMX, 190–92; "Four Convicts Turn Moslems, Get Calls Looking to Mecca," *Boston Herald*, 20 April 1950, 3; Perry, *Malcolm: The Life of a Man*, 133.

4. "Local Criminals, in Prison, Claim Moslem Faith Now: Grow Beards, Won't Eat Pork; Demand East-Facing Cells to Facilitate 'Prayers to Allah,' " *Springfield Union* (Springfield, Mass.), 21 April 1950, 1 and 7; "Four Convicts Turn Moslems, Get Calls Looking to Mecca"; Paul John Eakin, "Malcolm X and the Limits of Autobiography," *Criticism* (Summer 1976): 232–33; Betty Shabazz, "The Legacy of My Husband, Malcolm X," *Ebony* (June 1969), 176.

5. Letter of Malcolm Little to Commissioner MacDowell, Department of Corrections, State House, Boston, 18 April 1950, PF. All emphases in these excerpts are in the original manuscript.

6. Malcolm Little to MacDowell, 18 April 1950.

7. Malcolm Little to MacDowell, 18 April 1950.

8. Letter of Malcolm Little to Commissioner MacDowell, 6 June 1950, PF; letter from Malcolm Little to Commissioner MacDowell, ca. June 1950, PF. Cf. Malcolm's NOI teaching on the Masons in Hakim A. Jamal, *From the Dead Level: Malcolm X and Me* (New York: Random House, 1971), 181–84.

9. Letter from Malcolm Little to Commissioner MacDowell, 13 December 1950, PF; see Malcolm's interview on Stan Bernard's *Contact* (New York: WINS Radio, 18 February 1965), in Malcolm X, *February 1965: The Final Speeches*, ed. Steve Clark (New York: Pathfinder Press, 1992), 226–27; letter of Malcolm Little to Commissioner MacDowell, 13 December 1950, PF.

10. Letter of Commissioner MacDowell to Warden John J. O'Brien, Charlestown State Prison, 21 December 1950, *PF*; Massachusetts State Prison Report of Psychiatrist, 4 May 1951, *PF*; letter from Malcolm Little to Commissioner Grossman, 6 June 1951, *PF*; "Agreement of Prisoner When Permitted to Go to Another State," Massachusetts Department of Corrections, 7 August 1952, Parole File of Malcolm Little #22843. Henceforth, *PRF*.

11. Untitled departmental form, Massachusetts Department of Corrections, 7 July 1952, *PRF*; Wilfred Little Shabazz Interview, 14 August 1992; "Parole Officer's Report Sheet," n.d., *PRF*; *AMX*, 194 and 213; "Field Report, State of Michigan, Division of Pardons, Paroles and Probation, Lansing, Michigan; Godfrey G. Agriesti, Parole Officer," n.d., *PRF*; "Parole Board, Certification of Employer," n.d., *PRF*.

12. "Field Report, State of Michigan, Division of Pardons, Paroles & Probation, Lansing, Michigan, Godfrey G. Agriesti, Parole Officer," 14 February 1953, 2–3, *PRF*; Wilfred Little Shabazz Interview, 14 August 1992; "The Commonwealth of Massachusetts Parole Board Certificate of Discharge, Malcolm Little #8077," 4 May 1953, *PRF*.

13. *AMX*, 202; 204–5 (cf. Muhammad, *Message to the Blackman in America*, 179); Memo from SA [name redacted], to SAC, New York, "Malcolm K. Little; SM-MCI," 24 January 1955, 4–6, Malcolm X Little, FBI file, New York, 105–8999–61. Henceforth, *MX/NY*. Emphasis in the text for all quotations.

14. *AMX*, 205; SA [name redacted], to SAC, New York, "MKL; SM-MCI," 24 January 1955, 4–5, 7–8, *MX/NY-61*.

*Notes to Chapter 8*

1. Wilfred Little Shabazz Interview, 15 August 1992; *AMX*, 194–97.

2. "Field Report," 14 February 1953, 1, *PRF*; Cone, *Martin & Malcolm & America*, 91; *AMX*, 198, 200.

3. Wilfred Little Shabazz Interview, 15 August 1992; *AMX*, 201–3; New York Office Report, "[Malcolm K. Little; SM-MCI?]," 23 May 1955, 22, Reel 1, *SR*.

4. *AMX*, 213; Wilfred Little Shabazz Interview, 15 August 1992; *Malcolm X Speaks*, 40–41.

5. New York Office Report, "[MKL; SM-MCI?]," 23 May 1955, 24–25, Reel 1, *SR*; Wilfred Little Shabazz Interview, 15 August 1992; Cone, *Martin & Malcolm & America*, 92; *AMX*, 409, 216–17.

6. Airtel from SAC, Philadelphia to Director, "Muslim Mosque, Inc.; IS-X," 22 May 1964, 3–4, Muslim Mosque, Inc., FBI headquarters file, 100-441765-116. Henceforth, *MMI/HQ*; *AMX*, 217, 219–20; New York/Philadelphia Office Report, "Malcolm K. Little, was; Security Matter-MCI," 18 November 1954, 11, Reel 1, *SR*; Jeremiah Shabazz Interview.

7. Letter of Malcolm X, East Elmhurst, N.Y., 25 April 1955, *BEST*; Philadelphia Office Report, "[Malcolm K. Little?]," 23 August 1954, 1, Reel 1, *SR*; Goldman, *The Death and Life*, 55.

8. AMX, 220, 222–23; New York Office Report, "Malcolm Little, was; Security Matter-MCI," 31 January 1956, 4, Reel 1, *SR*; New York Office Report, "MKL; SM-NOI," 23 April 1957, 7, 37–38, and 50, Reel 1, *SR*; New York Office Report, "[MKL; SM-MCI?]," 23 May 1955, 12, Reel 1, *SR*; New York Office Report, "Malcolm Little, was Malcolm Shabazz; Malcolm X; Minister Malcolm; Brother Malcolm; Security Matter-NOI," 30 April 1958, 71, Reel 1, *SR*.

9. Tynnetta Muhammad, *Families of Muhammad: Study into the Birth of a Nation. Articles Based on Muhammad's History and the Holy Qur-an*, The Woman in Islam Educational Series (Phoenix, Ariz.: H.E.M.F., 1981), 13–14.

10. New York Office Report, "MKL; SM-NOI," 23 April 1957, 45, Reel 1, *SR*; New York Office Report, "[MKL; SM-MCI?]," 23 May 1955, 20, Reel 1, *SR*; SA [name redacted], to SAC, New York, "Malcolm K. Little; SM-MCI," 25 May 1955, 1, *MX/NY*-154. Cf. Goldman, *The Death and Life*, 42–43; Sahib, "The Nation of Islam," 94.

11. New York Office Report, "MKL; SM-NOI," 23 April 1957, 17 and 21, Reel 1, *SR*; letter from Mrs. J. Mims, St. Augustine, Fla., in "Voice of the People . . . What Courier Readers Think: 'Mr. Muhammad Speaks' Irks These Readers," *Pittsburgh Courier*, 14 July 1956, 10.

12. Letter from H. E. Fortsen, in "What Courier Readers Think: Muhammad Articles Called Undesirable," *Pittsburgh Courier*, 14 June 1957, sec. 2, 15; letter from Malcolm X, in "What Courier Readers Think, Malcolm X Fires Away at Principal," *Pittsburgh Courier*, 31 August 1957, sec. 2, 5.

13. AMX, 239–40; Essien-Udom, *Black Nationalism*, 168 and 177; Malcolm X, "We Arose from the Dead!" *Moslem World & The U.S.A.* (August–September 1956), 24–27 and 36.

14. Malcolm X, "God's Angry Men," *Herald-Dispatch* (Los Angeles), 10 October 1957, *MX/NY*-543.

15. "Certificate of Mr. Malcolm X. Little, Conducting Business under the Name of Temple #7 Luncheonette," County Clerk, N.Y. County, 14 November 1955; "Certificate of Incorporation of Muhammad's Temple of Islam, Inc.," County Clerk, N.Y. County, 11 May 1956; AMX, 224–25. Cf. Essien-Udom, *Black Nationalism*, 343–45.

16. New York Office Report, "ML; SM-MCI," 31 January 1956, 74-75, Reel 1, *SR*.


## Notes to Chapter 9

1. James L. Hicks, "Riot Threat as Cops Beat Moslem," *New York Amsterdam News*, 4 May 1957, 1; "Moslem Announces $ Million NY Suit," *Pittsburgh Courier*, 9 November 1957, 7; Perry, *Malcolm: The Life of a Man*, 164 and 437; AMX, 236; Goldman, *The Death and Life*, 56–58.

2. Author's transcript of *I Remember Harlem*, part 4: "Toward a New Day, 1965–

1980." Film by William Miles (Princeton, N.J.: Films for the Humanities, 1986); Goldman, *The Death and Life*, 57 and 59; James Hicks, "Another Angle: Sick of It All," *New York Amsterdam News*, 2 July 1960, 10; "Say Police Take Movies of Moslems," *New York Amsterdam News*, 11 May 1957. Clipping from the files of the New York City Police Department, Bureau of Special Services (BOSS); henceforth, *BOSS*.

3. *AMX*, 237; letters from Chief Inspector Nielson, New York City Police Department, 15 May 1957, *BOSS*; "Details of Brawl Aired in Court; Moslem, Beaten in N.Y. Cop Fracas, Acquitted," *Pittsburgh Courier*, 1 June 1957, sec. 2, 2, *BOSS*; "Moslems Ask Kennedy to Fire Two Cops," *New York Amsterdam News*, 9 November 1957, *BOSS*; "Charges Police with Brutality; Moslem Announces $ Million NY Suit," *Pittsburgh Courier*, 9 November 1957, 7, *BOSS*.

4. Telegram from Malcolm X to Commissioner Stephen P. Kennedy, New York City Police Department, 2 November 1957, 1 and 2, *BOSS*.

5. Malcolm X to S. P. Kennedy, 2, 3.

6. "Moslems Ask Kennedy to Fire Two Cops"; [Malcolm X], "Police Brutality in New York Exposed," *Mr. Muhammad Speaks* (May 1960, rpt. of 1st ed.), 13; *AMX*, 237; Goldman, *The Death and Life*, 256, 258–59.

7. David J. Garrow, *The FBI and Martin Luther King, Jr.* (New York: Penguin Books, 1981), 154; Clayborne Carson, *Malcolm X: The FBI File* (New York: Carroll and Graf, 1991), 26; Boston Office Report, "MKL; SM-C; SM-MCI," 4 May 1953, 3, Reel 1, *SR*; Memo from SA [redacted], to SAC, New York, "Malcolm K. Little, aka; IS-C," 12 August 1960, *MX/NY-1925*.

8. New York Office Report, "MKL: SM-NOI," 23 April 1957, 4, Reel 1, *SR*; *AMX*, 225; Cone, *Martin & Malcolm & America*, 91; TESUR summary, "[SAC Chicago, to SAC New York?]," "[?]; [Internal] Security-NOI," 25 April 1957, 1, *MX/NY-428*, emphasis in the text.

9. New York Office Report, "MKL; SM-NOI," 23 April 1957, 69, Reel 1, *SR*; New York Office Report, "ML; SM-NOI," 30 April 1958, 23, Reel 1, *SR*; "Malcolm X in Detroit for 2 Weeks," *New York Amsterdam News*, 31 August 1957, 16; "Malcolm X Making Hit in Detroit," *New York Amsterdam News*, 7 September 1957, 16; "Malcolm X Returns; Detroit Moslems Grow," *New York Amsterdam News*, 26 October 1957, 3.

10. *AMX*, 235; Wilfred Little Shabazz Interview, 15 August 1992; memorandum from Detective Walter Upshur to Commanding Officer, BOSS, "Meeting Sponsored by the Moslem Society," 7 November 1957, Case 55-M, *BOSS*; Perry, *Malcolm: The Life of a Man*, 170 and 439; "Malcolm X in Boston," *New York Amsterdam News*, 9 November 1957, 16; "Malcolm Shabazz Speaker at D.C. Brotherhood Feast," *New York Amsterdam News*, 30 November 1957, 4; "Malcolm X Speaks in Los Angeles," *New York Amsterdam News*, 7 December 1957, 17.

11. New York Office Report, "ML; SM-NOI," 30 April 1958, 2 and 38, Reel 1, *SR*; New York Office Report, "[MKL; SM-MCI ?]," 23 May 1955, 25, Reel 1, *SR*;

New York Office Report, "MKL; SM-NOI," 23 April 1957, 3, Reel 1, SR; Ted Watson and Paul E. N. Brown, "Moslems Stage Goodwill Tour," *Pittsburgh Courier*, 15 September 1956, 19; Abdul Basit Naeem, "Moslems 'Invade' Georgia," *The Moslem World & The U.S.A.* (October–December 1956), 36–38.

12. New York Office Report, "Malcolm K. Little, was; Internal Security-NOI," 19 November 1958, 9, 12, 18, and 19, Reel 1, SR; New York Office Report, [?], 10 November 1954, 1, Reel 1, SR; New York Office Report, "[MKL; SM-MCI?]," 23 May 1955, 12, Reel 1, SR; New York Office Report, "Nation of Islam, Internal Security-NOI," 21 February 1961, 5, Reel 1, SR.

13. "Moslems Fight R.R. Station Bias, Jailed," *Pittsburgh Courier*, 9 March 1957, sec. 2, 1; "Two Negroes Maul Chief in Flomaton," *Pensacola Journal* (Pensacola, Fla.), 23 February 1957, sec. A, 1 and 2; New York Office Report, "NOI; IS-NOI," 21 February 1961, 16, Reel 1, SR; Worthy, "The Nation of Islam: Impact and Prospects," 39–40; New York Office Report, "ML; SM-NOI," 30 April 1958, 6, Reel 1, SR.

14. Malcolm X was married to Betty Dean Sanders, a member of New York's Temple No. 7, on January 14, 1958. See "Malcolm X Married!" *Pittsburgh Courier*, 28 January 1958, 6; "Malcolm's Wed; It's a Surprise," *New York Amsterdam News*, 25 January 1958, 14; *AMX*, 228–235; Ann Geracimos, "Mrs. Malcolm X—Her Role as Wife," *New York Herald Tribune*, 30 June 1963, 6.

15. Memorandum from Det. William K. DeFossett to Commanding Officer, BOSS, "Incident at 25-46 99th Street, Corona, Involving Members of the Temple of Islam," 27 May 1958, #90-M, 1–8, BOSS; "3 Moslems Seized as Police Fighters; Home of 'X' Group's Leader Site of Battle," *New York Amsterdam News*, 24 May 1958, 21, BOSS; "Group Riled over Police Actions; Moslems Await 'D-Day' in N.Y. Court," *Pittsburgh Courier*, 24 May 1958, 7; "Moslems Plead 'Not Guilty,' " *New York Amsterdam News*, 18 October 1958, 21; "Muslims Win N.Y. Police Brutality Suit," *Pittsburgh Courier*, 17 February 1960, 9; "Trial of 5 N.Y. Moslems Draws Crowds," *Pittsburgh Courier*, 14 March 1959, 8; "Jury Deliberates 13 Hours; Moslems Freed, Cry for Arrest of Cops," *Pittsburgh Courier*, 28 March 1959, 3; and [Malcolm X], "Police Brutality in New York Exposed," 13.

16. "NY Cops Rip Moslem Leader's Home, Land in Hospital; Break in Malcolm X's Home; Followers Resent It," *Herald-Dispatch* (Los Angeles), 22 May 1958, BOSS; "Court Crowded; Postpone Moslem Hearing," *Pittsburgh Courier*, 31 May 1958, 3.

17. Cone, *Malcolm & Martin & America*, 93; emphasis in the text. "Moslem Speaker Electrifies Garvey Crowd," *New York Amsterdam News*, 10 August 1957, 4; SE [name redacted], to SAC, New York, "Nation of Islam, IS-NOI," 11 August 1957, 1, MX/NY-495.

18. New York Office Report, "ML; SM-MCI," 31 January 1956, 70, Reel 1, SR.

19. "ML; SM-MCI," 31 January 1956, 70.

20. "ML; SM-MCI," 31 January 1956, 72.

21. "ML; SM-MCI," 31 January 1956, 72.

22. Al Nall, "Indonesians Visit Harlem Landmarks," *New York Amsterdam News*, 20 July 1957, 7 and 33; "Malcolm X, Congressman Powell on Hand; Moslems Help Welcome Leaders from Indonesia," *Pittsburgh Courier* [New York edition], sec. 2, 1, MX/NY-480, in SAC, Los Angeles to FBI Director, "Nation of Islam, IS-NOI (OO: Chicago)," 23 July 1957, MX/NY-484; "2,000 at Moslem Feast in Harlem," *New York Amsterdam News*, 20 July 1957, 26.

23. "2,000 at Moslem Feast in Harlem."

24. New York Office Report, "ML; SM-NOI," 30 April 1958, 33–34, Reel 1, SR; also see "Breakfast in White House for Insulted African; Ike, Nixon Apologize to Negro over Delaware Racial Snub!" *Pittsburgh Courier*, 19 October 1957, 5.

## Notes to Prologue to Part Three

1. AMX, 341–42.

2. AMX, 345.

## Notes to Chapter 10

1. Memo from SAC, New York to Director, "Nation of Islam; IS-NOI (OO: Chicago)," 16 July 1959, 4–7, Reel 1, SR; also see Carson, *Malcolm X: The FBI File*, 163–64.

2. AMX, 240; "Is New York Sitting on a 'Powder Keg'? Racial Unrest Forces Its Way to the Surface," *U.S. News & World Report*, 3 August 1959, 48–51; "The Black Supremacists," *Time*, 10 August 1959, 24–25; "Moslems Fight Back; Bar White Press," *New York Amsterdam News*, 1 August 1959, 1 and 31; "Son Declares: Muslims' Critics Tell Falsehoods," *Pittsburgh Courier*, 29 August 1959, 8.

3. "Moslems Fight Back; Bar White Press," 31.

4. AMX, 333; Perry, *Malcolm: The Life of a Man*, 119; H. A. R. Gibb, *Mohammedanism* (New York: Oxford University Press, 1970), 127; Charles S. Braden, "Islam in America," *International Review of Missions* (July 1959): 310. An early historian of the Ahmadiyya, however, stated that Ahmad actually claimed a prophetic role of minor inspiration in contrast to that of the Prophet Muhammad. Despite his claim to prophethood solely in and through Muhammad, traditional Muslims apparently found Ahmad's assertion entirely unacceptable. H. A. Walter, *The Religious Life of India: The Ahmadiya Movement* (Calcutta: Association Press/London: Humphrey Milford, Oxford University Press, 1918; rpt., New Dehli: Manohar Publications, 1991), 55–56. Note that in my dissertation on the religious Malcolm X, I erroneously characterized the controversial distinction of the Ahmadiyya to be its claim that Ahmad was the Madhi. Such a "messianic" claim was not the problematic issue; rather, it was Ahmad's prophetic claim that is unacceptable to the Sunni Muslim world.

5. Richard B. Turner, "The Ahmadiyya Mission to Blacks in the United States in

the 1920s," *Journal of Religious Thought* 40 (1983): 55, 58–63; Gibb, *Mohammedanism*, 128; Braden, "Islam in America," 312–13.

6. Essien-Udom, *Black Nationalism*, 276–79. Abdul Basit Naeem, interview by [Detective Ernest B. Latty,] New York City Police Department, Bureau of Special Services, 5 August 1959, 2, BOSS; henceforth, Naeem Interview, 5 August 1959.

Unfortunately, in my dissertation on the religious Malcolm X, I have erred in associating Abdul Basit Naeem with the Ahmadiyya movement. Quite uncritically, I assumed Naeem's Pakistani background, his previous residence in Chicago, and his enthusiastic missionary spirit to be indicative of his affiliation with that movement. However, while my unscholarly assumption was reasonable, it is apparently incorrect. Subsequent tracing of Mr. Naeem has proven quite difficult, and efforts to confirm his particular affiliation have thus far been frustrated. However, a kind representative of the Ahmadiyya movement in New York City has tentatively assured me that he knows nothing of Mr. Naeem, nor of any Ahmadiyya missionary to the United States by that name. Telephone consultation with Nazir Ayaz, New York City, 20 September 1994.

7. AMX, 240; "The MUSLIMS of America Salute GHANA," *Pittsburgh Courier*, 9 March 1957, 26; "Mister Muhammad's Message to African-Asian Conference!" *Pittsburgh Courier*, 18 January 1958, 5; Essien-Udom, *Black Nationalism*, 279, n. 52.

8. Essien-Udom, *Black Nationalism*, 279. Abdul Basit Naeem, "Malcolm X as Nasser's Guest," interview by [Detective Ernest B. Latty?] New York City Police Department, Bureau of Special Services, 23 July 1959, 1, BOSS. Henceforth, Naeem Interview, 23 July 1959. Airtel from SAC, New York, to FBI Director, "Nation of Islam," 24 July 1959, 3, Reel 1, SR.

9. Naeem Interview, 5 August 1959, 1–2; Naeem Interview, 23 July 1959, 1–2; New York Office Report, "Malcolm K. Little; Internal Security-NOI," 17 November 1959, 23, Reel 1, SR.

10. Naeem Interview, 5 August 1959, 1–2.

11. Untitled clipping, *Pittsburgh Courier*, 1 August 1959, 22, BOSS; Naeem Interview, 23 July 1959, 1; Malcolm X, "Arabs Send Warm Greetings to 'Our Brothers' of Color in U.S.A.; Malcolm X Finds Africans, Arabs Fret More about Us Than Selves," *Pittsburgh Courier*, 15 August 1959, sec. 2, 5.

12. Letter from Malcolm X, "Africa Eyes Us," in "Pulse of the Public" column, *New York Amsterdam News*, 22 August 1959, 10.

13. Malcolm X, "Africa Eyes Us," 10.

14. Malcolm X, "Africa Eyes Us," 10.

15. Malcolm X, "Arabs Send Warm Greetings"; Malcolm X, "Africa Eyes Us"; Naeem Interview, 5 August 1959, 2; Wilfred Little Shabazz Interview, 15 August 1992; New York Office Report, "[Nation of Islam?]," 29 July 1959, 1, Reel 1, SR.

*Notes to Chapter 11*

1. Lincoln, *The Black Muslims*, 232–33, 250, and 246; Karim, *Remembering Malcolm*, 134.

2. Elijah Muhammad, "Muhammad's Trip to Mecca," *Salaam* (July 1960): 32–33, *BEST*; letter of Yusuf Ibrahim, "What Courier Readers Think," *Pittsburgh Courier*, 1 March 1958, sec. 2, 7; letter of Victor Brach, "What Courier Readers Think," *Pittsburgh Courier*, 31 May 1958, sec. 2, 7; Essien-Udom, *Black Nationalism*, 310–11.

3. Essien-Udom, *Black Nationalism*, 313 and n. 30, 314–15.

4. Telegram from Ahmad Jamal, *Time*, 31 August 1959, 5; "Dakota Staton Says: 'True Muslim Does Not Hate,' " *Pittsburgh Courier*, 26 September 1959, 24; "Muslim Leader Calls Moslem Leader 'Phony,' " *New York Amsterdam News*, 3 October 1959, 11; Essien-Udom, *Black Nationalism*, 314–17; "Fete for Toure, Booing Fiasco; Acid Thrown as 'Moslems' Clash," *Pittsburgh Courier*, 27 November 1959, 11.

5. Essien-Udom, *Black Nationalism*, 314 and 317; Howard Pulley, "Muslims a Fraud, Dakota, Hubby Charge," *Chicago Defender*, 8 June 1962, 1–2; "Dakota Staton, Hubby File Suit against Mr. Muhammad," *Pittsburgh Courier*, 9 June 1962, 1 and 4; John F. Hatchett, "The Moslem Influence among American Negroes," *Journal of Human Relations* (Summer 1962): 381–82; "Singer's Husband Issues Muhammad Debate Challenge," *Pittsburgh Courier*, 23 June 1962, 3; and Dakota Staton, "Why I'm against Elijah Muhammad," *Pittsburgh Courier*, 14 July 1962, 5.

6. Bob Queen, "Muhammad Bars 2 Orthodox Muslims," *Pittsburgh Courier*, 20 June 1962, 2; Alfredo Graham, "Suit against Muhammad Ridiculous; Is a Publicity Stunt,' Says Malcolm X," *Pittsburgh Courier*, 23 June 1962, 5; letter of Malcolm X, "Pulse of the Public" column, *New York Amsterdam News*, 1 December 1962, 10, NY/MX-3285; Lincoln, *The Black Muslims*, 232; Essien-Udom, *Black Nationalism*, 315.

7. Abdul B. Naeem, "Mr. Elijah Muhammad and The Moslem World & The U.S.A.," *The Moslem World & The U.S.A.* (October–December 1956), 8 and 9; Abdul Basit Naeem, "Pakistani Muslim Asserts: 'Will Forever Serve Messenger of Allah,' " *Muhammad Speaks*, 31 July 1964, 9; Abdul B. Naeem, "Moslem Convention—1957," *The Moslem World & The U.S.A.* (March–April 1957), 23 and 25.

8. Preface by Abdul Basit Naeem, *The Supreme Wisdom*, 5; emphasis and upper case in the text. Essien-Udom, *Black Nationalism*, 311–12; letter of Adib E. Nuruddin, "What Courier Readers Think," *Pittsburgh Courier*, 10 January 1959, sec. 2, 7; letter of Adib E. Nuruddin, "What Courier Readers Think," *Pittsburgh Courier*, 25 April 1959, sec. 2, 4.

9. Moses J. Newson, "Pakistani Says Black Muslims in U.S. Misrepresent Islam," *Afro-American* (Baltimore), 5 May 1962, 17; "Pakistan Moslem Blasts Muhammad," *Pittsburgh Courier*, 21 July 1962, 6; Essien-Udom, *Black Nationalism*, 313.

10. Essien-Udom, *Black Nationalism*, 318; "International Islam Ignores Skin Color," *Pittsburgh Courier*, 24 February 1962, sec. 2, 18.

11. *AMX*, 242; Harry S. Ashmore, "Negro Ghettos in the North, Part 4: Black Muslim Crusade a Parallel to the Klan," *New York Herald-Tribune*, 12 May 1960. From the clipping file of the Municipal Library, New York City, Borough of Manhattan; William Worthy, "The Angriest Negroes," *Esquire* (February 1961), 102; Krosney, "America's Black Supremacists," 390.

12. *AMX*, 250. Emphasis in the text.

13. Quigg, "Malcolm X, No. 2 Muslim, Says Black Man 'Original,' " 9.

14. Letter of Yahya Hawari, "What Courier Readers Think," *Pittsburgh Courier*, 25 August 1962, 12.

15. Letter of Malcolm X, "What Courier Readers Think," *Pittsburgh Courier*, 6 October 1962, 13.

16. Letter of Malcolm X, 13. Malcolm quoted Sûrah 5:51: "Oh you who believe, take not the Jew and the Christians for friends. They are friends of each other. And whoever amongst you takes them for friends he is indeed one of them. Surely Allah guides not the unjust people" (Muhammad Ali interpretation of the Qur'an).

17. Sahib, "The Nation of Islam," 183.

18. Letter of Malcolm X, "Amsterdam News Readers Write," *New York Amsterdam News*, 24 November 1962, 39. Malcolm quoted the Qur'an, Sûrah 20:102.

19. Robert Payne, "Why 400,000,000 Follow Mohammed," *New York Times Magazine*, 4 August 1963, 26; letter from Malcolm X, "Letters" section, *New York Times Magazine*, 25 August 1963, 2. Malcolm quoted from Sûrah 15:26 in the Muhammad Ali English interpretation of the Qur'an.

## Notes to Chapter 12

1. Malcolm X on *The Ben Hunter Show* (Los Angeles: Channel 11, 29–30 March 1963, 11:30 P.M. to 1:30 A.M.), LHM from Los Angeles Office, [caption redacted], 8 April 1963, 3, Reel 1, SR.

2. Malcolm X on *The Ben Hunter Show*, 3.

3. Malcolm X on *The Ben Hunter Show*, 3.

4. Lomax, *To Kill a Black Man*, 93–94; AMX, 269; H. D. Quigg, "Debate Muslim Claim to Be Legitimate Religion," *Daily Defender* (Chicago), 18 June 1963, 9; Albert B. Southwick, "Malcolm X: Charismatic Demagogue," *Christian Century*, 5 June 1963, 741.

5. Airtel from SAC, Chicago to Director, "Nation of Islam; IS-NOI," 11 March 1963, 4, MX/NY-3434; transcript of Malcolm X interview on *Focus* (Washington, D.C.: WUST Radio, 12 May 1963). LHM from Washington, D.C., field office, 23 May 1963, "Malcolm K. Little, Also Known as Malcolm X, Internal Security—Nation of Islam," 2 and 7, Reel 1, SR.

6. Malcolm X on *Focus*, 7 and 11; author's emphasis.

7. For example, George Breitman, *The Last Year of Malcolm X: The Evolution of a Revolutionary* (New York: Pathfinder Press, 1984), 13–21.

8. *The Last Speeches*, 44–45; Allen Howard, "The White Man Is Finished, Says Malcolm X," *Call & Post* (Cleveland), 29 June 1963, sec. A, 7. This article documents Malcolm's appearance on the *Discussion with Will Irvin Show*, KYW-TV, 22 June 1963; "Malcolm X Outlines Goal," *Michigan Daily* (Ann Arbor), 23 October 1963, 1.

9. Breitman, *The Last Year*, 9.

10. Cone, *Martin & Malcolm & America*, 165.

11. Cone, *Martin & Malcolm & America*, 154 and 155.

12. Cone, *Martin & Malcolm & America*, 157–59; AMX, 290–91.

13. *AMX*, 214.

14. Author's transcript of Malcolm X on *Program P.M.*, with host Jim Gordon (New York: WINS Radio, 13 June 1963), in archives of New York University, Institute of Afro-American Affairs; henceforth, *NYU*; "Malcolm X to Answer Calls," *New York Amsterdam News*, 15 June 1963, MX/NY-3687.

15. Malcolm X on *Program P.M.*; transcript of *Exposé* (Norfolk, Va.: WNOR Radio, 22–23 August 1963, 11 P.M. to 2:00 A.M.), Airtel and LHM from SAC, Norfolk to Director, "Nation of Islam, IS-NOI," 30 August 1963, 3–4, MX/NY-3084 and -3085.

16. For information about the Nation after Malcolm X, see Mamiya, "From Black Muslim to Bilalian: The Evolution of a Movement"; Martha F. Lee, *The Nation of Islam, an American Millenarian Movement* (Lewiston, N.Y.: Edwin Mellen Press, 1988); and Barboza, "A Divided Legacy."

17. Lincoln, *The Black Muslims*, 250.

18. Letter from Malcolm X to Alex Haley, 25 April 1964. Page 1 of this letter is reproduced in the original edition of *AMX*, insert, 336. Emphasis in original.

19. "Top Muslim Applauds Muhammad," *New Crusader* (Chicago), 12 November 1960, 20, MX/NY-2059; "Cairo Educator Says: 'All Muslims Are Brothers,' " *Pittsburgh Courier*, 12 November 1960, MX/NY-2061; "Moslem from Cairo Lauds Muslims Here," *New York Amsterdam News*, 15 November 1960, 1 and 11.

20. In February 1965, Malcolm said in a radio interview that Elijah Muhammad was "as anti-African as he was anti-white." He also declared, "Elijah Muhammad himself is anti-Arab; he's more anti-Arab than probably the Israelis are"; New York: WINS, *February 1965*, 205 and 208. Lincoln, *The Black Muslims*, 250.

21. See J. Milton Yinger, *Religion, Society and the Individual* (New York: Macmillan, 1957); reference to the numerical decline of the Nation's membership is made by Malcolm X in *February 1965*, 189; Lincoln, *The Black Muslims*, 240–44 (reference to Muhammad's quote from *The Supreme Wisdom*, 4).

22. Robert Booth Fowler, *Unconventional Partners: Religion and Liberal Culture in the United States* (Grand Rapids, Mich.: Eerdmans, 1989), 148; Hexham and Poewe, *Understanding Cults*, 7.

23. Lincoln, *Race, Religion, and the Continuing American Dilemma* (New York: Hill and Wang, 1984), 161. See Mustafa El-Amin, *The Religion of Islam and the Nation of Islam: What Is the Difference?* (Newark, N.J.: El-Amin Productions, 1990).

## Notes to Chapter 13

1. "Powell 'Very Flexible,' Race Waking Up: Malcolm X," *Daily Defender* (Chicago), 11 June 1963, 9; Howard, "The White Man Is Finished, Says Malcolm X."

2. "West Coast University Bars Malcom's [sic] Speech," *Afro-American* (Baltimore), 20 May 1961, 16; "UC Forbids Black Muslim to Give Scheduled Talk," *San Francisco Chronicle*, 5 May 1961, 5; "Malcolm X UC Ban Protested," *San Francisco Examiner*, 6 May 1961, 7; "Black Muslim Backed: ACLU Blasts UC Campus Talk Ban," *San Francisco Chronicle*, 7 May 1961, 5; William Boldenweck, " 'Christianity Failed Us,' Declares Black Muslim," *San Francisco Examiner*, 8 May 1961, 9; "Malcolm 'X' Raps UC, Asks Land," *San Francisco Chronicle*, 9 May 1961, 23.

3. James De Metro, "Malcolm X Predicts America Is Doomed," *Heights Daily News* (New York University, Bronx, N.Y.), 7 February 1962, 1; James De Metro, telephone interview by author, 8 June 1992; "Malcolm X, Abner Debate Integration," *Chicago Maroon* (University of Chicago), 20 February 1962; Jay Greenberg, "Muslims—Misunderstood Force," *Chicago Maroon*, 16 February 1962; "Invited by Campus NAACP; Malcolm X Howard U. Negro History Guest," *Pittsburgh Courier* [Southern Edition], 11 February 1961, 3; "Muslim Malcolm X Out as Howard U. History Speaker," *Pittsburgh Courier* [Southern Edition], 25 February 1961, sec. 2, 6.

4. Letter of Malcolm X to Elijah Muhammad, 15 February 1961; author's emphasis. "Black Muslim Chief Modifies Goal, Debates Integration at Howard U.," *Evening Star* (Washington, D.C.), 31 October 1961, sec. B, 1; Bayard Rustin, interview by Ed Edwin, 8 May 1985, "The Reminiscences of Bayard Rustin" (New York: Oral History Research Office, Columbia University, 1988), 217–18; AMX, 288 and 268; emphasis in the text. Malcolm dates Muhammad's admonition as having taken place after the Nation's first outreach in Atlanta, Georgia, in August 1956. Letter of Malcolm X to Elijah Muhammad, 19 July 1960, 2, *BEST*; Sahib, "The Nation of Islam," 241.

5. AMX, 285, 289–90, and 401; Malcolm X, *The End of White World Supremacy: Four Speeches by Malcolm X*, ed. Benjamin Karim (New York: Seaver Books, 1971), 19–20; Robert Little Interview; Joan V. Durham, "The Black Muslim Movement," MS, Hollins College, Roanoke, Va., April 1963, 37.

6. Charles Keil, "Remembering Malcolm," MS, 28 February 1990, 1–2.

7. Goldman, *The Death and Life*, 79; Hexham and Poewe, *Understanding Cults*, 14; Daniel G. Hill, "The Case against the Groups," in *New Religions and Mental Health*, ed. Herbert Richardson (New York: Edwin Mellen Press, 1980), 5; AMX,

213, 255, 292, and 270. Emphasis in the text; Robert S. Ellwood, *Religious and Spiritual Groups in Modern America* (Englewood Cliffs, N.J.: Prentice Hall, 1973), 18.

8. Malcolm later admitted that the Nation had "reached its peak in strength" in 1959–60, and "began to taper off" in 1961. *February 1965: The Final Speeches*, 189; Hentoff, "Elijah in the Wilderness," 40; letter from BEST to author, 5 August 1993, 3. One authority on the Nation observed that the black press had "acted with duplicity and opportunism toward the Nation of Islam," changing their opinion of the movement only after the larger press began to condemn the NOI. Essien-Udom, *Black Nationalism*, 307–8; Dan Day, "In the Nation's Capital: Muhammad's Muslims in Throes of Crisis," *Call & Post* (Cleveland), 23 November 1963, sec. B, 3.

9. Cone, *Martin & Malcolm & America*, 186; Malcolm X on *Exposé*, SAC, Norfolk to FBI Director, "NOI; IS-NOI," (Norfolk, Va.: WNOR Radio, 30 August 1963), 4, MX/NY-3804 and -3805; Gertrude Samuels, "Two Ways: Black Muslim and N.A.A.C.P.," *New York Times Magazine*, 12 May 1963, 27; Ralph Matthews, Jr., "Has Anything Really Changed since Malcolm X Talked to AFRO in 1963?" *Afro-American* (Baltimore), 23 May 1981, 14, BEST; AMX, 293–94; author's transcription of untitled videotape of panel discussion featuring Malcolm X with Herman Blake and unidentified host, University of California, Berkeley, 11 (?) October 1963. Malcolm's speech at Berkeley on 11 October 1963 is found in *The Last Speeches*, 59–79.

10. U.S. House, 87th Cong., 2d sess., H.R. 743 (2 August 1962), in General Correspondence, 1962, A: VIII, Congressional Investigating Committees, #18, Black Muslims (HUAC), ACLU; Elsie Carper, "Black Muslim Inquiry Tentatively Approved," *Washington Post*, 15 August 1962, ACLU; Poppy Cannon White, "Investigating the Muslims," *New York Amsterdam News*, 8 September 1962, 11.

11. Goldman, *The Death and Life*, 98; "Elijah Muhammad Offers $100,000," *Afro-American* (Baltimore), 17 August 1963, 1–2; and Balk and Haley, "Black Merchants of Hate," 68–74; "ACLU and Malcolm X Hit Muslim Firings," *Jet*, 8 August 1963, 54; "Civil Liberties Union Offers Aid to Black Muslims Fired by U. S.," *Washington Post*, 17 July 1963, sec. B, 2; "Black Muslims in Prison: Of Muslim Rites and Constitutional Rights," *Columbia Law Review* (1962): 1488–1504; "Criminal Anarchy—Louisiana; State of Louisiana v. Troy Bland Cade; Louisiana Supreme Court, 29 April 1963, 153 So. 2d 382," *Race Relations Law Reporter* 8 (1963): 411–18; Willard Clopton, "Black Muslims Tension Eases at Reformatory," *Washington Post*, 1 August 1963, sec. B, 1; *The Wisdom of Malcolm X* (Rahway, N.J.: Audiofidelity Enterprises, n.d.), recording of Nation rally, 10 August 1963, New York City.

12. Marc Crawford, interview by author, 30 August 1991, New York; henceforth, Marc Crawford Interview.

13. Wilfred Little Shabazz Interview, 15 August 1992; AMX, 266–67; Betty

Shabazz, "Malcolm X as a Husband and Father," in *Malcolm X: The Man and His Times*, 138; Worthy, "The Nation of Islam: Impact and Prospects," 35; Essien-Udom, *Black Nationalism*, 177.

14. *The Last Speeches*, 123; an FBI source confirms Malcolm's presence at the meeting. See memo from SAC, New Orleans, to Director, "Malcolm Little, aka; [caption redacted]," 15 November 1960, 19, Reel 1, *SR*; "White Fifth Crusader Aims Guns at Moslems," *Pittsburgh Courier*, 23 March 1957, magazine section, 6; "Mr. Muhammad Answers White Filth *[sic]* Crusader," *Pittsburgh Courier*, 30 March 1957, magazine section, 6. Both letters are reproduced in Muhammad, *Message to the Blackman in America*, 330–41.

15. *The Last Speeches*, 123; AMX, 268, 294, 296–97, 299–300; Wright, *Leaving Cults*, 8; New York Office Report, "MKL; IS-NOI," 16 November 1962, 13, Reel 1, *SR*.

16. Laurence Henry, "Malcolm X Lives," *Cavalier* (June 1966), 93, *BEST*; AMX, 295; emphasis in the text. Lomax, *When the Word Is Given*, 209; emphasis in the text. *Open Mind* with Eric Goldman (New York: WNBC-TV, 23 April 1961), audiocassette published as *The Disadvantaged American* (Hollywood, Calif.: The Center for Cassette Studies, 1971).

17. TESUR summary from SAC, Phoenix to SAC, Washington Field Office, "Nation of Islam; IS-NOI," 21 May 1963, 3, MX/NY-3631; TESUR summary from SAC [name redacted] to SAC, Chicago, "Nation of Islam; IS-NOI," 26 September 1963, 1, MX/NY-3811.

18. M. S. Handler, "Malcolm X Starting Drive in Washington," *New York Times*, 10 May 1963, 1, 14; M. S. Handler, "Malcolm X Scores Kennedy on Racial Policy; Says He Is 'Wrong Because His Motivation Is Wrong,' " *New York Times*, 17 May 1963, 14; "Kennedy Reported Concerned about Negro Extremism," *Washington Post*, 15 May 1963, A6; Ben Burns, "JFK Gags about TFX and Malcolm X," *Daily Defender* (Chicago), 5 June 1963, 13.

19. Karim, *Remembering Malcolm*, 147; Worthy, "The Nation of Islam: Impact and Prospects," 35.

In one open-air rally in Harlem, Malcolm exclaimed, "We are surrounded by agents posing as peace officers." "Malcolm X Scores JFK's Trip Abroad," *New York Amsterdam News*, 6 July 1963, 22; see also "FBI Keeping Close Watch on Malcolm X in Charlotte," *Afro-American* (Baltimore), 2 February 1963, 1; and "FBI Keeping Eye on Malcolm X's Visit to Charlotte; City Has Muslim Temple; Dixie Mission of Cult's No. 2 Man Disturbs Officials," *Journal and Guide* (Norfolk, Va.), 2 February 1963, 13; *Malcolm X: The Man and His Times*, 82.

20. "Coast Muslims Face Riot Charges," *Pittsburgh Courier*, 12 May 1962, 7; Julius W. Holer, "Los Angeles Tensions Up over Police Brutality; Shooting, Beatings, Gross Miscarriage, Muslims Declare," *Pittsburgh Courier*, 19 May 1962, 4; "Slain Muslim, 29, Buried; Cop Freed," *Afro-American* (Baltimore), 26 May 1962, 19; New York Office Report, "MKL; IS-NOI," 16 November 1962, Reel 1, *SR*; "L.A. Mus-

lims Face Trial over 'Riot,' " *Pittsburgh Courier*, 15 December 1962, 1 and 4; Bill Becker, "Muslims on Coast Fighting Riot Case," *New York Times*, 26 August 1962, 64; and "10 Coast Muslims Receive Jail Terms," *New York Times*, 1 August 1963, 12.

21. Kenneth Clark, interview by Ed Edwin, April–May 1985, "The Reminiscences of Kenneth Clark" (New York: Oral History Research Office, Columbia University, 1989), 213; Hakim A. Jamal, *From the Dead Level: Malcolm X and Me* (New York: Random House, 1971), 220–21; Goldman, *The Death and Life*, 99–100; Karim, *Remembering Malcolm*, 138; "The Crisis of Racism," New York City, 1 May 1962 (Hollywood, Calif.: Pacifica Radio Archive, #BB 3049 A and B); "The Ronald Stokes Incident: Brother Malcolm on WBAI with Richard Elman," in *Malcolm X: As They Knew Him*, ed. David Gallen (New York: Carroll and Graf, 1992), 101–8; Sue Solet, "Crime in Washington: Malcolm X on a Mission," *New York Herald Tribune*, 5 May 1963, 16; "Mayor Yorty Says Cult Backs 'Hate,' " *New York Times*, 27 July 1962, 8.

22. Bruce M. Tyler, "Black Radicalism in Southern California, 1950–1982" (Ph.D. diss., University of California, Los Angeles, 1983), 142; " 'Rights' Violated, Muslims Say," *Democrat & Chronicle* (Rochester, N.Y.), 8 January 1963, 19; letter of William M. Lombard, Chief of Police, Rochester, New York, to Inspector John L. Kinsella, BOSS, 19 February 1963, *BOSS*; "Muslim Assails Police 'Hostility,' " *Democrat & Chronicle* (Rochester, N.Y.), 15 February 1963, 19; memo from John L. Kinsella, Commanding Officer, BOSS, to Chief Inspector, "Arrest of Members of the Nation of Islam and Demonstrations in Connection Therewith," 12 January 1963, *BOSS*; "Muslims Protest Conviction of 2," *Democrat & Chronicle* (Rochester, N.Y.), 12 January 1963, 2; M. L. Stafford, "Jail Term for Black Muslim Arrested While Selling Paper," *Militant* (New York), 4 February 1963, 8; Nation flier, "America Has Become a Police-State for 20 Million Negroes," *BOSS*; author's emphasis.

23. Memo from John Kinsella to Chief Inspector, "Demonstration in Times Square by Members of the Nation of Islam," 12 February 1963, Supplementary #1, *BOSS*; memo from Detective Ernest B. Latty to Commanding Officer, BOSS, "Demonstration in Times Square by Members of the Nation of Islam," 13 February 1963, BSS 1-M, Final Report, *BOSS*; memo from Director to SAC, Buffalo, 5 March 1963, 6–7, Reel 1, *SR*.

24. Malcolm X on the *Barry Farber Show* (New York: WOR-AM Radio, [28 June? 9 August?] 1963), *BEST*; Jamal, *From the Dead Level*, 225; LHM from Los Angeles Office, [caption redacted], 8 April 1963, 4–5, Reel 1, *SR*.

25. LHM from New York Office, "MKL; IS-NOI," 16 November 1962, 22, Reel 1, *SR*.

26. Goldman, *The Death and Life*, 99; LHM from New York Office, "MKL; IS-NOI," 16 November 1962, 22, Reel 1, *SR*; Malcolm X on the *Barry Farber Show*; " 'Malcolm X Depraved'—Dr. Bunche," *Pittsburgh Courier*, 14 July 1962, 1 and 7; L. I. Brockenbury, "Ministers Call Muslims Hate Group," *Pittsburgh Courier*, 2 June

1962, 1 and 4; "Ministers Called 'Uncle Toms' Because of Stand," *Pittsburgh Courier*, 16 June 1962, sec. 2, 18; Bob Lucas, "First Magazine Interview with Elijah Muhammad Black Muslim Leader," *Cavalier* (January 1964), 91; Charles Portis, "Muslim Rally: Wave of Hate; Malcolm X Hits Kennedy, Jews and All Whites," *New York Herald Tribune*, 30 June 1963, 6; LHM from Los Angeles Office, [caption redacted], 8 April 1963, 5, Reel 1, SR; Malcolm X on the *Barry Farber Show*.

## Notes to Chapter 14

1. Shabazz, "Malcolm X as a Husband and Father," *Malcolm X: The Man and His Times*, 139; AMX, 298–300; Betty Shabazz, "Loving and Losing Malcolm," *Essence* (February 1992), 109. In a preface for Muhammad's publication, Malcolm X celebrated his leader as a divinely appointed "REFORMER," and the Nation as an "earth-shaking REFORMATION" among African Americans; *The Supreme Wisdom*, 7–8.

2. Goldman, *The Death and Life*, 115; AMX, 298–99, 301–2; Marc Crawford Interview.

3. AMX, 303 and 304; Airtel from SAC, Boston, to Director, "Nation of Islam; IS-NOI (OO: Chicago)," 15 June 1964, 4, *MMI/HQ*-N. R. behind 141; Spike Lee, with Ralph Wiley, *By Any Means Necessary: The Trials and Tribulations of the Making of Malcolm X* (New York: Hyperion, 1992), 61–62; Goldman, *The Death and Life*, 114; LHM from New York Office, "Malcolm K. Little; IS-NOI," 19 May 1959, 6, Reel 1, SR.

4. Malcolm X, *The End of White World Supremacy*, 21 and 121–48; AMX, 305; "Malcolm X Scores U.S. and Kennedy; Likens Slaying to 'Chickens Coming Home to Roost,' " *New York Times*, 2 December 1963, 21; Gertrude Wilson, "I Hate You!" *New York Amsterdam News*, 14 December 1963, 13. Malcolm X, interviewed by Joe Durso on *The World at Ten* (New York: WNDT-TV, 9 March 1964), in SA [name redacted] to SAC, New York, "Malcolm K. Little, aka; IS-NOI," 10 April 1964, 3 and 4, MX/NY-4346. Emendation of transcript, which reads: "I was just *waisting* away."

5. AMX, 307; memo from SAC, New York to Director, "Nation of Islam; [caption redacted] (OO: Chicago)," 20 January 1964, 1, Reel 2, SR.

6. Malcolm X to Elijah Muhammad, n.d., as read by Malcolm X in private February 1964 recording, in "The Loss of Our Warrior. . . Malcolm X," *Like It Is* (New York: WABC-TV, 3 May 1981), BEST.

7. Goldman, *The Death and Life*, 125; C. Alan Marshall, *The Life and Times of Louis Farrakhan* (Buffalo, N.Y.: Marshall Publishing, 1992), 105; Lee, *By Any Means Necessary*, 64; memo from SAC, Phoenix, to Director, "Nation of Islam; IS-NOI," 23 January 1964, in Carson, *Malcolm X: The FBI File*, 246–48.

8. Wilfred Little Shabazz, telephone interview by author, 20 May 1994; Baba Zak A. Kondo, *Conspiracys* [sic]: *Unravelling the Assassination of Malcolm X* (Wash-

ington, D.C.: Nubia Press, 1993), 66; *AMX*, 308–9; emphasis in the text; Wright, *Leaving Cults*, 5 and 6; emphasis in the text. Malcolm X, interview by Mike Wallace, 8 June 1964, author's transcript of audio track, *BEST*; intercepted telephone conversation with Mike Wallace, 8 June 1964, MX/ELSUR, 3, 5–6, MX/NY-1-6, *BEST*.

9. Henry, "Malcolm X Lives," 94; Goldman, *The Death and Life*, 120.

10. Wright, *Leaving Cults*, 53 and 75; *AMX*, 314–20.

11. M. S. Handler, "Malcolm X Sees Rise in Violence; Says Negroes Are Ready to Act in Self-Defense," *New York Times*, 13 March 1964, 20; M. S. Handler, "Malcolm X Splits with Muhammad; Suspended Muslim Leader Plans Black Nationalist Political Movement," *New York Times*, 9 March 1964, 1 and 43; Malcolm X, interview by Art Sears, evening of 9 March 1964. Transcript in the Allan Morrison Papers: 1948–1968, Research on Malcolm X, Schomburg Center for Research in Black Culture, New York City; henceforth, *AMP*. Malcolm's statement here, in response to the first interview question, was apparently read from the prepared press release he had issued the day before. A substantial part of this interview was published in Art Sears, Jr., "Malcolm X Charts New 'Negro Defense' Group without Clay," *Jet*, 2 April 1964, 54–56.

12. *Malcolm X Speaks*, 20–21. Less than a week later Malcolm spoke at the Leverett House Forum at Harvard University, declaring: "I am no longer an active member in the Nation of Islam, although I am myself still a Muslim. My religion is still Islam, and I still credit the Honorable Elijah Muhammad with being responsible for everything that I am." Malcolm X, *The Speeches of Malcolm X at Harvard*, ed. Archie Epps (New York: William Morrow, 1968), 140.

13. Malcolm X on Joe Rainey's *Listening Post* (Philadelphia: WDAS Radio, 20 March 1964), in *Malcolm X: As They Knew Him*, 156. Note that in his first independent press conference, Malcolm X spoke candidly of the opposition he had faced within the Nation: "Internal differences within the Nation of Islam forced me out of it. I did not leave of my own free will"; *Malcolm X Speaks*, 20.

14. Gertrude Samuels, "Feud within the Black Muslims," *New York Times Magazine*, 23 March 1964, 112. See Martin G. Berck, "Malcolm X—A Cry of War and Peace," *New York Herald Tribune*, 13 March 1964, 19; "Negroes Need Guns, Declares Malcolm X," *Daily Defender* (Chicago), 16 March 1964; Marc Crawford, "The Ominous Malcolm X Exits from the Muslims," *Life*, 20 March 1964, 40; "Malcolm's Brand X," *Newsweek*, 23 March 1964, 32; Albert Ellenberg, "Elijah Muhammad Weeps for the Loss of Malcolm X," *New York Post*, 10 March 1964, *AMP*; also Chicago Office Report, "Elijah Poole, Aka; IS-NOI," 9 October 1964, 2 and 19, EM/HQ-142; William Worthy, "Malcolm X Playing It 'Close to Chest,' " *Afro-American* (Philadelphia), 14 March 1964, 1–2.

15. Elijah Muhammad, "Mr. Muhammad Speaks: Divine Messengers Must Be Obeyed," *Gary Crusader* (Gary, Ind.), 28 March 1964, 5.

16. *AMX*, 310. For readings from this period, see *Malcolm X Speaks*, 23–57; *By*

*Any Means Necessary*, 1–32; and *The Speeches of Malcolm X at Harvard*, 131–60. Several important interviews typify Malcolm's black nationalist approach at this time: "Now It's A Negro Drive For Segregation," *U.S. News & World Report*, 30 March 1964; Carlos E. Russell, "Exclusive Interview with Brother Malcolm X," *Liberator* (May 1964), 12–13 and 16; and Malcolm X, interview by A. B. Spellman, 19 March 1964, in *By Any Means Necessary*, 1–13. See also Paul Lee, "A Study of the Evolution of Malcolm X's Black Nationalism," *Bulletin in Defense of Marxism* (December 1986): 25–29.

17. Goldman, *The Death and Life*, 48–49; Letter of Malcolm X to Elijah Muhammad, 19 July 1960.

18. *Malcolm X Speaks*, 40–41.

19. AMX, 320–21; Junius Griffin, "Malcolm X Plans Muslim Crusade; Tells Clerics He'll Preach as Billy Graham Does," *New York Times*, 3 April 1964, 23.

20. Griffin, "Malcolm X Plans Muslims Crusade"; Fred Powledge, "Brutality Cases Urged for Study," *New York Times*, 7 April 1964, 24.

## Notes to Chapter 15

1. AMX, 323; Lisa Chapman Jones, "Talking Book; Oral History of a Movement," *The Village Voice*, 26 February 1985, 21.

2. Memo from Frederick Jenoure, BOSS, to Commanding Officer, BOSS, "Muslim Rally," 17 July 1963, *BOSS*; Airtel from SAC, Chicago to Director, "Nation of Islam; IS-NOI," enclosing LHM from Chicago Office, "NOI; IS-NOI," 4 January 1965, 2, *MMI/HQ*-N.R. after 390; Ahmed S. Osman, "Malcolm X, 'A Brother,' " *The Dartmouth* (Dartmouth College, Hanover, N.H.), 5 March 1965, 5, *BEST*.

3. AMX, 323–25; "Top Muslim Applauds Muhammad"; also see "Cairo Educator Says: 'All Muslims Are Brothers' "; Jesse W. Lewis, Jr., "Islamic Leader Has a Stake in Sincerity; Man Who 'Tamed' Malcolm Is Hopeful," *Washington Post*, 18 May 1964, sec. A, 3, *BEST*; Goldman, *The Death and Life*, 163–65; New York Office Report, "Malcolm K. Little; IS-Muslim Mosque Incorporated," 20 January 1965, 90, Reel 2, *SR*.

4. Sandra Mackey, *The Saudis: Inside the Desert Kingdom* (N.p.: Meridian, 1987), 78–79; emphasis in the text. Bernard Lewis, ed., *Islam and the Arab World* (New York: Alfred A. Knopf, 1976), 27; Gibb, *Mohammedanism*, 44–45; AMX, 327; statistic given by Malcolm X on *Kup's Show*, with Irving Kupcinet (Chicago: WBKB-TV, 23 May 1964); Airtel from SAC Chicago to Director, "Muslim Mosque Incorporated; IS-MMI (OO:NY)," 19 June 1964, 40, *MMI/HQ*-151.

5. AMX, 326–31.

6. Mackey, *The Saudis*, 74; Abraham J. Heschel, *Between God and Man: An Interpretation of Judaism*, ed. Fritz A. Rothschild (New York: Free Press, 1965), 202.

7. AMX, 336–37; Charis Waddy, *The Muslim Mind* (New York: Longman,

1978), 107; emphasis in the text. Letter from Malcolm X, Jedda, Saudi Arabia, 20 April 1964 (New York: Muslim Mosque, Inc.), 3, *BEST*; see also New York Office Report, "MKL; IS-MMI," 20 January 1965, 100, Reel 2, *SR*.

8. Airgram from Richard W. Murphy, Second Secretary of the U.S. Embassy in Jedda, to U.S. Department of State, "Activities of Malcolm X," #A-90, 29 September 1964, 1, U.S. Department of State; henceforth, *DS/MX*. New York Office Report, "MKL; IS-MMI," 20 January 1965, 100, Reel 2, *SR*; letter from Malcolm X, Jedda, Saudi Arabia, 20 April 1964, 1; letter from Malcolm X, Jedda, Saudi Arabia, to Alex Haley, 25 April 1964, copy of first page in photo section of 1965 hardcover edition of *The Autobiography of Malcolm X*.

9. Author's transcript of Malcolm X on *The Barry Gray Show* (New York: WMCA Radio, 8–9 June 1964, an overnight program), *BEST*.

10. "Malcolm X on Islam, US, Africa," *Egyptian Gazette*, 17 August 1964, 5, *BEST*. Also in Airgram from Donald C. Bergus, Counselor of Embassy for Political Affairs, Cairo, Egypt, to Department of State, "Activities of Malcolm X in Cairo," #A-316, 7 November 1964, *DS/MX*; *Islam and the Arab World*, 29–30; *AMX*, 371–72; emphasis in the text. Waddy, *The Muslim Mind*, 107.

11. "Malcolm X says peace a miracle," *Afro-American* (Baltimore), 30 May 1964, 1; cf. James Farmer, *Lay Bare the Heart: An Autobiography of the Civil Rights Movement* (New York: Plume/New American Library, 1985), 229; M. S. Handler, "Malcolm X Pleased by Whites' Attitude on Trip to Mecca," *New York Times*, 8 May 1964, 1.

12. "For Malcom [*sic*] X, a Change of Heart," *New York Courier*, 16 May 1964, 4, *BEST*.

13. "Universal Brotherhood' View; Malcolm 'Converted' on Holy Land Visit," *Journal & Guide* (Norfolk, Va.), 6 March 1965, 9, *BEST*; "For Malcom [*sic*] X, a Change of Heart"; Handler, "Malcolm X Pleased by Whites' Attitude on Trip to Mecca"; letter from Malcolm X, Jedda, Saudi Arabia, 20 April 1964, 2.

14. Perry, *Malcolm: The Life of a Man*, 260; Oba T'Shaka, *The Political Legacy of Malcolm X* (Richmond, Calif.: Pan-Afrikan Publications, 1983), 212; Albert B. Cleage, Jr., *Black Christian Nationalism: New Directions for the Black Church* (New York: William Morrow, 1972), 113.

15. Albert Cleage, "Myths about Malcolm X," in *Malcolm: The Man and His Times*, 15.

## Notes to Chapter 16

1. Malcolm X, Bridson Interview.

2. Lotan, " 'No Peaceful Solution to Racialism,' " 5.

3. Lotan, " 'No Peaceful Solution to Racialism' "; emphasis in the text.

4. See also Cameron Duodo, "Malcolm X: Prophet of Harlem," *Drum* (Accra, Ghana), 1 October 1964; and *By Any Means Necessary*, 25.

5. New York Office Report, "ML; SM-MCI," 31 January 1956, 75, Reel 1, SR; emendations by the author. Malcolm X and Bayard Rustin on *A Choice of Two Roads*, hosted by John Donald (New York: WBAI-FM, 7 November 1960), source: Pacifica Tape Library #BB 3014; "Malcolm X On Islam, US, Africa"; "Why I Choose Islam; Malcolm X, who has become Haj Malek El-Shabazz interviewed by M. Ramzy Radwan," *Minbar Al-Islam* 4 (Cairo: The Supreme Council for Islamic Affairs) (November 1964): 56, *BEST*; Wright, *Leaving Cults: The Dynamics of Defection*, 77–78.

6. Peter Goldman, interview by author, 8 August 1991, New York; henceforth, Peter Goldman Interview. Goldman, *The Death and Life*, 166 and 169.

7. Note the remark made by a columnist about African American sympathizers of the Iraqis during the "Desert Storm" military campaign: "But then I've never understood the fascination of some American blacks with Islam, particularly men as intelligent as Malcolm X." Pete Hamill, "Gulf War Unfair to Blacks, but . . . It's Sick to Support Saddam," *New York Post*, 31 January 1991, 14.

8. Bernard Lewis, *Race and Color in Islam* (New York: Harper and Row, 1971), 3–4.

9. AMX, 349.

10. *Islam and the Arab World*, 27; *By Any Means Necessary*, 49.

11. Peter Goldman Interview.

12. AMX, 338.

13. AMX, 339–40; Peter Goldman Interview; Lewis, *Race and Color in Islam*; Davis, *Slavery and Human Progress*, 32–50; Draper, *The Rediscovery of Black Nationalism*, 88, n. 1.

14. Lewis, *Race and Color in Islam*, 102; Reply of Robert Payne following letter of Malcolm X, "Letters; Muslim Teachings," *New York Times Magazine*, 25 August 1963, 2; Chinweizu, *The West and the Rest of Us* (New York: Vintage Books, 1975), 3; William Montgomery Watt, *Muslim-Christian Encounters: Perceptions and Misperceptions* (New York: Routledge, 1991), 62.

15. *The Last Speeches*, 106–7.

16. AMX, 338–39, 343.

17. AMX, 304 and 353; Wright, *Leaving Cults*, 78.

*Notes to Chapter 17*

1. Ivan Van Sertima, ed., *Great Black Leaders: Ancient and Modern* (N.p.: Journal of African Civilizations, 1988), 8; Paul Lee, "The Magnitude of Malcolm, the Enormity of His Loss," transcript of speech in New York, 13 November 1992, *Bulletin in Defense of Marxism* 103 (February 1993): 15.

2. AMX, 353–66, 377; Malcolm did provide some additional detail and commentary on his second African tour of 1964 during a homecoming rally on 29 November 1964. See *By Any Means Necessary*, 133–48; Malcolm X, interview by

Claude Lewis, [31 December 1964], "The Final Views of Malcolm X," *National Leader* (Philadelphia, PA), 2 June 1983, 9; date of interview supplied in letter from *BEST* to author, 26 August 1993, 6.

3. Breitman, *The Last Year of Malcolm X*, 5 and 4.

4. AMX, 356; Airtel and LHM from SAC, Omaha, to Director, "Malcolm K. Little, also known as Malcolm X; [IS-MMI?]," 2 July 1964, 4, Reel 2, *SR*; Malcolm X, *Malcolm X Talks to Young People: Speeches in the U.S., Britain and Africa*, ed. Steve Clark (New York: Pathfinder Press, 1991), 11.

5. James Booker, "Is Mecca Trip Changing Malcolm?" *Amsterdam News*, 23 May 1964, 14. See also "Malcolm X's Letters to U.S. Describe Welcome in Africa," *Militant*, 25 May 1964, 6.

6. Julian Mayfield, *African Review* (May 1965): "Malcolm X: 1925–1965," 9; Donald Harris, "All Africa Was for Malcolm," *Militant*, 5 April 1965, 4; *Malcolm X: A Discussion*, with John Henrik Clark and James Shabazz, hosted by Joanne Grant (New York: WBAI-FM, 26 March 1965), source: Pacifica Radio Archive #BB 3085; *By Any Means Necessary*, 146.

7. Letter from Malcolm X, Accra, Ghana, 11 May 1964 (New York: Muslim Mosque, Inc.), *BEST*.

8. Duodo, "Malcolm X: Prophet of Harlem"; Lee, "A Study of the Evolution of Malcolm X's Black Nationalism," 28. See also "Malcolm on 'Zionist Logic,' " *Militant*, 25 February 1983, 8–9.

9. *By Any Means Necessary*, 137.

10. Martin Paris, "Negroes Are Willing to Use Terrorism, Says Malcolm X," *Columbia Spectator* (Columbia University, New York), 19 February 1965; *Malcolm X Speaks*, 130. See also *The Last Speeches*, 105; Malcolm X, Accra, Ghana, 11 May 1964, quoted in Paul Lee, "A Study of the Evolution of Malcolm X's Black Nationalism," 28.

11. New York Office Report, "Muslim Mosque, Incorporated; Internal Security," 6 November 1964, 4, *MMI/HQ*-348; *Voices from the Sixties: Twenty-Two Views of a Revolutionary Decade*, ed. Pierre Berton (Garden City, N.Y.: Doubleday, 1967), 37; Clarence Hunter, "Malcolm X Speaks: 'Guerilla Warfare Is Next,' " *Evening Star* (Washington, D.C.), 14 June 1964, 1, in memo from SAC, New York, to Director, "Afro-American Freedom Fighters; Internal Security-Miscellaneous," 18 June 1964, *OAAU/HQ*-1; Lee, "A Study of the Evolution of Malcolm X's Black Nationalism," 28; "Organization of Afro-American Unity: A Statement of Basic Aims and Objectives" (New York, July 1964), 3, *BEST*. Note the earlier version of this statement, as well as the "Basic Unity Program" of the OAAU, in the appendices of *The Last Year of Malcolm X*, 105–24.

12. "Mister X," *Arab Observer* (Cairo), 24 August 1964, 31–32, *BEST*; "Appeal to African Heads of State," 17 July 1964, *Malcolm X Speaks*, 72–77 and 79; "Malcolm X on Islam, US, Africa."

13. Clarence Hunter, "Dissident Muslim Expected to Be 'Silenced Forever,' "

*Evening Star* (Washington, D.C.), 22 February 1965, sec. A, 1, *BEST*; Malcolm X, Interview by Mike Wallace, 8 June 1964; "Malcolm X Tells of Death Threat," *New York Amsterdam News*, 21 March 1964, 50; "Muslims Planned His Death, Malcolm X Says," *New York Amsterdam News*, 4 April 1964, 1; Karim, *Remembering Malcolm*, 159–61; New York Office Report, "MKL; IS-MMI," 18 June 1964, 59–62, Reel 2, *SR*; Malcolm X, telephone interview by Art Sears, 26 May 1964, *AMP*; James Booker, "Seek to Evict Malcolm X from Home in Queens; Papers Already Filed in Court," *New York Amsterdam News*, 18 April 1964, 1 and 2; " 'My Next Move—' Malcolm X, an Exclusive Interview," *New York Amsterdam News*, 30 May 1964, 1 and 52.

14. "Malcolm X Tells Sordid Muslim Sex Scandal to N.Y. Courtroom," *Philadelphia Tribune*, 20 June 1964, 1 and 24; Airtel from SAC, Boston to Director, "Nation of Islam; IS-NOI (OO: Chicago)," 15 June 1964, 1–8, *MMI/HQ-N.R.* behind 141; Airtel from SAC, Philadelphia to Director, "Muslim Mosque, Inc.; IS-MMI," 25 June 1964, 1–2, *MMI/HQ*-156; New York Office Report, "MKL; IS-MMI," 20 January 1965, 3 and 59, Reel 2, *SR*; Malcolm X, Interview by Mike Wallace.

15. "Malcolm X Flees for Life; Muslim Factions at War," *New York Amsterdam News*, 20 June 1964, 1 and 2; "Muslim Factions Keep Fighting," *New York Amsterdam News*, 27 June 1964, 28; "Malcolm X Flees for Life; Accuses Muslims of Sordid Sex Misconduct," *Pittsburgh Courier*, 11 July 1964, 1; "Muslims Accused in Beatings," *Afro-American* (Philadelphia), 20 June 1964, 1 and 2; New York Office Report, "MMI; IS-MMI," 6 November 1964, 31, *MMI/HQ*-348; Airtel from SAC, Philadelphia, to Director, "Organization of Afro-American Unity; IS-MISC; OO: NY; Muslim Mosque Incorporated; IS-MMI; OO: NY," 15 July 1964, 16, *OAAU/HQ*-12.

16. "Malcolm X to Elijah: Let's End the Fighting," *New York Post*, 26 June 1964, 26; *By Any Means Necessary*, 66; "Women Accuse Muhammad; Muhammad Accuses Malcolm," *Cincinnati Herald*, 11 July 1964, 1 and 3; Stanley G. Robertson, "Two Local Women Ask Cult Leader for Child Support," *Los Angeles Sentinel*, 9 July 1964, 1 and 2; "Ex-Sweetheart of Malcolm X Accuses Elijah," *New York Amsterdam News*, 11 July 1964, 1 and 2; "False Charges Made against Muhammad," *New Crusader* (Chicago), 11 July 1964, 5.

17. New York Office Report, "MKL; IS-MMI," 20 January 1965, 56, Reel 2, *SR*; C. Eric Lincoln, *My Face Is Black* (Boston: Beacon Press, 1964), 109; New York Office Report, "Re: Malcolm K. Little," 3 September 1964, 1–3, Reel 2, *SR*; "Order Eviction of Malcolm X," *New York Amsterdam News*, 5 September 1964, 1.

18. *The Last Speeches*, 116–17.

19. *The Last Speeches*, 117–18; New York Office Report, "Muslim Mosque, Incorporated; IS-MMI," 21 May 1965, 46, *MMI/NY*-468; Karim, *Remembering Malcolm*, 181.

*Notes to Chapter 18*

1. Certificate of Incorporation of Muslim Mosque, Inc., County Clerk, N.Y. County, 16 March 1964, 3; letter from Malcolm X, Lagos, Nigeria, 11 May 1964 (New York: Muslim Mosque, Inc.), *BEST;* Breitman, *The Last Year of Malcolm X,* 31.

2. Malcolm X, Bridson Interview; Airtel from SAC, Philadelphia, to Director, "Muslim Mosque, Inc.; IS-MMI," 1 June 1964, 2, *MMI/HQ*-123; New York Office Report, "MKL; IS-MMI," 20 January 1965, 4–5, Reel 2, *SR;* New York Office Report, "MMI; IS-MMI," 6 November 1964, 12, *MMI/HQ*-348; Airtel from SAC, Philadelphia, to Director, "Muslim Mosque, Inc.; IS-MMI," 5 August 1964, 2, *MMI/HQ*-238.

3. New York Office Report, "MMI; IS-MMI," 6 November 1964, 1, 22, 41 and 42, *MMI/HQ*-348; New York Office Report, "MMI; IS-MMI," 21 May 1965, 17, 27–28, *MMI/HQ*-468; Timothy Lee, "Malcolm X and His Enemies," *New York Post,* 23 February 1965, 21; Malcolm X, interview by A. B. Spellman, 19 March 1964, in *By Any Means Necessary,* 5; New York Office Report, "MMI; IS-MMI," 21 May 1965, 26, *MMI/HQ*-468. For extracts from the *Blacklash,* see New York Office Report, "MKL; IS-MMI," 20 January 1965, 44–46, Reel 2, *SR.*

4. New York Office Report, "MMI; IS-MMI," 21 May 1965, 27, *MMI/HQ*-468.

5. *MMI/HQ*-468, 27, 29–30. With reference to the arrival of Hassoun, the FBI cited the 28 January 1965 edition of the *Herald-Dispatch.* Memo from SAC, New York, to Director, "Muslim Mosque, Inc.; IS-MMI," 26 April 1965, 2, *MMI/HQ*-461; memo from SAC, New York, to Director, "Muslim Mosque, Inc.; IS-MMI," 13 May 1965, 5, *MMI/HQ*-465; "Excerpts on Hajji Malik Shabazz," *Muslim Herald* (Philadelphia) (March–April 1965), 6.

6. *MMI/HQ*-468, 33; "Malcolm X Will Distribute 35 Scholarships," *Militant,* 2 November 1964, 8; "Malcolm X to Open Center Here," *New York Amsterdam News,* 17 October 1964, 3; "Malcolm X Reports He Now Represents World Muslim Unit," *New York Times,* 11 October 1964, 13; New York Office Report, "MKL; IS-MMI," 20 January 1965, 47, Reel 2, *SR.*

7. *Stokely Speaks: Black Power Back to Pan-Africanism* (New York: Random House, 1971), xiii; Carol Berger, "In Cairo, an Expatriate Black American Recalls Malcolm X," *Christian Science Monitor,* 10 February 1992, 11.

8. Letter of Malcolm X, 29 August 1964, Cairo, in *By Any Means Necessary,* 111.

9. Letter of Malcolm X, 29 August 1964; emphasis in the text. Moran, *Religious Education Development,* 153–54.

10. New York Office Report, "MMI; IS-MMI," 21 May 1965, 40, *MMI/HQ*-468; author's emphasis.

11. Moran, *Religious Education Development,* 155; Sara Mitchell, *Shepherd of*

*Black-Sheep: A Commentary on the Life of Malcolm X with an on the Scene Account of His Assassination* (Macon, Ga.: Sara Mitchell, 1981), 19.

12. Malcolm X, interview by Milton Henry, 25 [?] July 1964, Cairo, for broadcast on *The GOAL Show* (Detroit: WGPR), *BEST*; author's emphasis; henceforth, Malcolm X, Milton Henry Interview.

13. Malcolm X, Milton Henry Interview; Marc Crawford Interview; *Malcolm X Speaks*, 20; Lutfi Nasef, "A Meeting with Malcolm X; The Negro Leader Expected Assassination at Any Moment," *Gumhuriya*, 24 February 1965, 5, translated and transcribed in Airgram from Donald C. Bergus, Counselor of Embassy for Political Affairs, U.S. Embassy, Cairo, to Department of State, "Reaction to Death of Malcolm X in Cairo," #A-644, 3 March 1965, 3, *DS/MX*.

14. Nasef, "A Meeting with Malcolm X," 2.

15. Press release from James Shabazz, Secretary (New York: Muslim Mosque, Inc., 6 August 1964), 2, *BEST*; also see New York Office Report, "MKL; IS-MMI," 20 January 1965, 47–49, Reel 2, *SR*.

16. Press release from James Shabazz, 6 August 1964, 2–3; emphasis in the text.

17. Airgram from Richard W. Murphy, Second Secretary, U.S. Embassy at Jedda, "Activities of Malcolm X," #A-90, 29 September 1964, 2, *DS/MX*.

18. Airgram from Richard W. Murphy, 29 September 1964, 2–4.

19. M. S. Handler, "Malcolm Rejects Racist Doctrine; Also Denounces Elijah as a Religious 'Faker,' " *New York Times*, 4 October 1964, 59; see also "Malcolm X Hits Racism, Discards Former Stand as Black Muslim Boss," *Sunday Bulletin* (Philadelphia), 4 October 1964, sec. 1, 2.

20. Handler, "Malcolm Rejects Racist Doctrine."

21. TESUR summary from SAC, New York, to Director, "Malcolm K. Little aka; IS-MMI," 5 October 1964, 1, *MMI/HQ-N.R.* behind 343; M. S. Handler, "Malcolm X Reports He Now Represents World Muslim Unit," *New York Times*, 11 October 1964, 13; first-edition copy, *BEST*.

22. Certificate from the Office of the Supreme Imam, Sheikh Al-Azhar, 9 October 1964, in Airtel, SAC, Philadelphia, to Director, "MMI; IS-MMI," 22 October 1964, *MMI/HQ-343*. Also note that on 26 September 1964, the TESUR that had been placed on Malcolm's home phone recorded Dr. Shawarbi telling Malcolm's wife Betty that he had given her husband "further letters of introduction"; TESUR summary from SAC, New York, to Director, "MKL; IS-MMI," 5 October 1964, 1 and 4, *MMI/HQ-N. R.* behind 343.

23. Abdul Basit Naeem, " 'Obey Divine Leader,' " *Muhammad Speaks*, 17 July 1964, 1, 3; Abdul Basit Naeem, "Pakistani Muslim Asserts: 'Will Forever Serve Messenger of Allah,' " *Muhammad Speaks*, 31 July 1964, 9, 22.

24. Abdul Basit Naeem, "Pakistan Muslim Advises: March On under Messenger's Banner!" *Muhammad Speaks*, 5 February 1964, 4.

25. Abdul Basit Naeem, "Pakistan Muslim Advises: March On under Messenger's Banner!" *Muhammad Speaks*, 5 February 1964, 4, 9; Abdul Basit Naeem, " 'I'm

Ready to Meet Challenges of the Messenger's Foes,' " *Muhammad Speaks*, 12 February 1964, 4.

26. Peter J. Paris, *Black Leaders in Conflict* (New York: Pilgrim Press, 1978), 146.

## Notes to Chapter 19

1. Lebert Bethune, "Malcolm X in Europe," in *Malcolm X: The Man and His Times*, 233; Malcolm X, Bridson Interview; Malcolm X on *Kup's Show*, 25 May 1964, in Airtel from SAC, Chicago, to Director, "MMI; IS-MMI (OO: NY)," 19 June 1964, 40, *MMI/HQ*-151; Bryce B. Miller (UPI), "Seeking Freedom Like Dr. King, but Faster: Malcolm X Is No Longer 'Angriest Muslim' of All," *Journal and Guide* (Norfolk, Va.), 18 July 1964, 14.

2. Speech by Malcolm X, Muslim Mosque rally, 29 March 1964, Audubon Ballroom, New York City; transcript of NBC newsfilm, *BEST*; AMX, 229.

3. Robert Penn Warren, *Who Speaks for the Negro?* (New York: Vintage Books, 1966), 253.

4. Letter from Malcolm X, Lagos, Nigeria, 11 May 1964; see also "Malcolm's Letters to U.S. Describe Welcome in Africa," 6.

5. Christopher Langley, "Malcolm X Promises U.S. a Long, Bloody Summer," *The Dartmouth* (Dartmouth College, Hanover, N.H.), 27 January 1965, 1. The author is grateful to *BEST* for providing the emendation of this text, which incorrectly reads, "It is a situation which involves humans not *nationalists*"; Malcolm X, interviewed by Ken Sharpe (WDCR Radio, Dartmouth College, Hanover, N.H., 26 January 1965), author's transcription from audiotape, *BEST*; henceforth, Malcolm X, Dartmouth Interview.

6. Malcolm X, Dartmouth Interview.

7. The particular text of the Qur'an to which Malcolm referred is Sûrah II: 190; Lewis, "Islamic Leader Has a Stake in Sincerity; Man Who 'Tamed' Malcolm Is Hopeful."

8. Malcolm X, telephone interview by Art Sears, 26 May 1964, *AMP*.

9. Hunter, "Malcolm X Speaks: 'Guerilla Warfare Is Next.' "

10. Hunter, "Malcolm X Speaks: 'Guerilla Warfare Is Next.' "

11. Malcolm X, Mike Wallace Interview; Jones, "Talking Book; Oral History of a Movement," 20; SAC, New York, to Director, "MKL; IS-MMI," 5 October, 1964, 2, *MMI-HQ*-N.R. behind 343, author's emphasis.

12. Letter from Malcolm X, Cairo, to Alex Haley, 16 September 1964, all emphases in the text, transcribed and edited by *BEST*.

13. *Malcolm X Talks to Young People*, 21–22.

14. "London Letter" Column; "Militant Muslim," *Manchester Guardian Weekly*, 10 December 1964, 6. The author is grateful to *BEST* for providing the date and setting of this speech; Transcript of partially illegible copy of Airtel from SAC, New York, to Director, "MMI; IS-MMI," 10 September 1964, 1–2 (Confidential), *MMI/*

*HQ*-254, *BEST*. Malcolm's assassination brought an abrupt and tragic halt to the "Afro-American Freedom Brigade" plan. See Carlos Moore, *Castro, the Blacks, and Africa* (Los Angeles: Center for Afro-American Studies, University of California, 1988), 185–207; Washington Office Report, "Organization of Afro-American Unity," 2 December 1964, 3, in Airtel from SAC, Philadelphia, to Director, "OAAU; IS-Misc.; OO: NY," 2 December 1964, *OAAU/HQ*-44; Malcolm X on *Kup's Show*, 23 May 1964, Airtel from SAC, Chicago, to Director, "MMI; IS-MMI," 19 June 1964, 12, *MMI/HQ*-151.

15. Letter of Malcolm X, New York City, to Said Ramadan, 11 January 1965, *Al-Muslimoon* (Geneva, September 1965); emphasis in the text; *BEST*.

16. Malcolm X, New York, to Said Ramadan, Geneva, ca. 13–21 February 1965, in "Malik Shabazz (Malcolm X); Some Questions Answered" (Bloomington, Ind.: Muslim Students Association of the United States and Canada, n.d.); *BEST*. Malcolm's answer to question #5.

17. Malcolm X to Said Ramadan, 13–21 February 1965, question #7 and answer.

18. Malcolm X to Said Ramadan, answer to question #7.

19. Malcolm X to Said Ramadan, answer to questions #8 and 9.

20. LHM from SAC, New York to Director, "MKL; IS-MMI," 5 October 1964, 4, *MMI/HQ*-N.R. behind 343; AMX, 350.

21. Handler, "Malcolm Rejects Racist Doctrine"; Michael Abdul Malik, *From Michael de Freitas to Michael X* (London: Andre Deutsch, 1968), 146 and 156; Jamal, *From the Dead Level*, 254; Berger, "In Cairo, an Expatriate Black American Recalls Malcolm X"; David Graham Du Bois, . . . *And Bid Him Sing* (Palo Alto, Calif.: Ramparts Press, 1975), 136 and 134. Note reference that . . . *And Bid Him Sing* is a "remarkably faithful historical novel." *BEST* to author, 9 December 1992, 2; "Why I Choose Islam; Malcolm X, Who Has Become Haj Malek El-Shabazz Interviewed by M. Ramzy Radwan," 55.

22. Du Bois, . . . *And Bid Him Sing*, 151.

23. Mitchell, *Shepherd of Black-Sheep*, 17, emphasis in the text; AMX, 386; *The Speeches of Malcolm X at Harvard*, 164; Malcolm X at MMI rally, Audubon Ballroom, New York, 14 June 1964, transcribed from audiotape by *BEST*; letter from *BEST* to author, 1 September 1993, 1; emphasis in the text, which reads "*some* kind of God," but points out that "God" might be written in the lower case. I have done the latter in my reading of the text.

24. *The Speeches of Malcolm X at Harvard*, 164.

25. Gibb, *Mohammedanism*, 46–47.

26. Malcolm X, Bridson Interview.

27. AMX, 375; emphasis in the text. Malcolm X, Bridson Interview; author's emphasis. Lotan, " 'No Peaceful Solution to Racialism,' " 6; *The Last Speeches*, 103; *By Any Means Necessary*, 115.

## Notes to Chapter 20

1. *Malcolm X Speaks*, 82; Wright, *Leaving Cults*, 81; *The Last Speeches*, 147; Airtel from SAC, Chicago, to Director, "MKL, aka [caption redacted] (OO: NY)," 4 February 1965, 4 and 5, Reel 2, SR.

2. *The Last Speeches*, 139 and 174; Malcolm X, Bridson Interview; Lotan, " 'No Peaceful Solution to Racialism,' " 6. See also *Voices from the Sixties*, 36.

3. Malcolm X, telephone interview by Art Sears, 26 May 1964.

4. Malcolm X, Bridson Interview; *February 1965*, 204; *Malcolm X Talks to Young People*, 73.

5. Massaquoi, "Mystery of Malcolm X," 46; *The Last Speeches*, 84.

6. Malcolm X on *Contact*, with Stan Bernard (New York: WINS, 18 February 1965), in *February 1965*, 186.

7. *The Last Speeches*, 116; Malcolm X, "The Negro's Fight," *Egyptian Gazette*, 25 August 1964, 3, in Airgram from Donald C. Bergus, Counselor of Embassy for Political Affairs, Cairo, to Department of State, "Activities of Malcolm X in Cairo," #A-316, 7 November 1964, DS/MX. This article is reproduced, but with a different title, in "Racism: The Cancer That Is Destroying America," in *Malcolm X: The Man and His Times*, 302–6. Letter of Malcolm X to Alex Haley, 16 September 1964; emphasis in the text.

8. Wright, *Leaving Cults*, 91.

9. *The Last Speeches*, 132.

10. *The Last Speeches*, 132; *February 1965*, 207–8; Malcolm X, Mike Wallace Interview; Malcolm X, New York, to Said Ramadan, in "Malik Shabazz (Malcolm X); Some Questions Answered," answer to question #1; *Malcolm X Speaks*, 158.

11. Airtel from SAC, Chicago, to Director, "MKL, aka [caption redacted] (OO: NY)," 4 February 1965, 5, Reel 2, SR; Miller, "Seeking Freedom Like Dr. King, but Faster: Malcolm X Is No Longer 'Angriest Muslim' Of All"; *Voices from the Sixties*, 33; Malcolm X to Said Ramadan, "Some Questions Answered," answer to question #1.

12. *February 1965*, 208.

13. *The Last Speeches*, 125; *February 1965*, 189 and 206.

14. *The Last Speeches*, 133.

15. *The Last Speeches*, 132; Marlene Nadle, "Malcolm X: The Complexity of a Man in the Jungle," *The Village Voice*, 25 February 1965, 1; emendation of "$200" to preserve Malcolm's reference to Muhammad's costly suits.

16. "Why I Choose Islam; Malcolm X, Who Has Become Haj Malek El-Shabazz Interviewed by M. Ramzy Radwan," 56; Du Bois, . . . *And Bid Him Sing*, 125 and 134; "Malcolm X on Islam, US, Africa"; Malcolm X, "The Negro's Fight," 3; Langley, "Malcolm X Promises U.S.A. Long, Bloody Summer," 1; TESUR summary of conversation between Malcolm X and unidentified woman, 8 June 1964,

MX/ELSUR, in MX/NY-1; Carson, *Malcolm X: The FBI File*, 473; "Bloody Summer in '65 Is Seen by Malcolm X," *Valley News* (Hanover, N.H.), 27 January 1965.

17. *February 1965*, 22.

18. Malcolm X on *Kup's Show*, 30 January 1965; Airtel from SAC, Chicago, to Director, "MKL, aka; [redacted] (OO: New York)," 4 February 1965, 8–9, Reel 2, SR; Martin, *Race First*, 77.

## Notes to the Epilogue

1. Sidney Dominitz, "Manhattan Death Scene Visited," *Record* (Hackensack, N.J.), 22 February 1965, 5; David Goldberg, "Harlem Quiet after Slaying," *Record* (Hackensack, N.J.), 22 February 1965, 5; flier featuring photographs, directions, and layouts for New York dance/meeting facilities (New York: JPM Associates, ca. 1964).

2. Bernard Lewis, *Islam in History: Ideas, People, and Events in the Middle East* (Chicago: Open Court, 1993), 279–81; Albert Hourani, *A History of the Arab Peoples* (Cambridge, Mass.: The Belknap Press of Harvard University Press, 1991), 96.

3. The reader is advised to consult the following books to establish a basic understanding of the issues, questions, and theories pertaining to Malcolm's death: Baba Zak A. Kondo, *Conspiracys* [sic]: *Unravelling the Assassination of Malcolm X* (Washington, D.C.: Nubia Press, 1993); Karl Evanzz, *The Judas Factor: The Plot to Kill Malcolm X* (Emeryville, Calif.: Thunder's Mouth, 1992); Michael Friedly, *Malcolm X: The Assassination* (New York: Carroll and Graf, 1992); Peter Goldman, *The Death and Life of Malcolm X* (Chicago: University of Illinois Press, 1979); George Breitman, Herman Porter, and Baxter Smith, *The Assassination of Malcolm X* (New York: Pathfinder Press, 1986). Also note the intriguing reflections in James Farmer, *Lay Bare the Heart: An Autobiography of the Civil Rights Movement* (New York: Plume/New American Library, 1985), 230–38; Michael Abdul Malik, *From Michael de Freitas to Michael X* (Great Britain: Andre Deutsch, 1968), 174–78.

4. The recording of the first moments of the assassination was published on the audiotape, *Black Militant Ideologists* (N. Hollywood, Calif.: The Center for Cassette Studies, n.d.); Robert Allen, "Malcolm X 2/21/65," *The Village Voice*, 17 February 1966, 3, 10; Patricia M. Russell, "I Saw Malcolm X Killed," *Afro-American* (Baltimore), 27 February 1965, 1–2. Besides the assassination account provided in Alex Haley's epilogue, AMX, see the brief account of Thomas Skinner, "Murder of Malcolm X," in *American Violence: A Documentary History*, ed. Richard Hofstadter and Michael Wallace (New York: Vintage Books, 1971), 437–38; and Gordon Parks, "Violent End of a Man Called Malcolm X," *Life* (5 March 1965), 26–31. See sources in note 3.

5. Teletype from SAC, Detroit, to FBI Director, "Malcolm K. Little," 21 February 1965, 1–2, SR, Reel 2; telephone interview with Wilfred Little Shabazz, 20 May 1994.

6. George Murray, "Muslim Elite, Police Guard Muhammad," *Chicago's American*, 23 February 1965, 4; William Schaub, "Who Would Be Elijah's Successor?" *Chicago's American*, 24 February 1965, 5. See Aubrey Barnette, "The Black Muslims Are a Fraud," *The Saturday Evening Post* (27 February 1965), 23–29; see also the text of Malcolm's speech at the Audubon on 14 February 1965, and his radio interview with Aubrey Barnette, both in *February 1965*, 106–42, 184–229; and Les Matthews, "Muslims Charged in Death," *New York Amsterdam News*, 14 November 1964, 1–2; "Convict Muslims in Boston," *New York Amsterdam News*, 6 February 1965, 1–2.

7. In 1973, another ostensible "hypocrite" and ex-Nation member was targeted for a brutal attack. Like Malcolm, nine years before, Hamaas Abdul Khaalis had adopted orthodox Islam and condemned Elijah Muhammad as a religious fraud. In brutal retaliation for "messing with Elijah," seven members of Khaalis's family were murdered, including women, children, and a nine-day-old infant, who was drowned. Goldman, *The Death and Life*, 433–34; also see Kondo, *Conspiracys [sic]*, 339; *AMX*, 437; telephone interview with Wilfred Little Shabazz, 20 May 1994. Note reference to "hypocrites" in Hans J. Massaquoi, "Elijah Muhammad: Prophet and Architect of the Separate Nation of Islam," *Ebony* (August 1970), 88.

8. "Conventioneer?" Cartoon, *Chicago's American*, 26 February 1965, 8; Edward W. Baumann, "Black Muslims Meet 2d Day, Elijah Defiant," *Chicago's American*, 28 February 1965; Robert Jackson, "Muhammad's Son Pleads to Rejoin Black Muslims," *Chicago's American*, 25 February 1965, 4. Wallace's road to reconciliation with his father was quite rocky, however. In an interview, he later recalled he was excommunicated several times by his father, and that his ministerial privileges in the Nation were suspended between 1964 and 1969. See Marsh, *From Black Muslims to Muslims*, 112–13.

9. "Malcolm X," *New York Times*, 22 February 1965; "U.S. Justice and Malcolm X," *Plain Dealer* (Cleveland), 23 February 1965, 18; "Death of a Desperado," *Newsweek*, 8 March 1965, 25; "The Chickens Have Come Home to Roost," *Black Dispatch* (Omaha, Neb.), 26 February 1965, 6. Due to an omission in the text, I have supplied "rest" as it seems most congruous with the apparent sentiments of the columnist; however, one might wish to supply the more awkward "roost" in keeping with the theme; James L. Hicks, "Another Angle: Malcolm X," *New York Amsterdam News*, 27 February 1965, 9; "Baldwin Blames White Supremacy," *New York Post*, 22 February 1965, Malcolm X Scrapbook, vol. 1, Schomburg Center for Research in Black Culture, New York City. Henceforth, *MXS*; Whitney Young, "To Be Equal: Who Is to Blame for Death of Malcolm X?" *Call & Post* (Cleveland), 6 March 1965, B8.

10. "The Islamic Negro Nationalists," *Christianity Today* (12 March 1965): 644.

11. Joel Britton, "Describe Reaction to Malcolm X Speech: Interview with Selma Rights Fighters," *Militant* (New York), 8 March 1965, 3.

12. Walter Winchell, "Man Reading the Papers," *New York Journal American*, 28 February 1965, in *SR*, Reel 2; Jim Powell, "Malcolm X–Nat 'King' Cole, Two Men," *New Crusader* (Chicago), 21–27 February 1965, 10.

13. United Press International Report #161, in New York Office to FBI Director, "Malcolm K. Little and Bombing Matter Threat," 25 February 1965, *SR*, Reel 2; William Seraile, "The Assassination of Malcolm X: The View from Home and Abroad," *Afro-Americans in New York Life & History* (January 1981): 44–45; "Malcolm Called a Martyr Abroad," *New York Times*, 26 February 1965, 15; Gertrude Wilson, "White-On-White: Look Homeward, Mr. Rowan," *New York Amsterdam News*, 6 March 1965, 9. To no one's surprise, just prior to the release of Spike Lee's Malcolm X movie, Rowan defended his 1965 comments about Malcolm. "In real life," Rowan rationalized, "Malcolm X generated a feeble social hurricane of 'black power,' " and a "self-defeating madness for black America." Apparently, Mr. Rowan has yet to look homeward with clear vision. See Carl T. Rowan, "Commentary: What Did Malcolm X Ever Do for the Black People," *New York Post*, 3 September 1992, 25.

14. *Malcolm X Speaks*, 54–55; James A. Wechsler, "One Day After," *New York Post*, 13 April 1964, 24.

15. *By Any Means Necessary*, 28.

16. *By Any Means Necessary*, 25.

17. James A. Wechsler, "The Cult of Malcolm X," *The Progressive* (June 1964), 24–28; James Wechsler, "About Malcolm X," *New York Post*, 23 (?) February 1965, *MXS*, vol. 1; "Baldwin Blames White Supremacy"; "Baldwin Says Whites Share Assassins' Guilt," *Plain Dealer* (Cleveland), 23 February 1965, 21.

18. Ted Poston, "Widow Talks of Her Life with Malcolm," *New York Post*, 23 February 1965, 2, *MXS*, vol. 1; Gertrude Wilson, "White-On-White: Mrs. Malcolm X—'A Friend Of Mine,' " *New York Amsterdam News*, 27 February 1965, 9; Ara Piastro and Alfred Robbins, "Harlem Funeral Home Is Ringed by Police," *New York Journal-American*, 23 February 1965, 5; Carl J. Pelleck, "For Malcolm's Widow, Only His Work Is Left," *New York Post*, 22 February 1965, 2.

19. Death Certificate of Malcolm X, #56-65-104133. Signed by Chief Medical Examiner Milton Helpern, Bureau of Records and Statistics, Department of Health, New York, *PF*; *AMX*, 226. Note one person's recollection of Malcolm's teaching on afterlife in Essien-Udom, *Black Nationalism*, 91–92. "Guard Malcolm's Bier," *New York Post*, 23 February 1965, *MXS*, vol. 1; Piastro and Robbins, "Harlem Funeral Home Is Ringed by Police"; untitled clipping, *Chicago's American*, 23 February 1965, 4; "In State," photograph of Malcolm in death, *New York Amsterdam News*, 27 February 1965, 1; cf. photo of Malcolm in death, clearly showing the plate's "La Hajj" inscription, in Cone, *Martin & Malcolm & America*, photo insert section, [p. 12], bottom plate, and Haley's reference to the same plate, *AMX*, 440; Kenneth Gross, "The People Who Came to Mourn," *New York Post*, 24 (?) February 1965, *MXS*, vol. 1; Kenneth Gross, "Harlem Says Its Farewells," *New York Post*, 28

February 1965, *MXS*, vol. 2; Ossie Sykes, "The Week That Malcolm X Died," *Liberator* (New York) (April 1965), 5.

20. "Likens Malcolm X, Christ," *Chicago Defender* (National Edition), 27 February–5 March 1965, 1–2.

21. Sykes, "The Week That Malcolm X Died"; "Thousands Mourn Malcolm; A Violent Man Leaves in Peace," *Plain Dealer* (Cleveland), 28 February 1965, 1, 11; Poston, "Widow Talks of Her Life with Malcolm"; James Booker, "Exclusive: Malcolm X Speaks," *New York Amsterdam News*, 6 February 1965, 1–2; Theodore Jones, "Malcolm Knew He Was a 'Marked Man,' " *New York Times*, 23 February 1965, 1, 11; "Malcolm X Denies He Is Bomber," and photos, *New York Amsterdam News*, 20 February 1965, 1; Benfield, "His Work Will Go On, Wife Says"; *MXS*, 437; Goldman, *The Death and Life*, 364; (NPI), "Malcolm X Eulogized as a 'Black . . . Prince,' " *Call & Post* (Cleveland), 6 March 1965, A1, 2.

Note that on the day of the assassination, Malcolm X was awakened in his hotel room by a white man who called him at 8 A.M., a man who was very likely an FBI agent. Prof. Kondo astutely reveals that the purpose of the "wake-up call" may very well have been what the Bureau termed a "marking"—a mean-spirited ploy that only the most vindictive agent would stage. If the call was a "marking," it was intended to intensify Malcolm's sense of the imminence of his own death, and to taunt him with the notion that other forces were working behind the scenes to accomplish it. The ploy apparently worked, because when Malcolm drove uptown to the Audubon Ballroom, he parked his car a full twenty blocks south, at 146th Street and Broadway, in order to catch a bus the rest of the way—perhaps in an attempt to throw off his anticipated assailants. However, some people attending the rally spotted him from their car, and offered Malcolm a ride—inadvertently driving him to his appointment with death.

One of Malcolm's followers believes the reason Malcolm X parked twenty blocks south of the Audubon was so that he could walk the rest of the way, "to offer himself as a target, alone and away from his followers." Either way, it is clear that Malcolm's "wake-up" call was successful in its malicious intent; it also complements weightier evidence of the surveillance community's foreknowledge of the assassination. Cf. Kondo, *Conspiracys [sic]*, 79; Goldman, *The Death and Life*, 268–69; "Slain Malcolm's Missing Car Found," *Plain Dealer* (Cleveland), 23 February 1965, 21; Earl Grant, "The Last Days of Malcolm X," in *Malcolm X: The Man and His Times*, 92–93.

22. James Booker, "30,000 Mourn Malcolm X," *New York Amsterdam News*, 6 March 1965, 33; Goldman, *The Death and Life*, 271, 19; *AMX*, 433; New York Office Report, "Muslim Mosque, Incorporated; IS-MMI," 21 May 1965, 29–33, MMI/NY-468; *AMX*, 440, 300–301; Allen Woll, *Black Musical Theatre: From Coontown to Dreamgirls* (Baton Rouge: Louisiana State University Press, 1989), 256; "Malcolm X Eulogized as a 'Black . . . Prince' "; Marc Crawford Interview; Dick Gregory, *Up from Nigger* (New York: Stein & Day, 1976), 29; *Malcolm X Speaks*, 98–99.

23. *AMX*, 449–51; Osman, "Malcolm X, 'A Brother' "; "Thousands Mourn Malcolm"; Sykes, "The Week That Malcolm X Died"; Cathy White, "Personally and Socially," *New York Amsterdam News*, 6 March 1965, 10; Booker, "30,000 Mourn Malcolm X."

24. Letter of the Rev. W. E. Sanders, "Letters from Readers: Malcolm X Eulogy," *Call & Post* (Cleveland), 13 March 1965, B9; James Booker, "Exclusive Interview! Talk with Mrs. Malcolm X!" *New York Amsterdam News*, 13 March 1965, 4; "Mrs. Malcolm X Pens Us a Note," *New York Amsterdam News*, 10 April 1965, 2; Kenneth Gross, "The 40th Birthday of Malcolm X," *New York Post*, 20 May 1965, MXS, vol. 3.

# Selected Bibliography

*Books*

Baldwin, James. *The Fire Next Time*. New York: Delta, 1964.

Berton, Pierre. *Voices from the Sixties: Twenty-Two Views of a Revolutionary Decade*. Garden City, N.Y.: Doubleday, 1967.

Breitman, George. *The Last Year of Malcolm X: The Evolution of a Revolutionary*. New York: Pathfinder Press, 1984.

Buitrago, Ann Mari, and Leon Andrew Immerman. *Are You Now or Have You Ever Been in the FBI Files*. New York: Grove Press, 1981.

Carson, Clayborne. *Malcolm X: The FBI File*. New York: Carroll and Graf, 1991.

Clark, Kenneth B., ed. *The Negro Protest: James Baldwin, Malcolm X, Martin Luther King Talk with Kenneth B. Clark*. Boston: Beacon Press, 1963.

Clarke, John Henrik, ed. *Malcolm X: The Man and His Times*. New York: Collier Books, 1969.

Cone, James H. *Martin & Malcolm & America*. Maryknoll, N.Y.: Orbis Books, 1991.

Donner, Frank J. *The Age of Surveillance: The Aims and Methods of America's Political Intelligence System*. New York: Alfred A. Knopf, 1980.

345

Draper, Theodore. *The Rediscovery of Black Nationalism*. New York: Viking Press, 1969.

Du Bois, David Graham. *. . . And Bid Him Sing*. Palo Alto, Calif.: Ramparts Press, 1975.

Durham, Joan V. "The Black Muslim Movement." B.A. thesis, Hollins College, Roanoke, VA, 1963.

Essien-Udom, E. U. *Black Nationalism: The Search for an Identity in America*. Chicago: University of Chicago Press, 1963.

Goldman, Peter. *The Death and Life of Malcolm X*. Chicago: University of Illinois Press, 1979.

Golson, G. Barry, ed. *The Playboy Interview*, 2d ed. N.p.: Wideview, 1980.

Hauser, Thomas. *Muhammad Ali: His Life and Times*. New York: Simon and Schuster, 1991.

Hernton, Calvin C. *White Papers for Black Americans*. New York: Doubleday, 1966.

Hill, Roy L., ed. *Rhetoric of Racial Revolt*. Denver: Golden Bell Press, 1964.

Jamal, Hakim A. *From the Dead Level: Malcolm X and Me*. New York: Random House, 1971.

Jarrette, Alfred Q. *Muslims' Black Metropolis*. Los Angeles: Great Western Books, 1962.

Johnson, Timothy V. *Malcolm X: A Comprehensive Annotated Bibliography*. New York: Garland, 1986.

Karim, Benjamin. *Remembering Malcolm*. New York: Carroll and Graf, 1992.

Kondo, Baba Zak A. *Conspiracys* [sic]: *Unravelling the Assassination of Malcolm X*. Washington, D.C.: Nubia Press , 1993.

Lee, Martha F. *The Nation of Islam: An American Millenarian Movement*. N.p.: Edwin Mellen Press, 1988.

Lee, Spike, with Ralph Wiley. *By Any Means Necessary: The Trials and Tribulations of the Making of Malcolm X*. New York: Hyperion, 1992.

Lewis, Bernard, ed. *Race and Color in Islam*. New York: Harper and Row, 1971.

Lincoln, C. Eric. *The Black Muslims in America*. Boston: Beacon Press, 1960.

Lomax, Louis E. *The Negro Revolt*. New York: Signet Books, 1964.

———. *To Kill a Black Man*. Los Angeles: Holloway House, 1987.

———. *When the Word Is Given . . . .* Cleveland: World Publishing, 1963.

Malcolm X. *By Any Means Necessary: Speeches, Interviews and a Letter by Malcolm X*, ed. George Breitman. 12th ed. New York: Pathfinder Press, 1987.

———. *February 1965: The Final Speeches*, ed. Steve Clark. New York: Pathfinder Press, 1992.

———. *Malcolm X on Afro-American History*. New York: Pathfinder Press, 1988.

———. *Malcolm X Speaks: Selected Speeches and Statements*, ed. George Breitman. New York: Grove Press, 1982.

———. *Malcolm X Talks to Young People: Speeches in the U.S., Britain & Africa*, ed. Steve Clark. New York: Pathfinder Press, 1991.

————. *The End of White World Supremacy: Four Speeches by Malcolm X*, ed. Benjamin Karim. New York: Seaver Books, 1971.

————. *The Last Speeches*, ed. Bruce Perry. New York: Pathfinder Press, 1989.

————. *The Speeches of Malcolm X at Harvard*, ed. Archie Epps. New York: William Morrow, 1968.

Malcolm X, with Alex Haley. *The Autobiography of Malcolm X*. New York: Grove Press, 1965.

Malik, Michael Abdul. *From Michael de Freitas to Michael X*. Great Britain: Andre Deutsch, 1968.

Marsh, Clifton E. *From Black Muslims to Muslims: The Transition from Separatism to Islam, 1930–1980*. Metuchen, N.J.: Scarecrow Press, 1984.

McCauley, Mary Seibert. "Alex Haley, a Southern Griot: A Literary Biography," Ph.D. diss., George Peabody College for Teachers of Vanderbilt University, Nashville, Tenn., 1983.

Meier, August. *A White Scholar and the Black Community, 1945–1965*. Amherst: University of Massachusetts Press, 1992.

Mitchell, Sara. *Shepherd of Black-Sheep: A Commentary on the Life of Malcolm X with an on the Scene Account of His Assassination*. Macon, Ga.: Sara Mitchell, 1981.

Moore, Carlos. *Castro, the Blacks, and Africa*. Los Angeles: Center for Afro-American Studies, University of California, 1988.

O'Neill, Daniel J., ed. *Speeches by Black Americans*. Encino, Calif.: Dickenson, 1971.

Paris, Peter J. *Black Leaders in Conflict*. New York: Pilgrim Press, 1978.

Perry, Bruce. *Malcolm: The Life of a Man Who Changed Black America*. Barrytown, N.Y., 1991.

Pinkney, Alphonso. *Red, Black, and Green: Black Nationalism in the United States*. New York: Cambridge University Press, 1976.

Sahib, Hatim. "The Nation of Islam." Master's thesis, University of Chicago, 1951.

Sales, William W., Jr. *From Civil Rights to Black Liberation: Malcolm X and the Organization of Afro-American Unity*. Boston: South End Press, 1994.

Silberman, Charles E. *Crisis in Black and White*. New York: Vintage Books, 1964.

Van Sertima, Ivan, ed. *Great Black Leaders: Ancient and Modern*. N.p.: Journal of African Civilizations, 1988.

Waddy, Charis. *The Muslim Mind*. New York: Longman, 1978.

Warren, Robert Penn. *Who Speaks for the Negro?* New York: Vintage Books, 1966.

Williams, D. E., and C. Brown, eds. *Howard University Bibliography of African and Afro-American Religious Studies*. Wilmington, Del.: Scholarly Resources, 1977.

Wolfenstein, Eugene V. *Victims of Democracy*. London: Free Association Books, 1989.

*Newspaper and Magazine Articles*

Ashmore, Harry S. "Negro Ghettos in the North, Part 4: Black Muslim Crusade a Parallel to the Klan." *New York Herald-Tribune,* 12 May 1960.

Bailey, A. Peter. "Malcolm: A White Man's View." *Emerge* (February 1992), 57.

Balk, Alfred. "Who Are the Black Muslims? Part I: Clay Conversion Spotlights Sect." *Citizen-Journal* (Columbus, Ohio), 6 April 1964, 19.

———. "Who Are the Black Muslims? Part II: Look on Selves as Superior People." *Citizen-Journal* (Columbus, Ohio), 7 April 1964, 19.

———. "Who Are the Black Muslims? Part III: Sect Not as Strong as Believed." *Citizen-Journal* (Columbus, Ohio), 8 April 1964, 17.

Balk, Alfred, and Alex Haley, "Black Merchants of Hate." *Saturday Evening Post* (26 January 1963), 74.

Barnes, Jack. "Malcolm X: Recollections of a Visit." *Militant* (New York), 21 February 1966, 3.

Barnette, Aubrey. "The Black Muslims Are a Fraud." *Saturday Evening Post* (27 February 1965), 23–29.

Berger, Carol. "In Cairo, an Expatriate Black American Recalls Malcolm X." *Christian Science Monitor,* 10 February 1992, 11.

Berger, Morroe. "The Black Muslims." *Horizon* (Winter 1964), 48–64.

Boldenweck, William. " 'Christianity Failed Us,' Declares Black Muslim." *San Francisco Examiner,* 8 May 1961, 9.

Booker, James. "As Jimmy Booker Knew Him: Real Malcolm X." *New York Amsterdam News,* part 1, 20 March 1965, 39; part 2, 27 March 1965, 11.

———. "How I Got to Know Malcolm Intimately." *New York Amsterdam News,* 6 March 1965, 3.

———. "Is Mecca Trip Changing Malcolm?" *New York Amsterdam News,* 23 May 1964, 14.

———. "Malcolm X Ignores Brother." *New York Amsterdam News,* 4 April 1964, 1, 2.

———. "Malcolm X Speaks." *New York Amsterdam News,* 6 February 1965, 1–2.

———. "Malcolm X: 'Why I Quit and What I Plan Next." *New York Amsterdam News,* 14 March 1964, 1, 51.

———. "Seek to Evict Malcolm X from Home in Queens; Papers Already Filed in Court." *New York Amsterdam News,* 18 April 1964, 1–2.

Boyd, Herb. "Family of Malcolm X Denounces White Author of New Book." *New York Amsterdam News,* 30 November 1991, 5.

Bradley, Edward. "How Malcolm X Escaped One Death Trap." *Chicago's American* (Final Edition), 24 February 1965, 1, 28.

Cooper, Clarence, Jr. "Aftermath: The Angriest Negroes Revisited." *Esquire* (June 1961), 164–66.

Crawford, Marc. "The Ominous Malcolm X Exits from the Muslims." *Life*, 20 March 1964, 40–41.

Cunningham, Bill, and Daniel Golden. "Malcolm: The Boston Years." *Boston Globe Magazine*, 16 February 1992, 16.

DeCaro, Louis A., Jr. "Bruce Perry's Malcolm: Biography or Pathography?" *Daily Challenge* (Brooklyn), part 1, 27 January 1992, 6 and 18; part 2, 28 January 1992, 5; part 3, 29 January 1992, 6 and 15; and part 4, 30 January 1992, 8 and 18.

Dudar, Helen. "The Muslims and Black Nationalism." *New York Post*, part 2, 7 April 1964, 29.

———. "The Muslims and Black Nationalism: The Question of Violence." *New York Post*, part 4, 9 April 1964, 27.

———. "The Muslims and Black Nationalism: What Does Malcolm Want?" *New York Post*, part 5, 10 April 1964, 49.

———. "The Return of Malcolm X." *New York Post*, 22 May 1964, 3.

Duodo, Cameron. "Malcolm X: Prophet of Harlem." *Drum* (Accra, Ghana), 1 October 1964.

Eakin, John Paul. "Malcolm X and the Limits of Autobiography." *Criticism* (Summer 1976): 230–42.

Ellenberg, Albert. "Elijah Muhammad Weeps for the Loss of Malcolm X." *New York Post*, 10 March 1964, 5.

Evans, Orrin. "Malcolm X Comes to Phila[delphia] to 'Reorganize Muslims.' " *Evening Bulletin* (Philadelphia), 30 December 1964, 3.

"Excerpts on Hajji Malik Shabazz." *Muslim World* (Philadelphia) (March–April 1965), 3–9.

"The Final Views of Malcolm X." *National Leader* (Philadelphia), 2 June 1983, 6.

Friscia, Joseph T. "Malcolm X and His Black Muslims." *Saga* (July 1962), 30.

Garland, Phyl. "Has Mr. Muhammad Ousted Malcolm?" *Pittsburgh Courier*, 2 November 1963, 1, 4.

Geracimos, Ann. "Mrs. Malcolm X—Her Role as Wife." *New York Herald Tribune*, 30 June 1963, 6.

Greenberg, Jay. "Muslims—Misunderstood Force." *Chicago Maroon* (University of Chicago), 16 February 1962.

Handler, M. S. "Assertive Spirit Stirs Negroes, Puts Vigor in Civil Rights Drive." *New York Times*, 23 April 1963, 20.

———. "Black Muslims Asked to Help Treat Addicts Here." *New York Times*, 10 January 1964, 84.

———. "Cites Jews' Progress." *New York Times*, 24 May 1964, 61.

———. "Malcolm Absent as Muslims Meet; Power Struggle Is Believed Mounting in Movement." *New York Times*, 27 February 1964, 23.

———. "Malcolm Rejects Racist Doctrine; Also Denounces Elijah as a Religious 'Faker.' " *New York Times*, 4 October 1964, 59.

Handler, M. S. "Malcolm X Cites Role in U.N. Fight." 2 January 1965, 6.

————. "Malcolm X Pleased by Whites' Attitude on Trip to Mecca." *New York Times*, 8 May 1964, 1.

————. "Malcolm X Scores Kennedy on Racial Policy; Says He Is 'Wrong Because His Motivation Is Wrong.' " *New York Times*, 17 May 1963, 14.

————. "Malcolm X Sees Rise in Violence; Says Negroes Are Ready to Act in Self-Defense." *New York Times*, 13 March 1964, 20.

————. "Malcolm X Seeks U.N. Negro Debate; He Asks African States to Cite U.S. Over Rights." *New York Times*, 13 August 1964, 22.

————. "Malcolm X Splits with Muhammad; Suspended Muslim Leader Plans Black Nationalist Political Movement." *New York Times*, 9 March 1964, 1, 43.

————. "Malcolm X Starting Drive in Washington." *New York Times*, 10 May 1963, 1, 14.

————. "Malcolm X Terms Dr. King's Tactics Futile." *New York Times*, 11 May 1963, 9.

————. "Malcolm X's Role Dividing Muslims; New York Leader May Shun Group's Chicago Parley." *New York Times*, 26 February 1964, 34.

————. "Muhammad Predicts Final Victory for Muslims; Believes Negroes Will Accept Separation from Whites." *New York Times*, 17 June 1963, 14.

[Handler, M. S.] "Malcolm X Reports He Now Represents World Muslim Unit." *New York Times*, 11 October 1964, 13.

Harris, Donald. "All Africa Was for Malcolm X." *Militant*, 5 April 1965, 4.

Henry, Laurence. "Malcolm X Lives." *Cavalier* (June 1966), 36, 91–95.

Hentoff, Nat. "Elijah in the Wilderness." *The Reporter*, 4 August 1960, 37–40.

————. "Remembering Malcolm." *The Village Voice*, 26 February 1985, 24–26.

Horne, Gerald. "Hostile, Unsympathetic Book on Malcolm X Published. " *New York Amsterdam News*, 30 November 1991, 5, 37.

Howard, Allen. "The White Man Is Finished, Says Malcolm X." *Call & Post* (Cleveland), 29 June 1963, sec. A, 7.

Hughes, Langston. "Malcolm X in Cairo." *New York Post*, 17 July 1964, 32.

Hunter, Clarence. "Dissident Muslim Expected to Be 'Silenced Forever.' " *Evening Star* (Washington, D.C.), 22 February 1965, sec. A, 1.

————. "Malcolm X Speaks: 'Guerilla Warfare Is Next.' " *Evening Star* (Washington, D.C.), 14 June 1964, 1.

Joel, Gil S. "Black Muslim Approach." *Patent Trader* (Mt. Kisco, N.Y.), 25 April 1963, 3.

————. "Negroes 'Aren't Americans.' " *Patent Trader* (Mt. Kisco, N.Y.), 28 April 1963, 3.

————. "Attack on 'White Liberals.' " *Patent Trader* (Mt. Kisco, N.Y.), 5 May 1963, 3.

————. "America—Negro 'Prison.' " *Patent Trader* (Mt. Kisco, N.Y.), 12 May 1963, 3.

Jones, Lisa Chapman. "Talking Book: Oral History of a Movement." *The Village Voice*, 26 February 1985, 18–22.

Knebel, Fletcher. "A Visit with the Widow of Malcolm X." *Look* (4 March 1969), 74–80.

Krosney, Herbert. "America's Black Supremacists." *The Nation*, 6 May 1961, 390–92.

Langley, Christopher. "Malcolm X Explains Stand of "Militant Militants"; Says Negroes Are "Just as Human as All Others.' " *The Dartmouth* (Dartmouth College, Hanover, N.H.), 28 January 1965, 1.

———. "Malcolm X Promises U.S. a Long, Bloody Summer." *The Dartmouth* (Dartmouth College, Hanover, N.H.), 27 January 1965, 1.

Lee, Timothy. "Malcolm X and His Enemies." *New York Post Daily Magazine*, 23 February 1965, 21.

Lewis, Jesse W., Jr. "Islamic Leader Has a Stake in Sincerity; Man Who 'Tamed' Malcolm Is Hopeful." *Washington Post*, 18 May 1964, sec. A, 3.

Lincoln, C. Eric. "Extremist Attitudes in the Black Muslim Movement." *New South* (Atlanta) (January 1963), 3–10.

———. "The Black Muslims." *The Progressive* (December 1962), 43–48.

———. "The Meaning of Malcolm X." *Christian Century*, 7 April 1965, 431–33.

"Local Criminals, in Prison, Claim Moslem Faith Now: Grow Beards, Won't Eat Pork; Demand East-Facing Cells to Facilitate 'Prayers to Allah.' " *Springfield Union* (Springfield, Mass.), 21 April 1950, 1, 7.

Loh, Jules. "Malcolm Knew of Peril; Said a Year Ago Foes Out to Get Him." *Newark Evening News* (Newark, N.J.), 22 February 1965, 3.

Lotan, Yael. " 'No Peaceful Solution to Racialism': An Exclusive Interview with Malcolm X." *Sunday Gleaner Magazine*, 12 July 1964, 5–6.

Lucas, Bob. "First Magazine Interview with Elijah Muhammad, Black Muslim Leader." *Cavalier* (January 1964), 11–12, 89–93.

Major, Clarence. "A Personal Memoir: Malcolm the Martyr." *Negro Digest* (December 1966), 37–42.

Malcolm X. "Africa Eyes Us," in "Pulse of the Public." *New York Amsterdam News*, 22 August 1959, 10.

———. "I'm Talking to You, White Man." *Saturday Evening Post* (12 September 1964), 31.

———. Letter to Editor. "Amsterdam News Readers Write . . . ," *New York Amsterdam News*, 24 November 1962, 39.

———. Letter to Editor. "Letters." *New York Times Magazine*, 25 August 1963, 2.

———. Letter to Editor. "Pulse of the Public." *New York Amsterdam News*, 1 December 1962, 10.

———. Letter to Editor. "What Courier Readers Think." *Pittsburgh Courier*, 6 October 1962, 13.

———. Letter to Editor. "What Courier Readers Think, Malcolm X Fires Away at Principal. " *Pittsburgh Courier*, 31 August 1957, sec. 2, 5.

[Malcolm X]. "Police Brutality in New York Exposed." *Mr. Muhammad Speaks* (May 1960; rpt. of first ed.), 2, 5, 13.

————. "We Are All Blood Brothers." *Liberator* (New York) (July 1964), 4–6.

————. [Guest Columnist] "The Way the Ball Bounces: Your 'Shiftiness' Still Dazzling, Malcolm X Tells Jackie Robinson." *Philadelphia Tribune*, part 1, 10 December 1963, 6; part 2, 14 December 1963, 8.

"Malcolm X: A Clear Perception." *Black Praxis* (Dartmouth College, Hanover, N.H.), 2 February 1976.

"Malcolm X on Islam, US, Africa." *Egyptian Gazette*, 17 August 1964.

Martin, Abram V. "Apartheid and Malcolm X." *New Leader*, 22 June 1964, 7–9.

Massaquoi, Hans J. "Mystery of Malcolm X." *Ebony* (September 1964), 38.

Matthews, Ralph, Jr. "Has Anything Really Changed since Malcolm X Talked to AFRO in 1963?" *Afro-American* (Baltimore), 23 May 1981, 14.

Mayfield, Julian. "Malcolm X: 1925–1965." *African Review* (Accra, Ghana) (May 1965), 8–9.

Miller, Bryce B. "Seeking Freedom Like Dr. King, but Faster: Malcolm X No Longer 'Angriest Muslim' Of All." *Journal and Guide* (Norfolk, Va.), 18 July 1964, 14.

Miller, Gene. "A Misunderstood Man? Us Hate the White Man? Not So, Says Malcolm X; A Black Muslim's White Paper." *Miami Herald*, 21 February 1964.

"Mister X." *Arab Observer* (United Arab Republic), 24 August 1964, 31–32.

" 'My Next Move—' Malcolm X, an Exclusive Interview." *New York Amsterdam News*, 30 May 1964, 1, 52.

Nadle, Marlene. "Malcolm X: The Complexity of a Man in the Jungle." *The Village Voice*, 25 February 1965, 1.

Naeem, Abdul Basit. " 'I'm Ready to Meet Challenges of the Messenger's Foes.' " *Muhammad Speaks*, 12 February 1964, 4.

————. " 'Obey Divine Leader.' " *Muhammad Speaks*, 17 July 1964, p. 1.

————. "Pakistan Muslim Advises: March On under Messenger's Banner!" *Muhammad Speaks*, 5 February 1964, 4.

Nasef, Lutfi. "A Meeting with Malcolm X; The Negro Leader Expeted Assassination at Any Moment." *Gumhuriya* (Cairo), 24 February 1965, p. 5.

Osman, Ahmed S. "Malcolm X, 'A Brother.' " *The Dartmouth* (Dartmouth College, Hanover N.H.), 5 March 1965, p. 5.

Plimpton, George. "Miami Notebook: Cassius Clay and Malcolm X." *Harper's* (June 1964), 54–61.

Quigg, H. D. "Finds Black Muslims Keep Morally Straight." *Daily Defender* (Chicago), 17 June 1963, 9.

————. "Debate Muslim Claim to Be Legitimate Religion." *Daily Defender* (Chicago), 18 June 1963, 9.

————. "Malcolm X, No. 2 Muslim, Says Black Man 'Original.' " *Daily Defender* (Chicago), 19 June 1963, 9.

————. "The 'Devil' Catches Hell When Black Muslims Meet." *Daily Defender* (Chicago), 20 June 1963, 9.

Russell, Carlos E. "Exclusive Interview with Brother Malcolm X." *Liberator* (May 1964), 12–13, 16.

Samuels, Gertrude. "Feud within the Black Muslims." *New York Times Magazine*, 23 March 1964, 11.

———. "Two Ways: Black Muslim and N.A.A.C.P." *New York Times Magazine*, 12 May 1963, 26.

Shabaka, Segun, ed. *Black News Reprints on Malcolm X* (February 1986).

Shabazz, Betty. "The Legacy of My Husband, Malcolm X." *Ebony* (June 1969), 172.

———. "Loving and Losing Malcolm." *Essence* (February 1992), 50.

Topor, Tom. "Harlem Youth Backs Malcolm X, but He Irks Cops, Rights Chiefs." *The Record* (Hackensack, N.J.), 15 June 1964, 5.

———. "Rebel with a Cause: Malcolm X Trims His Tenets to the Times." *The Record* (Hackensack, N.J.), 16 June 1964, 5.

———. "Negro Revolution In America? Malcolm X Can See It Brewing." *The Record* (Hackensack, N.J.), 17 June 1964, 5.

"Why I Choose Islam: Malcolm X, Who Has Become Haj Malek El-Shabazz Interviewed by M. Ramzy Radwan." *Minbar Al-Islam* (Cairo: The Supreme Council for Islamic Affairs) (November 1964), 55–57.

Wiley, Charles W. "Who Was Malcolm X?" *National Review*, 23 March 1965, 239–40.

Worthy, William. "The Angriest Negroes." *Esquire* (February 1961), 102–5.

## Scholarly Journals

Calverley, Edwin E. "Negro Muslims in Hartford." *The Muslim World* (October 1965): 340–45.

Eakin, Paul John. "Malcolm X and the Limits of Autobiography." *Criticism* (Wayne State University, Detroit) 18 (3) (Summer 1976): 230–42.

Hatchett, John F. "The Moslem Influence Among American Negroes." *Journal of Human Relations* (Summer 1962): 381–82.

Lee, Paul. "A Study of the Evolution of Malcolm X's Black Nationalism." *Bulletin in Defense of Marxism* (December 1986): 25–29.

———. "The Magnitude of Malcolm, the Enormity of His Loss." Transcript of speech at a "Malcolm X forum," New York, 13 November 1992. *Bulletin in Defense of Marxism* (February 1993): 15.

Miller, Ross. "Autobiography As Fact and Fiction: Franklin, Adams, Malcolm X." *Centennial Review* (Summer 1972): 221–32.

Vincent, Ted. "The Garveyite Parents of Malcolm X." *The Black Scholar* (April 1989): 10–13.

Worthy, William. "The Nation of Islam: Impact and Prospects." *Midstream* (Spring 1962): 26–44.

Yaker, Henri M. "The Black Muslims in the Correctional Institution." *Welfare Reporter* (Trenton, N.J.) (October 1962): 158–65.

## Unpublished Government Documents

Federal Bureau of Investigation (FBI). Files on Malcolm X, the Nation of Islam, the
Muslim Mosque, Inc., the Organization of Afro-American Unity, and Elijah
Muhammad, 1953–65. Best Efforts Inc., Highland Park, Mich.

New York City Police Department, Bureau of Special Services (BOSS). Files on
Malcolm X and the Nation of Islam, 1957–65.

United States, Department of State. Files on Malcolm X, 1964–65.

## Audio/Video Recordings

*Bell & Howell Close-Up: Walk in My Shoes.* Features footage of Malcolm X speaking
at the Uline Arena, Washington, D.C., 25 June 1961. Originally broadcast on
ABC-TV, 19 September 1961. Video in the Museum of Television and Radio,
New York.

*CBS Reports: The Harlem Temper,* with Harry Reasoner. Features footage of Malcolm X speaking at undated Harlem rally. Originally broadcast on CBS-TV, 11
December 1963. Video in the Museum of Television and Radio, New York.

*A Choice of Two Roads.* Malcolm X and Bayard Rustin, hosted by John Donald.
New York, WBAI-FM, 7 November 1960. Los Angeles: Pacifica Tape Library
#BB 3014.

Farrakhan, Louis. Easter Sunday message, 26 March 1989. Copy of unpublished cassette.

*I Remember Harlem,* part 4: "Toward a New Day, 1965–1980." Film by William
Miles. Princeton, N.J.: Films for the Humanities, 1986.

Malcolm X. Interviewed by Ken Sharpe. Dartmouth College, Hanover, N.H.,
WDCR Radio, 26 January 1965. Best Efforts, Inc., Highland Park, Mich.

Malcolm X. Interviewed by Mike Wallace, 8 June 1964, New York. Author's transcript of audiotrack from unedited CBS film footage. Best Efforts, Inc., Highland
Park, Mich.

Malcolm X. Interviewed by Milton Henry, 25 (?) July 1964, Cairo. Broadcast on *The
Goal Show,* Detroit: WGPR Radio. Best Efforts, Inc., Highland Park, Mich.

Malcolm X. Interviewed by Herman Blake and unidentified host. University of
California, Berkeley, 11 (?) October 1963. Untitled, unpublished videotape.

Malcolm X on *City Desk.* Chicago, WMBQ-TV, 17 March 1963. Videotape in the
Schomburg Center for Research in Black Culture, New York.

Malcolm X on *The Barry Farber Show.* New York, WOR-AM Radio, 29 June (?) 9
August (?) 1963. Best Efforts, Inc., Highland Park, Mich.

Malcolm X on *The Barry Gray Show.* New York, WMCA-AM Radio, 9 June 1964.
Best Efforts, Inc., Highland Park, Mich.

Malcolm X on *Program P.M.* New York, WINS Radio, 13 June 1963. Audiotape in
New York University, Institute of Afro-American Affairs, New York.

*Malcolm X: A Discussion.* John Henrik Clark and James Shabazz, hosted by

Joanne Grant, 26 March 1965. N. Hollywood, Calif.: Pacifica Radio Archive, #BB 3085.

"Malcolm X." Panel discussion on *The Charlie Rose Show*, featuring Betty Shabazz, James Turner, Peter Bailey, William Sales, Benjamin Karim, and "Sister Souljah." New York, WNET-TV, 19 May 1992. Audiotrack from broadcast.

*Open Mind.* New York, WNBC-TV, 23 April 1961. Published on audiocassette as *The Disadvantaged American.* Hollywood, Calif.: Center for Cassette Studies, 1971.

*The Crisis of Racism.* Audiotape of panel discussion featuring Malcolm X, James Farmer, and William Worthy, hosted by Murray Kempton. Palm Gardens, New York, 1 May 1962. N. Hollywood, Calif.: Pacifica Radio Archive, #BB 3049, A & B.

"The Loss of Our Warrior . . . Malcolm X." *Like It Is.* New York, WABC-TV, 3 May 1981. Audiotape of television program. Best Efforts, Inc., Highland Park, Mich.

*The Wisdom of Malcolm X.* Malcolm X at Nation of Islam Rally, 10 August 1963, New York. Rahway, N.J.: Audiofidelity Enterprises, n.d.


*Unpublished Interviews*

Atkins, Clarence. Interview by author, 17 July 1992, New York.

Clark, Kenneth. Interview by Ed Edwin, April–May 1985, "The Reminiscences of Kenneth Clark." New York: Oral History Research Office, Columbia University, 1989.

Crawford, Marc. Interview by author, New York University, 30 August 1991, New York.

Goldman, Peter. Interview by author, 8 August 1991, New York.

Little, Robert, Commissioner of New York City Child Welfare Administration. Interview by author, 2 April 1992, New York.

Little Shabazz, Wilfred. Interview by author, with Paul Lee, 14 August 1992, Detroit.

———. Interview by author, 15 August 1992, Detroit.

———. Telephone interview by author, 27 November 1992.

———. Telephone interview by author, 20 May 1994.

Malcolm X. Interview by Art Sears, 9 March 1964. Transcript in Allan Morrison Papers: 1948–1968, Research on Malcolm X. Schomburg Center for Research in Black Culture, New York.

———. Telephone interview by Art Sears, 26 May 1964. Transcript in Allan Morrison Papers: 1948–1968, Research on Malcolm X. Schomburg Center for Research in Black Culture, New York.

———. Interview by Douglas Geoffrey Bridson. London, BBC Broadcasting House, 2 December 1964. Transcribed and edited by Paul Lee. Best Efforts, Inc., Highland Park, Mich.

Malcolm X. Interview by Carter Davidson on *At Random* television program. Chicago, 2 March 1963. Transcript in SAC Chicago Airtel to Director, "Nation of Islam; IS-NOI," 11 March 1963. FBI New York Office file on Malcolm X #3434.

———. Interview by Joe Durso on *World at Ten*. New York, WNDT-TV, Channel 13, 9 March 1964. Transcript in SA [name redacted] (412) to SAC, New York, "Malcolm K. Little, aka; IS-NOI," 10 April 1964. FBI New York Office file on Malcolm X #4346.

———. Interview by William Kunstler on *Pro and Con*, with the Rev. William M. James. New York, WMCA Radio, 3 March 1960. Transcript in Report from SA[redacted], New York Office, "Malcolm K. Little; Internal Security-NOI," 17 November 1959. Reel 1, Scholarly Resources edition of FBI Headquarters file on Malcolm X.

———. Interview by Irving Kupcinet on *Kup's Show*. Chicago, WBKB-TV, 23 May 1964. Transcript in Airtel from SAC Chicago to Director, "Muslim Mosque, Incorporated; IS-MMI (OO: NY)," 19 June 1964. FBI Headquarters file on the Muslim Mosque, Inc. #151.

———. Interview by Irving Kupcinet on *Kup's Show*. Chicago, WBKB-TV, 30 January 1965 [televised 31 January 1965]. Transcript in Airtel from SAC, Chicago to Director, "Malcolm K. Little, aka; (OO: New York)," 4 February 1965. Reel 2, Scholarly Resources edition of FBI headquarters file on Malcolm X.

———. Interview on *Exposé*. Norfolk, VA, WNOR Radio, 22–23 August 1963, 11 P.M. to 2 A.M. Transcript in LHM from SAC, Norfolk to Director, "Nation of Islam, IS-NOI," 30 August 1963, in SAC, Norfolk to Director, "NOI; IS-NOI," 30 August 1963, FBI New York Office file on Malcolm X #3084 and #3085.

———. Interview on *Focus*. Washington, D.C., WUST Radio, 12 May 1963. Transcript in Washington, D.C., Office Report, 23 May 1963. "Malcolm K. Little, Also Known As Malcolm X, Internal Security-Nation of Islam," Reel 1, Scholarly Resources edition of FBI Headquarters file on Malcolm X.

———. Interview on *The Ben Hunter Show*. Los Angeles: Channel 11, 29–30 March 1963, 11:30 P.M. to 1:30 A.M. Transcript in LHM from Los Angeles office [caption redacted], 8 April 1963, Reel 1, Scholarly Resources edition of FBI Headquarters file on Malcolm X.

Naeem, Abdul Basit. "Malcolm X as Nasser's Guest." Interview by [Detective Ernest B. Latty (?),] New York City Police Department, Bureau of Special Services, 23 July 1959. Files of the Bureau of Special Services, New York City Police Department.

———. Interview by [Detective Ernest B. Latty,] New York City Police Department, Bureau of Special Services, 5 August 1959. Files of the Bureau of Special Services, New York City Police Department.

Rustin, Bayard. Interview by Ed Edwin, 8 May 1985, "The Reminiscences of Bayard Rustin." New York: Oral History Research Office, Columbia University, 1988.

## Archives and Collections

African American newspaper collection in the Black Studies Department of the Ohio State University Library, Columbus, Ohio.

Allan Morrison Papers: 1948–1968, Research on Malcolm X. Schomburg Center for Research in Black Culture, New York.

American Civil Liberties Union Archives, Seeley G. Mudd Manuscript Library of Princeton University, Princeton, N.J.

Best Efforts, Inc., Highland Park, Mich.

Malcolm X Audiotape Collection, Archives of the Institute of Afro-American Affairs, New York University, New York.

Malcolm X Scrapbooks, vols. 1–3, Archives of the Schomburg Center for Research in Black Culture, New York.

Moorish Science Temple of America Collection, Archives of the Schomburg Center for Research in Black Culture, New York.

Newark Public Library, Newark, N.J. Clipping files.

New York City Municipal Library. Clipping files.

New York City Public Library. Newspaper collection.

Rare Book and Manuscript Collection, Columbia University, New York.

## Other Primary Sources

"Certificate of Incorporation of Muhammad's Temple of Islam, Inc., Pursuant to Article 10 of the Religious Corporation Law of the State of New York." County Clerk, N.Y. County, 11 May 1956.

"Certificate of Mr. Malcolm X. Little, Conducting Business Under the Name of Temple #7 Luncheonette." County Clerk, N.Y. County, 14 November 1955.

Malcolm X, Accra, Ghana, 11 May 1964. New York, Muslim Mosque, Inc. Typewritten copy. Best Efforts, Inc., Highland Park, Mich.

Malcolm X, Jedda, Saudi Arabia, 20 April 1964. New York, Muslim Mosque, Inc. Best Efforts, Inc., Highland Park, Mich.

Malcolm X, Lagos, Nigeria, 11 May 1964. New York, Muslim Mosque, Inc. Typewritten copy. Best Efforts, Inc., Highland Park, Mich.

Malcolm X, Queens, N.Y., to Elijah Muhammad, Chicago, 15 February 1961, typewritten letter, signed. Copy in author's files.

Malcolm X, Queens, N.Y., 25 April 1955, typewritten letter, signed. Best Efforts, Inc., Highland Park, Mich.

Malik Shabazz [Malcolm X], New York, to Said Ramadan, Geneva, 11 January 1965. *Al-Muslimoon* (Geneva), September 1965. Best Efforts, Inc., Highland Park, Mich.

"Organization of Afro-American Unity: A Statement of Basic Aims and Objectives." New York, July 1964. Best Efforts, Inc., Highland Park, Mich.

Parole File of Malcolm Little, the Department of Correction, the Commonwealth of Massachusetts.

Prison File of Malcolm Little, the Department of Correction, the Commonwealth of Massachusetts.

## Published Primary or Rare Sources

"Abolishment of Capital Punishment: The Death Penalty Is Ineffective as a Deterrent; 2nd Speaker, Malcom [sic] Little." *The Colony* (1 January 1950), 9. Best Efforts, Inc., Highland Park, Mich.

*F.B.I. Surveillance Files on Malcolm X*. Wilmington, Del.: Scholarly Resources, 1978, Reels 1 and 2.

Shabazz, Betty. "Betty Shabazz Remembers Malcolm." Interview on *Like It Is* by Gil Noble. New York, WABC-TV, 19 May 1991. Journal Graphics #810.

## Miscellaneous Materials

Keil, Charles. "Remembering Malcolm." MS, 28 February 1990.

Speech by Malcolm X, Muslim Mosque, Incorporated, rally, 29 March 1964, at Audubon Ballroom, New York. Transcript of NBC newsfilm. Best Efforts, Inc., Highland Park, Mich.

# Index